FORENSIC EXAMINATION

OF WINDOWS®-SUPPORTED FILE SYSTEMS

DOUG ELRICK

Forensic Examination of Windows-Supported File Systems by Doug Elrick

Additional copies may be purchased by contacting the author at:
FEWSFS@gmail.com

Cover Design: Drew Elrick | ***drewelrick.com***
Cover Photo: Lane Pelovsky | ***lpvisuals.com***
Interior Design: Drew Elrick
Editors: Lauren Elrick, Paula Beckman
ISBN: 978-0-359-37072-6
Second Edition - March 21, 2019
Printed in the U.S.A.

MENU

FOREWORD

It's when you've "bumped in to someone" in the Charles De Gaulle Airport, or spent multiple weeks with that someone in another country, been stuck in an elevator with the person, watched a space shuttle take off together, and even watched your favorite sports team lose–in their own stadium–that you begin to realize all the ways you've benefited from your relationship with that person.

In compiling a foreword for Doug's latest excursion of knowledge delivery, I wanted to reflect on things relative to the book's content. If you're reading this writing, chances are fair you've spent a small amount of time with me, talking about topics ranging from partition table reconstruction with disk level editing tools to vendor related technology that might be in your toolbox at this very moment. Chances are even better that you've spent an amount of time learning something from Doug.

While I could work hard to embellish several things relative to this book or Doug's capability to instill knowledge, I can take a much easier road speaking directly from my past experience with Doug as a mentor (the days at the Iowa crime lab), Doug as a teacher (the many moons spent together volunteering time for the International Association of Computer Investigative Specialists – IACIS), Doug as a peer in our community (his current life) and most importantly, Doug as a friend, resource, or, as many of you know, someone to whom you can just drop a line for some help.

Anything with the words "Forensic" and "Examination" in the title automatically elicits the conversation around schooling an investigator to be a geek, or molding the geek in to an investigator. I'll throw Doug under the bus as being excellent at both, and with that admission will summarily advise this book as recommended reading. Ideally we learn something new every time we try. I made it to page #1. I didn't know Doug's middle name began with a G. By the time I got to the first practical exercise, I was completely ready to run back to automated technology and Google, but my recollection of "Doug-speak" and "Doug-thought" as pitted against many years of personal instruction in this field, combined with many nights of these same conversations with Doug, rang like familiar bells as the pages take the reader down "that path." You know the one; where you come out the other end having traded your "I just learned something" light bulb from incandescent to fluorescent. Not only are you still "seeing the light," you're doing it much more effectively and efficiently than before.

Doug: thanks for the gratuitous use of pictures, the knowledge dump, and the exercises with which to practice and validate that data assimilation. In the world of being a super genius but not being able to convey a point to save your life, or being an expert conveyor of completely irrelevant knowledge, you continue to strike the perfect harmony of the best of both worlds.

Keith Lockhart
Vice President, Global Training
AccessData Group

ABOUT THE AUTHOR

Doug has worked in the area of digital forensics for over twenty-five years. Doug worked for thirteen years as a forensic scientist for the Iowa Division of Criminal Investigation where he conducted forensic examinations in the areas of drug analysis, toxicology, arson, trace evidence, serology, DNA and crime scene investigation. He started the computer forensic unit for the DCI laboratory in 1992. He transitioned to the public sector, working for Digital Intelligence, a Digital Forensic company from 2002–2018 as the Director of Forensic Services. Doug is now an instructor of digital forensics/cybersecurity and general networking at Des Moines Area Community College.

Doug has been involved in computer forensic training since 1995. He instructs law enforcement and corporate security investigators in proper forensic methodologies and in the use of common computer forensic applications. He has conducted presentations in basic and advanced computer evidence collection and processing for the Iowa Department of Public Safety, Malaysian National Police, Japanese National Police, Italian National Police and law enforcement officials from all twenty-seven countries in the European Union during IACIS training events. Doug has also presented at the American Academy of Forensic Sciences, American Society of Crime Laboratory Directors, FBI National Academy Re-trainer, and the US Department of Justice Science and the Law Conference.

Doug holds a master's degree in digital forensics from the University of Central Florida and has obtained the following digital forensic certifications: CFCE and CAWFE from IACIS, EnCE from Guidance Software. Doug is currently working towards a Ph.D. in education at Iowa State University, specializing in instructional technology.

ABOUT THE DESIGNER

Drew Elrick is a graphic designer from St. Paul, Minnesota. Drew earned his Bachelor of Arts degree in Design from the University of Northwestern – St. Paul. He specializes in design and marketing for higher education, as well as branding and identity design.

DEDICATION

To the memory of my Dad, Gordon Elrick, who passed away during the final writing of this text. He was always an encourager of both myself and my son, Drew, who designed this book.

THANK YOU

Many thanks go out to my loving wife, Lori, who patiently put up with my time spent working on this project instead of spending family time or completing the projects around the house. I also want to thank Lauren Bernhagen and Paula Beckman for their tremendous job editing and for compensating for my sleeping through English class for twelve years.

Doug Elrick
2019

DOWNLOAD RESOURCES

STUDENT PRACTICAL EXERCISE FILES

To obtain a copy of the practical exercise files, please send an email to **FEWSFS@gmail.com** and you will receive a link to download the files.

Subject line: *Practical Files*

Message Body
Name of Institution:
Course Name/Number:
Instructor:

INSTRUCTOR RESOURCES

To obtain a copy of the instructor resource files, please send an email to **FEWSFS@gmail.com** and you will receive a link to download the files.

Subject line: *Instructor Resources*

Message Body
Name:
Institution Email Address:
Name of Institution:
Type of Institution:
Institution Address:

Department:
Supervisor Name:
Supervisor Email Address:
Supervisor Phone Number:

01 BITS & BYTES

The question arises as to how the computer can recognize what keystrokes are recorded and how to translate them into meaningful data. When the letter "A" is hit on the keyboard, a signal is sent and interpreted by the system and displayed on the monitor or saved to the storage device.

Most people are now familiar with the fact that computers use "1s"and "0s" to represent information, but the question is, how is that done? What is the correlation between these two values and the Twitter posts and cat videos on the Internet? This chapter will describe the process that computers use for interpreting and storing data. The forensic implications will also be covered.

Binary Data

The smallest unit of measurement that a computer can understand is the ***bit***, which stands for ***binary digit***. Binary implies that there are two possible options; YES/NO, TRUE/FALSE, 0/1, +5V/-5V. A traditional analogy is the light switch, where it is either in the "ON" or "OFF" position. There is no in-between for the light bulb; this is a base-2 system or binary. If a single bit represented each character in the alphabet, then it would be limited to two letters: A or B. This limited alphabet will not be adequate. For each additional bit that is added to represent a character, the number of possibilities is expanded exponentially by a factor of two. If 2 bits are used for each character, then the alphabet expands to four characters 2^2 (2x2). Note that in the computer world, counting typically starts with 0 instead of 1, so the four characters are numbered 0, 1, 2, and 3.

Bit
Binary digit and the smallest unit of data

#	Bits	Letters
0	00	A
1	01	B
2	10	C
3	11	D

If the set is expanded to 3 bits per letter or 2^3 (2x2x2), then there will be eight possibilities.

#	Bits	Letters
0	000	A
1	001	B
2	010	C
3	011	D
4	100	E
5	101	F
6	110	G
7	111	H

ASCII
American Standard Code for Information Interchange that defines 128 characters based upon 7 bits

Extended ASCII
An additional 128 characters in the ASCII table based upon 8 bits

Byte
8 bits that represent a single character

When the early teletypewriters were invented, they used either 5 or 6 bits to represent each character that was sent. The limitation to a five-bit system is that only 32 characters are allowed (2^5)(2x2x2x2x2). This would accommodate the 26 letters of the alphabet and up to six numbers. An obvious problem comes about when the numbers 7, 8, 9, or 0 need to be used or to distinguish between upper and lowercase letters. Also, there would be no possibilities for punctuation or special characters. The 6-bit system allowed for 64 characters (2^6) (2x2x2x2x2x2), which would handle 26 lowercase letters, 26 uppercase letter, ten numbers and two special characters. Eventually a 7-bit system (2^7) (2x2x2x2x2x2x2) was adopted allowing for 128 characters. The standard became known as the ***American Standard Codes for Information Interchange*** or ***ASCII (pronounced ASK-EE)***. This standard allowed for 96 symbols as well as 32 special control characters such as a carriage return and a line feed. As time passed and computers became more widespread and widely used for various applications, an eighth bit was added. This increased the character possibilities to 256 (0-255). The additional 100 characters are known as the ***Extended ASCII*** set. Many of these additional characters are graphic symbols. This code is stored in the computer's BIOS chip and handles the translation.

The term used to describe these 8 bits is the ***byte***. So 1 byte is equivalent to 1 character or symbol. In the ASCII table the first 32 entries are assigned to special characters and codes. Starting with entry 32, the characters found on the keyboard are defined including a SPACE. The capital letter "A" is the 65th entry in the table, and the lowercase letter "a" is the 97th entry. These are displayed in the excerpt below.

The full Extended ASCII table is located in the appendix of this book.
What is the relationship between the decimal number and the binary number? This relationship can be shown by creating a binary table.

As stated above, there are always 8 bits per ASCII byte, so there will be eight columns in our table.

As a reminder, for each bit, there are two options: 0 or 1. The column header will be 2 raised to the power of the column number.

2^7	2^6	2^5	2^4	2^3	2^2	2^1	2^0

Calculating this out, the headers are as follows:

128	64	32	16	8	4	2	1

Now add a row beneath this and enter in the binary value of the byte "A" from the ASCII table excerpt above (01000001).

128	64	32	16	8	4	2	1
0	1	0	0	0	0	0	1

Decimal
Base 10 counting system

Wherever a "1" occurs, add the value of the column. In this example, 64 and 1 equals 65. This is the ***decimal*** value for this byte. This is distinguished from the lowercase "a", which is represented by 01100001, which is decimal 97. If applied to the table, the following is displayed:

128	64	32	16	8	4	2	1
0	1	1	0	0	0	0	1

Adding 64 + 32 + 1 equals 97.

If all the bits were "1," then the table would look as follows:

128	64	32	16	8	4	2	1
1	1	1	1	1	1	1	1

The decimal value would be: 128 + 64 + 32 + 16 + 8 + 4 + 2 + 1 equaling 255. This is the last entry in the extended ASCII character set and represents the NULL character.

PRACTICAL EXERCISE 1

Convert the following binary values to decimal values.

	128	64	32	16	8	4	2	1	Decimal value
a) 10110101									
b) 01101010									
c) 11110000									
d) 01010111									
e) 11111101									
f) 00000011									
g) 10000001									
h) 00110011									
i) 11001100									
j) 01011111									
k) 01011110									
l) 01111111									
m) 00111000									
n) 11100001									
o) 01000010									
p) 01000100									
q) 11000010									
r) 00100010									
s) 00000010									
t) 10000000									
u) 01100000									
v) 10101010									
w) 01010101									
x) 11011111									
y) 00011001									
z) 01100011									

The process can be reversed and converted from decimal to binary. Use decimal 159.

Start with the binary table:

128	64	32	16	8	4	2	1

Take the decimal and subtract the largest column value that will leave a positive remainder.

159 – 128 = 31, then place a 1 under the column that was used.

128	64	32	16	8	4	2	1
1							

Continue the process using 31where 64 or 32 cannot be subtracted without getting a negative value, so place 0 in those two columns.

128	64	32	16	8	4	2	1
1	0	0					

Subtract 16. 31-16 =15, so place a 1 in that column. 15-8=7. Place 1 in that column. 7-4=3, 3-2=1, and 1-1=0, so put a 1 in all five remaining columns.

128	64	32	16	8	4	2	1
1	0	0	1	1	1	1	1

159 decimal equals 10011111 binary.

An example would be converting decimal 46.

128	64	32	16	8	4	2	1

128 or 64 cannot be used. 46-32=14, 14-8=6, 6-4=2, 2-2=0, so 1 cannot be used

128	64	32	16	8	4	2	1
0	0	1	0	1	1	1	0

PRACTICAL EXERCISE 2

Convert the following decimal values to binary.

Decimal Value	128	64	32	16	8	4	2	1
a) 73								
b) 126								
c) 52								
d) 199								
e) 231								
f) 92								
g) 108								
h) 81								
i) 66								
j) 117								
k) 45								
l) 129								
m) 184								
n) 212								
o) 36								
p) 222								
q) 99								
r) 12								
s) 255								
t) 4								
u) 89								
v) 70								
w) 247								
x) 13								
y) 32								
z) 201								

Hexadecimal

In order to "simplify" things, programmers wanted a code system that takes up less space. In doing so, they changed from a base 10 system of counting to a base 16 method of counting known as ***hexadecimal***.

Hexadecimal
Base 16 method of counting, values are 0-9 and A-F.

Decimal	Hexadecimal
0	0
1	1
2	2
3	3
4	4
5	5
6	6
7	7
8	8
9	9
10	A
11	B
12	C
13	D
14	E
15	F

Note that starting with decimal 10 the hexadecimal values use letters. Do not confuse these letters with the ASCII characters of A through Z. Each hexadecimal value listed above is represented by 4 bits.

Decimal	Hexadecimal	Binary
0	0	0000
1	1	0001
2	2	0010
3	3	0011
4	4	0100
5	5	0101
6	6	0110
7	7	0111
8	8	1000
9	9	1001
10	A	1010
11	B	1011
12	C	1100
13	D	1101
14	E	1110
15	F	1111

This means that there are two hexadecimal values for each byte. To gain an understanding of this, go back to the binary table. The lower case "z" is represented by 01111010. Entering this information into the table results in the following:

128	64	32	16	8	4	2	1
0	1	1	1	1	0	1	0

The decimal value is 64 + 32 + 16 + 8 + 2 equaling 122. Now split this byte in half, giving two sets of 4 bits.

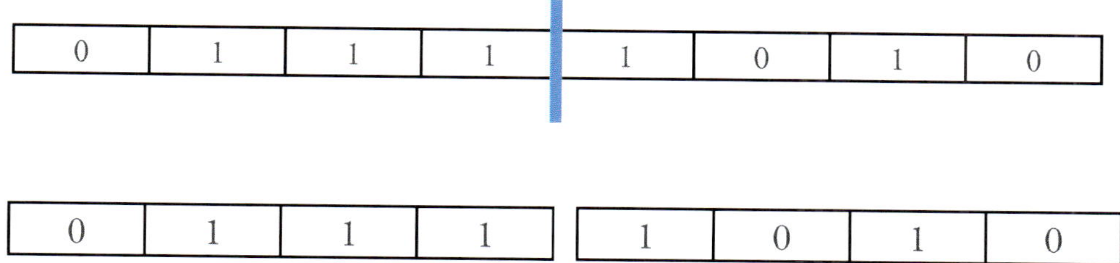

In classical programmer (nerd) humor, this half byte is referred to as a ***nibble***. If each nibble is treated separately and applied to the table, decimal values for each can be discovered:

Nibble
Half of a byte or 4 bits.

8	4	2	1

Add in our first nibble values:

8	4	2	1
0	1	1	1

The decimal value is 4 + 2 + 1= 7. Apply the second nibble values:

8	4	2	1
1	0	1	0

The decimal value is 8 + 2 equaling 10; thus the two values, 7 and 10; however, the programmers wanted each nibble to only take up one space. Therefore 10, 11, 12, 13, 14, and 15 (the largest nibble value: 8+4+2+1) do not fit into this model. This is where the hexadecimal counting scheme comes into play. Remember that the counting method is as follows: 0, 1, 2, 3, 4, 5, 6, 7, 8, 9, A, B, C, D, E, and F.

Using this counting method, each nibble can be represented with a single value. In the example, there were 7 and 10 decimal values; in hexadecimal, or hex for short, it would be 7 and A. 7A or 7Ah represent the whole byte. The "h" is used to denote that it is a hex value. This is used to avoid confusion between decimal and hexadecimal values. The hex value for a lowercase "d" is 64. Sixty-four in decimal is the "@"symbol.

Using 64h indicates the type of counting method used. Apply this method of conversion to larger numbers to arrive at the hex values. Another way to express hexadecimal values would be 0x64.

Try another example of converting from binary to hexadecimal. Start with the value of 10111101 (decimal 189).

1	0	1	1	1	1	0	1

The nibbles are as follows:

8	4	2	1
1	0	1	1

8	4	2	1
1	1	0	1

The first nibble decimal value is 8 + 2 + 1 equaling 11. The hex value is B.

The second nibble decimal value is 8 + 4 + 1 equaling 13. The hex value is D.

The hexadecimal value for decimal 189 is 0xBD.

PRACTICAL EXERCISE 3

Convert the following binary values to hexadecimal values.

		8	4	2	1		8	4	2	1		Hex Value
a)	10110101											
b)	01101010											
c)	11110000											
d)	01010111											
e)	11111101											
f)	00000011											
g)	10000001											
h)	00110011											
i)	11001100											
j)	01011111											
k)	01011110											
l)	01111111											
m)	00111000											
n)	11100001											
o)	01000010											
p)	01000100											
q)	11000010											
r)	00100010											
s)	00000010											
t)	10000000											
u)	01100000											
v)	10101010											
w)	01010101											
x)	11011111											
y)	00011001											
z)	01100011											

Now look at converting back from hexadecimal to decimal.

Start with 0xFC.

Hex F equals decimal 15 (15-8=7, 7-4=3, 3-2=1, 1-1=0).
Hex C equal decimal 12 (12-8=4, 4-4=0).
The nibbles are as follows:

8	4	2	1
1	1	1	1

8	4	2	1
1	1	0	0

Combine the two nibbles.

128	64	32	16	8	4	2	1
1	1	1	1	1	1	0	0

128 + 64 + 32 + 16 + 8 + 4 = 252

There is another method for converting hexadecimal to decimal using a mathematical formula.

Using the hex value FC, use the formula Nibble1 * 16^1 + Nibble0 * 16^0.

16^1 equals 16 and 16^0 equals 1.

Restating the formula, Nibble1 (left nibble) * 16 + Nibble0 (right nibble) * 1.

(15 * 16) + (12*1) = 252

Convert 0x24 to decimal.

(2 * 16) + (4*1) = 36

Multi-byte Data

So far, there has only been one byte of data per character; however, this is limited to 255 characters. This works well for just the English language, but there are approximately 68,000 languages used worldwide. In order to be universally accessible, the different programs must accommodate all the possible characters. To make allowances for all the various languages, ***Unicode*** was developed. Unicode uses 16 bits (or 2 bytes) to represent each symbol, which allows up to 65,536 possible characters. This is referred to as UCS-2. But, even 65,536 characters may not be enough, so a 4-byte option is also employed into Unicode (UCS-4). UCS-4 is used for specialized character sets, which allows for millions of additional characters. Unicode is utilized in the Microsoft Windows operating system and Microsoft Office products. For more additional information regarding Unicode, see ***www.unicode.org.***

Unicode
An encoding system that uses at least 16 bits to represent a single character and is intended to allow international languages

Fortunately, the Unicode character starts with the ASCII characters and pads them with 0x00. For example, capital "A" is 0x41 (65 decimal) in ASCII. In Unicode, this would be 0x0041. In binary, this would be:

32768	16384	8192	4096	2048	1024	512	256	128	64	32	16	8	4	2	1
0	0	0	0	0	0	0	0	0	1	0	0	0	0	0	1

Note that the decimal value is still 65 even though a second byte is added.

There are many other instances where more than one byte of information is needed to express a value. When writing code, a programmer will define how many bytes are needed for specific values. For example, a Windows date and time value requires 8 bytes.

As discussed above, 4 bits is referred to as a nibble, and 8 bits is a byte. There are other references for multi-byte values shown on the following page.

# of Bits	# of Bytes	Name
8	1	Byte
16	2	Word or Short
32	4	Double Word (DWord) or Long
64	8	QWord or Long Long

Little Endian
Reading data on the drive from right to left.

Big Endian
Reading data on the drive from left to right.

The next issue associated with multi-bytes is how to read them properly. On some systems the bytes are read off the media from right to left, (RTL) and on other systems they are read from left to right (LTR). RTL systems such as Intel based computers are referred to as ***Little Endian*** systems. These make up the vast majority of computer systems available (Windows, Macintosh, and most Linux). The LTR systems are known as ***Big Endian*** systems, and there are far fewer systems available.

When reading from a Little Endian system, the bytes will be stored such as 0x7A43. To read this value properly, the bytes must be reversed to be 0x437A.

Below is the binary representation.

32768	16384	8192	4096	2048	1024	512	256	128	64	32	16	8	4	2	1
0	1	0	0	0	0	1	1	0	1	1	1	1	0	1	0

The decimal value is 17274. If the bytes were read incorrectly by not reversing the order, the table would show:

32768	16384	8192	4096	2048	1024	512	256	128	64	32	16	8	4	2	1
0	1	1	1	1	0	1	0	0	1	0	0	0	0	1	1

The decimal value would be 31299, which is substantially different.

As shown above, capital "A" is 0x0041 in Unicode. In the media, this would be stored as 0x4100. Again, if read incorrectly, the decimal value would be 16640 instead of 65.

PRACTICAL EXERCISE 4

Interpret the following bytes as read directly off a drive.

1. 0x54AA		2. 0xCFD3		3. 0x00FF
4. 0x9241		5. 0x86EC		6. 0x2197
7. 0x0568		8. 0xDB82		9. 0x465C
10. 0x3553		11. 0x1001		12. 0x7600

32768	16384	8192	4096	2048	1024	512	256	128	64	32	16	8	4	2	1

Provide the decimal values for each.

1. ____________ 2. ____________ 3. ____________

4. ____________ 5. ____________ 6. ____________

7. ____________ 8. ____________ 9. ____________

10. ____________ 11. ____________ 12. ____________

Converting multi-byte binary values to hexadecimal or decimal is done in the same manner as with a single byte.

Take the binary value of 1101101010101011.

Split the value into nibbles 1101 1010 1010 1011. The decimal values of each nibble are 13 10 10 11. The hexadecimal value would be 0xDAAB.

Converting the multi-byte to decimal is a bit more complex. A binary table like the one above with 16 columns is an option, but this becomes cumbersome if expanded to 32 or 64 bit values.

The method above regarding the mathematical formula for converting a byte can be used for multi-bytes as well.

$(Nibble3 * 16^3) + (Nibble2 * 16^2) + (Nibble1 * 16^1) + (Nibble0 * 16^0)$
A table can be generated to assist in this.

16^7	16^6	16^5	16^4	16^3	16^2	16^1	16^0	Total
268435456	16777216	1048576	65536	4096	256	16	1	
				13	10	10	11	
				53248	2560	160	11	55979

PRACTICAL EXERCISE 5

Convert the following binary values to hexadecimal.

1. 10110110111101111100001111011010 ____________
2. 01000000110110101110011010101111 ____________
3. 11001101001010101110101010111110 ____________
4. 00001110101101010110101101010011 ____________
5. 11010101101010101111010101110100 ____________
6. 01101111010100101011101011101011 ____________
7. 10101110101010101011110101000000 ____________
8. 11111111111111111100000000000001 ____________
9. 00111110111101111110000110101000 ____________
10. 00000000000000011010101111000111 ____________
11. 10101101011101011101011010000010 ____________
12. 11111100000000001111111110000001 ____________

Convert the following hexadecimal values to decimal.

1. 0x01A2 2. 0xFEDC 3. 0x1122

4. 0xB3A9 5. 0x43210A 6 0x12121200

16^7	16^6	16^5	16^4	16^3	16^2	16^1	16^0	Total
268435456	16777216	1048576	65536	4096	256	16	1	

There are many other issues that can be delved into relating to computer data. One such topic is signed versus unsigned numbers. The values shown thus far have been positive, and thus, unsigned. Recognize, however, that in certain circumstances numbers can also be negative. When programmers design code, they will define a number as either signed or unsigned. For example, a person's age is defined as an unsigned value because an age cannot be negative. However, if the code is calling for temperature in Fahrenheit, then it certainly can be negative. This issue of signed and unsigned values will be dealt with in more detail when the NTFS file system is covered in Chapter 11.

The big question now is, "Who cares?" Forensic examiners do. The reality is that many commonly used forensic programs will express values in hexadecimal. Not everything that is examined will be photographs, Word documents or web pages. Forensic examiners are regularly called upon to analyze information at a lower level or regions of data that cannot be displayed in any other method.

The next chapter will look at specific examples of how this information is applied.

CHAPTER SUMMARY

Bits and Bytes A bit is a binary digit and the smallest unit of data. A bit is represented by either a 1 or a 0. A byte is made up of 8 bits and can represent a single ASCII character. Half a byte is referred to as a ***nibble***. Each of the 2 nibbles per byte has 4 bits.

ASCII stands for the American Standard Code for Information Interchange. There are 128 characters in the ASCII table and Extended ASCII adds an additional 128 characters for a total of 256.

Each byte has a ***decimal value*** and a ***hexadecimal value***. The decimal value is calculated by establishing eight columns with headers of 128, 64, 32, 16, 8, 4, 2, and 1 from left to right. The 8 bits are placed under these column headers. Wherever there is a 1, the column header is added. For example, 01101011 is 64+32+8+2+1 = 107. Hexadecimal values are 0-9 and A-F for 0-16 decimal. The hexadecimal value for a byte can be calculated by determining the decimal value of each nibble from the byte. Using the same byte as above, the nibbles are 0110 and 1011. The decimal values are 6 and 11. In hexadecimal, this would be 6 and B, so the hexadecimal value of the byte is 6B.

Unicode uses at least 2 bytes and is replacing ASCII has the standard encoding format. For English characters the decimal values in Unicode are the same as in ASCII. This is done by padding the ASCII byte with a byte of 0.

When multiple bytes of data are read as a group, the order in which they are read is critical. On Motorola-based systems, the data is read from left to right, known as ***Big Endian***. On Intel-based systems, the data is read from right to left, or ***Little Endian***.

AT HOME PRACTICAL EXERCISES

1. What is the binary value for the decimal number 137?

2. What are the nibble values?

3. What is the hexadecimal value from decimal 137?

4. What ASCII character does the above hex value represent?

5. What is the binary value for the decimal number 216?

6. What are the nibble values?

7. What is the hexadecimal value from decimal 216?

8. What ASCII character does the above hex value represent?

9. What are the binary values for the letters

F								
o								
R								
E								
n								
S								
I								
c								

10. Convert 1 1 0 1 0 1 1 1 to Decimal and Hex

Dec_________________

Hex _________________

11. Convert BE to Decimal and Binary

Dec ____________________

Bin ____________________

12. Reading data off a Motorola-based Macintosh (Big Endian), convert the following unsigned 2-byte segments to decimal and binary in the space below.

1) FE 15 Dec ________

2) 01 E2 Dec ________

3) 76 A6 Dec ________

4) 26 54 Dec ________

5) 54 26 Dec ________

6) DD 01 Dec ________

7) 78 EA Dec ________

8) CF CB Dec ________

													4	2	1

13. Reading data off an Intel-based Macintosh (Little Endian), convert the following unsigned 2-byte segments to decimal and binary in the space provided below.

1) FE 15 Dec ____________

2) E2 01 Dec ____________

3) C8 55 Dec ____________

4) 31 86 Dec ____________

5) AE B9 Dec ____________

6) 11 00 Dec ____________

7) 00 11 Dec ____________

8) FB BF Dec ____________

ADVANCED PRACTICAL

Using the mathematical formula, convert the following hexadecimal values to decimal. (Show your work)

1) D7

2) 68 AB

3) 8C EF 21

4) 99 48 32 17

5) 76 4B 51 A1 FD

6) A2 11 3C C3 1D E6

REFERENCES

1. Sammes, T., & Jenkinson, B. (2007). *Forensic Computing, A Practitioner's Guide*. (2nd ed., pp. 7-11). London: Springer Publishing.

2. Norton, P., & Goodman, J. (1999). Inside the PC. (8th ed.). Indianapolis: SAMS Publishing.

3. ASCII table, ASCII Codes. (n.d.). Retrieved from http://www.theasciicode.com.ar/.

4. Hexadecimal Numbering System, (n.d.). Retrieved from http://www.computerhope.com/jargon/h/hex.htm

5. Nibble , (n.d.). Retrieved from http://www.computerhope.com/jargon/n/nibble.htm

6. The Unicode Consortium. (n.d.) Retrieved from http://www.unicode.org

7. Sammes, T., & Jenkinson, B. (2007). F*orensic Computing, A Practitioner's Guide*. (2nd ed., pp. 14-17). London: Springer Publishing.

8. Big-Endian and Little-Endian . (n.d.). Retrieved from http://searchnetworking.techtarget.com/definition/big-endian-and-little-endian

02 USES OF COMPUTER DATA

Chapter 1 discussed how computers utilize data. This chapter will look into practical uses of this knowledge, examining the basics of encryption, how file types are identified, and data verification through hashing.

Encryption

This is the process of obfuscating data through some encoding methodology or mathematical formula[1]. This can be at the bit, nibble, or byte level.

Bit Shifting: The process of moving the bits in a byte left or right.

Bit Shifting
The process of moving the bits in a byte left or right.

Plaintext
The decrypted data.

Cyphertext
Data after encryption.

Non-looping Bit Shift
01000110 Shift 1 to the left **10001100**
Note the left-most bit is lost and the right-most bit becomes a 0.

The process changed decimal 70 to decimal 140 or ASCII character F to î.

01111010 Shift two to the right 00011110 changes z to a Right Shift key.

Take the word EXAMPLE and shift one to the left.

01000101 01011000 01000001 01001101 01010000 01001100 01000101

Shift one to the left.

10001010 10110000 10000010 10011010 1010000 10011000 10001010

è░éÜÉÿè

While this is not a strong encryption, this does obfuscate the message. This example can be reversed by shifting 1 bit back to the right. Not all shifting can be reversed.

10000001 shifted 1 bit to the left gives 00000010; shifting 1 bit to the right gives 00000001. In this case, the original message is lost in the process so this would not make a very effective encryption scheme.

There is also a process of looping bit shifting, where instead of dropping off the end bit, it is looped back around. For example, start with 10100001 and bit shift 1 bit to the left, so it becomes 01000011. Also, 11001100 bit shifted 2 bits to the right becomes 00110011. Looping bit shifting can be reversed since no bits are lost.

PRACTICAL EXERCISE 1

Using non-looping bit shifts, shift the following by 3 bits to the left. Give the beginning and ending decimal values.

Original Bits	Shifted Bits	Original Decimal	New Decimal
11111000			
01011100			
00110110			
10101010			

Using looping bit shifts, shift the following by 2 bits to the right. Give the beginning and ending decimal values.

Original Bits	Shifted Bits	Original Decimal	New Decimal
11111000			
01011100			
00110110			
10101010			

Encrypt: "*Test Message*" by shifting 1 bit to the left. (Show work)

___ ___ ___ ___ ___ ___ ___ ___ ___ ___ ___

Nibble Swapping

This process switches the 2 nibbles in each byte. For example, the letter *x* is decimal 88, binary 01011000, and hexadecimal 58. Swapping the nibbles results in binary 10000101, hexadecimal 85, decimal 133, and ASCII character à.

Note that at the binary level,

0101 1000 swapped 1000 0101.

At the hex level, 58 becomes 85.

From an encryption perspective, this process is completely reversible.

PRACTICAL EXERCISE 2

Swap the nibbles from each byte. Give the beginning and ending decimal, binary and hex values.

Byte	Original Binary	Original Decimal	Original Hex	New Binary	New Decimal	New Hex	New Byte
T							
e							
s							
t							
<space>							
M							
e							
s							
s							
a							
g							
e							

XORing
Adding bytes

Nibble Swapping
The process of switching the 2 nibbles in each byte

Adding Bytes (XORing)

This process is the basis for using pass phrases.

Addition is done at the bit level.

Bit 1	Bit 2	Equals
0	0	0
0	1	1
1	0	1
1	1	0

This is applied by adding one byte to another.

Start with the capital letter *A*, binary 01000001, and encrypt it using the "key" lowercase *a*, binary 01100001.

```
  01000001
+ 01100001
__________
  00100000
```

This results in a decimal value of 32, <space> in ASCII.

This key can be applied to an entire word or message.

```
01000101 01011000 01000001 01001101 01010000 01001100

01100001 01100001 01100001 01100001 01100001 01100001
_____________________________________________________
00100100 00111001 00100000 00101100 00110001 00101101

Dec. 36        57       32     44       49       45
```

Result: $9 ,1-

While this is drastically different, it is still not very strong encryption. To make this stronger, the key length should be increased from 1 byte to multiple bytes. The longer the key value, the more difficult it will be to crack and reverse the process.

Use the key "abc" 01100001 01100010 01100011

E X A M P L E
a b c a b c a

01000101 01011000 01000001 01001101 01010000 01001100 01000101
01100001 01100010 01100011 01100001 01100010 01100011 01100001

00100100 00111010 00100010 00101100 00110010 00101111 00100100

Dec 36 58 34 44 50 47 36

Result: $:",2/$

Using the key "abcdefg," the following will occur:

01000101 01011000 01000001 01001101 01010000 01001100 01000101
01100001 01100010 01100011 01100100 01100101 01100110 01100111
00100100 00111010 00100010 00101001 00110101 00101010 00100010

Dec. 36 58 34 41 53 42 34

Result: $:")5*"

PRACTICAL EXERCISE 3

Go to Chapter 1 and copy the first two words of the first paragraph.

_____ ____________

Use this as the key to encrypt the following phrase between the quotes:

"We the people of the United States,"

Remember to include the <*space*> between the words as part of the key and encrypt the <*space*> between words in the sentence. For characters in the ASCII table with hex values of 0x00 through 0x20, use < > (i.e. <SPC>).

Plaintext Letter	W	e	<SPC>	t	h	e
Orig. Binary						
Key Letter						
Key Binary						
Cypher Binary						
Cypher Character						
Plaintext Letter						
Orig. Binary						
Key Letter						
Key Binary						
Cypher Binary						
Cypher Character						
Plaintext Letter						
Orig. Binary						
Key Letter						
Key Binary						
Cypher Binary						
Cypher Character						
Plaintext Letter						
Orig. Binary						
Key Letter						
Key Binary						
Cypher Binary						
Cypher Character						

Plaintext Letter						
Orig. Binary						
Key Letter						
Key Binary						
Cypher Binary						
Cypher Character						
Plaintext Letter						
Orig. Binary						
Key Letter						
Key Binary						
Cypher Binary						
Cypher Character						

Hex Editors

Before moving on to additional forensics implications of bits and bytes, there is much to learn about some of the software tools that will help in conducting examinations. One such tool is a hex editor that allows byte level access to files and physical drives. There are a number of hex editor programs available for DOS, Windows, Macintosh, and Linux operating systems. They each have different features, but what they have in common is that they display the data in both ASCII and Hexadecimal formats.

While there are some very good programs available, many come at a substantial price. A free program named **HxD**© is a recommended alternative. This program has basic editor features and can be downloaded at ***www.mh-nexus.de***. The tool has many functions and the main ones will be explained in this book. In future chapters, additional functionality will be discussed and utilized.

Another valuable tool is a text editor named **Notepad++**. This is similar to the text editor that comes with Windows, but has a ability to write both ASCII files as well as Unicode files. This is also a free program that can be download at ***www.notepad-plus-plus.org***.

FOLLOW-ALONG EXERCISE

Download and install the two programs mentioned on the previous page onto a Windows computer system.

1) Run Notepad++

2) Select File > New

3) Type the following sentence:

> *Outside of a dog, a book is man's best friend.*
> *Inside of a dog, it's too dark to read. - Groucho Marx*

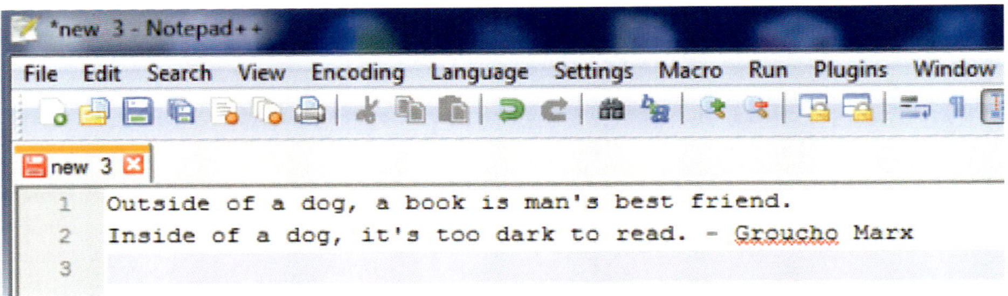

4) Select File>Save and save the file as ASCII.txt onto the desktop. The extension is added for you.

Based upon what is typed above, estimate how many bytes are in this file.

5) Next, select Encoding and Convert to UCS-2 Little Endian. This is Unicode, Little Endian format. Recall from Chapter One that this means data is read and written from right to left.

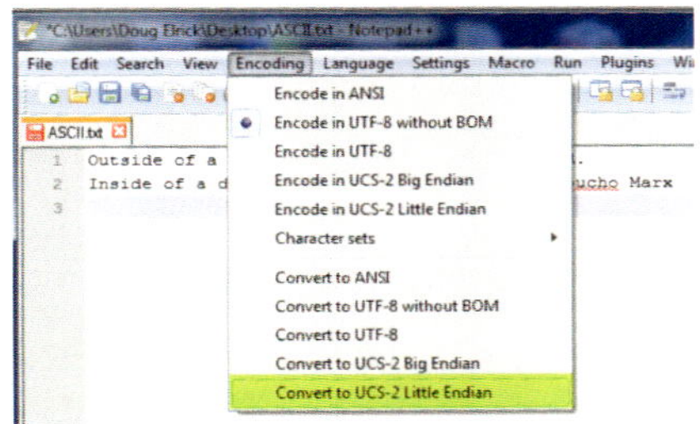

6) Select File As > Unicode.txt to your Desktop.

There will be no changes to the file. Exit Notepad++.

Estimate the number of bytes in the Unicode text file. ___________

7) Right click on the ASCII.txt file from the desktop, select Properties and note the file size.

How does this number compare to your estimate? Remember that each character is a single byte, even spaces and punctuation count.

Even while counting these bytes, you may come up a couple bytes short.

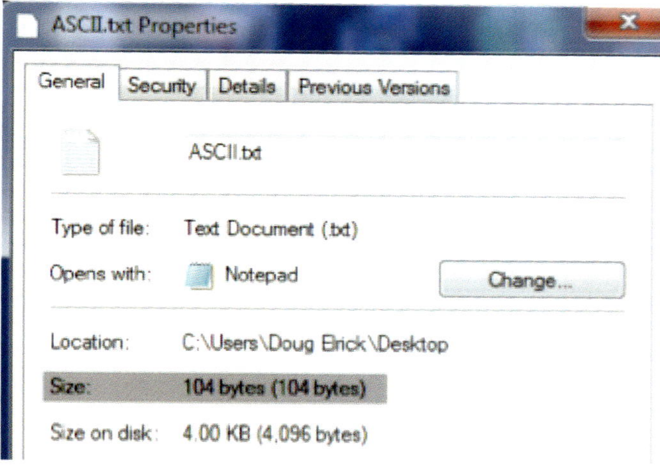

Take a look at this text file with the use of the hex editor to help explain the additional bytes.

Run HxD
Select File > Open, and select the ASCII.txt file.

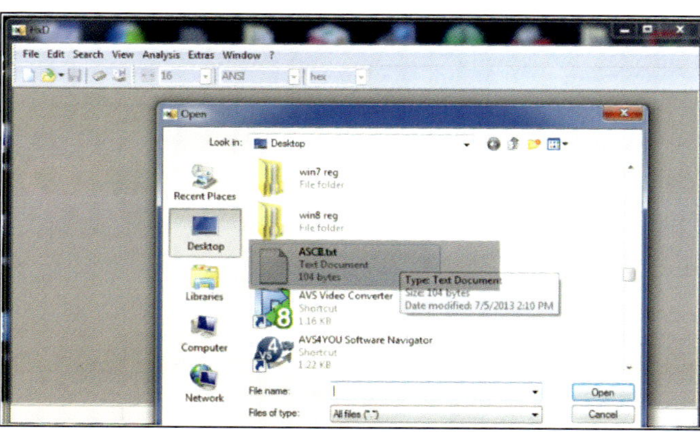

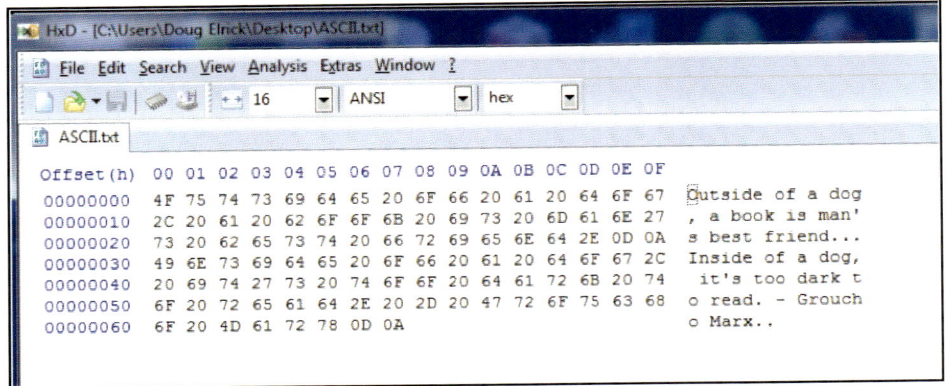

Offset

There are several features that should be noted. From the left side, there is the offset. The offset is the number of bytes from the beginning of a set point. Counting always begins with zero. The offset may be from the beginning of a file, a drive, or a partition. Throughout the remainder of this textbook, data will be referenced from various offsets. By default HxD displays the offsets in hexadecimal values. Note the (h) notation. This can be changed to decimal values by selecting View > Offset base.

Offset
Number of bytes from the the beginning of a set point, starting from zero.

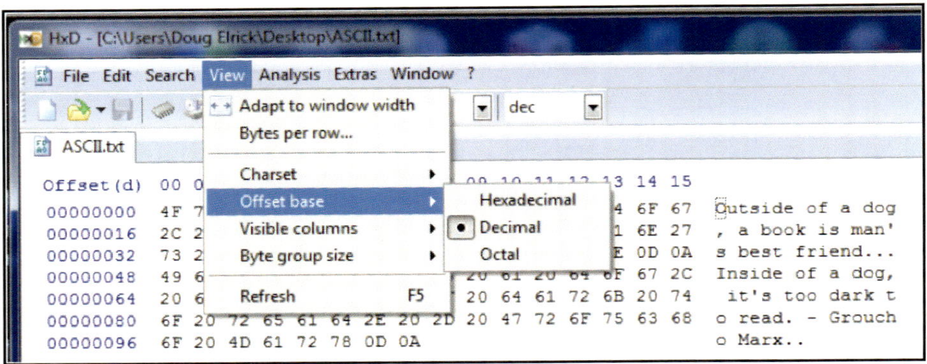

The next selection in the middle of the display is the hexadecimal view. Note that each row is 16 bytes in length. Hex editors typically display 16 bytes per row as this correlates to the fact that there 16 possible hex values. By examining the hexadecimal offsets displayed above, you will note the values of 0x00, 0x10, 0x20, 0x30 etc. or 0, 16, 32, 48 in decimal. The first row contains bytes 0 through 15, row two has bytes 16 through 31, row three has bytes 32 through 47, and row four has bytes 48 through 63.

The third section of the display has the ASCII values for each byte. As you move your cursor from byte to byte in the hex display, note that the corresponding ASCII value is highlighted. Go to offset 45 from the beginning of the file and provide the hexadecimal value.

You should have observed 0x2E. If you consult the ASCII table, you will find this to be a period *(.)*. Note the next 2 bytes 0x0D and 0x0A. Again consulting your ASCII table, you will find them to be a carriage return and a line feed. The carriage return sends the cursor back to the beginning of the line. The line feed jumps to the next line. These 2 bytes are entered when you hit the Enter key. The CR and LF go back to the days of typewriters. These account for the additional bytes in our file.

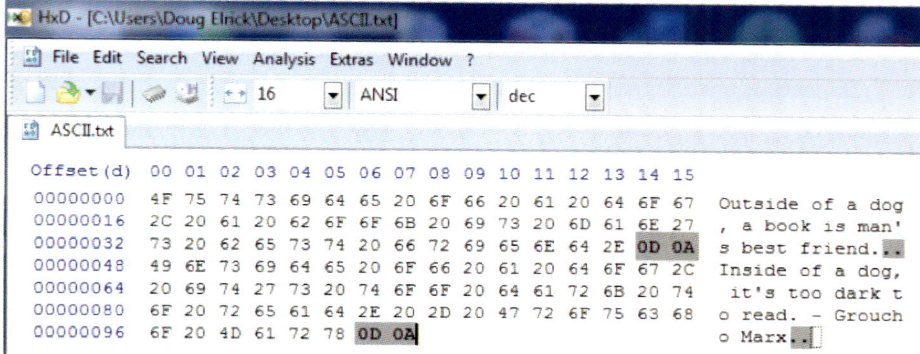

Since the CR and LF do not have display characters, HxD simply displays ".." in their place in the ASCII section.

Besides viewing the data, the hex editor will allow for modification of data as well. Go to offset 90. If you highlight the data from the beginning of the file, you will see the length of the highlighted portion so that you can identify the offset more easily.

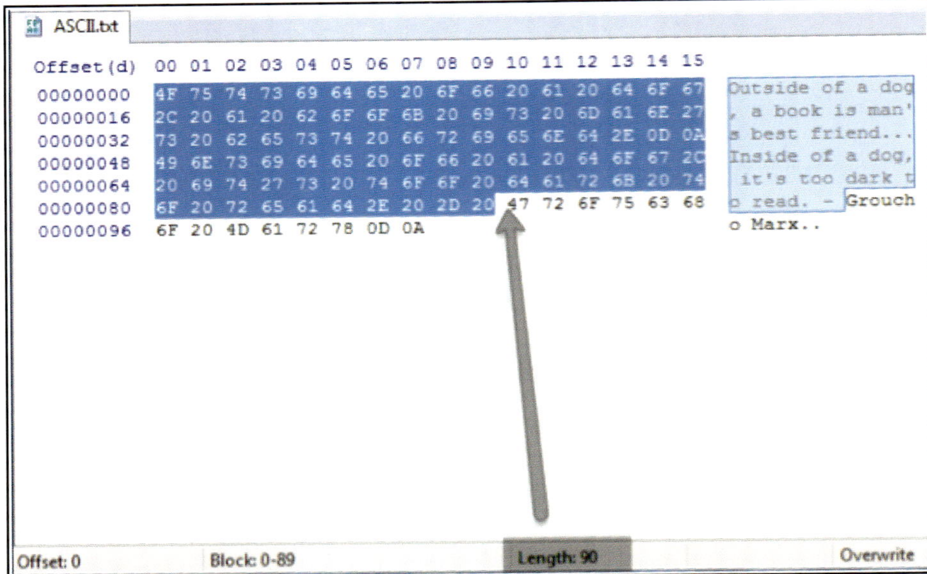

Offset 90 takes you to the G in Groucho. Hit the Tab key to move your editing cursor from the Hex section to the ASCII section. Replace Groucho Marx with your name even if it goes beyond the previous text.

```
Offset(d) 00 01 02 03 04 05 06 07 08 09 10 11 12 13 14 15
00000000  4F 75 74 73 69 64 65 20 6F 66 20 61 20 64 6F 67  Outside of a dog
00000016  2C 20 61 20 62 6F 6F 6B 20 69 73 20 6D 61 6E 27  , a book is man'
00000032  73 20 62 65 73 74 20 66 72 69 65 6E 64 2E 0D 0A  s best friend...
00000048  49 6E 73 69 64 65 20 6F 66 20 61 20 64 6F 67 2C  Inside of a dog,
00000064  20 69 74 27 73 20 74 6F 6F 20 64 61 72 6B 20 74   it's too dark t
00000080  6F 20 72 65 61 64 2E 20 2D 20 44 6F 75 67 6C 61  o read. - Dougla
00000096  73 20 45 6C 72 69 63 6B                          s Elrick
```

You then select File > Save to write these changes, or go to Edit >Undo to reverse what you type. Once you save the changes, the text will go from red to black, and the Undo option will no longer be available. There is a backup file, however, that will display the original text.

Next open up the Unicode.txt file in HxD. You can open up this file without closing the ASCII file.

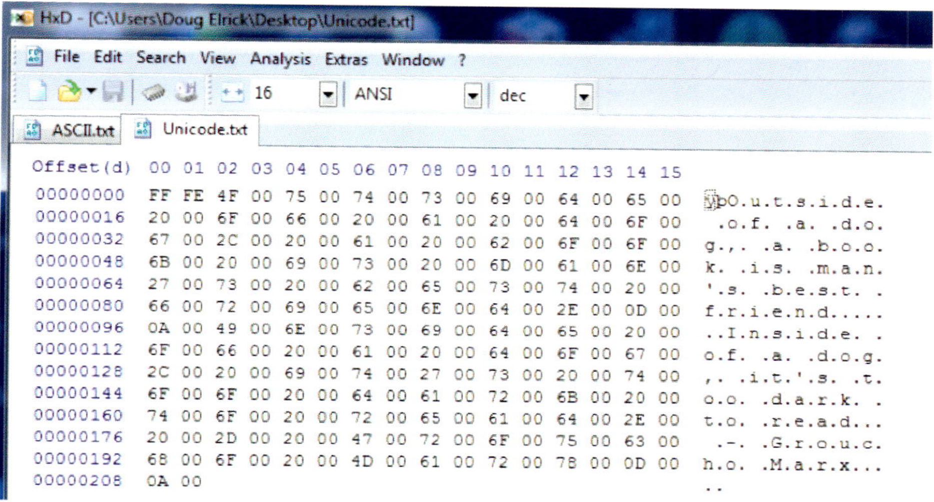

There are some very obvious differences between the two files. Note that there are 2 bytes added at the beginning. Data at the beginning of the file will be discussed file shortly. Next, note that there is a 0x00 byte between each letter. Remember that we saved this file in Unicode Little Endian format and this means that there are 2 bytes for each character and each are read from right to left. So starting with offset 2, the data will be read as follows: 0x004F 0x0075 0x0074 0x0073 0x0069 etc. Note on the ASCII section, there is a (.) for the extra byte. In a program that properly interprets Unicode, you will not see the (.). Finally, note the size of the Unicode file.

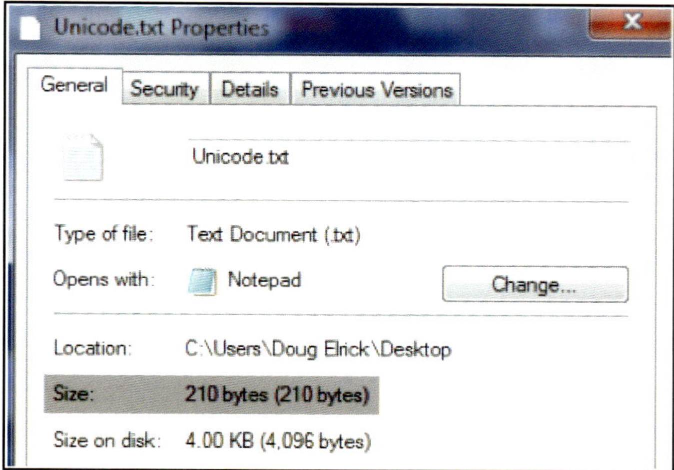

The ASCII file was 104 bytes in size. In the Unicode file, each character is twice the size: 208 bytes, plus the 2 bytes added at the beginning, which equals 210 bytes in size.

This effect was seen in the late 1990s when Microsoft Word began utilizing Unicode. The sizes of all the files doubled.

PRACTICAL EXERCISE 4

Provide the hex values at the decimal offsets.

Offset(d)	00	01	02	03	04	05	06	07	08	09	10	11	12	13	14	15
00000000	D4	C3	B2	A1	02	00	04	00	00	00	00	00	00	00	00	00
00000016	00	20	00	00	00	00	00	00	D2	09	5E	4B	8C	A4	09	00
00000032	34	00	00	00	34	00	00	00	02	00	00	00	45	C0	00	30
00000048	00	00	00	00	01	11	74	D2	20	E1	22	40	4A	4C	B6	BE
00000064	07	C1	07	C1	00	1C	4A	3F	00	00	10	02	07	78	48	00
00000080	76	6C	61	6E	37	32	00	00	AB	40	48	01	D3	09	5E	4B
00000096	2A	F0	00	00	34	00	00	00	34	00	00	00	02	00	00	00
00000112	45	C0	00	30	00	00	00	00	01	11	74	D1	20	E1	22	41
00000128	4A	4C	B6	BE	07	C1	07	C1	00	1C	52	52	00	00	08	02
00000144	07	64	48	00	76	6C	61	6E	37	32	00	00	AB	40	48	01
00000160	D3	09	5E	4B	EE	6C	07	00	EC	00	00	00	EC	00	00	00
00000176	02	00	00	00	45	00	00	E8	00	00	00	00	80	11	B3	14
00000192	20	E1	22	AE	20	E1	22	81	00	8A	00	8A	00	D4	E1	BA
00000208	11	02	C0	3A	AB	40	48	C9	00	8A	00	BE	00	00	20	45
00000224	4C	45	4A	46	49	43	41	43	41	43	41	43	41	43	41	43
00000240	41	43	41	43	41	43	41	43	41	43	41	43	41	43	41	00
00000256	20	45	44	46	47	45	42	43	4E	45	4F	46	45	43	41	43
00000272	41	43	41	43	41	43	41	43	41	43	41	43	41	43	41	42
00000288	4F	00	FF	53	4D	42	25	00	00	00	00	00	00	00	00	00
00000304	00	00	00	00	00	00	00	00	00	00	00	00	00	00	00	00
00000320	00	00	11	00	00	24	00	00	00	00	00	00	00	00	00	E8
00000336	03	00	00	00	00	00	00	00	00	24	00	56	00	03	00	01
00000352	00	00	00	02	00	35	00	5C	4D	41	49	4C	53	4C	4F	54
00000368	5C	42	52	4F	57	53	45	00	0F	00	80	FC	0A	00	4B	49
00000384	58	00	00	00	04	F4	B8	64	AE	A4	D1	11	B7	B6	05	02

Offset 23 – 1 byte :

Offset 59 – 3 bytes (LE):

Offset 99 – 4 bytes (LE):

Offset 131 – 2 bytes (BE):

Offset 195 – 1 bytes:

Offset 246 – 5 bytes (LE):

Offset 377 – 8 bytes (LE):

Using HxD open the file \Chapter Two\Offset File 1.txt.

Provide the ASCII text for the following decimal offsets.

Offset 37 – 6 bytes:

Offset 309 – 15 bytes:

Offset 472 – 6 bytes:

Offset 638 – 9 bytes:

Offset 890 – 10 bytes:

Offset 1175 – 15 bytes:

File Headers

Files can be identified in two different manners. The first method is by file extension. The extension is typically added to a file by whatever application was used to create it. For example, Microsoft Word creates files with .DOC extensions, Adobe Acrobat creates files with .PDF extensions, and compilers create programs with .EXE extensions. When coming across different files during a forensic examination, the file extensions can be useful in determining what types of files you have. There are several websites available that can be helpful in identifying extensions that are not familiar to you:

www.garykessler.net/library/file_sigs.html
www.filext.com
http://en.wikipedia.org/wiki/List_of_file_signatures
However, these extensions are not required. A Word document does

not have to have a .DOC extension in order to for it to be a Word document. Many files have several bytes at the beginning that uniquely identify the type of file that it is. This is referred to as the File Header, File Signature, or Magic Number.
These bytes are typically hexadecimal values that may be as short as 2 bytes or may be as long as 16 to 20 bytes. Most headers begin at offset 0, but there are some that begin several bytes into the file.

Below is a list of a few common file headers from ***www.filesignatures.net:***

Extension	Header (signature) (Hex)	Associated Program
DOC	D0 CF 11 E0 A1 B1 1A E1 00	Microsoft Office
EML	46 72 6F 6D	Generic Email
EXE	4D 5A	Windows Executable
GIF	47 49 46 38	Graphic Interchange Format
JPG	FF D8 FF E0	JPEG Graphics Format
MOV	73 6B 69 70	Quicktime Movie
PDF	25 50 44 46	Adobe Acrobat
ZIP	50 4B 07 08	PK Zip File

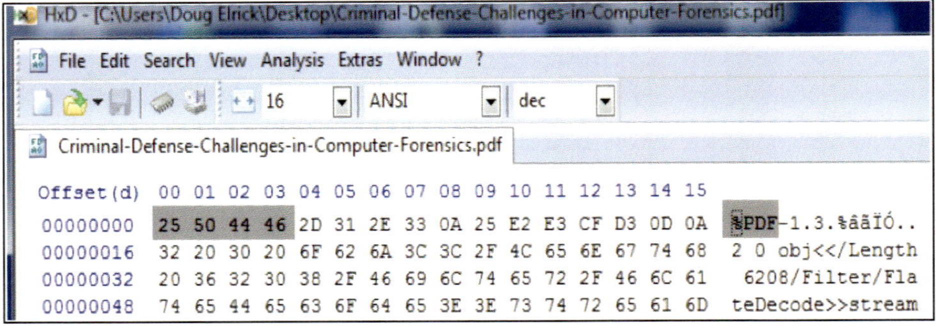

Note the file signature for the Adobe Acrobat file.

PRACTICAL EXERCISE 5

Using HxD, open the file Chapter Two File 2.txt
Search for the header for a JPEG file. Select search and change the data type to Hex values.

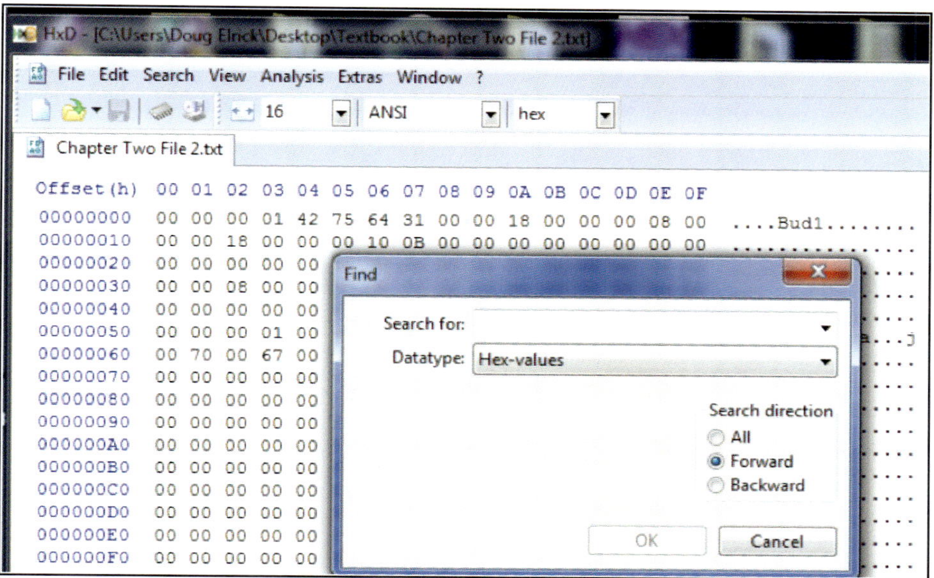

How many headers did you find?

Hash Values

The last byte-based issue we will look at is ***hash values***. A hash is a value expressed in hexadecimal that is calculated based upon the content of the item examined. This item may be a file, a forensic image, or a physical storage device. Forensic hash values are used for verification of data and for file comparison. A hash has been likened to a fingerprint in that it is a unique value. There are several types of hash calculations, but the most common utilized in forensics are the MD5, the SHA-1, and the SHA-2 methods. When two files have the same hash value, it is known as a collision. With MD5, there have been collisions generated in test facilities.

Hash
Value expressed in hexadecimal that is calculated based upon the content of the item examined

As mentioned, forensic hash values are used for file comparison. This is done in two different fashions. First, they can be used to eliminate files that have to be reviewed. Second, they can be used to identify specific files of evidentiary value. On a typical drive, there are hundreds of thousands of files. Many files can be eliminated for inspection if they can be shown to be exact matches to a known standard. For example, there is no need to examine all the Microsoft operating system files if they match the files from the installation disc. This will tell you that the files have not been altered by the subject.

Evidence files can also be identified by searching files for the hash values. An example of this would be the use of a hash database by the National Center for Missing and Exploited Children (NCMEC). The center has taken thousands of known child pornography images and created a hash value database for each. Evidence files can be searched against this database. A match can definitively prove the presence of a child pornography picture in the possession of the subject. Another example is when a death threat document is sent to a politician. This document can be hashed and then searched for across a drive.

To demonstrate the hashing process we will use a free tool named HashCalc from http://www.slavasoft.com/hashcalc/. There are many free hashing tools available, and the feature is incorporated into full forensic programs such as EnCase and FTK.

FOLLOW ALONG EXERCISE 2

Download and install HashCalc on to your Windows computer.

Go to ***www.usconstitution.net/const.pdf*** and save a copy of the US Constitution to your desktop.

This example can actually be done with any file of your choosing, but in order to start and end with the same values, we will use the same file.

Open HashCalc, and make sure the following hash types are checked: MD5, SHA1 and CRC32.

Drag and drop the CONST.PDF file onto the HashCalc window.

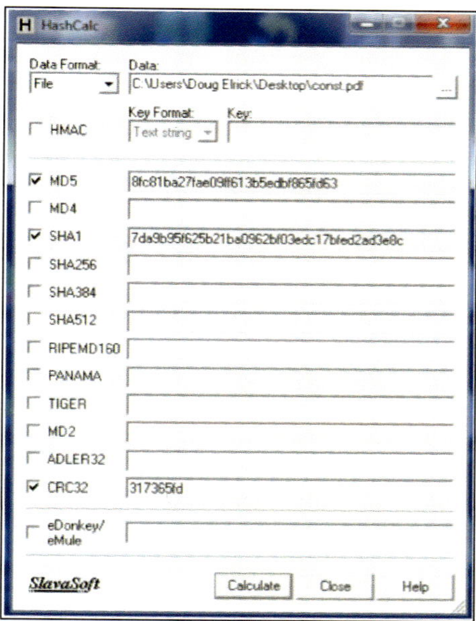

Open up CONSTAT.PDF in HxD, and go to offset 55867, and change the byte from 32 to 33. This is a change from 00110010 to 00110011. We are simply flipping a single bit.

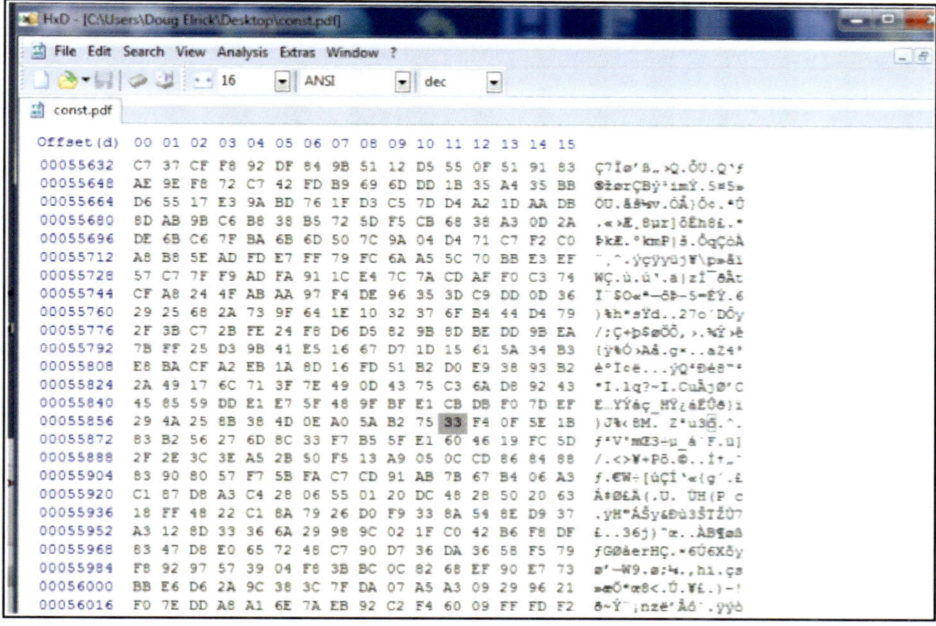

Save the file and drop it again onto Hashcalc.

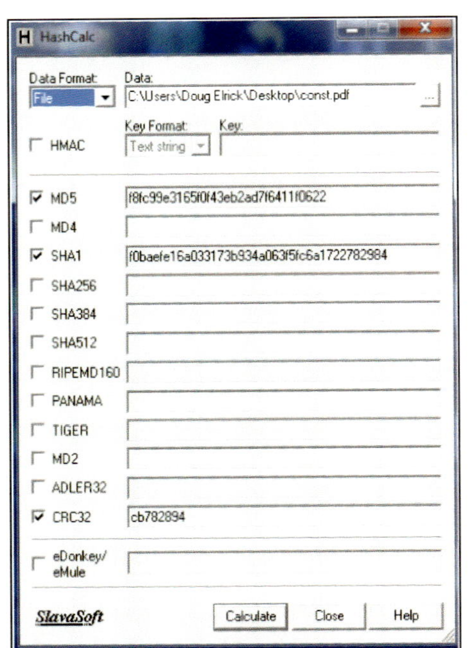

This shows that a change in a single bit will cause a change in the hash values.

Note that all three hash values are expressed in hexadecimal.

CHAPTER SUMMARY

1. ***Encryption*** is the process of obscuring data in a method that can be reversed. The unencrypted data is referred to as plaintext, and the encrypted data is referred as cyphertext.

2. There are several methods of encrypting data at the bit or hexadecimal level, such as ***bit shifting*** or ***nibble swapping.***

3. Adding bits together can also encrypt data. This process is known as ***XORing***. In this process, adding two 0s or two 1s results in a 0. Adding a 0 and 1 or a 1 and 0 processes a 1.

4. ***Hex editors*** are programs that provide hexadecimal access to files and drives. These tools allow the use to edit and change data. Data is identified by ***offsets***, which is the number of bytes from the beginning of the section of data.

5. ***File headers*** (signatures) are the first few bytes in a file that identify the type. These headers can be either in hexadecimal or ASCII characters. Searching for file headers can help examiners find previously deleted files.

6. ***Hashing*** is a mathematical process that provides a digital fingerprint of a file or a drive. If any bits or bytes are changed in a file then the hash value will change. There are different algorithms, but the common ones used forensically are CRC32, MD5 and SHA-1.

AT HOME EXERCISES

1. Encrypt the following text using a non-looping bit-shift 2 bytes to the left.

*Digital*Forensics*

2. Encrypt the same text above using the nibble-swap technique.

3. Decrypt the following 13 nibble-swapped characters.

R ç 4 T ╞ ─ T µ E u ù ' ╢

4. Decrypt the following hex values with the key *password.* Provide their decrypted ASCII characters.

0x25 0D 06 53 13 06 16 44 11 41 14 01 12 0D 06 44 3A 0D 11

5. Provide the requested offsets from Intel-based system.

Dec Offset	Hex Offset	# Bytes	Type	HEX
a) 35	23	2	uShort	
b) 104	68	2	uShort	
c) 170	AA	2	uShort	
d) 236	EC	4	uINT	
e) 296	128	8	uLong	

```
00000000 33 c0 8e d0 bc 00 7c 8e-c0 8e d8 be 00 7c bf 00
00000010 06 b9 00 02 fc f3 a4 50-68 1c 06 cb fb b9 04 00
00000020 bd be 07 80 7e 00 00 7c-0b 0f 85 10 01 83 c5 10
00000030 e2 f1 cd 18 88 56 00 55-c6 46 11 05 c6 46 10 00
00000040 b4 41 bb aa 55 cd 13 5d-72 0f 81 fb 55 aa 75 09
00000050 f7 c1 01 00 74 03 fe 46-10 66 60 80 7e 10 00 74
00000060 26 66 68 00 00 00 00 66-ff 76 08 68 00 00 68 00
00000070 7c 68 01 00 68 10 00 b4-42 8a 56 00 8b f4 cd 13
00000080 9f 83 c4 10 9e eb 14 b8-01 02 bb 00 7c 8a 56 00
00000090 8a 76 01 8a 4e 02 8a 6e-03 cd 13 66 61 73 1e fe
000000a0 4e 11 0f 85 0c 00 80 7e-00 80 0f 84 8a 00 b2 80
000000b0 eb 82 55 32 e4 8a 56 00-cd 13 5d eb 9c 81 3e fe
000000c0 7d 55 aa 75 6e ff 76 00-e8 8a 00 0f 85 15 00 b0
000000d0 d1 e6 64 e8 7f 00 b0 df-e6 60 e8 78 00 b0 ff e6
000000e0 64 e8 71 00 b8 00 bb cd-1a 66 23 c0 75 3b 66 81
000000f0 fb 54 43 50 41 75 32 81-f9 02 01 72 2c 66 68 07
00000100 bb 00 00 66 68 00 02 00-00 66 68 08 00 00 00 66
00000110 53 66 53 66 55 66 68 00-00 00 00 66 68 00 7c 00
00000120 00 66 61 68 00 00 07 cd-1a 5a 32 f6 ea 00 7c 00
00000130 00 cd 18 a0 b7 07 eb 08-a0 b6 07 eb 03 a0 b5 07
00000140 32 e4 05 00 07 8b f0 ac-3c 00 74 fc bb 07 00 b4
00000150 0e cd 10 eb f2 2b c9 e4-64 eb 00 24 02 e0 f8 24
```

6. Open Chapter Two Signature Files.zip. Under the folder Ext Change there are nine files that have had their extension changed. Research the file header (signatures), and provide the correct extension.

Using Hashcalc (***www.slavasoft.com/hashcalc***), calculate the MD5 for each file after the extension change.

Name	Header	Correct Extension	MD5 Hash
EnCase v615.xls			
faq.txt			
FlickAnimation.dat			
George.exe			
hashcalc.act			
Penguins.swp			
sample.zif			
spinner[1].doc			
wizard.emf			

7. Under the folder Sig Change, there are 10 files that have had their file header (signature) changed to X (hex 58). Research the file extension and using a hex editor like HxD, put in the correct header.

Open any media files to test.

Using Hashcalc, calculate the MD5 for each file after the header change.

Name	Correct Header	MD5
Clip_1080_5sec_10mbps_h264.mp4		
Clip_1080_5sec_MPEG2_HD_15mbps.mpg		
ehiUserXp.dll		
favicon[1].ico		
gc2.rar		
imkren.chm		
PreviewEffect.png		
RUNDLL32.EXE-007BDBE0.pf		
Windows Error.wav		
Youtube.swf		

ADVANCED PRACTICAL

Devise your own encryption method at the bit or byte level. Describe your encryption scheme, and provide an example.

CASE STUDY 1: ENCRYPTING FILES

Several years back, a sixteen-year-old boy was accused of sexually abusing his younger stepsister. Police executed a warrant against the family's home and seized a Macintosh computer from the boy's room along with an external hard drive. During the interview, the suspect laid down the gauntlet to the police by saying that they would never get access to the external Lacie hard drive. It was password-protected, prohibiting mounting without the key.

Cracking the password protected drive required identifying the program utilized. In this case, the program found on the suspect's program was related to the Lacie external hard drive. Using this program, a new drive was protected with a password of AAAAAAAA. No files were added and the drive was imaged. The drive was wiped and setup again, this time the password of BBBBBBBB was added. The drive was reimaged and compared to the first image made. Based upon the comparison, it was noted that only eight bytes near the beginning of the drive were different. Using this information, we went to the same location on the copy of the original evidence and changed all the data to 0, which allowed full access to the data.

Since the suspect had laid down the challenge, just getting access was not enough. Deciphering the password needed to be done to put him in his place. It was noted in the examination that in the first image, the eight bytes stored were DDDDDDDD and the eight bytes in the second image were EEEEEEEE. This appeared to be a character shift of four bytes. Adding a password of ABCDEFGH resulted in LKJIHGFED. This again showed the password was shifted four bytes and stored in reverse order on the drive. Reversing the process on the original drive showed the password was PICARD001. Relevant information was recovered from the drive and the suspect pled guilty.

CASE STUDY 2: TRIAL VERSION

Another case involved a man accused possessing child pornography. A large number of encrypted pictures were found on his computer drive. Examination of the file headers of the pictures revealed that a shareware encryption program was used. Shareware is a program that is copyrighted but allows some level of access before purchasing. In this case, the full version of the program ran around $20. The suspect was unaware that when using the trial version, the header of each file has the following: *This file was encrypted using the password: XXXXXXXX*, giving the password used. The suspect was amazed that his encryption was defeated and, of course, was never told of his blunder so that word would not get out that you could hide pictures for $20. This case ended in a plea agreement.

03 PHYSICAL & LOGICAL STRUCTURES: PART I

The primary focus of digital forensics is the examination of media and one of the most common media types is the hard disk. This chapter will cover the general process of how data can be organized and stored.

When we refer to a physical drive, we are referring to something you can hold in your hand. The humorist and columnist Dave Barry wrote, "Hard Drive: The part of the computer that stops working when you spill beer on it."

Physical hard disks are made up of platters, heads and voice coil actuators. For our purposes we are going to be examining the data structure laid out on the platters.

A drive may have one or more platters. Early hard drives could be found with three or four platters. There is a floating head over each side of each platter. So if a drive has three platters then there will be six heads. Heads actually float on a cushion of air about 15 nanometers thick and the platters commonly spin beneath them at rates of 5400, 7200, or 10,000 revolutions per second.

Each platter is referenced by top and bottom ***sides***. Each side is broken down into concentric circles called ***tracks***. Both sides and tracks are numbered starting with 0.

The numbering of the tracks starts at the outer ring and moves inward. If there are multiple platters in the drive, then they will be numbered starting with 0 as well.

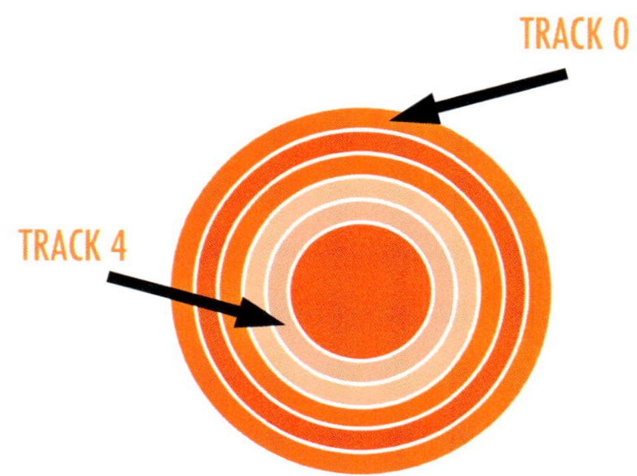

Head
Floats above hard drive platters and reads data

Platter
Disks within a hard drive that store datea

Sides
Top and bottom of a platter

Tracks
Concentric circles of a platter

Cylinder
Group of same-numbered tracks on all platters

Sectors
Units of data that hold 512 bytes

Grouping the platters, we take all the same tracks for each side, and these are referred to together as a ***cylinder***.

Notice in this figure, there is a Track 0 on Head 0, 1, 2, 3, 4, 5, 6, and 7. These combine to make Cylinder 0.

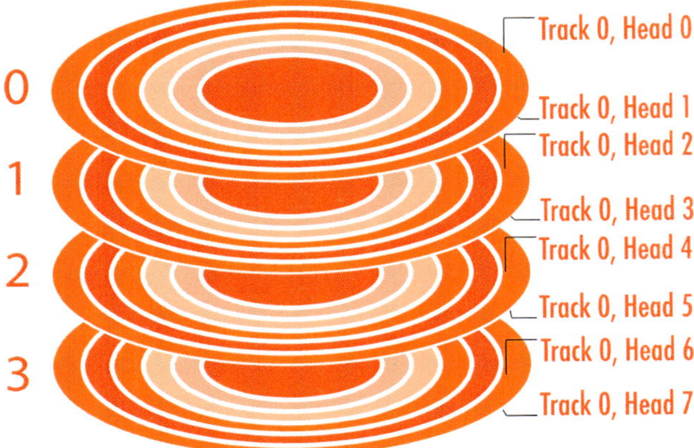

Progressing inward on the platters will be each of the cylinders.

In this case, there will be Cylinders 0, 1, 2, 3, and 4.

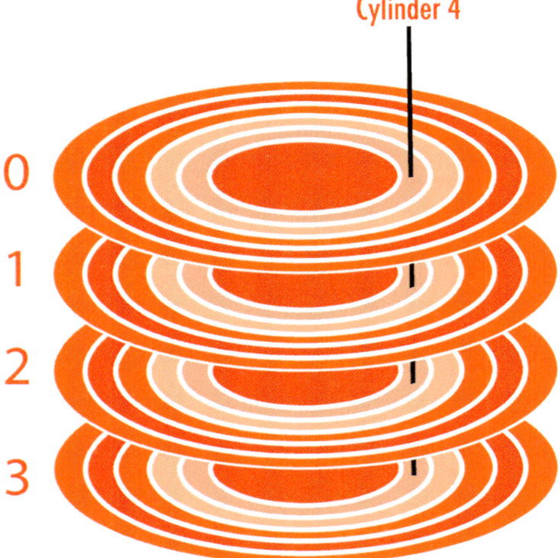

We are going to break down the tracks into pie-shaped components called ***sectors***. A sector is a unit of data that typically holds 512 bytes of data. Unlike the heads, tracks, cylinders and platters, which start counting at 0, sectors begin with 1.

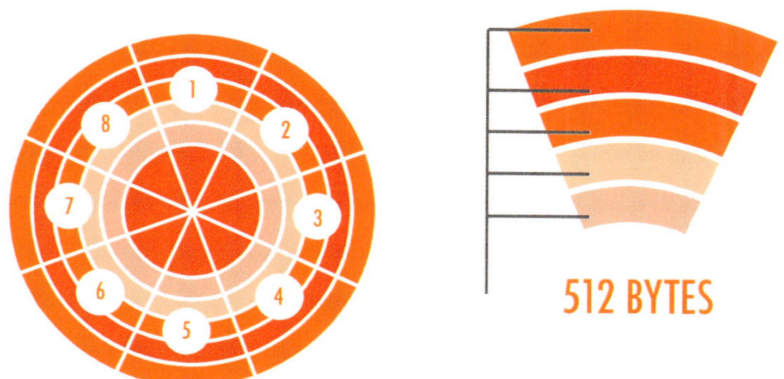

Note that the sectors in the outer tracks are visually larger than those in the inner tracks.

Despite the size difference in appearance, each still holds 512 bytes of data.

Besides the 512 bytes of data, there is also additional information such as a header or footer and data CRC.

Header, Address, CRC	512 Bytes of Data	Footer, CRC

Based upon the information above, we now have a three-dimensional coordinate system to find data – cylinder, head and sector.

For example, lets find data at Cylinder 4, Head 4 and Sector 4 (CHS 4/4/4)
First we start with the Cylinder.

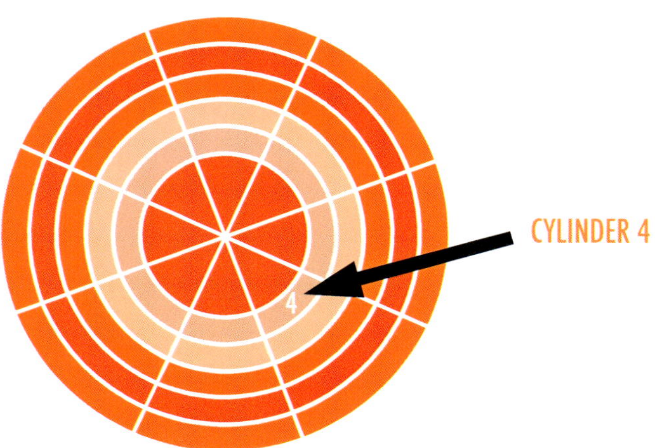

Next we identify Head 4.

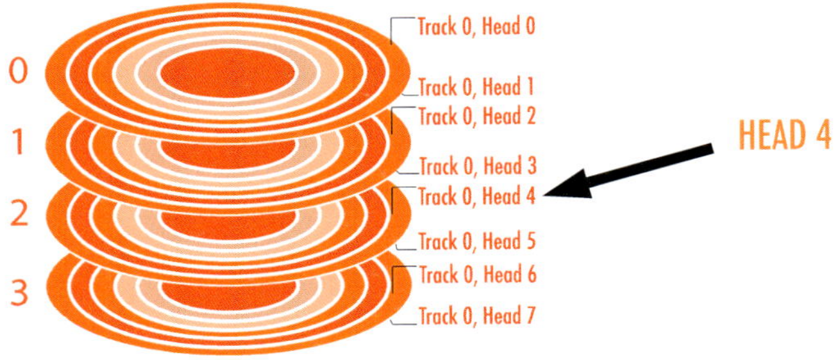

Finally we identify Sector 4

Logical Block Address (LBA)
A unique number given to each sector for identification of its location.

Now we have specifically identified a region of data on the hard drive.

For years, this was the method for locating and identifying data. This has changed now to give each sector (still typically 512 bytes of data) a unique number starting with 0. These are referred to as a ***Logical Block Addresses (LBA)***. Utilizing LBA, each sector is sequentially numbered making identification much easier.

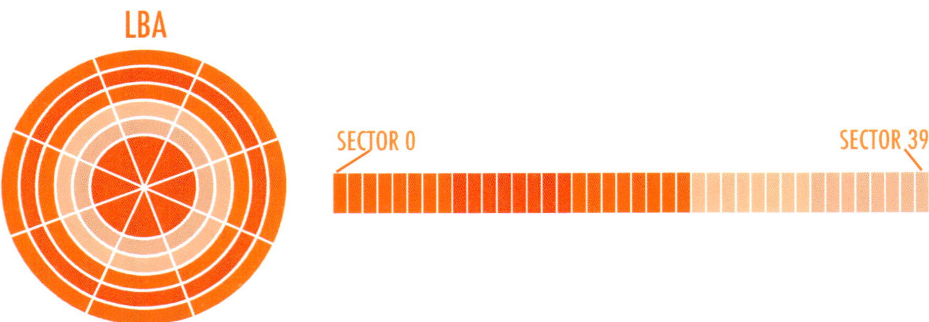

Drive capacities can be calculated by multiplying the number of sectors by 512.

LBA sectors 235,345,630 * 512 bytes per sector = 120,496,962,560 (120 gigabytes).

Partitioning (Master Boot Record)

To get to the point of understanding how files can be saved and tracked we must first understand the organizational structure of the drive. Files can only be stored on a file system, and a file system must exist on a partition. Imagine you are filing paper. The papers go into file folders and the folders go into file cabinets. There are different ways of designing file cabinets. Historically, the structural system used is referred to as the ***Master Boot Record (MBR)*** method. In the next chapter we will cover a different method that is likely to become the standard.

Master Boot Record (MBR)
Method of organizing a hard drive

To understand the MBR system we start with the structure of the disk. We previously discussed the concept of disk tracks: the concentric rings around the platters. Recall that we start counting the tracks with 0. In the MBR system, we reserve the entire Track 0 for the partitioning structure. On current drives, this means there will be either 63 sectors reserved or 1024 sectors. Even though we have reserved this many sectors, only one of them will be used (LBA sector 0). This is the very first sector of the drive.

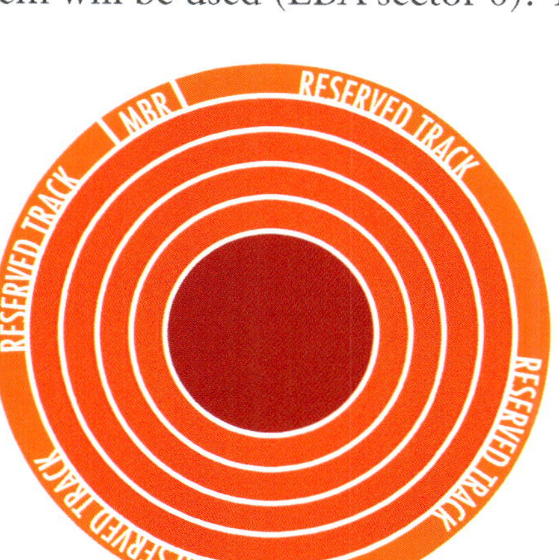

If there are 63 sectors per track (spt), then Sector 0 will contain the structural information (MBR), and the remaining 62 sectors will typically contain all 0s.

If there are 1024 sectors per track (spt), then Sector 0 will contain the structural information (MBR), and the remaining 1023 sectors will typically contain all 0s.

Also recall that typically, each sector contains 512 bytes of data. In this first sector, there will be 446 bytes of what is referred to as boot code. This is specific data placed in the sector by the system that set up the structure. The boot code has the instructions on starting up the drive to be read properly. One piece of information that Microsoft Windows places in this section is the drive serial number.

```
Offset(d)   00 01 02 03 04 05 06 07 08 09 10 11 12 13 14 15
0000000000  33 C0 8E D0 BC 00 7C FB 50 07 50 1F FC BE 1B 7C  3ÀŽĐ¼.|ûP.P.ü¾.|
0000000016  BF 1B 06 50 57 B9 E5 01 F3 A4 CB BD BE 07 B1 04  ¿..PW¹å.ó¤Ë½¾.±.
0000000032  38 6E 00 7C 09 75 13 83 C5 10 E2 F4 CD 18 8B F5  8n.|.u.ƒÅ.âôÍ.‹õ
0000000048  83 C6 10 49 74 19 38 2C 74 F6 A0 B5 07 B4 07 8B  ƒÆ.It.8,tö µ.´.‹
0000000064  F0 AC 3C 00 74 FC BB 07 00 B4 0E CD 10 EB F2 88  ð¬<.tü»..´.Í.ëòˆ
0000000080  4E 10 E8 46 00 73 2A FE 46 10 80 7E 04 0B 74 0B  N.èF.s*þF.€~..t.
0000000096  80 7E 04 0C 74 05 A0 B6 07 75 D2 80 46 02 06 83  €~..t. ¶.uÒ€F..ƒ
0000000112  46 08 06 83 56 0A 00 E8 21 00 73 05 A0 B6 07 EB  F..ƒV..è!.s. ¶.ë
0000000128  BC 81 3E FE 7D 55 AA 74 0B 80 7E 10 00 74 C8 A0  ¼.>þ}Uªt.€~..tÈ
0000000144  B7 07 EB A9 8B FC 1E 57 8B F5 CB BF 05 00 8A 56  ·.ë©‹ü.W‹õË¿..ŠV
0000000160  00 B4 08 CD 13 72 23 8A C1 24 3F 98 8A DE 8A FC  .´.Í.r#ŠÁ$?˜ŠÞŠü
0000000176  43 F7 E3 8B D1 86 D6 B1 06 D2 EE 42 F7 E2 39 56  C÷ã‹Ñ†Ö±.ÒîB÷â9V
0000000192  0A 77 23 72 05 39 46 08 73 1C B8 01 02 BB 00 7C  .w#r.9F.s.¸..».|
0000000208  8B 4E 02 8B 56 00 CD 13 73 51 4F 74 4E 32 E4 8A  ‹N.‹V.Í.sQOtN2äŠ
0000000224  56 00 CD 13 EB E4 8A 56 00 60 BB AA 55 B4 41 CD  V.Í.ëäŠV.`»ªU´AÍ
0000000240  13 72 36 81 FB 55 AA 75 30 F6 C1 01 74 2B 61 60  .r6.ûUªu0öÁ.t+a`
0000000256  6A 00 6A 00 FF 76 0A FF 76 08 6A 00 68 00 7C 6A  j.j.ÿv.ÿv.j.h.|j
0000000272  01 6A 10 B4 42 8B F4 CD 13 61 61 73 0E 4F 74 0B  .j.´B‹ôÍ.aas.Ot.
0000000288  32 E4 8A 56 00 CD 13 EB D6 61 F9 C3 49 6E 76 61  2äŠV.Í.ëÖaùÃInva
0000000304  6C 69 64 20 70 61 72 74 69 74 69 6F 6E 20 74 61  lid partition ta
0000000320  62 6C 65 00 45 72 72 6F 72 20 6C 6F 61 64 69 6E  ble.Error loadin
0000000336  67 20 6F 70 65 72 61 74 69 6E 67 20 73 79 73 74  g operating syst
0000000352  65 6D 00 4D 69 73 73 69 6E 67 20 6F 70 65 72 61  em.Missing opera
0000000368  74 69 6E 67 20 73 79 73 74 65 6D 00 00 00 00 00  ting system.....
0000000384  00 00 00 00 00 00 00 00 00 00 00 00 00 00 00 00  ................
0000000400  00 00 00 00 00 00 00 00 00 00 00 00 00 00 00 00  ................
0000000416  00 00 00 00 00 00 00 00 00 00 00 00 00 00 00 00  ................
0000000432  00 00 00 00 00 2C 44 63 93 7F F1 4D 00 00 80 01  .....,Dc".ñM..€.
```

This is a 4-byte value written in Little Endian. This serial number is located at sector offset 440. Remember that we start counting at 0 when looking for an offset.

The serial number in the example graphic is 0x4D F1 7F 93 when read in Little Endian.

This leaves 66 remaining bytes (512-446=66). Sixty-four of these bytes are used for a partition table. Partitions are defined areas on a drive that can hold a file system. We will discuss files systems in later chapters. Partitions are used to segregate data. In the past, partitions were used to separate programs from the files that were created. Today, if there are multiple partitions on a drive, then one will be the main boot partition containing Microsoft Windows and your files. A second partition may be a system-restore partition containing the files needed to set the drive back to factory specifications. Another reason to find a multiple partitions is because there are multiple operating systems on the same drive, such as Windows and Linux. It is very common to just find a single partition on a drive.

The Partition Table contains four 16-byte records. This means there can be four partitions defined for each drive. However, a drive does not require four partitions; it only needs one in order to store files. Each record defines the type of partition it is, the size and the location on the drive.

Byte offset 0 – This byte is used to indicate whether the drive is bootable or not. To be bootable means that if the drive contains an operating system such as Windows 8, then the drive can be used to start up. If the drive is not bootable, then it can be used to stored data when connected to a computer that has a boot drive. For example, an external USB hard drive will not be set to be bootable. There will be two optional values that can be used in this byte, either 0x00 for non-bootable or 0x80 for bootable.

Byte offset 1 – There are 3 bytes used for the starting Cylinder, Head, and Sector. Here is an example of the legacy use of CHS values. The starting CHS is obtained as follows: byte 1 is the Head, and the first 6 bits from byte 2 are for the Sector location, and the remaining 2 bits from byte 2 plus the 8 bits from byte 3 are used to obtain the Cylinder location.

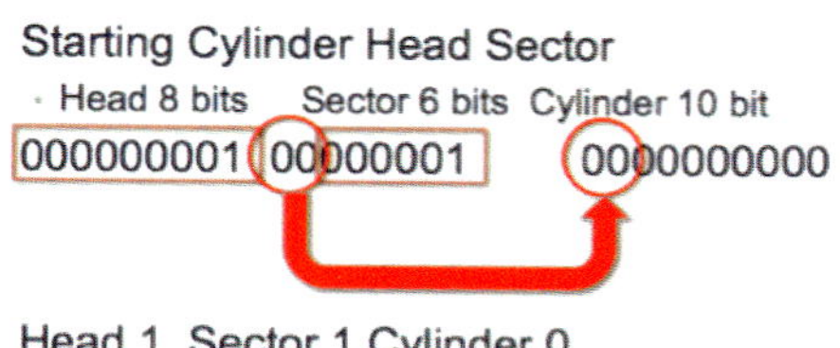

With 8 bits for the Head, 6 bits for the Sector, and 10 bits for the Cylinder, then there are limits of:

255 Heads (11111111), 63 Sectors (111111) and 1023 Cylinders (1111111111)

Typically the first partition will start at Head 0, Sector 1, and Cylinder 1. Note that it is reported as CHS, it is recorded in the data as HSC.

Byte Offset 4 – System Indicator or partition type. There is a listing of partition types in Appendix B identified by a single byte. Below is a sampling of the partition types:

www.win.tue.nl/~aeb/partitions/partition_types-1.html
00 Empty
01 DOS 12-bit FAT (up to 15 M)
02 XENIX root
03 XENIX /usr
04 DOS 3.0+ 16-bit FAT (up to 32M)
05 DOS 3.3+ Extended Partition
06 DOS 3.31+ 16-bit FAT (over 32M)
07 Windows NT NTFS
08 Commodore DOS
09 AIX data partition
0a OS/2 Boot Manager
0b WIN95 OSR2 32-bit FAT
0c WIN95 OSR2 32-bit FAT, LBA-mapped
0e WIN95: DOS 16-bit FAT, LBA-mapped
0f WIN95: Extended partition, LBA-mapped

In Windows environments the hard drives typically have a partition type of 0x07.

Byte Offset 5 – Ending CHS value. Bytes 5, 6, and 7 contain the last location of the partition. The values are calculated in the same manner as the starting CHS. Again, it is stored as HSC.

Byte Offset 8 – Starting LBA sector. This is a 32-bit, unsigned integer (4 bytes) providing the starting sector of the partition. This value is much easier to interpret than the CHS values.

Byte Offset 12 – This is the number of sectors in the partitions. Again this is a 32-bit, unsigned integer (4 bytes). Multiplying this value times the bytes per sector (typically 512) will provide the size of the partition. Below is an example of a partition table with three partitions in it.

OFFSET 446

```
00000000416  00 00 00 00 00 00 00 00 00 00 00 00 00 00 00 00  ................
00000000432  00 00 00 00 00 2C 44 63 93 7F F1 4D 00 00 80 01  .....,Dc".ñM..€.
00000000448  01 00 0B FE 3F 3F 3F 00 00 00 01 B0 0F 00 00 00  ...þ???....°....
00000000464  01 40 05 FE 3F 76 40 B0 0F 00 77 7B 0D 00 00 00  .@.þ?v@°..w{....
00000000480  01 77 07 FE 3F A3 B7 2B 1D 00 ED 07 0B 00 00 00  .w.þ?£·+..í.....
00000000496  00 00 00 00 00 00 00 00 00 00 00 00 00 00 55 AA  ..............Uª
```

Below is a graphical representation of the partition scheme.

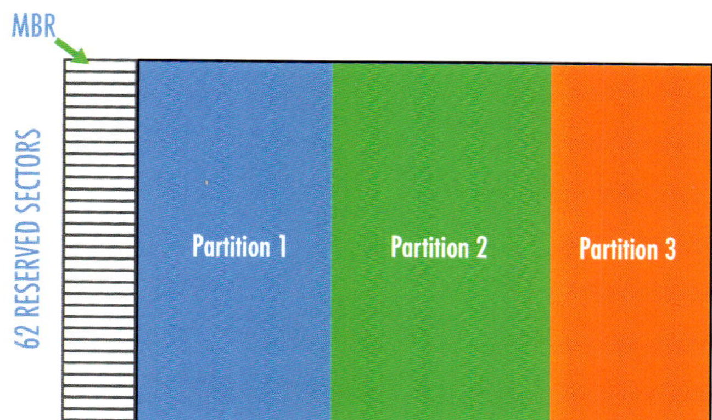

Partition 1:

Offset 0: 0x80 - this partition is bootable

Offset 1-3: 01 01 00 Head: 00000001 Sector: 000001 Cylinder: 0000000000 CHS: 0/1/1

Offset 4: 0x0B – 32 bit FAT (FAT32)

Offset 5: 0xFE 3F 3F Head: 11111110 Sector: 111111 Cylinder: 0000111111
CHS: 254/63/63

Offset 8: 0x3F 00 00 00 – Little Endian 0x00 00 00 3F – LBA sector 63

Offset 12: 0x01 B0 0F 00 – Little Endian 0x00 0F B0 01 – 1028097 sectors x 512 = 526,385,664 bytes

PRACTICAL EXERCISE 1:

Interpret the information from the remaining two partitions.

Partition 2

Offset 0: Bootable: Non-bootable:

Offset 1-3: Head: Sector:

Cylinder: CHS:

Offset 4: Partition Type Description:

Offset 5-7: Head: Sector:

Cylinder: CHS:

Offset 8: – Little Endian:

LBA sector:

Offset 12: – Little Endian:

sectors x 512 =

Partition 3

Offset 0: Bootable: Non-bootable:

Offset 1-3: Head: Sector:
Cylinder: CHS:

Offset 4: Partition Type Description:

Offset 5-7: Head: Sector:

Cylinder: CHS:

Offset 8: – Little Endian:

LBA sector:

Offset 12: – Little Endian:

PRACTICAL EXERCISE 2:

Using HxD, open the file MBR-Part_Example.001 by selecting the menu option Extras > Open disk image.

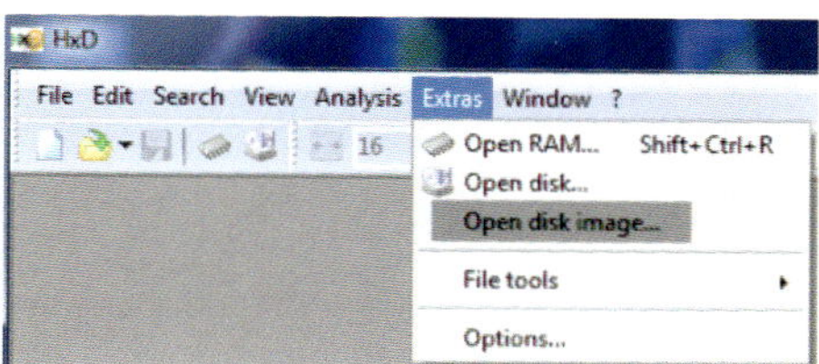

What Physical LBA sector is the MBR located at?

How many reserved sectors are there?

What sector offset does the serial number begin at?

What is the serial number of this drive in proper notation?

What sector offset does the partition table begin at?

Interpret the information for the partitions:

Partition 1: Offset 0: Bootable: Non-bootable:

Offset 1-3: Head: Sector:

Cylinder: CHS:

Offset 4: Partition Type Description:

Offset 5-7: Head: Sector:

Cylinder: CHS:

Offset 8: – Little Endian:

LBA sector:

Offset 12: – Little Endian:

sectors x 512 =
Partition 2: Offset 0: Bootable: Non-bootable:

Offset 1-3: Head: Sector:

Cylinder: CHS:

Offset 4: Partition Type Description:

Offset 5-7: Head: Sector:

Cylinder: CHS:

Offset 8: – Little Endian:

LBA sector:

Offset 12: – Little Endian:

sectors x 512 =

Partition 3: Offset 0: Bootable: Non-bootable:

Offset 1-3: Head: Sector:

Cylinder: CHS:

Offset 4: Partition Type Description:

Offset 5-8: Head: Sector:

Cylinder: CHS:

Offset 8: – Little Endian:

LBA sector:

Offset 12: – Little Endian:

sectors x 512 =

Partition 4: Offset 0: Bootable: Non-bootable:

Offset 1-3: Head: Sector:

Cylinder: CHS:

Offset 4: Partition Type Description:

Offset 5-7: Head: Sector:

Cylinder: CHS:

Offset 8: – Little Endian:

LBA sector:

Offset 12: – Little Endian:

sectors x 512

Master Boot Record Signature

We discussed file signatures in the previous chapter, but a master boot record signature is not in the header but at the end of the sector. We have discussed the 446 bytes of the boot code and the four partition table records that are each 16 bytes (64 bytes total): this is a total of 510 bytes out of 512. The last 2 bytes of the sector contain the signature of 0x55 AA. This signature will always be found after the partition table, and the drive will not initiate properly if this signature is not present.

```
0000000464  01 40 05 FE 3F 76 40 B0 0F 00 77 7B 0D 00 00 00  .@.þ?v@°..w{....
0000000480  01 77 07 FE 3F A3 B7 2B 1D 00 ED 07 0B 00 00 00  .w.þ?£·+..í.....
0000000496  00 00 00 00 00 00 00 00 00 00 00 00 00 00 55 AA  ..............Uª
```

Adding a New Hard Drive

When adding a new or wiped hard drive to a Microsoft Windows system it must be set up before data can be placed on it. Once properly connected, right-click on the My Computer icon on the Desktop or click on Start and then right-click on Computer from the menu. Select Manage to access the Computer Management window.

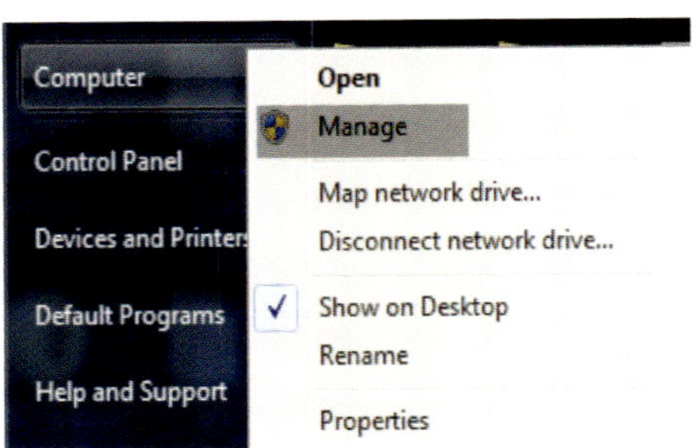

Next select the Disk Management option under Storage.

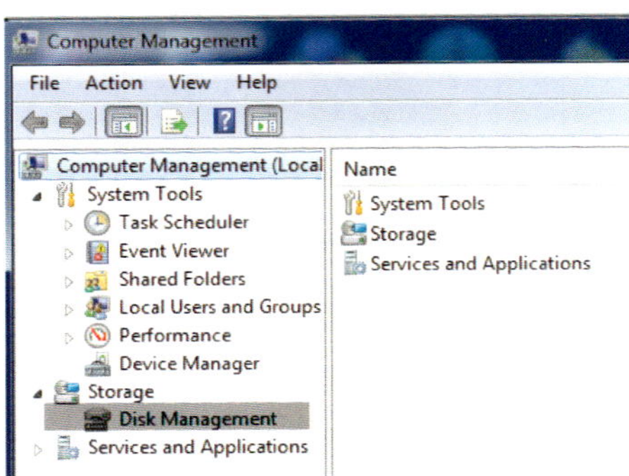

You should have a window popup for initializing the disk. This process does nothing more than add the serial number that we discussed earlier. MS Windows will not recognize the drive unless this serial number is present.

Note that the drive is identified with a number, starting with 0. Beware that some programs start counting physical hard drives with 1 instead of 0 so it is easy to get them mixed up when jumping between these programs. This can be very problematic when wiping or formatting drives.

Also note that this window provides the option for setting up the drive with the MBR partitioning method we have been discussing or for useing the GPT method, which will be covered in the next chapter of this text. If you are running an older version of Windows, such as XP, you will not have this option.

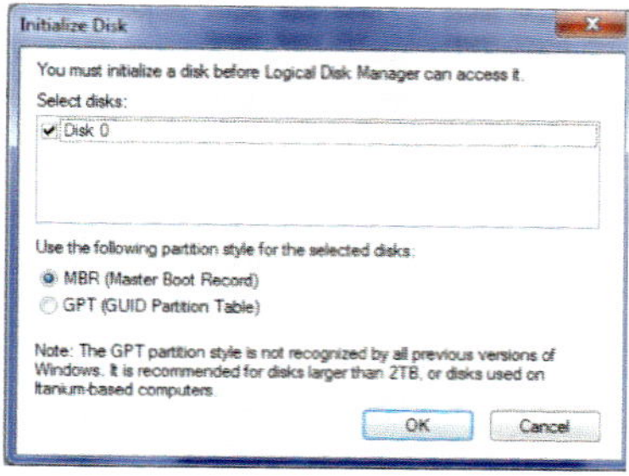

After the drive has been initialized, right-click on the drive area of Disk 0 and select New Simple Volume.

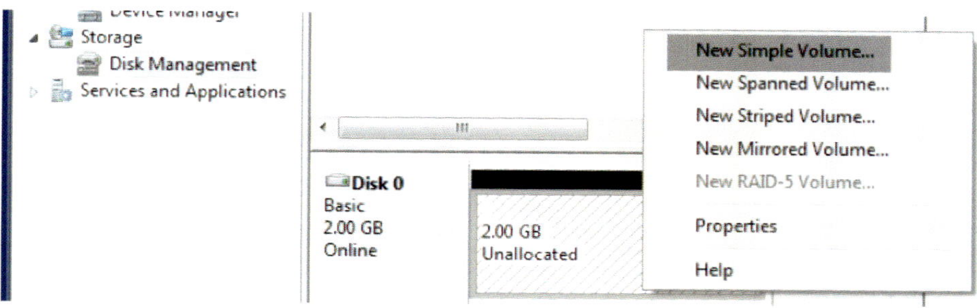

There are other options such as, Spanned Volume or Striped Volume or Mirroring. These are software RAID options that are going to be outside the scope of this discussion.

The New Simple Volume option will create a partition on the drive. The next window will allow you to set the size of the partition. If the maximum size is not set then additional partitions can be added by going through the same procedure.

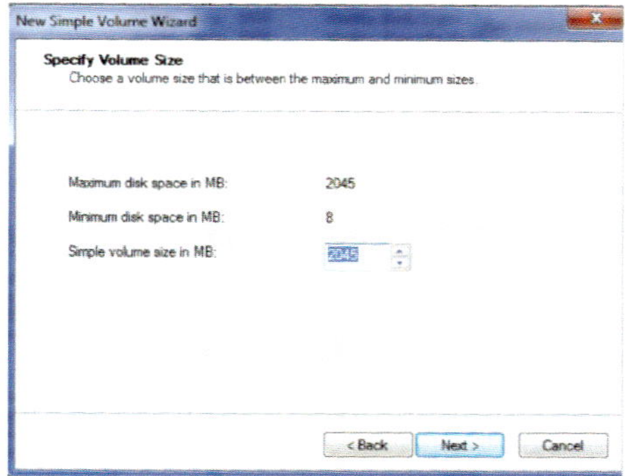

Once the size is set then the file system of choice can be selected. The differences between the file systems with the pros and cons will be dealt with later in this book.

For now, simply select FAT32. You can also provide a volume label at this point if you choose. The default is New Volume.

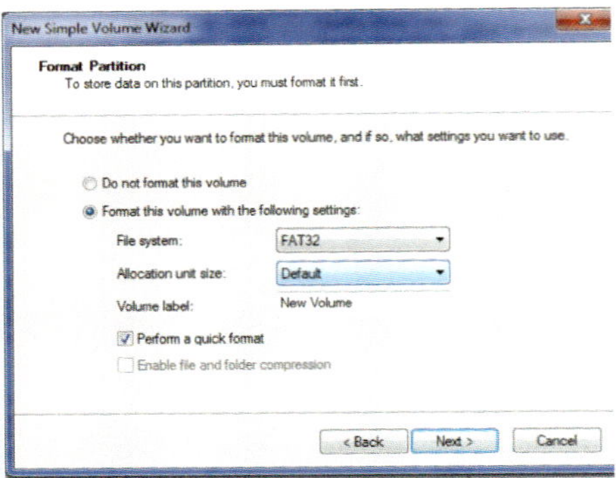

Once this is completed the drive letter should be provided.

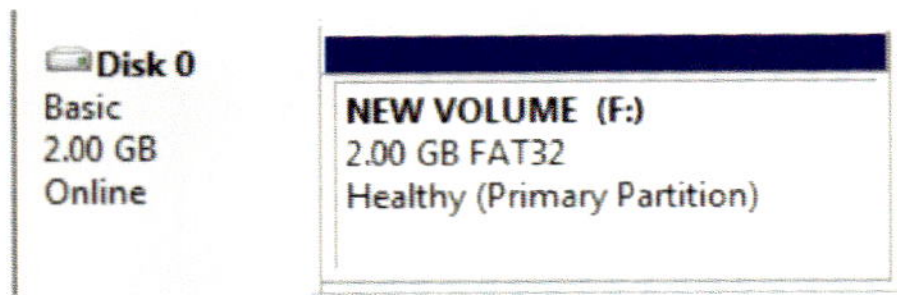

Once the partition is created, we can now examine it at the hex level using HxD. If you are running Windows Vista, 7 or 8 you have to run HxD with administrative privileges, as Windows will not allow access to a level on the disk without it.

Right-click on HxD and select Run as administrator.

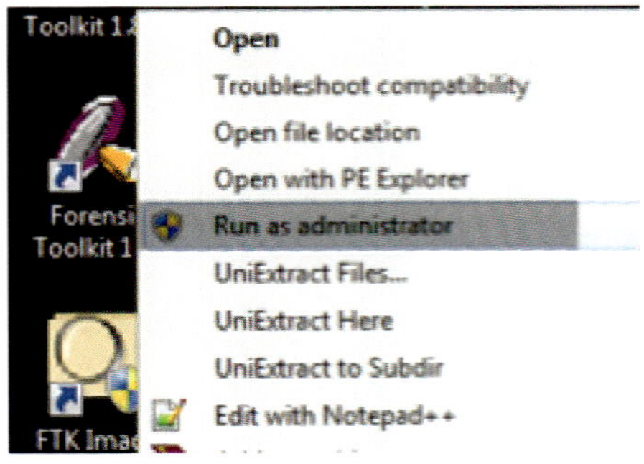

In this case we are going to open a disk, so select Extras > Open disk.

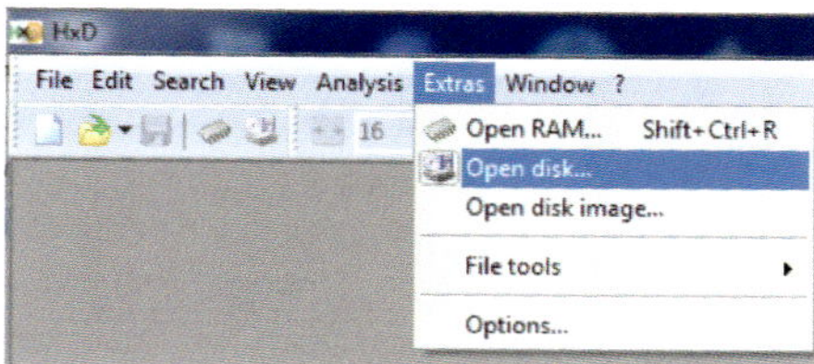

Note that with HxD, physical disks start counting with 1 instead of 0 as discussed earlier. For my example, Windows identified my disk as 0 so I will select drive 1 in HxD.

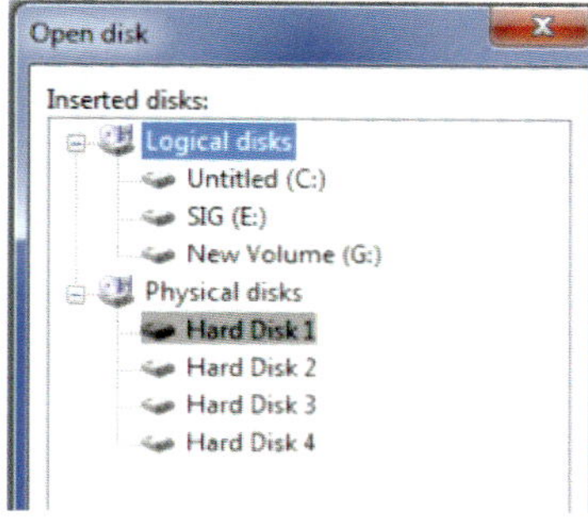

Also note that the drive is set as Read Only so we cannot make any changes inadvertently.

When the drive is opened up it will display the beginning of the drive at sector 0.

As a reminder, the first 446 bytes (offset 0-445) will contain boot code entered in by Windows. The next 64 bytes (offset 446-509) will be the partition table and the last 2 bytes (offset 510-511) will be the Master Boot Record signature of 0x55AA.

You may need to change your offset view from hex to decimal by selecting View > offset base > decimal

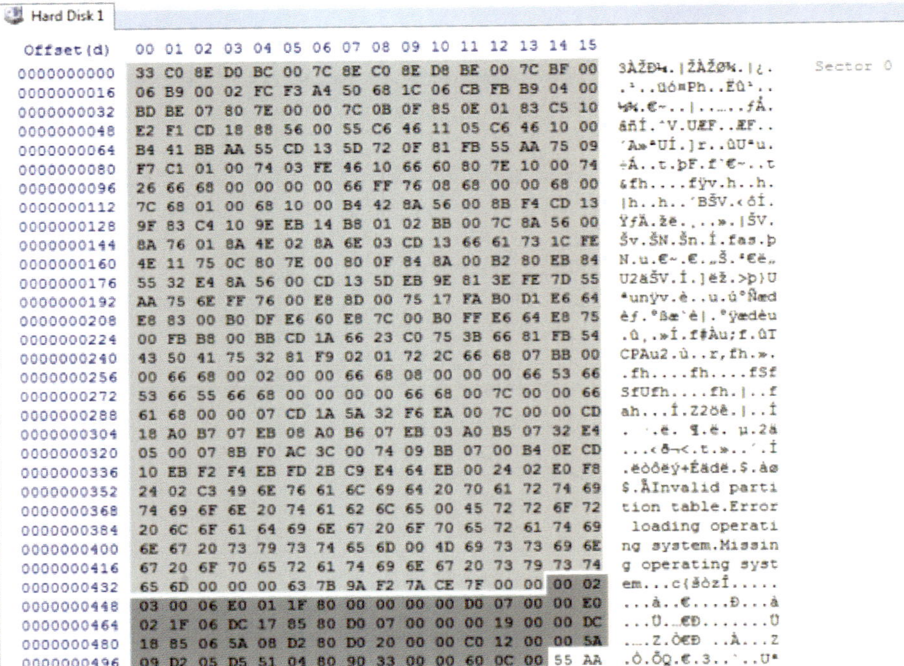

Primary Partitions
First four partitions of a drive

Extended Partition
A non-bootable partition that can be further split into volumes or logical partitions

We created four partitions on the drive and remember that each partition entry is 16 bytes. Your numbers may vary.

	Bootable	CHS	Type	CHS	Start Sec.	# of Sec.
Partition1	00	020300	06	E0011F	80000000	00D00700
Partition2	00	E0021F	06	DC1785	80D00700	00001900
Partition3	00	DC1885	06	5A08D2	80D02000	00C01200
Partition4	00	5A09D2	05	D55104	80903300	00600C00

Interpret the values for the following.

Starting sector number for partition 1:

Number of sectors in partition 2:

Size of partition 3 in MB (Divide bytes by 1048576 bytes per megabyte):

Partition type of partition 4:

Primary versus Extended Partitions

One of the original limitations of the MBR partitioning system was that there was only space to define four partitions known as ***Primary Partitions***. This meant that you could only have a C, D, E and F drive (A and B were reserved for floppy disks). In the early days of personal computing, it was common to utilize a number of partitions to segregate data - either by data type or by user.

In order to allow more partitioning, a method was introduced that created a special partition known as an ***Extended Partition.*** There could only be one extended partition on a drive and this partition could not be set as bootable, but it could be split into a large number of volumes or logical partitions. So, on the drive there could be one to three Primary Partitions and then one Extended Partition that could be broken down into several logical partitions.

Creating these logical partitions is accomplished by using a series of partition tables. There is still the table in the Master Boot Record, but then there is an additional table at the beginning of each logical partition. The sector containing the logical partition tables is laid out like the Master Boot Record where the table starts at offset 446. There is no boot code in these sectors, so the first 445 bytes are all 0. These tables will only have two 16-byte entries. Entry One defines the logical partition size and the second will point to the location of the next logical partition. Following the logical partition table will be a number of reserved sectors just like with the Master Boot Record. The last logical partition table will only have one 16-byte entry as no additional pointer is needed.

Physical Sector: 1028160

Boot Selector	STARTING HEAD	STARTING SECTOR	STARTING CYLINDER	PARTITION TYPE	ENDING HEAD	ENDING SECTOR	ENDING CYLINDER	STARTING SECTOR	SEC IN PARTITION
0	1	1	64	06	254	63	108	63	681345
0	0	1	109	05	254	63	113	681354	80325

Physical Sector: 1751085

Boot Selector	STARTING HEAD	STARTING SECTOR	STARTING CYLINDER	PARTITION TYPE	ENDING HEAD	ENDING SECTOR	ENDING CYLINDER	STARTING SECTOR	SEC IN PARTITION
0	1	1	109	06	254	63	113	63	80262
0	0	1	114	05	254	63	118	762024	80325

Physical Sector: 1831410

Boot Selector	STARTING HEAD	STARTING SECTOR	STARTING CYLINDER	PARTITION TYPE	ENDING HEAD	ENDING SECTOR	ENDING CYLINDER	STARTING SECTOR	SEC IN PARTITION
0	1	1	114	06	254	63	113	63	80262

One thing to note in examining and tracing logical partition tables is that the starting sector is calculated from the location of the table itself and not from the beginning of the drive as in the Master Boot Record table. Adding the number of sectors in the logical partition to the physical sector that the table is in will provide the location of the next table.

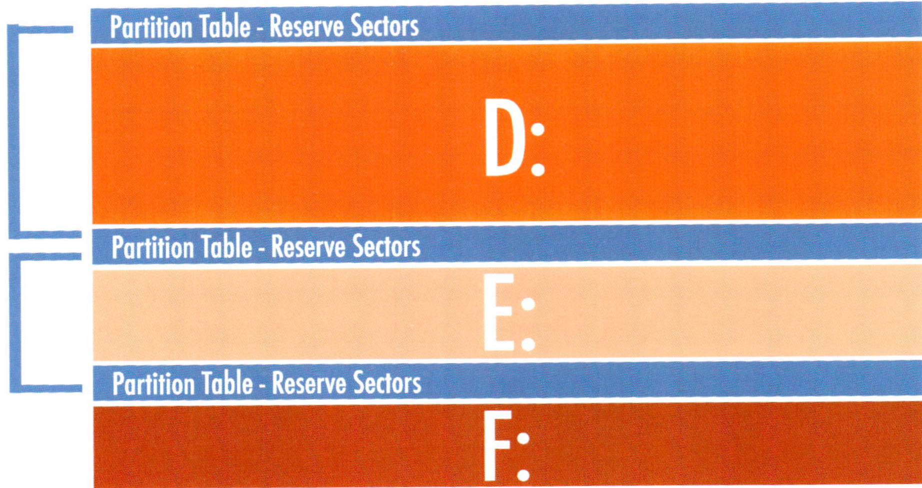

Because of the size of drives and the reduced need for partitioning, Extended Partitions have been eliminated in Windows Vista, 7 and 8. Primary Partitions are now referred to as Simple Volumes. Be aware that in forensics, an examiner must be able to examine not only the latest technologies but also the old as well. One can never predict what type of systems, new or old, a subject may have.

CHAPTER SUMMARY

Hard disks are physically made up of ***platters*** that can hold data on both sides. The platters are broken down to ***tracks*** and ***sectors.***

Tracks are concentric circles on each side of the platters. ***Sectors*** are units that typically hold 512 bytes of data but may also hold larger amounts.

In order to hold data on a drive, there must be at least one partition established. A ***partition*** is defined as continuous group of sectors on a drive that will hold a file system and if meant to be bootable, then it can also hold an operating system.

Partitions are set up in the first sector of the hard drive; physical sector 0. This sector is known as the ***Master Boot Record***. In this sector there are 446 bytes of boot code established by the operating system that set up the drive. There are also 64 bytes for the partition table made up of four 16-byte entries. Finally, there is a ***signature*** of 0x55AA in the last 2 bytes of the sector. This signature must be present for the partitions to be recognized. The partition entries are made up the of following components:

Bootable or Non-bootable
Starting CHS values
Partition Type
Ending CHS values
Starting Sector
Number of sectors in the partition

There are two types of partitions, ***primary*** and ***extended.*** There can only be up to four Primary Partitions. A drive can have only one Extended Partition and then from zero to three Primary Partitions. Only Primary Partitions can be bootable. Extended Partitions are designed to be broken into a number of logical volumes. Each logical volume begins with a partition table. Extended Partitions are no longer used and cannot be created in Windows Vista/7/8.

AT HOME EXERCISE

```
Offset(h) 00 01 02 03 04 05 06 07 08 09 0A 0B 0C 0D 0E 0F
00000000  33 C0 8E D0 BC 00 7C 8E C0 8E D8 BE 00 7C BF 00  3ÀŽÐ¼.|ŽÀŽØ¾.|¿.   Sector 0
00000010  06 B9 00 02 FC F3 A4 50 68 1C 06 CB FB B9 04 00  .¹..üó¤Ph..Ëû¹..
00000020  BD BE 07 80 7E 00 00 7C 0B 0F 85 0E 01 83 C5 10  ½¾.€~..|......ƒÅ.
00000030  E2 F1 CD 18 88 56 00 55 C6 46 11 05 C6 46 10 00  âñÍ.ˆV.UÆF..ÆF..
00000040  B4 41 BB AA 55 CD 13 5D 72 0F 81 FB 55 AA 75 09  ´A»ªUÍ.]r..ûUªu.
00000050  F7 C1 01 00 74 03 FE 46 10 66 60 80 7E 10 00 74  ÷Á..t.þF.f`€~..t
00000060  26 66 68 00 00 00 00 66 FF 76 08 68 00 00 68 00  &fh....fÿv.h..h.
00000070  7C 68 01 00 68 10 00 B4 42 8A 56 00 8B F4 CD 13  |h..h..´BŠV.‹ôÍ.
00000080  9F 83 C4 10 9E EB 14 B8 01 02 BB 00 7C 8A 56 00  ŸƒÄ.žë.¸..».|ŠV.
00000090  8A 76 01 8A 4E 02 8A 6E 03 CD 13 66 61 73 1C FE  Šv.ŠN.Šn.Í.fas.þ
000000A0  4E 11 75 0C 80 7E 00 80 0F 84 8A 00 B2 80 EB 84  N.u.€~.€.„Š.²€ë„
000000B0  55 32 E4 8A 56 00 CD 13 5D EB 9E 81 3E FE 7D 55  U2äŠV.Í.]ëž.>þ}U
000000C0  AA 75 6E FF 76 00 E8 8D 00 75 17 FA B0 D1 E6 64  ªunÿv.è..u.ú°Ñæd
000000D0  E8 83 00 B0 DF E6 60 E8 7C 00 B0 FF E6 64 E8 75  èƒ.°ßæ`è|.°ÿædèu
000000E0  00 FB B8 00 BB CD 1A 66 23 C0 75 3B 66 81 FB 54  .û¸.»Í.f#Àu;f.ûT
000000F0  43 50 41 75 32 81 F9 02 01 72 2C 66 68 07 BB 00  CPAu2.ù..r,fh.».
00000100  00 66 68 00 02 00 00 66 68 08 00 00 00 66 53 66  .fh....fh....fSf
00000110  53 66 55 66 68 00 00 00 00 66 68 00 7C 00 00 66  SfUfh....fh.|..f
00000120  61 68 00 00 07 CD 1A 5A 32 F6 EA 00 7C 00 00 CD  ah...Í.Z2öê.|..Í
00000130  18 A0 B7 07 EB 08 A0 B6 07 EB 03 A0 B5 07 32 E4  . ·.ë. ¶.ë. µ.2ä
00000140  05 00 07 8B F0 AC 3C 00 74 09 BB 07 00 B4 0E CD  ...‹ð¬<.t.»..´.Í
00000150  10 EB F2 F4 EB FD 2B C9 E4 64 EB 00 24 02 E0 F8  .ëòôëý+Éädë.$.àø
00000160  24 02 C3 49 6E 76 61 6C 69 64 20 70 61 72 74 69  $.ÃInvalid parti
00000170  74 69 6F 6E 20 74 61 62 6C 65 00 45 72 72 6F 72  tion table.Error
00000180  20 6C 6F 61 64 69 6E 67 20 6F 70 65 72 61 74 69   loading operati
00000190  6E 67 20 73 79 73 74 65 6D 00 4D 69 73 73 69 6E  ng system.Missin
000001A0  67 20 6F 70 65 72 61 74 69 6E 67 20 73 79 73 74  g operating syst
000001B0  65 6D 00 00 00 63 7B 9A F2 7A CE 7F 00 00 00 02  em...c{šòzÎ.....
000001C0  03 00 07 61 1B 06 80 00 00 00 00 90 01 00 00 61  ...a..€........a
000001D0  1C 06 0B 9A 15 C5 80 90 01 00 00 E0 2E 00 00 9A  ...š.Å€....à...š
000001E0  16 C5 07 B4 70 04 80 70 30 00 00 78 0F 00 00 00  .Å.´p.€p0..x....
000001F0  00 00 00 00 00 00 00 00 00 00 00 00 00 00 55 AA  ..............Uª
```

1. How many partitions are defined?

2. Were any of the partitions bootable?

3. Provide the starting sector for each of the partitions

    1. ____________________

    2. ____________________

    3. ____________________

    4. ____________________

4. Provide the size for each of the partitions on MB.

    1. ____________________

    2. ____________________

    3. ____________________

4. ________________

5. Provide the partition type for each of the partitions.

    1. ________________
    2. ________________
    3. ________________
    4. ________________

Unzip and open the file MBR_Part-Homework1.001 in HxD.

6. How many partitions are defined? __________

7. Were any of the partitions bootable? __________

8. Provide the starting sector for each of the partitions.

    1. ________________
    2. ________________
    3. ________________
    4. ________________

9. Provide the size for each of the partitions on MB.

    1. ________________
    2. ________________
    3. ________________

4. ____________________

10. Provide the partition type for each of the partitions.

    1. ____________________
    2. ____________________
    3. ____________________
    4. ____________________

ADVANCED HOMEWORK

Unzip and open the file MBR_Part-Homework2.001 in HxD.

Partition 1
Bootable or Non-bootable:

Starting CHS:

Partition Type Description:

Ending CHS:

Starting LBA sector:

Number of sectors in the partition:

Examine Partition 2

Partition Type Description:

How many logical volumes are contained in the Extended Partition?

Provide the starting physical sector and size in MB of each of the log-

REFERENCES

1. Barry, D. (1998). *Dave Barry in Cyberspace*. Ballantine Books.

2. Mueller, S. (1991). *Que's guide to data recovery*. (pp. 50-75). Carmel: Que Publishing.

3. *Enterprise hard drive featured items*. (n.d.). Retrieved from http://www.newegg.com/New-Release/PromotionStore/ID-2128382?name=Enterprise-HDD

4. Mueller, S. (1991). *Que's guide to data recovery.* (pp. 12-15). Carmel: Que Publishing.

5. Carrier, B. (2005). *File system forensic analysis.* (pp. 31). Upper Sad dle River: Addison-Wesley

6. Carrier, B. (2005). *File system forensic analysis.* (pp. 82-96). Upper Saddle River: Addison-Wesley

7. *To assign, change, or remove a drive letter. (n.d.).* Retrieved from http://www.microsoft.com/resources/documentation/windows/xp/all/proddocs/en-us/dm_drive_letter.mspx?mfr=trueamendement purposes?. (n.d.). Retrieved from http://www.ibls.com

04 PHYSICAL & LOGICAL STRUCTURES: PART II

In the previous chapter, we looked at using the MBR method for partitioning a hard drive. Microsoft has utilized this method since it started allowing hard drives. However, there are several limitations to this method, requiring a new method for setting up partitions.

As a review, let's revisit the MBR structure. At offset 446 of the Physical Sector 0, there is the partition table that has four 16-byte records, a total of 64 bytes.

Boot Selector	Starting Head	Starting Sector	Starting Cylinder	Partition Type	Ending Head	Ending Cylinder	Starting Sector	Sec. in Partition

One of the obvious limitations is that there are only four primary partitions allowed. As mentioned in the previous chapter, there is a workaround to this by incorporating an Extended Partition and logical volumes, but these cannot be set as bootable.

A second limitation and one that has become problematic in the last couple years, is the limitation on the size of partitions. In the current MBR structure, the partition size entry in the table is a 32-bit value (4 bytes). The largest single byte value is 0xFF making the largest 4-byte value 0xFF FF FF FF. This would be the largest possible partition size.

Converting this to decimal, it is 4294967295 sectors. Multiplying by 512 bytes per sector gives the following:

4294967295 sectors
x 512 bytes per sector

2,199,023,255,040 bytes

2.2 Terabytes

As of the writing of this text, there are 4 terabyte drives on the market and capacities will continue to grow[1]. The MBR system is simply obsolete when compared to the new technology.

GPT Partitioning
GUID Partitioning Table

GUID
Global Unique Identifier.

GPT Partitioning

Microsoft began using GPT partitions that were bootable with Windows 2003.[2] GPT stands for GUID Partitioning Table. A GUID, pronounced like druid or squid, is a Global Unique Identifier. A GUID is a 128-bit or 16-byte number. GUIDs are used throughout Windows, Linux, MacOS and applications.[3]

There are various ways of generating GUIDs. One way incorporates the date and time of creation as well as the MAC address of the computer, which is a unique identifier from the network interface card.[4] This MAC address can be traced to a specific computer. A GUID in a Microsoft Word document was used against David Smith, the creator of the Melissa virus.[5]

As stated, the GUID is a 16-byte number and is typically displayed in five groups and in the following format:[4]

{1111-22-33-44-555555}

Something unusual about the format is that groups 1, 2 and 3 are are multi-byte values written in Little Endian format and groups 4 and 5 are individual bytes so they are read in the displayed order(R. Nordvik, email, June 2015). Data found on the drive may look like the following:

0x3A215F8816924C4B67DE23E4DF76BA36

and displayed as:

{885F213A-9216-4B4C-67DE-23E4DF76BA36}

GUIDs are utilized in the partitioning scheme by assigning a unique value to the drive itself and to each partition created. Since this is a 128-bit value it means that the number of possible values is 2^{128} or 3.4×10^{38}. In most situations the GUIDs are unique; however there are some specific GUID values that have been assigned to certain types of partitions. We will begin to look at configuring a GPT drive and then at the structure, starting at the beginning of the drive.

Setting up a GPT drive

Like we saw in the last chapter, when adding a blank drive you will be prompted to choose the partitioning scheme.

Also, if you have a drive that is set up with a MBR partition table but with no partitions, then the scheme can be converted to GPT.

Right-clicking on a MBR drive will provide the menu option to convert to a GPT partitioning scheme.

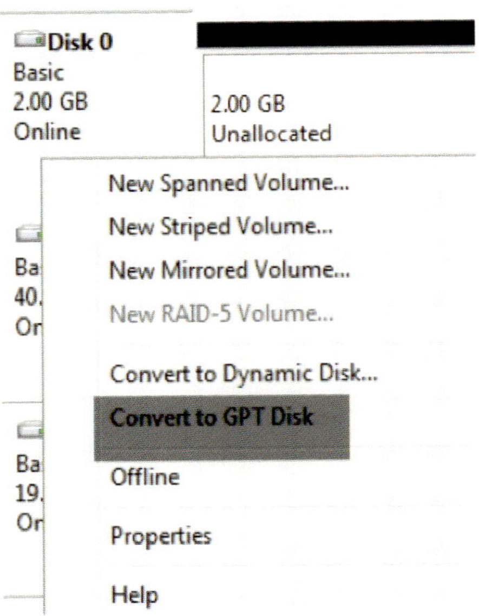

Once the GPT partitioning scheme is set up, then the partitioning can be done.

Below is an example of seven partitions setup.

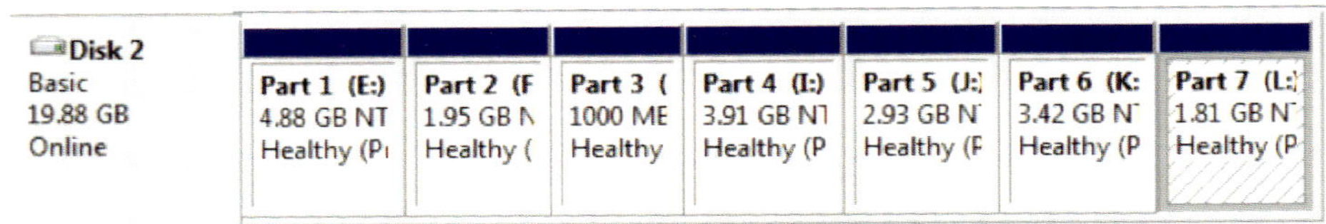

Protective/Legacy MBR
Physical Sector 0 in a GPT scheme. Has a partition table at offset 446 with a single record entry, preventing the drive from being overwritten when connected to an older computer.

Physical Sector 0 – Protective (Legacy) MBR

Under the MBR system, the first sector of the drive contains the Master Boot Record with boot code, the partition table, and the signature of 0x55 AA. Under GPT scheme, Physical Sector 0 contains what is known as a Protective or Legacy MBR. This sector has a partition table at offset 446 with a single record entry. The purpose of the table is to prevent the drive from being overwritten when connected to an older (legacy) computer.[2] GPT partitions can be recognized on Windows XP

64-bit and newer systems, but not on a Windows XP 32-bit system or older.[2] If a 3-terabyte external USB hard drive is set up on a Windows 7 system with GPT partitioning and then connected to a Windows XP 32-bit system, the partitions will not be recognized. However, with the Protective MBR, Windows XP will recognize that there is some type of partitioning filling the entire drive and not allow a new partition to be created. Without the Protective MBR, if this drive was connected, Windows would not see a partition and would allow the user to create a new partition, overwriting the existing data.

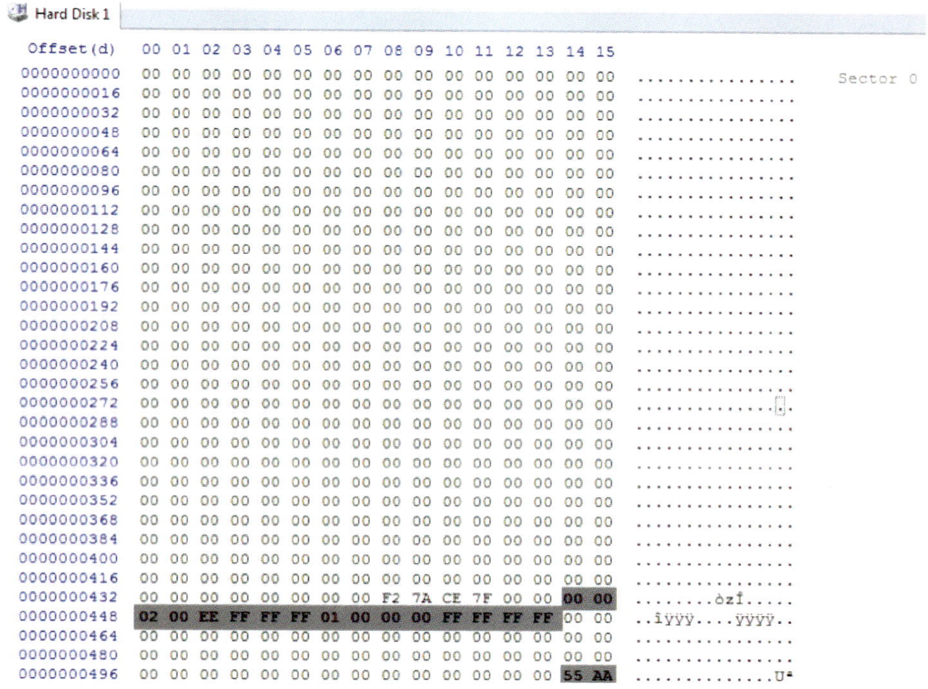

Note that there is no boot code, but there is the 4-byte serial number. The 16 bytes of the partition entry are as follows:

Non-bootable

Starting CHS: Cylinder 0 Head 0 and Sector 2

Partition Type: EE – This signifies a GPT Partition

Ending CHS: Cylinder 1023 Head 255 and Sector 63
Starting Sector: 1

Sectors in the Partition: 4294967295
As discussed previously, this is the maximum number of sectors allowable, setting up a 2.2TB partition. It does not matter how large the drive is, the Protective MBR will show a 2.2TB partition, even on a 20GB drive.

The last two bytes of the sector have the MBR signature of 0x55AA.

Physical Sector 1 – GPT Header

The next sector on the drive contains 92 bytes of information as shown in the table below:

GPT Header - Physical Sector 1			
DEC OFFSET	HEX OFFSET	SIZE (BYTES)	DESCRIPTION
0	00	8	Signature "EFI PART"
8	08	4	Revision (1)
12	0C	4	Header Size - typically 92 Bytes
16	10	4	Header CRC32
20	14	4	Reserved - 00
24	18	8	Current LBA sector
32	20	8	Sector Location of Backup
40	28	8	1st sector for partition (34)
48	30	8	Last sector for partitions
56	38	16	Physical Disk GUID
72	48	8	1st Partition Table sector (2)
80	50	4	# of Partition Table Entries (128)
84	54	4	Size of Partition Table Entries (128 bytes)
88	58	4	Partition Table CRC32

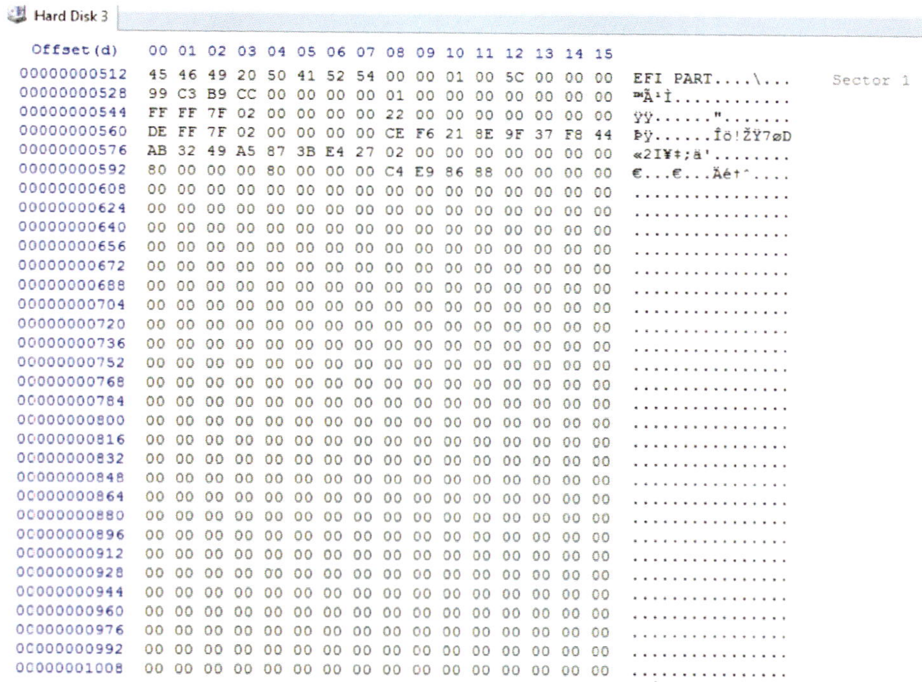

Offset 0-7 – signature – EFI PART, this will always be the signature. EFI stands for Extensible Firmware Interface.

Offset 8-11 – revision of EFI partitioning – 0x00 01 00 00

Offset 12-15 – header size – 0x00 00 00 5C or 92 bytes

Offset 16-19 – header CRC32 – 0xCC B9 C3 99, this is a calculated value based upon the 92 bytes in the header. This is similar in theory to a hash value, but just not as unique. CRC32 values are commonly used to verify sections of data.

Offset 20- 23 – reserved bytes – 0x00 00 00 00, not used.

Offset 24-31 – sector location – 0x00 00 00 00 00 00 00 01 or sector 1. This is the current location of the header.

Offset 32-39 – backup sector – 0x00 00 00 00 2F 7F FF FF or sector 796917759. There is a backup copy of the GPT Header at this location.

Offset 40-47 – first sector for partitions – 0x00 00 00 00 00 00 00 22 or sector 34. The first partition typically begins in sector 34. Remember in MBR partitions they typically start in sector 63 or 2048.

Offset 48-55 – last sector that is usable – 0x00 00 00 00 2F 7F FF DE or sector 796917726. Note that the last usable sector is 33 sectors away from the backup copy of the GPT header.

Offset 56-71 – disk GUID - 0xCE F6 21 8E 9F 37 F8 44 AB 32 49 A5 87 3B E4 27 or {8E21F6CE-379F-44F8-AB32-49A5873BE427}, this is effectively a serial number for the disk.

Offset 72-79 – sector for beginning of the partition table – 0x00 00 00 00 00 00 00 02 or sector 2. The partitions start at sector 34 but the partition table itself starts at sector 2.

Offset 80-83 – number of partitions allowed – 0x00 00 00 80 or 128. Remember the MBR allows 4 primary partitions, GPT allows 128 partitions.

Offset 84-87 – size of partition table entries – 0x00 00 00 80 or 128 bytes. In MBR the partition table entry is 16 bytes, in GPT it is 128 bytes long. This means 4 entries will fit in each sector (4x128=512 bytes).

Offset 88-91 – CRC32 of the partition table – 0x88 86 E9 C4. There are 4 entries per sector and 128 entries. 128/4=32 sectors in the partition table. This CRC value is based upon the data in the 32 sectors.

GPT Partition Table Entry - Physical Sector 2-33			
DEC OFFSET	**HEX OFFSET**	**SIZE (BYTES)**	**DESCRIPTION**
0	00	16	Partition Type GUID
16	10	16	Unique Partition GUID
32	20	8	1st LBA Sector of Partition
40	28	8	Last LBA Sector of Partition
48	30	8	Attributes (typically 00)
56	38	72	Partition Name in Unicode

Physical Sectors 2-33 –Partition Table

Note that while the partition entries are quite a bit longer in GPT partition tables than in MBR partitions tables, they are actually much simpler. There are no longer any meaningless CHS values in the table.

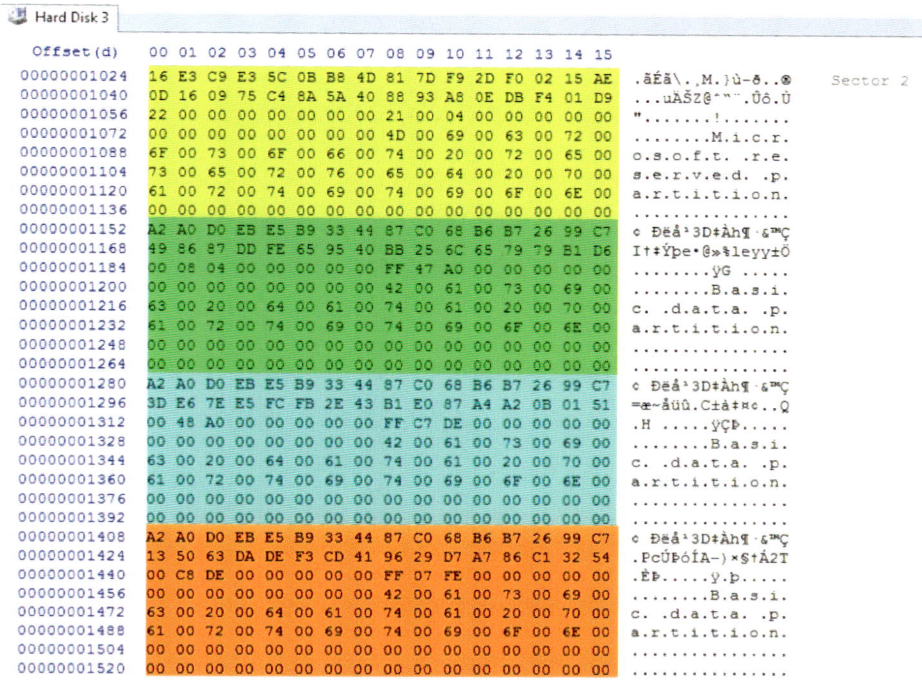

In sector 2, there are four partition entries.

Offset 0-15 – Partition type GUID. These GUIDs are not unique as they are defined values to identify partition types. These values are not like the MBR types like 0B, 07 or 05. These define the types such as Basic disk or Dynamic disk[6].

These five partitions types are the only ones available for Windows drives. There are other GUID types available for other operating systems such as MacOS and Linux[6].

Looking at the first partition above, the partition type GUID is:

0x16 E3 C9 E3 5C 0B B8 4D 81 7D F9 2D F0 02 15 AE or

{E3C9E316-0B5C-4DB8-817D-F92DF00215AE} and identified as

Microsoft Reserved Partition (MSR)
Automatically created by Microsoft. 128 MB in size for drives larger than 16 GB.

the Microsoft Reserved Partition (MSR). This partition is automatically created by Microsoft and is 128 megabytes in size for drives that are larger than 16 gigabytes. If the drive is smaller than 16 gigabytes, then the partition size will be 32 megabytes.

Offset 16-31 – Partition GUID –

0x0D 16 09 75 C4 8A 5A 40 88 93 A8 0E D4 4F 01 D9
{7509160D-8AC4-5A8A-4088-93A80ED44F01D9}

This is a unique value that is effectively a serial number for the partition. Even though every drive has an MSR, the Partition GUID will be different for each.

Offset 32-39 – First sector of the partition – 0x00 00 00 00 00 00 00 22 or sector 34.

Offset 40-47 – Last sector of the partition – 0x00 00 00 00 00 04 00 21 or sector 262177. This gives a 128 MB partition. Note that this is a 64-bit value and the largest possible number would be 0xFF FF FF FF FF FF FF FF or 18446744073709552000. Multiplying by 512 bytes per sector gives 9 Zetabytes.

Offset 48-55 – Attributes – These are typically all 0x00 00 00 00 00 00 00 00.

Offset 56-127 – Partition Name – Microsoft reserved partition. This name comes from the partition type table and not from the user.

PRACTICAL EXERCISE 1

There are three remaining partitions defined above, provide the following information:

Partition 2: Partition type GUID in proper notation

Partition 2: Unique GUID in proper notation

Partition 2: Starting Physical Sector

Partition 2: Ending Physical Sector

Size of the Partition in megabytes:

Partition 2: Partition Name

Partition 3: Partition type GUID in proper notation

Partition 3: Unique GUID in proper notation

Partition 3: Starting Physical Sector

Partition 3: Ending Physical Sector

Size of the Partition in megabytes:

Partition 3: Partition Name

Partition 4: Partition type GUID in proper notation

Partition 4: Unique GUID in proper notation

Partition 4: Starting Physical Sector

Partition 4: Ending Physical Sector

Size of the Partition in megabytes:

Partition 4: Partition Name

See the remainder of the partition below and provide the details on those partitions.

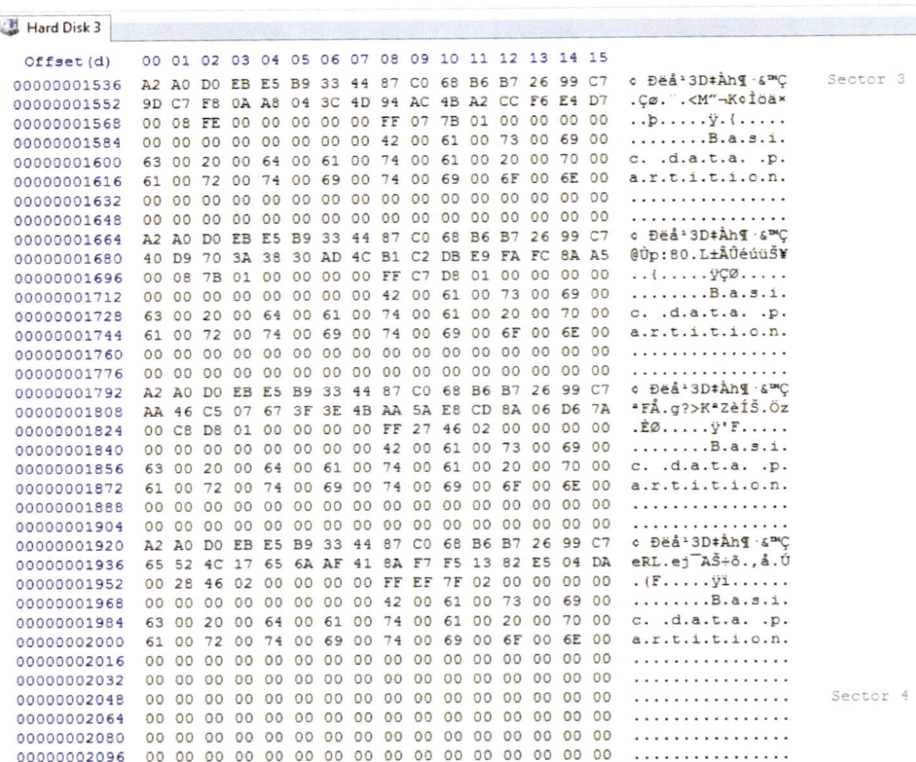

```
Hard Disk 3

Offset(d)    00 01 02 03 04 05 06 07 08 09 10 11 12 13 14 15
0000001536   A2 A0 D0 EB E5 B9 33 44 87 C0 68 B6 B7 26 99 C7   ¢ Ðëå¹3D‡Àh¶·&™Ç   Sector 3
0000001552   9D C7 F8 0A A8 04 3C 4D 94 AC 4B A2 CC F6 E4 D7   .Çø.¨.<M"¬K¢Ìöä×
0000001568   00 08 FE 00 00 00 00 00 FF 07 7B 01 00 00 00 00   ..þ.....ÿ.{.....
0000001584   00 00 00 00 00 00 00 00 42 00 61 00 73 00 69 00   ........B.a.s.i.
0000001600   63 00 20 00 64 00 61 00 74 00 61 00 20 00 70 00   c. .d.a.t.a. .p.
0000001616   61 00 72 00 74 00 69 00 74 00 69 00 6F 00 6E 00   a.r.t.i.t.i.o.n.
0000001632   00 00 00 00 00 00 00 00 00 00 00 00 00 00 00 00   ................
0000001648   00 00 00 00 00 00 00 00 00 00 00 00 00 00 00 00   ................
0000001664   A2 A0 D0 EB E5 B9 33 44 87 C0 68 B6 B7 26 99 C7   ¢ Ðëå¹3D‡Àh¶·&™Ç
0000001680   40 D9 70 3A 38 30 AD 4C B1 C2 DB E9 FA FC 8A A5   @Ùp:80.L±ÂÛéúüŠ¥
0000001696   00 08 7B 01 00 00 00 00 FF C7 D8 01 00 00 00 00   ..{.....ÿÇØ.....
0000001712   00 00 00 00 00 00 00 00 42 00 61 00 73 00 69 00   ........B.a.s.i.
0000001728   63 00 20 00 64 00 61 00 74 00 61 00 20 00 70 00   c. .d.a.t.a. .p.
0000001744   61 00 72 00 74 00 69 00 74 00 69 00 6F 00 6E 00   a.r.t.i.t.i.o.n.
0000001760   00 00 00 00 00 00 00 00 00 00 00 00 00 00 00 00   ................
0000001776   00 00 00 00 00 00 00 00 00 00 00 00 00 00 00 00   ................
0000001792   A2 A0 D0 EB E5 B9 33 44 87 C0 68 B6 B7 26 99 C7   ¢ Ðëå¹3D‡Àh¶·&™Ç
0000001808   AA 46 C5 07 67 3F 3E 4B AA 5A E8 CD 8A 06 D6 7A   ªFÅ.g?>KªZèÍŠ.Öz
0000001824   00 C8 D8 01 00 00 00 00 FF 27 46 02 00 00 00 00   .ÈØ.....ÿ'F.....
0000001840   00 00 00 00 00 00 00 00 42 00 61 00 73 00 69 00   ........B.a.s.i.
0000001856   63 00 20 00 64 00 61 00 74 00 61 00 20 00 70 00   c. .d.a.t.a. .p.
0000001872   61 00 72 00 74 00 69 00 74 00 69 00 6F 00 6E 00   a.r.t.i.t.i.o.n.
0000001888   00 00 00 00 00 00 00 00 00 00 00 00 00 00 00 00   ................
0000001904   00 00 00 00 00 00 00 00 00 00 00 00 00 00 00 00   ................
0000001920   A2 A0 D0 EB E5 B9 33 44 87 C0 68 B6 B7 26 99 C7   ¢ Ðëå¹3D‡Àh¶·&™Ç
0000001936   65 52 4C 17 65 6A AF 41 8A F7 F5 13 82 E5 04 DA   eRL.ej¯AŠ÷õ.‚å.Ú
0000001952   00 28 46 02 00 00 00 00 FF EF 7F 02 00 00 00 00   .(F.....ÿï......
0000001968   00 00 00 00 00 00 00 00 42 00 61 00 73 00 69 00   ........B.a.s.i.
0000001984   63 00 20 00 64 00 61 00 74 00 61 00 20 00 70 00   c. .d.a.t.a. .p.
0000002000   61 00 72 00 74 00 69 00 74 00 69 00 6F 00 6E 00   a.r.t.i.t.i.o.n.
0000002016   00 00 00 00 00 00 00 00 00 00 00 00 00 00 00 00   ................
0000002032   00 00 00 00 00 00 00 00 00 00 00 00 00 00 00 00   ................
0000002048   00 00 00 00 00 00 00 00 00 00 00 00 00 00 00 00   ................   Sector 4
0000002064   00 00 00 00 00 00 00 00 00 00 00 00 00 00 00 00   ................
0000002080   00 00 00 00 00 00 00 00 00 00 00 00 00 00 00 00   ................
0000002096   00 00 00 00 00 00 00 00 00 00 00 00 00 00 00 00   ................
```

Partition 5: Partition type GUID in proper notation

Partition 5: Unique GUID in proper notation

Partition 5: Starting Physical Sector

Partition 5: Ending Physical Sector

Size of the Partition in megabytes:

Partition 5: Partition Name

Partition 6: Partition type GUID in proper notation

Partition 6: Unique GUID in proper notation

Partition 6: Starting Physical Sector

Partition 6: Ending Physical Sector

Size of the Partition in megabytes:

Partition 6: Partition Name

Partition 7: Partition type GUID in proper notation

Partition 7: Unique GUID in proper notation

Partition 7: Starting Physical Sector

Partition 7: Ending Physical Sector

Size of the Partition in megabytes:

Partition 7: Partition Name

Partition 8: Partition type GUID in proper notation

Partition 8: Unique GUID in proper notation

Partition 8: Starting Physical Sector

Partition 8: Ending Physical Sector

Size of the Partition in megabytes:

Partition 8: Partition Name

PRACTICAL EXERCISE 2

Unzip and open GWPart_HW.001 in HxD as an image file and answer the following questions.

What is the drive serial number listed in the Protective MBR?
What is the partition type in the Protective MBR?

What is the disk GUID in the GPT header?

What is the CRC32 value of the GPT header?

How many bytes are used in the GPT header?

What sector contains the backup of the header?

What is the last available sector on the drive that can be partitioned?

How many possible partitions are there?

How many partitions are defined?

Write out the starting sector and ending sector for each partition and list the Unique GUID in proper format.

GPT Header and Partition Table Backup

The GPT header indicates the sector containing a backup copy. This is always the very last addressable sector of the drive. The Partition Table is backed up 33 sectors from the end of the drive. The Protective MBR is not backed up.

GPT Header – 41943040 sectors (0 through 41943039)

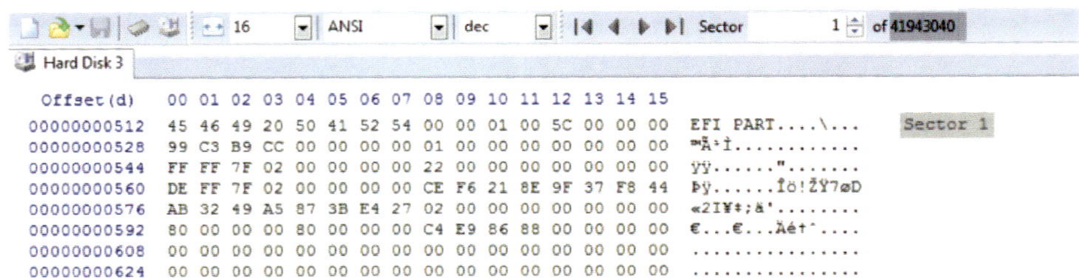

Backup GPT Header – Sector 41943039

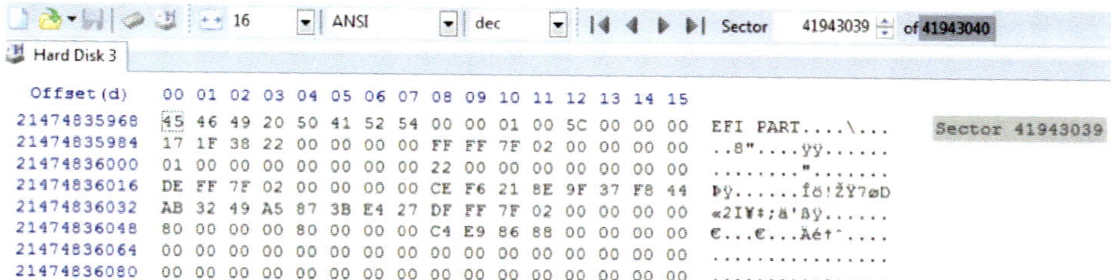

Compare the value of the two sectors

Offset 0-7 signature is identical

Offset 8-11 revision is identical

Offset 12-15 header size is identical

Offset 16-19 CRC32 of the header is different

Offset 20-23 reserved sectors are identical

Offset 24-31 current LBA sector (header = 1, backup =41943039)

Offset 32-39 sector location of the backup (header=41943039, backup=1). *Note each copy points to the other

Offset 40-47 First sector for partitions is identical

Offset 48-55 Last sector for partitions is identical

Offset 56-71 disk GUID is identical

Offset 72-79 starting sector of the partition table is identical

Offset 80-83 number of partition entries is identical

Offset 84-87 size of the partition entries is identical

Offset 88-91 CRC32 of the partition table is identical

Below depicts the layout of the drive:

Sector 0 – Protective MBR
Sector 1 – GPT Header
Sectors 2 through 32 -Partition Table
Sector 34 -beginning of first partition
Sector X – last sector of drive and backup copy of GPT Header
Sectors X-32 through X-1- backup of Partition Table

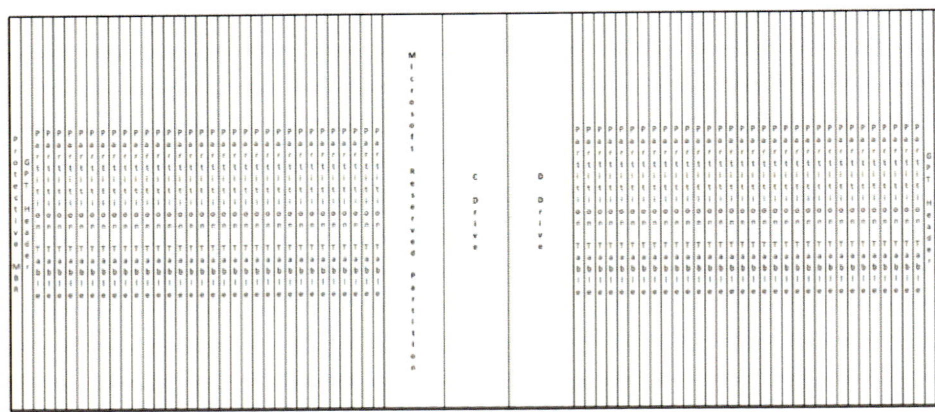

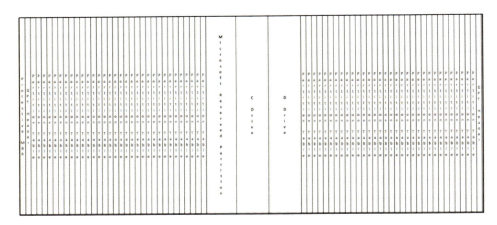

With the backup copy, if the beginning of the drive is wiped out then it can be reconstructed from the backup copy. The sector references just have to be reversed in the GPT header.

PRACTICAL EXERCISE 3

Using GPTPart_HW.001 in HxD from Practical 2 answer the following questions:

What sector is the backup copy of the GPT Header in?

Provide a comparison of the information between the Header and the Backup.

Signature:

Revision:

Size of Header:

CRC32 of the header (explain why there may be a difference):

Current Sector:

Sector location of the backup:

Disk GUID:

Starting location of the Partition table:

Last available sector for partitions:

Number of entries in the Partition Table:

Size of the Partition Table Entries:

CRC32 of the Partition Table:

What sector does the backup Partition table start in?

How many entries are there?

Provide the Unique Partition GUIDs for each entry.

CHAPTER SUMMARY

The limitation of the MBR partition scheme is that it can only handle four primary (bootable) partitions and there is a limit to only 2.2 terabytes as the value for the partition size is only 4 bytes (32-bit)

GPT Partitioning uses ***GUID***s to identify drives and partitions. ***GUIDs*** are 128-bit numbers broken down into 5 groups of values {1111-22-33-44-555555} expressed in hexadecimal. Groups 1, 2, and 3 are written in Little Endian as read from the drive and groups 4 and 5 are written in Big Endian. Most GUIDs are unique, but some are set for specific purposes such as partitions types.

The GPT structure uses the first 34 sectors of the drive.

Sector 0 has the ***Protective MBR*** also known as a legacy MBR. This protects the drive from being repartitioned by an older system not recognizing GPT.

Sector 1 has the ***GPT Header.*** This sector has the GUID for the drive and the number of usable sectors on the drive.

Sectors 2-33 hold the ***partition table***. Each entry is 128 bytes, and there are 128 entries. The entries contain the partition type GUID and a unique GUID. There is also the starting sector and the ending sector.

There is a backup copy of the GPT header in the last sector of the drive and a backup of the partition table starting 33 sectors from the end of the drive. The Protective MBR is not backed up.

AT HOME EXERCISE

Unzip and open GPTPart_HW2.zip in HxD.

What is the drive serial number listed in the Protective MBR?

What is the partition type in the Protective MBR?

What is the disk GUID in the GPT header?

What is the CRC32 value of the GPT header?

How many bytes are used in the GPT header?

What sector contains the backup of the header?

What is the last available sector on the drive that can be partitioned?

How many possible partitions are there?

How many partitions are defined?

What sector does the backup of the Partition Table begin in?

Write out the starting sector and ending sector for each odd numbered (0-3-5, etc.) partition and list the Unique GUID in proper format.

ADVANCED HOMEWORK

Unzip and open GPTPart_HW3.zip in HxD.

Scenarios: This drive suffered a malware attack.

Examine the 34 sectors of the drive image.

What data is found?

Recover the partition structure (sectors 0-34) and write the changes. Reload in the saved image in HxD.

Write out the last 66 bytes of Sector 0 in hex after your changes.

Write out the first 92 bytes of Sector 1 in hex after your changes and corrections for recovery.

How many partition entries were recovered? What types?

REFERENCES

1. (2013, September 09). Retrieved from http://www.newegg.com/Product/ProductList.aspx?Submit=ENE&N=100007603600457700&IsNodeId=1&name=4T-Bandhigher

2. (2012, November 30). Retrieved from http://msdn.microsoft.com/en-us/library/windows/hardware/gg463525.aspx

3. Nikkel, B. (2009). Forensic Analysis of GPT Disks and Partition Tables. *The International Journal for Digital Forensics and Incident Response*, 6(102), doi: doiL10.1016/j.diin.2009.07.001

4. P. Leach, M. Mealling, R. Salz. "A Universally Unique IDentifier (UUID) URN Namespace". Internet Engineering Task Force Request for Comment (RFC) 4122. Retrieved from http://www.ietf.org/rfc/rfc4122.txt on May 5, 2009.

5. Reiter, L. (1999, April 2). *Tracking Melissa's Alter Egos*. Retrieved from http://www.zdnet.com/news/tracking-melissas-alter-egos/101974

6. *Guid partition table.* (n.d.). Retrieved from http://en.wikipedia.org/wiki/GUID_Partition_Table

CASE STUDY 3: MISSING PARTITIONS

In one civil matter I was involved in, I was asked to travel to a client site to oversee the work done by forensic examiners from the opposing side in the case. It is not uncommon for courts to allow opposing forensic examiners to come in and copy or view data of a client. I often play that same role of examiner in other cases.

In this matter, the client was being sued by a competitor for hiring a former employee and was being accused of obtaining and using proprietary information. The plaintiff (the competing company) hired forensic examiners to come to examine specific hard drive in the defendant's (my client) office for the proprietary data. These hard drives were one that had been previously used and were no longer installed in computer systems. These drives were suspected of having data from the former employee.

The examiners brought in their own forensic systems to examine the drives and were the industry standard forensic tool. They connected the hard drives and viewed then in the forensic program. The program reported that there were no partitions and did not display any files. After viewing all the drives with the same result, the examiners were satisfied that there were no suspicious files present and packed up their equipment and left.

The client was confused because he believed that were files present on the drive, not that he admitted there was anything suspicious, just that there were files. I then showed them that the forensic tool utilized was only as good as the examiner using it. By default, it only reads the partition in the first sector of the drive, physical sector 0. However, in this case the drives were not set up in a standard single drive configuration and the partition information was present in a different location. Using the data at the alternate location allowed the partitions to be mounted and all the files to be viewed and accessed.

There may have been evidentiary files in these partitions the examiners completely missed because of relying on forensic tools and not on the knowledge of partition structures.

05 FILE SYSTEMS: FAT PART I

Until this point, we have dealt with the physical structure of a hard drive and the layout of the partitions. From this point forward, the focus will be on what is referred to as the logical structure of the drives. In order to store files on the one of the partitions that we created in the previous chapters (either MBR or GPT), there must first be a file system present. A file system is a file organizational method that controls how files and folders are named and stored. A file system may also be responsible for managing file ownership, encryption and security[1].

Different operating systems will support working with different file systems. For example, Microsoft Windows supports the following file systems[2]:

File Allocation Table – 12bit (FAT12)

File Allocation Table – 16bit (FAT16)

File Allocation table – 32bit (FAT32)

New Technology File System (NTFS)

Extended File Allocation Table (exFAT)

Resilient File System (ResFS)

There are other file systems such as EXT, HFS, HFS+, RieserFS, JFS, and many others. These files systems are not supported by Microsoft Windows. This means that when a drive containing a partition with one of these file systems is connected to a Windows computer, a drive letter will not be assigned and the files will not be available.

Some operating systems have support for a large number of file systems. Linux, for example, supports more than 15[3]. Other operating systems, like Macintosh OS X, will support several file systems, but some – like NTFS – are only supported in Read-Only mode. Natively, the Macintosh operating system cannot write to drives with NTFS[4].

In this chapter, we will begin examining the FAT file system. While this is the oldest of the Windows file systems and not utilized on hard drives any longer, FAT will be encountered on the thousands of flash drives that are floating around and used by suspects on a daily basis.

The original version of FAT was developed between 1976 and 1977 by Bill Gates and Marc McDonald and utilized by Microsoft for floppy disks. It was limited in its ability and capability[5]. The first version was a 12-bit file system. This leads us to the introduction of a cluster. A cluster is the smallest unit of data that can be written or read by the operating system. A cluster is made up of one or more contiguous sectors (sectors next to each other). The cluster size in FAT will vary based upon the size of the partition.

An analogy for a cluster is a page in a book. In this analogous book, each page has a fixed number of paragraphs, and the paragraph is a sector on our drive.

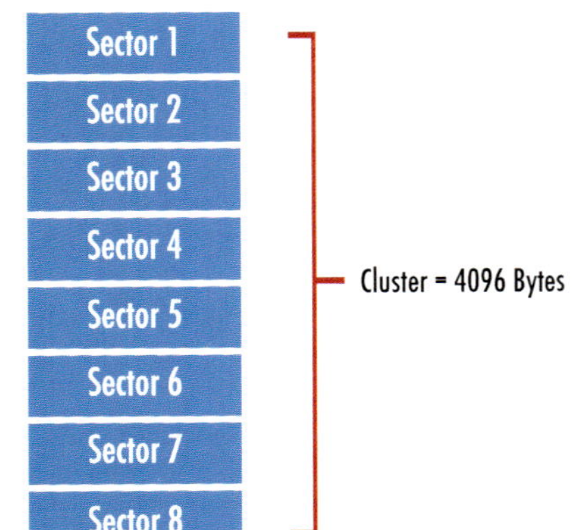

Each file takes up one or more clusters and no cluster can contain data from more than one file.

One of the major functions of the FAT file system is to track the usage of each and every cluster on the volume.

The FAT12 file system can manage 2^{12} clusters.

2x2x2x2x2x2x2x2x2x2x2x2 = 4096 clusters

Actually, on a disk some of the area is reserved so that for practical purposes there are 4086 clusters available[6].

On floppy disks, the cluster sizes are one or two sectors. On hard drives, the clusters can be as large as 64 sectors (Windows NT allows for clusters as large as 512 sectors)[7].

FAT16 can manage 2^{16} clusters (65636-10 reserved) and FAT32 can manage 2^{28} clusters. Four of the bits were reserved for future purposes that never came about[6].

Getting back to our partition (volume), let's take a look at how the clusters and the file are managed and tracked.

We will use an MBR drive as an example, but at the file system level, the partition structure does not matter.

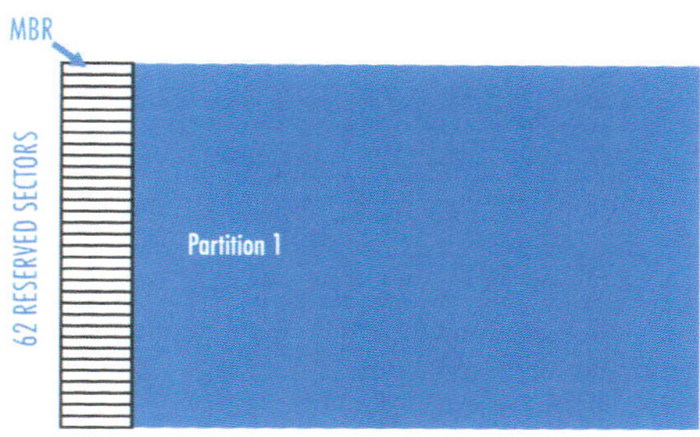

After the reserved sectors, the first partition will begin. The first sector of the partition will contain reference information. One thing that should be noted is that removable media, such a flash drives, cannot be partitioned and contains no MBR or reserved sectors. The first sector of removable drive will be just like the first sector of a hard drive partition.

Volume Boot Record (VBR)
First sector of a partition, which contains reference information.

This reference sector is referred to as a ***Volume Boot Record.*** This VBR (not to be confused with a MBR) will be at least one sector in length.

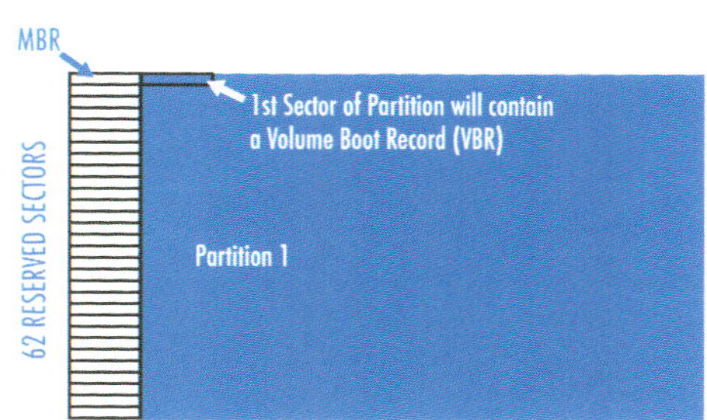

We will now walk through the VBR information.

FAT 12/16 VBR			
DEC OFFSET	HEX OFFSET	SIZE (BYTES)	DESCRIPTION
0	00	3	Jump to bootstrap. (The position of the bootstrap varies.)
3	03	8	OEM name/version (e.g. "IBM 3.3", "IBM 20.0", "MSDOS5.0", "MSWIN4.0").
11	0B	2	Number of bytes per sector (512) Must be one of 512, 1024, 2048, 4096.
13	0D	1	Number of sectors per cluster (1) Must be one of 1, 2, 4, 8, 16, 32, 64, 128. A cluster should have at most 32768 bytes.
14	0E	2	14-15 Number of reserved sectors (1).
16	10	1	Number of FAT copies (2).
17	11	2	Number of root directory entries (224) 0 for FAT32; 512 is recommended for FAT16.
19	13	2	Total number of sectors in the file system for smaller sector numbers.
21	15	1	Media descriptor type (f0: 1.4 MB floppy, f8: hard disk).
22	16	2	Number of sectors per FAT (9).
24	18	2	Number of sectors per track (12).
26	1A	2	Number of heads (2, for diskette).
28	1C	4	Number of hidden sectors (0). Hidden sectors are sectors preceding the partition.
32	20	4	Total number of sectors in the file system for larger sector numbers.
36	24	1	Logical drive number (00 for floppy and 80 for hard drive).
37	25	1	Reserved.
38	26	1	Extended Signature (29).
39	27	4	Volume Serial Number
43	2B	11	Volume Label – ("NO NAME").
54	36	8	File system type.
62	3E	441	Bootstrap code.
510	1FE	2	Signature ("55 AA").

Below is the first sector containing the Volume Boot Record.

```
000000 EB 3C 90 4D 53 44 4F 53-35 2E 30 00 02 01 01 00 ë<·MSDOS5.0·····
000010 02 E0 00 40 0B F0 09 00-12 00 02 00 00 00 00 00 ·à·@·ð··········
000020 00 00 00 00 00 00 29 A6-06 AE BE 4E 4F 20 4E 41 ······)¦·®¾NO NA
000030 4D 45 20 20 20 20 46 41-54 31 32 20 20 20 33 C9 ME    FAT12   3É
000040 8E D1 BC F0 7B 8E D9 B8-00 20 8E C0 FC BD 00 7C ·Ñ¼ð{·Ù¸· ·Àü½·|
000050 38 4E 24 7D 24 8B C1 99-E8 3C 01 72 1C 83 EB 3A 8N$}$·Á·è<·r··ë:
000060 66 A1 1C 7C 26 66 3B 07-26 8A 57 FC 75 06 80 CA f¡·|&f;·&·Wüu··Ê
000070 02 88 56 02 80 C3 10 73-EB 33 C9 8A 46 10 98 F7 ··V··Ã·së3É·F··÷
000080 66 16 03 46 1C 13 56 1E-03 46 0E 13 D1 8B 76 11 f··F··V··F··Ñ·v·
000090 60 89 46 FC 89 56 FE B8-20 00 F7 E6 8B 5E 0B 03 `·Fü·Vþ¸ ·÷æ·^··
0000a0 C3 48 F7 F3 01 46 FC 11-4E FE 61 BF 00 00 E8 E6 ÃH÷ó·Fü·Nþa¿··èæ
0000b0 00 72 39 26 38 2D 74 17-60 B1 0B BE A1 7D F3 A6 ·r9&8-t·`±·¾¡}ó¦
0000c0 61 74 32 4E 74 09 83 C7-20 3B FB 72 E6 EB DC A0 at2Nt··Ç ;ûræëÜ 
0000d0 FB 7D B4 7D 8B F0 AC 98-40 74 0C 48 74 13 B4 0E û}´}·ð¬·@t·Ht·´·
0000e0 BB 07 00 CD 10 EB EF A0-FD 7D EB E6 A0 FC 7D EB »··Í·ëï ý}ëæ ü}ë
0000f0 E1 CD 16 CD 19 26 8B 55-1A 52 B0 01 BB 00 00 E8 áÍ·Í·&·U·R°·»··è
000100 3B 00 72 E8 5B 8A 56 24-BE 0B 7C 8B FC C7 46 F0 ;·rè[·V$¾·|·üÇFð
000110 3D 7D C7 46 F4 29 7D 8C-D9 89 4E F2 89 4E F6 C6 =}ÇFô)}·Ù·Nò·NöÆ
000120 06 96 7D CB EA 03 00 00-20 0F B6 C8 66 8B 46 F8 ··}Ëê··· ·¶Èf·Fø
000130 66 03 46 1C 66 8B D0 66-C1 EA 10 EB 5E 0F B6 C8 f·F·f·ÐfÁê·ë^·¶È
000140 4A 4A 8A 46 0D 32 E4 F7-E2 03 46 FC 13 56 FE EB JJ·F·2ä÷â·Fü·Vþë
000150 4A 52 50 06 53 6A 01 6A-10 91 8B 46 18 96 92 33 JRP·Sj·j···F···3
000160 D2 F7 F6 91 F7 F6 42 87-CA F7 76 1A 8A F2 8A E8 Ò÷ö·÷öB·Ê÷v··ò·è
000170 C0 CC 02 0A CC B8 01 02-80 7E 02 0E 75 04 B4 42 ÀÌ··Ì¸···~··u·´B
000180 8B F4 8A 56 24 CD 13 61-61 72 0B 40 75 01 42 03 ·ô·V$Í·aar·@u·B·
000190 5E 0B 49 75 06 F8 C3 41-BB 00 00 60 66 6A 00 EB ^·Iu·øÃA»··`fj·ë
0001a0 B0 42 4F 4F 54 4D 47 52-20 20 20 20 0D 0A 52 65 °BOOTMGR    ··Re
0001b0 6D 6F 76 65 20 64 69 73-6B 73 20 6F 72 20 6F 74 move disks or ot
0001c0 68 65 72 20 6D 65 64 69-61 2E FF 0D 0A 44 69 73 her media.ÿ··Dis
0001d0 6B 20 65 72 72 6F 72 FF-0D 0A 50 72 65 73 73 20 k errorÿ··Press 
0001e0 61 6E 79 20 6B 65 79 20-74 6F 20 72 65 73 74 61 any key to resta
0001f0 72 74 0D 0A 00 00 00 00-00 00 00 AC CB D8 55 AA rt·········¬ËØUª
```

For FAT12 and FAT16, the VBR is a single sector (512 bytes). Walking through each of the items of information, the areas that could be of forensic importance will be highlighted.

The first 3 bytes (decimal offsets 0-2) are jump code directing the system pointer to bootstrap code. The bootstrap will be addressed later.

```
000000 EB 3C 90 4D 53 44 4F 53-35 2E 30 00 02 01 01 00 ë<·MSDOS5.0·····
000010 02 E0 00 40 0B F0 09 00-12 00 02 00 00 00 00 00 ·à·@·ð··········
000020 00 00 00 00 00 00 29 A6-06 AE BE 4E 4F 20 4E 41 ······)¦·®¾NO NA
000030 4D 45 20 20 20 20 46 41-54 31 32 20 20 20 33 C9 ME    FAT12   3É
000040 8E D1 BC F0 7B 8E D9 B8-00 20 8E C0 FC BD 00 7C ·Ñ¼ð{·Ù¸· ·Àü½·|
000050 38 4E 24 7D 24 8B C1 99-E8 3C 01 72 1C 83 EB 3A 8N$}$·Á·è<·r··ë:
000060 66 A1 1C 7C 26 66 3B 07-26 8A 57 FC 75 06 80 CA f¡·|&f;·&·Wüu··Ê
000070 02 88 56 02 80 C3 10 73-EB 33 C9 8A 46 10 98 F7 ··V··Ã·së3É·F··÷
000080 66 16 03 46 1C 13 56 1E-03 46 0E 13 D1 8B 76 11 f··F··V··F··Ñ·v·
```

Decimal Offsets 3 – 10 have the Original Equipment Manufacturer (OEM) ID and version. Since Windows 2000, the OEM ID has been set as MSDOS5.0 for FAT volumes that were formatted through Windows.

```
000000 EB 3C 90 4D 53 44 4F 53-35 2E 30 00 02 01 01 00 ë<·MSDOS5.0·····
000010 02 E0 00 40 0B F0 09 00-12 00 02 00 00 00 00 00 ·à·@·ð··········
000020 00 00 00 00 00 00 29 A6-06 AE BE 4E 4F 20 4E 41 ······)¦·®¾NO NA
000030 4D 45 20 20 20 20 46 41-54 31 32 20 20 20 33 C9 ME    FAT12   3É
000040 8E D1 BC F0 7B 8E D9 B8-00 20 8E C0 FC BD 00 7C ·Ñ¼ð{·Ù¸· ·Àü½·|
000050 38 4E 24 7D 24 8B C1 99-E8 3C 01 72 1C 83 EB 3A 8N$}$·Á·è<·r··ë:
000060 66 A1 1C 7C 26 66 3B 07-26 8A 57 FC 75 06 80 CA f¡·|&f;·&·Wüu··Ê
000070 02 88 56 02 80 C3 10 73-EB 33 C9 8A 46 10 98 F7 ··V··Ã·së3É·F··÷
000080 66 16 03 46 1C 13 56 1E-03 46 0E 13 D1 8B 76 11 f··F··V··F··Ñ·v·
```

Decimal Offsets 11-12 have the number of bytes per sector. 0x0200 = 512.

```
000000 EB 3C 90 4D 53 44 4F 53-35 2E 30 00 02 01 01 00 ë<·MSDOS5.0·····
000010 02 E0 00 40 0B F0 09 00-12 00 02 00 00 00 00 00 ·à·@·ð··········
000020 00 00 00 00 00 00 29 A6-06 AE BE 4E 4F 20 4E 41 ······)¦·®¾NO NA
000030 4D 45 20 20 20 20 46 41-54 31 32 20 20 20 33 C9 ME    FAT12   3É
000040 8E D1 BC F0 7B 8E D9 B8-00 20 8E C0 FC BD 00 7C ·Ñ¼ð{·Ù¸· ·Àü½·|
000050 38 4E 24 7D 24 8B C1 99-E8 3C 01 72 1C 83 EB 3A 8N$}$·Á·è<·r··ë:
000060 66 A1 1C 7C 26 66 3B 07-26 8A 57 FC 75 06 80 CA f¡·|&f;·&·Wüu··Ê
000070 02 88 56 02 80 C3 10 73-EB 33 C9 8A 46 10 98 F7 ··V··Ã·së3É·F··÷
000080 66 16 03 46 1C 13 56 1E-03 46 0E 13 D1 8B 76 11 f··F··V··F··Ñ·v·
```

Decimal Offset 13 is the number of sectors per cluster. This value is forensically important in the recovery of deleted files, which will be shown in Chapter 8.

```
000000 EB 3C 90 4D 53 44 4F 53-35 2E 30 00 02 01 01 00 ë<·MSDOS5.0·
000010 02 E0 00 40 0B F0 09 00-12 00 02 00 00 00 00 00 ·à·@·ð······
000020 00 00 00 00 00 00 29 A6-06 AE BE 4E 4F 20 4E 41 ······)¦·®¾N
000030 4D 45 20 20 20 20 46 41-54 31 32 20 20 20 33 C9 ME    FAT12
000040 8E D1 BC F0 7B 8E D9 B8-00 20 8E C0 FC BD 00 7C ·Ñ¼ð{·Ù¸· ·À
000050 38 4E 24 7D 24 8B C1 99-E8 3C 01 72 1C 83 EB 3A 8N$}$·Á·è<·r
000060 66 A1 1C 7C 26 66 3B 07-26 8A 57 FC 75 06 80 CA f¡·|&f;·&·Wü
000070 02 88 56 02 80 C3 10 73-EB 33 C9 8A 46 10 98 F7 ··V··Ã·së3É·
```

Decimal Offsets 14-15 are the number of reserved sectors. Typically the value is 1 in FAT12 and FAT16.

```
000000 EB 3C 90 4D 53 44 4F 53-35 2E 30 00 02 01 01 00 ë<·MSDOS5.0·····
000010 02 E0 00 40 0B F0 09 00-12 00 02 00 00 00 00 00 ·à·@·ð··········
000020 00 00 00 00 00 00 29 A6-06 AE BE 4E 4F 20 4E 41 ······)¦·®¾NO NA
000030 4D 45 20 20 20 20 46 41-54 31 32 20 20 20 33 C9 ME    FAT12   3É
000040 8E D1 BC F0 7B 8E D9 B8-00 20 8E C0 FC BD 00 7C ·Ñ¼ð{·Ù¸· ·Àü½·|
000050 38 4E 24 7D 24 8B C1 99-E8 3C 01 72 1C 83 EB 3A 8N$}$·Á·è<·r··ë:
000060 66 A1 1C 7C 26 66 3B 07-26 8A 57 FC 75 06 80 CA f¡·|&f;·&·Wüu··Ê
000070 02 88 56 02 80 C3 10 73-EB 33 C9 8A 46 10 98 F7 ··V··Ã·së3É·F··÷
000080 66 16 03 46 1C 13 56 1E-03 46 0E 13 D1 8B 76 11 f··F··V··F··Ñ·v·
```

Decimal Offset 16 is the number of copies of the File Allocation Table. In FAT12, FAT 16, and FAT32 there is a redundant copy immediately following the first table, so this value should always be 2.

```
000000 EB 3C 90 4D 53 44 4F 53-35 2E 30 00 02 01 01 00 ë<·MSDOS5.0·····
000010 02 E0 00 40 0B F0 09 00-12 00 02 00 00 00 00 00 ·à·@·ð··········
000020 00 00 00 00 00 00 29 A6-06 AE BE 4E 4F 20 4E 41 ······)¦·®¾NO NA
000030 4D 45 20 20 20 20 46 41-54 31 32 20 20 20 33 C9 ME    FAT12   3É
000040 8E D1 BC F0 7B 8E D9 B8-00 20 8E C0 FC BD 00 7C ·Ñ¼ð{·Ù¸· ·Àü½·|
000050 38 4E 24 7D 24 8B C1 99-E8 3C 01 72 1C 83 EB 3A 8N$}$·Á·è<·r··ë:
000060 66 A1 1C 7C 26 66 3B 07-26 8A 57 FC 75 06 80 CA f¡·|&f;·&·Wüu··Ê
000070 02 88 56 02 80 C3 10 73-EB 33 C9 8A 46 10 98 F7 ··V··Ã·së3É·F··÷
000080 66 16 03 46 1C 13 56 1E-03 46 0E 13 D1 8B 76 11 f··F··V··F··Ñ·v·
```

Decimal Offsets 17-18 are the number of entries allowed in the root directory. Under FAT12 and FAT16 there is a limited number of entries. In FAT12 it is 224 entries and 512 for FAT16. There is no such limitation for FAT32.

```
000000 EB 3C 90 4D 53 44 4F 53-35 2E 30 00 02 01 01 00 ë<·MSDOS5.0·····
000010 02 E0 00 40 0B F0 09 00-12 00 02 00 00 00 00 00 ·à·@·ð··········
000020 00 00 00 00 00 00 29 A6-06 AE BE 4E 4F 20 4E 41 ······)¦·®¾NO NA
000030 4D 45 20 20 20 20 46 41-54 31 32 20 20 20 33 C9 ME    FAT12   3É
000040 8E D1 BC F0 7B 8E D9 B8-00 20 8E C0 FC BD 00 7C ·Ñ¼ð{·Ù¸· ·Àü½·|
000050 38 4E 24 7D 24 8B C1 99-E8 3C 01 72 1C 83 EB 3A 8N$}$·Á·è<·r··ë:
000060 66 A1 1C 7C 26 66 3B 07-26 8A 57 FC 75 06 80 CA f¡·|&f;·&·Wüu··Ê
000070 02 88 56 02 80 C3 10 73-EB 33 C9 8A 46 10 98 F7 ··V··Ã·së3É·F··÷
000080 66 16 03 46 1C 13 56 1E-03 46 0E 13 D1 8B 76 11 f··F··V··F··Ñ·v·
```

Decimal Offsets 19-20 are the total number of sectors in the partition for FAT12 and FAT16. This value is needed if recovering deleted partitions. For this case, it is 2880 sectors.

```
000000 EB 3C 90 4D 53 44 4F 53-35 2E 30 00 02 01 01 00 ë<·MSDOS5.0·····
000010 02 E0 00 40 0B F0 09 00-12 00 02 00 00 00 00 00 ·à·@·ð··········
000020 00 00 00 00 00 00 29 A6-06 AE BE 4E 4F 20 4E 41 ······)¦·®¾NO NA
000030 4D 45 20 20 20 20 46 41-54 31 32 20 20 20 33 C9 ME    FAT12   3É
000040 8E D1 BC F0 7B 8E D9 B8-00 20 8E C0 FC BD 00 7C ·Ñ¼ð{·Ù¸· ·Àü½·|
000050 38 4E 24 7D 24 8B C1 99-E8 3C 01 72 1C 83 EB 3A 8N$}$·Á·è<·r··ë:
000060 66 A1 1C 7C 26 66 3B 07-26 8A 57 FC 75 06 80 CA f¡·|&f;·&·Wüu··Ê
000070 02 88 56 02 80 C3 10 73-EB 33 C9 8A 46 10 98 F7 ··V··Ã·së3É·F··÷
000080 66 16 03 46 1C 13 56 1E-03 46 0E 13 D1 8B 76 11 f··F··V··F··Ñ·v·
```

Decimal Offset 21 is the Media Descriptor. F0 is for floppy disks and F8 is for Hard disks.

```
000000 EB 3C 90 4D 53 44 4F 53-35 2E 30 00 02 01 01 00 ë<·MSDOS5.0·····
000010 02 E0 00 40 0B F0 09 00-12 00 02 00 00 00 00 00 ·à·@·ð··········
000020 00 00 00 00 00 00 29 A6-06 AE BE 4E 4F 20 4E 41 ······)¦·®¾NO NA
000030 4D 45 20 20 20 20 46 41-54 31 32 20 20 20 33 C9 ME    FAT12   3É
000040 8E D1 BC F0 7B 8E D9 B8-00 20 8E C0 FC BD 00 7C ·Ñ¼ð{·Ù¸· ·Àü½·|
000050 38 4E 24 7D 24 8B C1 99-E8 3C 01 72 1C 83 EB 3A 8N$}$·Á·è<·r··ë:
000060 66 A1 1C 7C 26 66 3B 07-26 8A 57 FC 75 06 80 CA f¡·|&f;·&·Wüu··Ê
000070 02 88 56 02 80 C3 10 73-EB 33 C9 8A 46 10 98 F7 ··V··Ã·së3É·F··÷
000080 66 16 03 46 1C 13 56 1E-03 46 0E 13 D1 8B 76 11 f··F··V··F··Ñ·v·
```

Decimal Offsets 22-23 are the number of sectors per FAT.

```
000000 EB 3C 90 4D 53 44 4F 53-35 2E 30 00 02 01 01 00 ë<·MSDOS5.0·····
000010 02 E0 00 40 0B F0 09 00-12 00 02 00 00 00 00 00 ·à·@·ð··········
000020 00 00 00 00 00 00 29 A6-06 AE BE 4E 4F 20 4E 41 ······)¦·®¾NO NA
000030 4D 45 20 20 20 20 46 41-54 31 32 20 20 20 33 C9 ME    FAT12   3É
000040 8E D1 BC F0 7B 8E D9 B8-00 20 8E C0 FC BD 00 7C ·Ñ¼ð{·Ù¸· ·Àü½·|
000050 38 4E 24 7D 24 8B C1 99-E8 3C 01 72 1C 83 EB 3A 8N$}$·Á·è<·r··ë:
000060 66 A1 1C 7C 26 66 3B 07-26 8A 57 FC 75 06 80 CA f¡·|&f;·&·Wüu··Ê
000070 02 88 56 02 80 C3 10 73-EB 33 C9 8A 46 10 98 F7 ··V··Ã·së3É·F··÷
000080 66 16 03 46 1C 13 56 1E-03 46 0E 13 D1 8B 76 11 f··F··V··F··Ñ·v·
```

Decimal Offsets 24-25 are the number sectors per track. In this case, 18.

```
000000 EB 3C 90 4D 53 44 4F 53-35 2E 30 00 02 01 01 00 ë<·MSDOS5.0·····
000010 02 E0 00 40 0B F0 09 00-12 00 02 00 00 00 00 00 ·à·@·ð··········
000020 00 00 00 00 00 00 29 A6-06 AE BE 4E 4F 20 4E 41 ······)¦·®¾NO NA
000030 4D 45 20 20 20 20 46 41-54 31 32 20 20 20 33 C9 ME    FAT12   3É
000040 8E D1 BC F0 7B 8E D9 B8-00 20 8E C0 FC BD 00 7C ·Ñ¼ð{·Ù¸· ·Àü½·|
000050 38 4E 24 7D 24 8B C1 99-E8 3C 01 72 1C 83 EB 3A 8N$}$·Á·è<·r··ë:
000060 66 A1 1C 7C 26 66 3B 07-26 8A 57 FC 75 06 80 CA f¡·|&f;·&·Wüu··Ê
000070 02 88 56 02 80 C3 10 73-EB 33 C9 8A 46 10 98 F7 ··V··Ã·së3É·F···÷
000080 66 16 03 46 1C 13 56 1E-03 46 0E 13 D1 8B 76 11 f··F··V··F··Ñ·v·
```

Decimal Offsets 26-27 are the number of heads (2 for a floppy disk).

```
000000 EB 3C 90 4D 53 44 4F 53-35 2E 30 00 02 01 01 00 ë<·MSDOS5.0·····
000010 02 E0 00 40 0B F0 09 00-12 00 02 00 00 00 00 00 ·à·@·ð··········
000020 00 00 00 00 00 00 29 A6-06 AE BE 4E 4F 20 4E 41 ······)¦·®¾NO NA
000030 4D 45 20 20 20 20 46 41-54 31 32 20 20 20 33 C9 ME    FAT12   3É
000040 8E D1 BC F0 7B 8E D9 B8-00 20 8E C0 FC BD 00 7C ·Ñ¼ð{·Ù¸· ·Àü½·|
000050 38 4E 24 7D 24 8B C1 99-E8 3C 01 72 1C 83 EB 3A 8N$}$·Á·è<·r··ë:
000060 66 A1 1C 7C 26 66 3B 07-26 8A 57 FC 75 06 80 CA f¡·|&f;·&·Wüu··Ê
000070 02 88 56 02 80 C3 10 73-EB 33 C9 8A 46 10 98 F7 ··V··Ã·së3É·F···÷
000080 66 16 03 46 1C 13 56 1E-03 46 0E 13 D1 8B 76 11 f··F··V··F··Ñ·v·
```

Decimal Offsets 28-31 are the number of hidden sectors.

```
000000 EB 3C 90 4D 53 44 4F 53-35 2E 30 00 02 01 01 00 ë<·MSDOS5.0·····
000010 02 E0 00 40 0B F0 09 00-12 00 02 00 00 00 00 00 ·à·@·ð··········
000020 00 00 00 00 00 00 29 A6-06 AE BE 4E 4F 20 4E 41 ······)¦·®¾NO NA
000030 4D 45 20 20 20 20 46 41-54 31 32 20 20 20 33 C9 ME    FAT12   3É
000040 8E D1 BC F0 7B 8E D9 B8-00 20 8E C0 FC BD 00 7C ·Ñ¼ð{·Ù¸· ·Àü½·|
000050 38 4E 24 7D 24 8B C1 99-E8 3C 01 72 1C 83 EB 3A 8N$}$·Á·è<·r··ë:
000060 66 A1 1C 7C 26 66 3B 07-26 8A 57 FC 75 06 80 CA f¡·|&f;·&·Wüu··Ê
000070 02 88 56 02 80 C3 10 73-EB 33 C9 8A 46 10 98 F7 ··V··Ã·së3É·F···÷
000080 66 16 03 46 1C 13 56 1E-03 46 0E 13 D1 8B 76 11 f··F··V··F··Ñ·v·
```

Decimal Offsets 32-35 are the total number of sectors in the partition. This is used for larger than in offset 19-20.

```
000000 EB 3C 90 4D 53 44 4F 53-35 2E 30 00 02 01 01 00 ë<·MSDOS5.0·····
000010 02 E0 00 40 0B F0 09 00-12 00 02 00 00 00 00 00 ·à·@·ð··········
000020 00 00 00 00 00 00 29 A6-06 AE BE 4E 4F 20 4E 41 ······)¦·®¾NO NA
000030 4D 45 20 20 20 20 46 41-54 31 32 20 20 20 33 C9 ME    FAT12   3É
000040 8E D1 BC F0 7B 8E D9 B8-00 20 8E C0 FC BD 00 7C ·Ñ¼ð{·Ù¸· ·Àü½·|
000050 38 4E 24 7D 24 8B C1 99-E8 3C 01 72 1C 83 EB 3A 8N$}$·Á·è<·r··ë:
000060 66 A1 1C 7C 26 66 3B 07-26 8A 57 FC 75 06 80 CA f¡·|&f;·&·Wüu··Ê
000070 02 88 56 02 80 C3 10 73-EB 33 C9 8A 46 10 98 F7 ··V··Ã·së3É·F···÷
000080 66 16 03 46 1C 13 56 1E-03 46 0E 13 D1 8B 76 11 f··F··V··F··Ñ·v·
```

Decimal Offset 36 is the logical drive number for hard drives.

```
000000 EB 3C 90 4D 53 44 4F 53-35 2E 30 00 02 01 01 00 ë<·MSDOS5.0·····
000010 02 E0 00 40 0B F0 09 00-12 00 02 00 00 00 00 00 ·à·@·ð··········
000020 00 00 00 00 00 00 29 A6-06 AE BE 4E 4F 20 4E 41 ······)¦·®¾NO NA
000030 4D 45 20 20 20 20 46 41-54 31 32 20 20 20 33 C9 ME    FAT12   3É
000040 8E D1 BC F0 7B 8E D9 B8-00 20 8E C0 FC BD 00 7C ·Ñ¼ð{·Ù¸· ·Àü½·|
000050 38 4E 24 7D 24 8B C1 99-E8 3C 01 72 1C 83 EB 3A 8N$}$·Á·è<·r··ë:
000060 66 A1 1C 7C 26 66 3B 07-26 8A 57 FC 75 06 80 CA f¡·|&f;·&·Wüu··Ê
000070 02 88 56 02 80 C3 10 73-EB 33 C9 8A 46 10 98 F7 ··V··Ã·së3É·F··÷
000080 66 16 03 46 1C 13 56 1E-03 46 0E 13 D1 8B 76 11 f··F··V··F··Ñ·v·
```

Decimal Offset 37 is reserved.

```
000000 EB 3C 90 4D 53 44 4F 53-35 2E 30 00 02 01 01 00 ë<·MSDOS5.0·····
000010 02 E0 00 40 0B F0 09 00-12 00 02 00 00 00 00 00 ·à·@·ð··········
000020 00 00 00 00 00 00 29 A6-06 AE BE 4E 4F 20 4E 41 ······)¦·®¾NO NA
000030 4D 45 20 20 20 20 46 41-54 31 32 20 20 20 33 C9 ME    FAT12   3É
000040 8E D1 BC F0 7B 8E D9 B8-00 20 8E C0 FC BD 00 7C ·Ñ¼ð{·Ù¸· ·Àü½·|
000050 38 4E 24 7D 24 8B C1 99-E8 3C 01 72 1C 83 EB 3A 8N$}$·Á·è<·r··ë:
000060 66 A1 1C 7C 26 66 3B 07-26 8A 57 FC 75 06 80 CA f¡·|&f;·&·Wüu··Ê
000070 02 88 56 02 80 C3 10 73-EB 33 C9 8A 46 10 98 F7 ··V··Ã·së3É·F··÷
000080 66 16 03 46 1C 13 56 1E-03 46 0E 13 D1 8B 76 11 f··F··V··F··Ñ·v·
```

Decimal Offset 38 is an extended signature of 29

```
000000 EB 3C 90 4D 53 44 4F 53-35 2E 30 00 02 01 01 00 ë<·MSDOS5.0·····
000010 02 E0 00 40 0B F0 09 00-12 00 02 00 00 00 00 00 ·à·@·ð··········
000020 00 00 00 00 00 00 29 A6-06 AE BE 4E 4F 20 4E 41 ······)¦·®¾NO NA
000030 4D 45 20 20 20 20 46 41-54 31 32 20 20 20 33 C9 ME    FAT12   3É
000040 8E D1 BC F0 7B 8E D9 B8-00 20 8E C0 FC BD 00 7C ·Ñ¼ð{·Ù¸· ·Àü½·|
000050 38 4E 24 7D 24 8B C1 99-E8 3C 01 72 1C 83 EB 3A 8N$}$·Á·è<·r··ë:
000060 66 A1 1C 7C 26 66 3B 07-26 8A 57 FC 75 06 80 CA f¡·|&f;·&·Wüu··Ê
000070 02 88 56 02 80 C3 10 73-EB 33 C9 8A 46 10 98 F7 ··V··Ã·së3É·F··÷
000080 66 16 03 46 1C 13 56 1E-03 46 0E 13 D1 8B 76 11 f··F··V··F··Ñ·v·
```

Decimal Offsets 39-42 are the volume serial number (BEAE06A6). This can be valuable evidence in tracking data and is different from the drive serial number.

```
000000 EB 3C 90 4D 53 44 4F 53-35 2E 30 00 02 01 01 00 ë<·MSDOS5.0·····
000010 02 E0 00 40 0B F0 09 00-12 00 02 00 00 00 00 00 ·à·@·ð··········
000020 00 00 00 00 00 00 29 A6-06 AE BE 4E 4F 20 4E 41 ······)¦·®¾NO NA
000030 4D 45 20 20 20 20 46 41-54 31 32 20 20 20 33 C9 ME    FAT12   3É
000040 8E D1 BC F0 7B 8E D9 B8-00 20 8E C0 FC BD 00 7C ·Ñ¼ð{·Ù¸· ·Àü½·|
000050 38 4E 24 7D 24 8B C1 99-E8 3C 01 72 1C 83 EB 3A 8N$}$·Á·è<·r··ë:
000060 66 A1 1C 7C 26 66 3B 07-26 8A 57 FC 75 06 80 CA f¡·|&f;·&·Wüu··Ê
000070 02 88 56 02 80 C3 10 73-EB 33 C9 8A 46 10 98 F7 ··V··Ã·së3É·F··÷
000080 66 16 03 46 1C 13 56 1E-03 46 0E 13 D1 8B 76 11 f··F··V··F··Ñ·v·
```

Decimal Offsets 43-53 are the volume label, but this is filled with NO NAME

```
000000 EB 3C 90 4D 53 44 4F 53-35 2E 30 00 02 01 01 00 ë<·MSDOS5.0·····
000010 02 E0 00 40 0B F0 09 00-12 00 02 00 00 00 00 00 ·à·@·ð··········
000020 00 00 00 00 00 00 29 A6-06 AE BE 4E 4F 20 4E 41 ······)¦·®¾NO NA
000030 4D 45 20 20 20 20 46 41-54 31 32 20 20 20 33 C9 ME    FAT12   3É
000040 8E D1 BC F0 7B 8E D9 B8-00 20 8E C0 FC BD 00 7C ·Ñ¼ð{·Ù¸· ·Àü½·|
000050 38 4E 24 7D 24 8B C1 99-E8 3C 01 72 1C 83 EB 3A 8N$}$·Á·è<·r··ë:
000060 66 A1 1C 7C 26 66 3B 07-26 8A 57 FC 75 06 80 CA f¡·|&f;·&·Wüu··Ê
000070 02 88 56 02 80 C3 10 73-EB 33 C9 8A 46 10 98 F7 ··V··Ã·së3É·F··÷
000080 66 16 03 46 1C 13 56 1E-03 46 0E 13 D1 8B 76 11 f··F··V··F··Ñ·v·
```

Decimal Offsets 54-61 are for the file system type name.

```
000000 EB 3C 90 4D 53 44 4F 53-35 2E 30 00 02 01 01 00 ë<·MSDOS5.0·····
000010 02 E0 00 40 0B F0 09 00-12 00 02 00 00 00 00 00 ·à·@·ð··········
000020 00 00 00 00 00 00 29 A6-06 AE BE 4E 4F 20 4E 41 ······)¦·®¾NO NA
000030 4D 45 20 20 20 20 46 41-54 31 32 20 20 20 33 C9 ME    FAT12   3É
000040 8E D1 BC F0 7B 8E D9 B8-00 20 8E C0 FC BD 00 7C ·Ñ¼ð{·Ù¸· ·Àü½·|
000050 38 4E 24 7D 24 8B C1 99-E8 3C 01 72 1C 83 EB 3A 8N$}$·Á·è<·r··ë:
000060 66 A1 1C 7C 26 66 3B 07-26 8A 57 FC 75 06 80 CA f¡·|&f;·&·Wüu··Ê
000070 02 88 56 02 80 C3 10 73-EB 33 C9 8A 46 10 98 F7 ··V··Ã·së3É·F··÷
000080 66 16 03 46 1C 13 56 1E-03 46 0E 13 D1 8B 76 11 f··F··V··F··Ñ·v·
```

Decimal Offset 62-509 is the bootstrap code mentioned in the first offset. This has the code for booting the file system if needed.

Decimal Offsets 510-511 are the VBR signature, which is the same as that of the MBR 0x 55AA.

```
0001a0 B0 42 4F 4F 54 4D 47 52-20 20 20 20 0D 0A 52 65 °BOOTMGR    ··Re
0001b0 6D 6F 76 65 20 64 69 73-6B 73 20 6F 72 20 6F 74 move disks or ot
0001c0 68 65 72 20 6D 65 64 69-61 2E FF 0D 0A 44 69 73 her media.ÿ··Dis
0001d0 6B 20 65 72 72 6F 72 FF-0D 0A 50 72 65 73 73 20 k errorÿ··Press
0001e0 61 6E 79 20 6B 65 79 20-74 6F 20 72 65 73 74 61 any key to resta
0001f0 72 74 0D 0A 00 00 00 00-00 00 00 AC CB D8 55 AA rt·········¬ËØUª
```

PRACTICAL EXERCISE 1

Utilizing the FAT16 VBR Below, interpret the requested information.

```
000 EB 3C 90 4D 53 44 4F 53-35 2E 30 00 02 01 04 00 ë<·MSDOS5.0·····
010 02 00 02 00 FC F8 FA 00-3F 00 FF 00 00 00 00 00 ····üøú·?·ÿ·····
020 00 00 00 00 80 00 29 3D-41 5D 04 4E 4F 20 4E 41 ······)=A]·NO NA
030 4D 45 20 20 20 20 46 41-54 31 36 20 20 20 33 C9 ME    FAT16   3É
040 8E D1 BC F0 7B 8E D9 B8-00 20 8E C0 FC BD 00 7C ·Ñ¼ð{·Ù¸· ·Àü½·|
050 38 4E 24 7D 24 8B C1 99-E8 3C 01 72 1C 83 EB 3A 8N$}$·Á·è<·r··ë:
060 66 A1 1C 7C 26 66 3B 07-26 8A 57 FC 75 06 80 CA f¡·|&f;·&·Wüu··Ê
070 02 88 56 02 80 C3 10 73-EB 33 C9 8A 46 10 98 F7 ··V··Ã·së3É·F··÷
080 66 16 03 46 1C 13 56 1E-03 46 0E 13 D1 8B 76 11 f··F··V··F··Ñ·v·
090 60 89 46 FC 89 56 FE B8-20 00 F7 E6 8B 5E 0B 03 `·Fü·Vþ¸ ·÷æ·^··
0a0 C3 48 F7 F3 01 46 FC 11-4E FE 61 BF 00 00 E8 E6 ÃH÷ó·Fü·Nþa¿··èæ
0b0 00 72 39 26 38 2D 74 17-60 B1 0B BE A1 7D F3 A6 ·r9&8-t·`±·¾¡}ó¦
0c0 61 74 32 4E 74 09 83 C7-20 3B FB 72 E6 EB DC A0 at2Nt··Ç ;ûræëÜ 
0d0 FB 7D B4 7D 8B F0 AC 98-40 74 0C 48 74 13 B4 0E û}´}·ð¬·@t·Ht·´·
0e0 BB 07 00 CD 10 EB EF A0-FD 7D EB E6 A0 FC 7D EB »··Í·ëï ý}ëæ ü}ë
0f0 E1 CD 16 CD 19 26 8B 55-1A 52 B0 01 BB 00 00 E8 áÍ·Í·&·U·R°·»··è
100 3B 00 72 E8 5B 8A 56 24-BE 0B 7C 8B FC C7 46 F0 ;·rè[·V$¾·|·üÇFð
110 3D 7D C7 46 F4 29 7D 8C-D9 89 4E F2 89 4E F6 C6 =}ÇFô)}·Ù·Nò·NöÆ
120 06 96 7D CB EA 03 00 00-20 0F B6 C8 66 8B 46 F8 ··}Ëê··· ·¶Èf·Fø
130 66 03 46 1C 66 8B D0 66-C1 EA 10 EB 5E 0F B6 C8 f·F·f·ÐfÁê·ë^·¶È
140 4A 4A 8A 46 0D 32 E4 F7-E2 03 46 FC 13 56 FE EB JJ·F·2ä÷â·Fü·Vþë
150 4A 52 50 06 53 6A 01 6A-10 91 8B 46 18 96 92 33 JRP·Sj·j···F···3
160 D2 F7 F6 91 F7 F6 42 87-CA F7 76 1A 8A F2 8A E8 Ò÷ö·÷öB·Ê÷v··ò·è
170 C0 CC 02 0A CC B8 01 02-80 7E 02 0E 75 04 B4 42 ÀÌ··Ì¸···~··u·´B
180 8B F4 8A 56 24 CD 13 61-61 72 0B 40 75 01 42 03 ·ô·V$Í·aar·@u·B·
190 5E 0B 49 75 06 F8 C3 41-BB 00 00 60 66 6A 00 EB ^·Iu·øÃA»··`fj·ë
1a0 B0 42 4F 4F 54 4D 47 52-20 20 20 20 0D 0A 52 65 °BOOTMGR    ··Re
1b0 6D 6F 76 65 20 64 69 73-6B 73 20 6F 72 20 6F 74 move disks or ot
1c0 68 65 72 20 6D 65 64 69-61 2E FF 0D 0A 44 69 73 her media.ÿ··Dis
1d0 6B 20 65 72 72 6F 72 FF-0D 0A 50 72 65 73 73 20 k errorÿ··Press 
1e0 61 6E 79 20 6B 65 79 20-74 6F 20 72 65 73 74 61 any key to resta
1f0 72 74 0D 0A 00 00 00 00-00 00 00 AC CB D8 55 AA rt·········¬ËØUª
```

What is the OEM version that was used to setup this volume?

How many bytes are there per sector?

How many sector are there per cluster?

Based upon the previous answer, how many bytes per cluster?

How many sectors are there in the partition?

How many sectors per FAT are there?

What is the partition (volume) serial number?

What is the volume label?

What is the file system type?

What is the VBR signature?

FAT32

The FAT32 Volume Boot Record is different in that it incorporates 6 sectors instead of just 1, and there is a backup copy of those 6 sectors immediately following the first copy.

The first sector is very similar to the FAT12/16 VBR with a few differences.

FAT 32 VBR	FS INFO		
DEC OFFSET	HEX OFFSET	SIZE (BYTES)	DESCRIPTION
0	00	36	Identical to FAT12/16
36	24	4	Sectors per FAT
40	28	2	Mirror Flags
42	2A	2	Filesystem Version
44	2C	4	1st Cluster of Root Directory (2)
48	30	2	FS Information sector (usually 1)
50	32	2	Backup Boot Sector
52	34	12	Reserved
64	40	1	Logical Drive Number (0x00 or 0x80)
65	41	1	Reserved
66	42	1	Extended signature (0x29)
67	43	4	Serial number of partition
71	47	11	Volume Label
82	52	8	Filesystem type
90	5A	421	Bootstrap
510	3E	2	Signature 0x55 AA

Note that the first 36 bytes are identical to the FAT12/16 VBR. The next six entries are new and then the remainder of the items of information is the same as with FAT12/16 but at different offsets.
The next sector in the VBR is referred to as the File System Information (FS INFO).

FAT 32 VBR FS INFO			
DEC OFFSET	HEX OFFSET	SIZE (BYTES)	DESCRIPTION
0	00	4	Signature of 0x52526141
4	04	480	Blank
484	1E4	4	Secondary Signature of 0x72726141
488	1E8	4	Free cluster count
492	1EC	4	Next free count
496	1F0	14	Reserved bytes
510	1FE	2	Signature 0x55 AA

The third sector is the FAT32 VBR only has a signature at offset 510 (0X55AA). The fourth, fifth and sixth sectors are all blank, and are not even a signature.

PRACTICAL EXERCISE 2

Utilizing the FAT32 VBR below, interpret the requested information.

```
Offset(d)   00 01 02 03 04 05 06 07 08 09 10 11 12 13 14 15

0000000000  EB 58 90 4D 53 44 4F 53 35 2E 30 00 02 04 A6 01  ëX.MSDOS5.0...¦.
0000000016  02 00 00 00 00 F8 00 00 3F 00 FF 00 00 00 00 00  .....ø..?.ÿ.....
0000000032  00 78 1E 00 2D 0F 00 00 00 00 00 00 02 00 00 00  .x..-...........
0000000048  01 00 06 00 00 00 00 00 00 00 00 00 00 00 00 00  ................
0000000064  80 00 29 45 0D F0 80 4E 4F 20 4E 41 4D 45 20 20  €.)E.ð€NO NAME
0000000080  20 20 46 41 54 33 32 20 20 20 33 C9 8E D1 BC F4    FAT32   3ÉŽÑ¼ô
0000000096  7B 8E C1 8E D9 BD 00 7C 88 4E 02 8A 56 40 B4 41  {ŽÁŽÙ½.|ˆN.ŠV@´A
0000000112  BB AA 55 CD 13 72 10 81 FB 55 AA 75 0A F6 C1 01  »ªUÍ.r..ûUªu.öÁ.
0000000128  74 05 FE 46 02 EB 2D 8A 56 40 B4 08 CD 13 73 05  t.þF.ë-ŠV@´.Í.s.
0000000144  B9 FF FF 8A F1 66 0F B6 C6 40 66 0F B6 D1 80 E2  ¹ÿÿŠñf.¶Æ@f.¶Ñ€â
0000000160  3F F7 E2 86 CD C0 ED 06 41 66 0F B7 C9 66 F7 E1  ?÷â†ÍÀí.Af.·Éf÷á
0000000176  66 89 46 F8 83 7E 16 00 75 38 83 7E 2A 00 77 32  f‰Føƒ~..u8ƒ~*.w2
0000000192  66 8B 46 1C 66 83 C0 0C BB 00 80 B9 01 00 E8 2B  f‹F.fƒÀ.».€¹..è+
0000000208  00 E9 2C 03 A0 FA 7D B4 7D 8B F0 AC 84 C0 74 17  .é,. ú}´}‹ð¬„Àt.
0000000224  3C FF 74 09 B4 0E BB 07 00 CD 10 EB EE A0 FB 7D  <ÿt.´.»..Í.ëî û}
0000000240  EB E5 A0 F9 7D EB E0 98 CD 16 CD 19 66 60 80 7E  ëå ù}ëà˜Í.Í.f`€~
0000000256  02 00 0F 84 20 00 66 6A 00 66 50 06 53 66 68 10  ...„ .fj.fP.Sfh.
0000000272  00 01 00 B4 42 8A 56 40 8B F4 CD 13 66 58 66 58  ...´BŠV@‹ôÍ.fXfX
0000000288  66 58 66 58 EB 33 66 3B 46 F8 72 03 F9 EB 2A 66  fXfXë3f;Før.ùë*f
0000000304  33 D2 66 0F B7 4E 18 66 F7 F1 FE C2 8A CA 66 8B  3Òf.·N.f÷ñþÂŠÊf‹
0000000320  D0 66 C1 EA 10 F7 76 1A 86 D6 8A 56 40 8A E8 C0  ÐfÁê.÷v.†ÖŠV@ŠèÀ
0000000336  E4 06 0A CC B8 01 02 CD 13 66 61 0F 82 75 FF 81  ä..Ì¸..Í.fa.‚uÿ.
0000000352  C3 00 02 66 40 49 75 94 C3 42 4F 4F 54 4D 47 52  Ã..f@Iu”ÃBOOTMGR
0000000368  20 20 20 20 00 00 00 00 00 00 00 00 00 00 00 00      ............
0000000384  00 00 00 00 00 00 00 00 00 00 00 00 00 00 00 00  ................
0000000400  00 00 00 00 00 00 00 00 00 00 00 00 00 00 00 00  ................
0000000416  00 00 00 00 00 00 00 00 00 00 00 00 0D 0A 52 65  ..............Re
0000000432  6D 6F 76 65 20 64 69 73 6B 73 20 6F 72 20 6F 74  move disks or ot
0000000448  68 65 72 20 6D 65 64 69 61 2E FF 0D 0A 44 69 73  her media.ÿ..Dis
0000000464  6B 20 65 72 72 6F 72 FF 0D 0A 50 72 65 73 73 20  k errorÿ..Press
0000000480  61 6E 79 20 6B 65 79 20 74 6F 20 72 65 73 74 61  any key to resta
0000000496  72 74 0D 0A 00 00 00 00 00 AC CB D8 00 00 55 AA  rt.......¬ËØ..Uª
```

What is the OEM version that was used to set up this volume?

How many bytes are there per sector?

How many sectors are there per cluster?

Based upon the previous answer, how many bytes per cluster?

How many sectors are there in the partition?

How many sectors per FAT are there?

What cluster does the Root Directory begin in?

What sector is the FS Info Block in?

What sector does the backup copy of the VBR begin in?

What is the partition (volume) serial number?

What is the volume label?

What is the file system type?

What is the VBR signature?

Below is the FS Info Block.

Offset(d)	00	01	02	03	04	05	06	07	08	09	10	11	12	13	14	15	
0000000512	52	52	61	41	00	00	00	00	00	00	00	00	00	00	00	00	RRaA............
0000000528	00	00	00	00	00	00	00	00	00	00	00	00	00	00	00	00	....
0000000544	00	00	00	00	00	00	00	00	00	00	00	00	00	00	00	00	....
0000000560	00	00	00	00	00	00	00	00	00	00	00	00	00	00	00	00	....
0000000576	00	00	00	00	00	00	00	00	00	00	00	00	00	00	00	00	....
0000000592	00	00	00	00	00	00	00	00	00	00	00	00	00	00	00	00	....
0000000608	00	00	00	00	00	00	00	00	00	00	00	00	00	00	00	00	....
0000000624	00	00	00	00	00	00	00	00	00	00	00	00	00	00	00	00	....
0000000640	00	00	00	00	00	00	00	00	00	00	00	00	00	00	00	00	....
0000000656	00	00	00	00	00	00	00	00	00	00	00	00	00	00	00	00	....
0000000672	00	00	00	00	00	00	00	00	00	00	00	00	00	00	00	00	....
0000000688	00	00	00	00	00	00	00	00	00	00	00	00	00	00	00	00	....
0000000704	00	00	00	00	00	00	00	00	00	00	00	00	00	00	00	00	....
0000000720	00	00	00	00	00	00	00	00	00	00	00	00	00	00	00	00	....
0000000736	00	00	00	00	00	00	00	00	00	00	00	00	00	00	00	00	....
0000000752	00	00	00	00	00	00	00	00	00	00	00	00	00	00	00	00	....
0000000768	00	00	00	00	00	00	00	00	00	00	00	00	00	00	00	00	....
0000000784	00	00	00	00	00	00	00	00	00	00	00	00	00	00	00	00	....
0000000800	00	00	00	00	00	00	00	00	00	00	00	00	00	00	00	00	....
0000000816	00	00	00	00	00	00	00	00	00	00	00	00	00	00	00	00	....
0000000832	00	00	00	00	00	00	00	00	00	00	00	00	00	00	00	00	....
0000000848	00	00	00	00	00	00	00	00	00	00	00	00	00	00	00	00	....
0000000864	00	00	00	00	00	00	00	00	00	00	00	00	00	00	00	00	....
0000000880	00	00	00	00	00	00	00	00	00	00	00	00	00	00	00	00	....
0000000896	00	00	00	00	00	00	00	00	00	00	00	00	00	00	00	00	....
0000000912	00	00	00	00	00	00	00	00	00	00	00	00	00	00	00	00	....
0000000928	00	00	00	00	00	00	00	00	00	00	00	00	00	00	00	00	....
0000000944	00	00	00	00	00	00	00	00	00	00	00	00	00	00	00	00	....
0000000960	00	00	00	00	00	00	00	00	00	00	00	00	00	00	00	00	....
0000000976	00	00	00	00	00	00	00	00	00	00	00	00	00	00	00	00	....
0000000992	00	00	00	00	72	72	41	61	DC	8A	07	00	D7	11	00	00	....rrAaÜŠ..×...
0000001008	00	00	00	00	00	00	00	00	00	00	00	00	00	00	55	AA	..............Uª

How many free clusters are there?

What is the next free cluster?

Graphically, the FAT32 structure is as below.

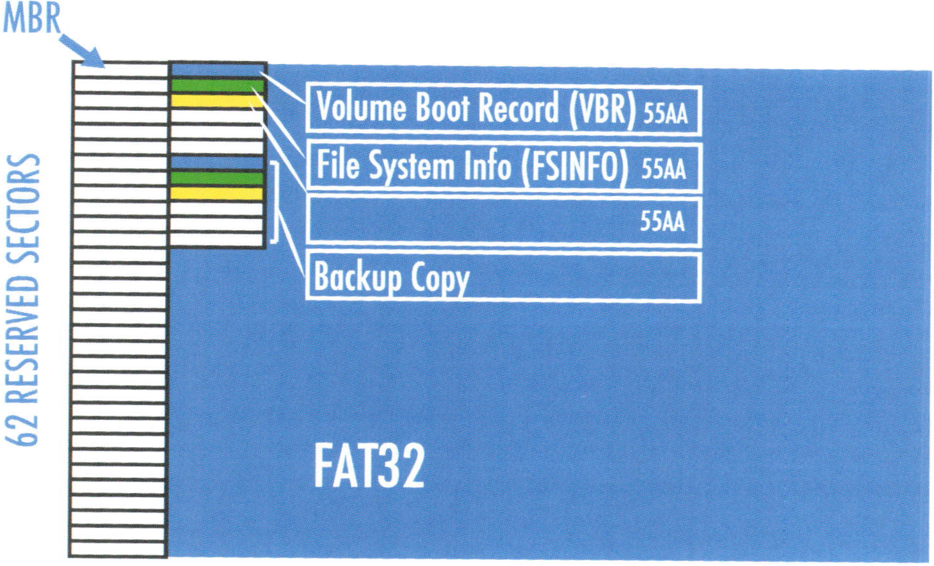

FTK Imager

It is time to use another tool as we dig deeper into the file system. HxD will still be useful but what is needed is a tool that can interpret file system information.

FTK Imager is a free tool from AccessData Corporation (***www.accessdata.com***), and besides being an excellent forensic imaging program, it also provides a hex viewer (not an editor) and a data interpreter.

The tool can be downloaded at:
www.accessdata.com/support/product-downloads
Do not confuse this tool with the full forensic utility name FTK, Forensic Toolkit.

Once downloaded and installed, you can double click on the icon to start.

One thing to be aware of in dealing with some versions of Microsoft Windows is that you need an administrative level of access in order to view the contents of a connected hard drive.

If you are going to be viewing a forensic image file then the elevated accessed is not necessary.

There are four panes within FTK Imager:

Pane 1 is the Evidence Tree

Pane 2 is the File List

Pane 3 is the Combination View

Pane 4 is the Viewer window

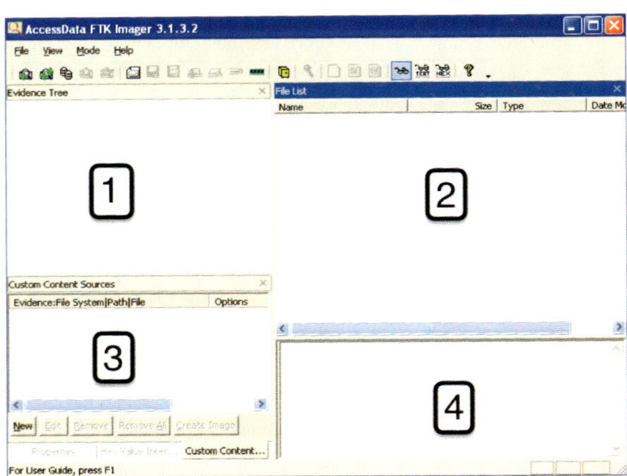

Add a forensic image by selecting File>Add Evidence Item.

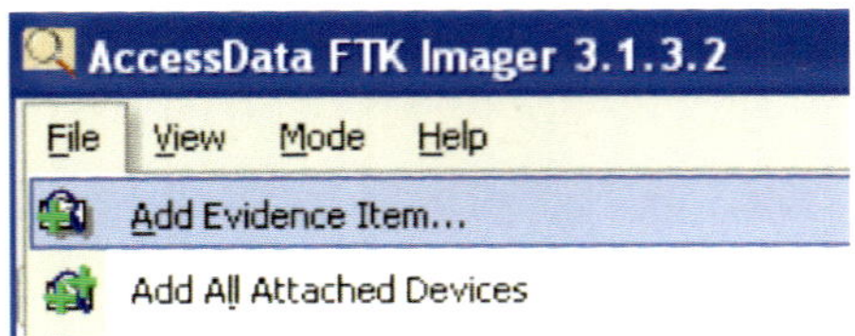

Then choose the type of evidence to add; in this study we will often be adding Image Files.

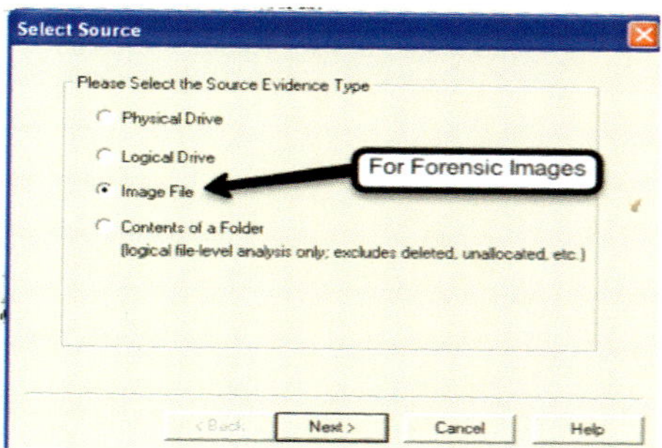

Browse to the path of the image file. FTK Imager supports various image formats including Raw, EnCase, and Smart file types. See the user manual for a complete list.

Once the image is added, the partitions will be displayed and can be expanded to show the contents.

Note that the image file added below is named FATVBR1.E01. This is an EnCase image format, which is the industry standard forensic format. In this case, there is one primary partition (Partition 1) and one extended partition with three logical volumes (Partition 5, 6 and 7). FTK Imager reserves 1-4 for primary partitions and 5 on up for logical volumes.

Click on the + next to each partition to open up the contents. Click on the Volume Label in the Evidence Tree Pane. You should note the VBR in the File List Pane. Highlight the VBR in the File List Pane and you will see the contents in the Viewer Pane.

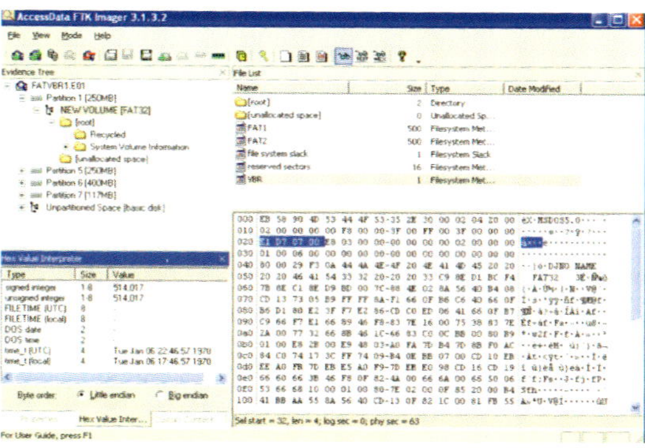

When highlighting offsets 32-35 in the Viewer Pane, the content will be interpreted in the Combination Pane if you choose the Hex Value Interpreter. Note that the number of sectors in the partition is 514,017. No more copying the bytes and reversing the order in a hex converter.

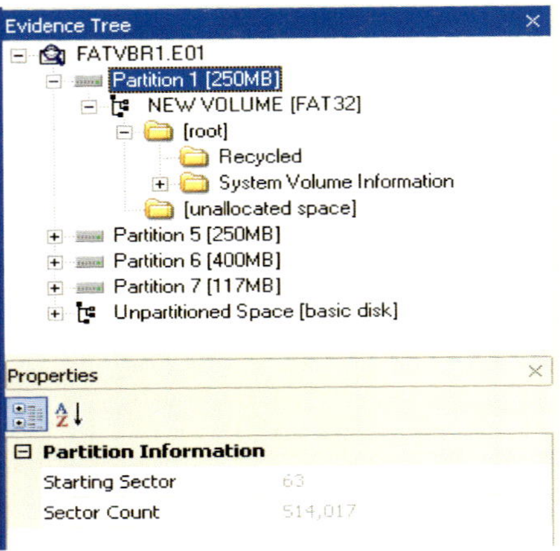

Click on Partition 1 in the Evidence Tree and then on Properties in the Combination Pane. The hex value interpreter value is confirmed in the properties tab in the Combination Pane. Also provided is the sector location of the VBR, which is also the first sector of the partition. Remember that in MBR, partitioning the first partition typically starts in either LBA sector 63 or 2048.

PRACTICAL EXERCISE 3

Add image file FATVBR.001 to FTK Imager and provide the following information on each of the three partitions.

	1	2	3
OEM			
Sector Size			
Sec/Cluster			
Total Sectors			
Sectors per FAT			
Location of Backup VBR (if applicable)			
Serial #			
File System			
VBR Signature			
# of Free Clusters (if applicable)			
Next Free Cluster (if applicable)			

Deleted Partitions

The value of understanding the VBR is that if one or more partitions are deleted or wiped out intentionally or accidently, it can be rebuilt from data contained in the Volume Boot Record. A virus or other malware can wipe out the entire Master Boot Record or GPT structure, including the backup copy. A subject may also selectively delete a partition.
Let's first look at recovery from a MBR system.

As a reminder, the information in the MBR partition table that is needed to recover the partition is:

Starting at offset 446 in sector 0 (16 bytes per entry)

Byte 1: Bootable or non-bootable (forensically not necessary to know)

Bytes 2-4: Starting CHS (not necessary to know)

Byte 5: Partition type (contain obtain from the File System Type in the VBR)

Bytes 6-8: Ending CHS (not necessary to know)

Bytes 9-12: Starting Sector (location of the VBR)

Bytes 13-16: Sectors in the partition (total sectors value found in the VBR)

MBR Signature: 0x55AA at offset 510

Using a tool like HxD or FTK Imager, a search can be run for information that can be found in the VBR. Terms as NO NAME, or FAT12, FAT16, or FAT32 would be good examples of what to search for. Finding the VBR will provide you with the starting sector of the partition and the additional information listed above.

One thing to aware of is that the backup copy of the VBR in FAT32 will provide a search hit, but is NOT the beginning of the partition. As stated above, the backup copy is located 6 sectors after the first copy. So running a search can provide hits for FAT32 at sector s1028064 and 1028070. The first hit would be the beginning of the partition and the second hit would be the backup.

Recovery from a GPT System

Since the overall structure is more complex, involving multiple sectors, it can be more time consuming for recovery if the entire partitioning scheme is wiped out.

Explore reviewing the structure of the GPT scheme.

Sector 0 has the Protective MBR.

The information needed in this sector: the partition type (EE), starting sector of 0x01, the number of sectors in the partition (0xFFFFFFFF), and signature of 0x55AA

Sector 1 has the GPT header. There are 92 bytes of data in the header, including the disk GUID and header and partition table CRCs. Most of the header information is standard, such as the signature, starting sector of the partition table, location of the header, size of the header, and size and number of partition entries. The unique information is the location of the backup header, which is in the last sector of the drive; and the last usable sector of partitions, which is located in the last sector minus 34 (the last 33 sectors are for the backup partition table and header). You do not need to fill in the Header CRC, the Disk GUID or the Partition Table CRC.

Sectors 2-32 contain the Partition Table. Each entry is 128 bytes in length. The first entry is for the Microsoft Reserved Partition; this entry will be the same on each drive, and with the exception of the unique partition GUID, this can be left blank.

For the next entries, the type GUID will be for a Basic data partition. The unique partition GUID does not need to be entered. The first sector of the partition can be found at the location of the VBR you found and the last sector can be determined by the number of sectors in the partition, found in the VBR. The next partition will start immediately following the previous partition.

Let's look at what happens when a GPT partition is deleted. For our example, Partition 1 will be the Microsoft Reserved, Partition 2 will the first user-created, and Partition 3 will be the second user-created.

Sector 2
Partition 1 Microsoft Reserved info (128 bytes)
Partition 2 User Partition 1 info (128 bytes)
Partition 3 User Partition 2 info (128 bytes)

If Partition 2 is deleted by the suspect, then in the partition table, the Partition 3 entry is shifted up 128 bytes and will overwrite Partition 2 info. The partition data itself still exists on the drive at its original location.

Sector 2
Partition 1 Microsoft Reserved info (128 bytes)
Partition 2 **User Partition 2 info (128 bytes)**

To recover the partition, copy the Partition 3 table info back to its original location and in the Partition 2 entry, zero out the unique partition GUID. Change the starting and ending sectors to match that of Partition 2. The starting sector will be the next sector after the end of Microsoft Reserve and the ending sector will be one sector before the beginning of Partition 3.

CHAPTER SUMMARY

File systems are structures for storing and naming files. They can also provide file security, compression, encryption and ownership. While there are a large number of file systems, there are certain ones that are supported by the operating system that is booted.

For example, Microsoft Windows 7 only supports a limited number of file systems, such as FAT12, FAT16, FAT32, exFAT, and NTFS.

FAT12, FAT16 and FAT32 file systems are named based upon the number of clusters that can be referenced (212, 216, 228).

Files are written and read in units named ***clusters.*** Clusters are made up of contiguous sector groups. The number of sectors per cluster varies based upon the size of the drive. Only one file can be stored in a cluster and a file may use more than one cluster.

Volume Boot Records (VBR) contain the information about partitions. The VBR is located in the very first sector of the partition. For FAT12 and FAT16 files systems the VBR is a single sector. The FAT32 VBR is six sectors in length and has a backup copy immediately following. The second sector in the VBR is referred to as the FSInfo Block.

The VBR contains the number of sectors in the partition, the file system type and a serial number for the partition, among other items of information.

Finding VBRs can help recover deleted partitions from either the MBR or GPT partitioning schemes.

AT HOME EXERCISE

1. Using Del_Part1.001 image, search for deleted volume boot records using HxD or FTK Imager.

How many deleted partitions did you find?

Rebuild the partition table in HxD and save.

	File System	Starting Sector	# of Sectors
Part 1			
Part 2			
Part 3			
Part 4			

View the Del_Part1.001 in FTK Imager. In each recovered partition, expand the [root] in the tree pane. There should be a JPG picture listed. Highlight the JPG file in the file list pane.

Provide the filename and a brief description of what the file depicts from the view pane.

2. Using Del_Part2.001 image, first view the image in FTK Image.

How many partitions are visible?

Search for the one deleted volume boot record.

What sector is it in?

How many sectors are in the partition?

Reconstruct the deleted partition table entry in HxD.

What is the partition type GUID?

What is the starting sector?

What is the ending sector?

What is the partition label?

Once you have reconstructed the partition table entry, view the image in FTK Imager.

What partition number is assigned to the recovered partition?

In the recovered partition, expand the [root] in the tree pane. There should be a JPG picture listed. Highlight the JPG file in the file list pane.

Provide the filename and a brief description of what the file depicts from the view pane.

ADVANCED HOMEWORK

1. Take what you have learned about the MBR partition structure and Volume Boot Records and recover the logical volumes in the Extended Partition of the image file Del_Part3.001.

How many logical volumes did you find and what sectors were they found in?

For each logical volume, list the File System, number of sectors in the volume, and the serial number.

List the sectors that should contain Logical Volume Partition tables.

Rebuild each of the Logical Volume Partition tables.

View the image in FTK Imager.

What Partition numbers are given for each recovered partition?

In each recovered partition, expand the [root] in the tree pane. There should be a JPG picture listed. Highlight the JPG file in the file list pane.

Provide the filename and a brief description of what the file depicts from the view pane.

2. Smart malware wiped out the first 34 sectors and the last 33 sectors of the GPT partitioned drive in image Del_Part4.001.

Provide the partition type code, the starting sector and number of sectors for the Protective MBR.

How many sectors are in the drive?

What sector will the backup copy of the GPT header reside?

Recover any deleted partitions.

How many partitions did you find?

List the starting and ending sectors of each partition.

View the image in FTK Imager. What are the partition numbers for each recovered partition?

In each recovered user partition, expand the [root] in the tree pane. There should be a JPG picture listed. Highlight the JPG file in the file list pane.

Provide the filename and a brief description of what the file depicts from the view pane.

REFERENCES

1. (2010). Digital Forensic Examiner's Training Manual. New Berlin: Digital Intelligence, LLC.

2. Understanding File System. (2013). Retrieved from http://www.ufsexplorer.com/und_fs.php

3. Linux Programmer's Manual. (n.d.). Retrieved from http://man7.org/linux/man-pages/man5/filesystems.5.html

4. Apple Support Communities. (2013, August 19). Retrieved from https://discussions.apple.com/thread/5076451

5. Kirps, J. (2008, March 19). A Short History of the Windows FAT File System. Retrieved from http://www.kirps.com/cgi-bin/web.pl?blog_record=84

6. FAT Sizes: FAT12, FAT16 and FAT32. (n.d.). Retrieved from http://www.pcguide.com/ref/hdd/file/partSizes-c.html

7. (n.d.). Retrieved from http://www.win.tue.nl/~aeb/linux/fs/fat/fat-1.html

06 FILE SYSTEMS: FAT PART II

In the previous chapter, we began looking at the FAT File System from the Volume Boot Record. We are now going to take a step backwards and look into how the VBR information gets placed on the drive and the logical volume setup. This is done through a process known as ***formatting***.

There are two different types of formatting, low and high. Low-level formatting is typically done by the manufacturer of the drive and sets up the tracks and sectors structure. In contrasting, high-level formatting is what occurs when we click on or type the Format command. A high-level format will write out the Volume Boot Record information based upon the version of the operating system that is booted; for example, Windows 7 versus DOS 3.3. Each operating system will write out the VBR and provide its own unique information. We saw that the OEM ID was written in the VBR and that from Windows XP forward would write the OEM ID as MSDOS 5.0; other versions of Windows or DOS would write out different OEM ID values.

What also occurs when a high-level format is initiated is that an area known as the ***System Area*** is set up. This area includes the Volume Boot Record, the File Allocation Table and, in some circumstances, the Root Directory.

In FAT12 and FAT16 the Root Directory is part of the system area. The ***Data Area*** is where the content of files and folders get written. Think back to our discussion of the VBR for FAT12 and FAT16, there was a limited number of entries for the Root Directory.

16	10	Number of FAT copies (2)
17-18	11-12	Number of root directory entries (224) 512 is recommended for FAT16.
19-20	13-14	Total number of sectors in the filesystem

Formatting
Process of setting the System Area and Data Area of a partition by writing a Volume Boot Record and zeroing out the File Allocation Table and all or part of the Root Directory.

System Area
Area of the partition containing file system information.

Data Area
Area of the partition where the content of files and folders is written.

This limitation is there because the Root Directory is in the System Area and that is a fixed size. In FAT32 the Root Directory is part of the Data Area so the only limitation to the directory size is the size of the disk. The directory could continue to expand until the drive is full.

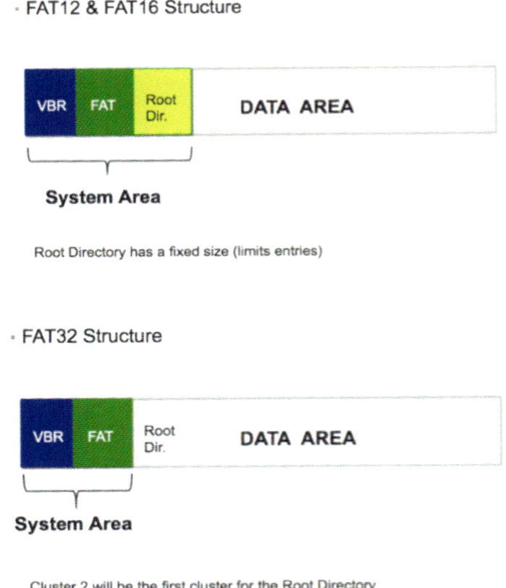

During the high-level format the VBR is rewritten, the FAT is zeroed out (we will discuss this in detail during the next chapter) and the Root Directory for FAT12/16 is completely zeroed and for FAT32 the first sector is zeroed. This is all that is written during the high-level format. Note that other than the first sector of the Root Directory in FAT32, the Data Area is not touched. This means if we have files saved and the drive is formatted, then the file names are lost but the data is still safe. Below is a FAT16 system:

VBR: Note the OEM ID and Serial Number

```
 Offset(d)   00 01 02 03 04 05 06 07 08 09 10 11 12 13 14 15
0000000000   EB 3C 90 4D 53 44 4F 53 33 2E 33 00 02 40 08 00   ë<.MSDOS3.3..@..     Sector 0
0000000016   02 00 02 00 00 F8 BC 00 3F 00 FF 00 80 00 00 00   .....ø¼.?.ÿ.€...
0000000032   00 E0 2E 00 80 00 29 CA 29 6E B2 4E 4F 20 4E 41   .à..€.)Ê)n²NO NA
0000000048   4D 45 20 20 20 20 46 41 54 31 36 20 20 20 33 C9   ME    FAT16   3É
```

FAT: (Note that there are hex values in this; we will cover this in the next chapter.)

```
 Offset(d)   00 01 02 03 04 05 06 07 08 09 10 11 12 13 14 15
0000004096   F8 FF FF FF FF FF 00 00 00 00 00 00 00 00 00 00   øÿÿÿÿÿ..........     Sector 8
0000004112   00 00 00 00 00 00 00 00 00 00 00 00 00 00 00 00   ................
0000004128   00 00 00 00 00 00 00 00 00 00 00 00 00 00 00 00   ................
0000004144   00 00 00 00 00 00 00 00 00 00 00 00 00 00 00 00   ................
0000004160   00 00 00 00 00 00 00 00 00 00 00 00 00 00 00 00
```

Root Directory

Lastly, we will look at the contents of the Data Area, which is where the content of Seuss.txt will be.

Data Area: Note the sector location

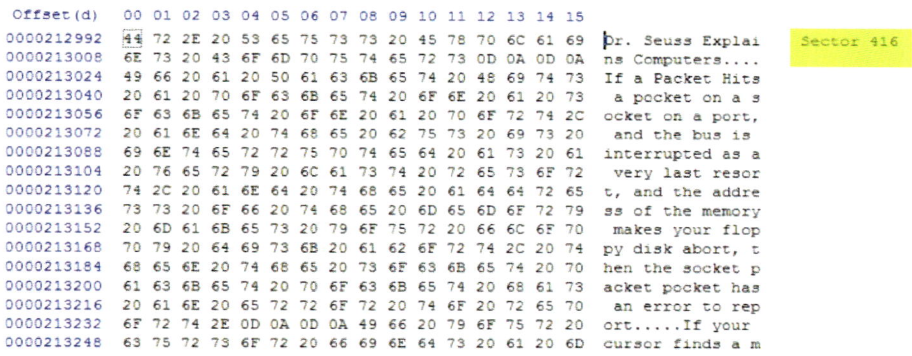

We will now reformat the volume and review the results. The formatting can be done on the Disk Management utility.

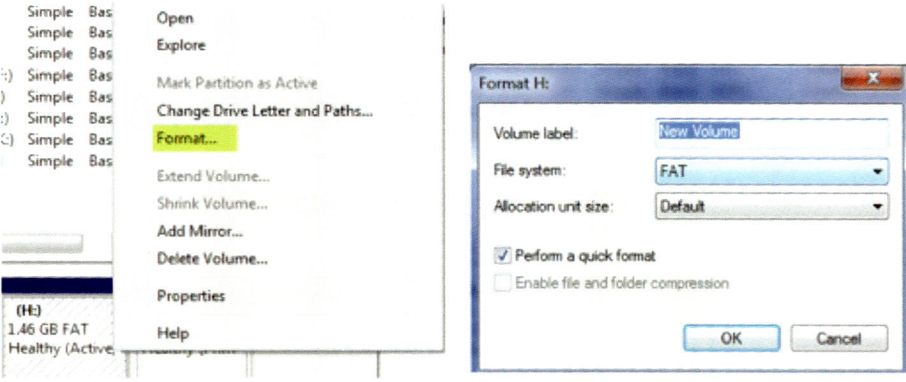

It can also through the Windows Explorer.

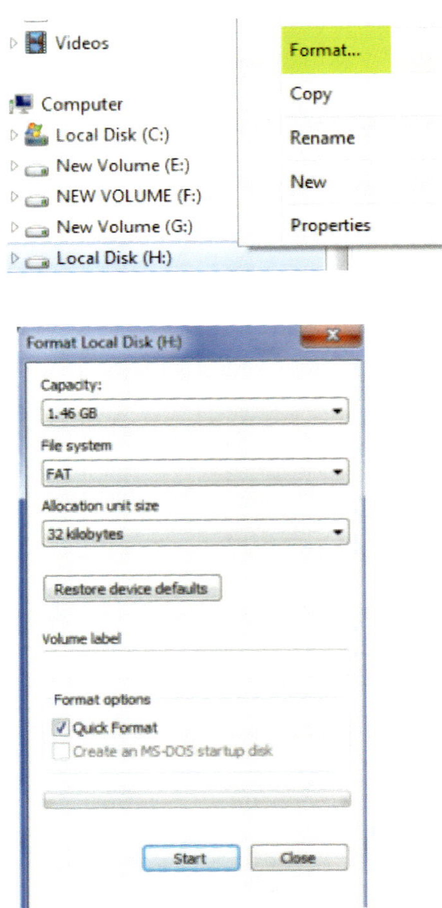

VBR: Note the change to the OEM ID and Serial Number

```
Offset(d)   00 01 02 03 04 05 06 07 08 09 10 11 12 13 14 15
0000000000  EB 3C 90 4D 53 44 4F 53 35 2E 30 00 02 40 08 00  ë<.MSDOS5.0..@..    Sector 0
0000000016  02 00 02 00 00 F8 BC 00 3F 00 FF 00 80 00 00 00  .....ø¼.?.ÿ.€...
0000000032  00 E0 2E 00 80 00 29 E2 E9 68 D0 4E 4F 20 4E 41  .à..€.)âéhÐNO NA
0000000048  4D 45 20 20 20 20 46 41 54 31 36 20 20 20 33 C9  ME    FAT16   3É
```

FAT: Note that the first 4 bytes contain the same data as before. This is effectively a signature for the File Allocation Table and will always be set to F8 FF FF FF during formatting for the FAT16.

```
Offset(d)   00 01 02 03 04 05 06 07 08 09 10 11 12 13 14 15
0000004096  F8 FF FF FF 00 00 00 00 00 00 00 00 00 00 00 00  øÿÿÿ............    Sector 8
0000004112  00 00 00 00 00 00 00 00 00 00 00 00 00 00 00 00  ................
```

Root Directory: empty

Evidence Tree	File List			
H:	Name	Size	Type	Date Modified

Data Area: Note that the data is still present.

```
Offset(d)    00 01 02 03 04 05 06 07 08 09 10 11 12 13 14 15
0000212992   44 72 2E 20 53 65 75 73 73 20 45 78 70 6C 61 69  Dr. Seuss Explai    Sector 416
0000213008   6E 73 20 43 6F 6D 70 75 74 65 72 73 0D 0A 0D 0A  ns Computers....
0000213024   49 66 20 61 20 50 61 63 6B 65 74 20 48 69 74 73  If a Packet Hits
0000213040   20 61 20 70 6F 63 6B 65 74 20 6F 6E 20 61 20 73   a pocket on a s
0000213056   6F 63 6B 65 74 20 6F 6E 20 61 20 70 6F 72 74 2C  ocket on a port,
0000213072   20 61 6E 64 20 74 68 65 20 62 75 73 20 69 73 20   and the bus is
0000213088   69 6E 74 65 72 72 75 70 74 65 64 20 61 73 20 61  interrupted as a
0000213104   20 76 65 72 79 20 6C 61 73 74 20 72 65 73 6F 72   very last resor
0000213120   74 2C 20 61 6E 64 20 74 68 65 20 61 64 64 72 65  t, and the addre
0000213136   73 73 20 6F 66 20 74 68 65 20 6D 65 6D 6F 72 79  ss of the memory
0000213152   20 6D 61 6B 65 73 20 79 6F 75 72 20 66 6C 6F 70   makes your flop
```

Be aware that under some conditions, formatting can overwrite the data. For example, if the quick format under Windows 7 is not checked (checked by default), then the data area will be overwritten[1]; however, under XP, the data area will not be overwritten even if the quick format is not checked[2].

For review, we have extensively looked at the VBR (backup only present on FAT32). We will explore the FAT in the next chapter, so we will skip over that and look at the Root Directory structure and file naming conventions.

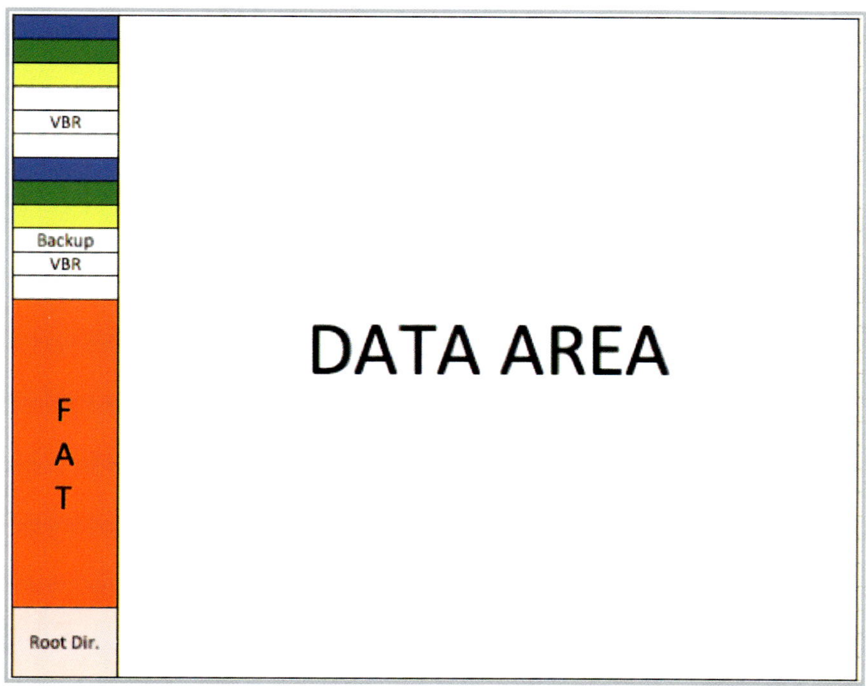

Root Directory
Primary folder for filenames and metadata about the files.

During the format process, there is the option to add a volume label. Originally the label was to put in the VBR, but as we have seen in the last chapter, the volume label in the VBR is NO NAME. When the user creates a label it is placed in the Root Directory and can be up to 11 characters in length.

Root Directory

This is the top-level directory on a system, often referred to simply as Root. A FAT directory will hold the following 32 bytes of information:

FAT DIRECTORY STRUCTURE			
DEC OFFSET	HEX OFFSET	SIZE (BYTES)	DESCRIPTION
0	00	8	File name (1-8 bytes)
8	08	3	Extension (0-3 bytes)
11	0B	1	Attribute - a bitvector. Bit 0: read only. Bit 1: hidden.
			Bit 2: system file. Bit 3: volume label. Bit 4: subdirectory.
			Bit 5: archive. Bits 6-7: unused.
12	0C	1	Case – >0 if needs to be converted to upper case
13	0D	1	Created Time 1/10 of a Second - FAT32
			Reserved - FAT12/16
14	0E	2	Created Time - FAT32
			Reserved - FAT12/16
16	10	2	Created Date - FAT32
			Reserved - FAT12/16
18	12	2	Last Accessed Date - FAT32
			Reserved - FAT12/16
20	14	2	High Bytes for Cluster location - FAT32
			Reserved - FAT12/16
22	16	2	Modified Time (5/6/5 bits, for hour/minutes/halfseconds)
24	18	2	Modified Date (7/4/5 bits, for year-since-1980/month/day)
26	1A	2	Starting cluster (0 for an empty file)
			Low Bytes for Cluster location - FAT32
28	1C	4	Filesize in bytes

Below is the Root Directory, as shown by FTK Imager displaying the hex contents and the interpreted data.

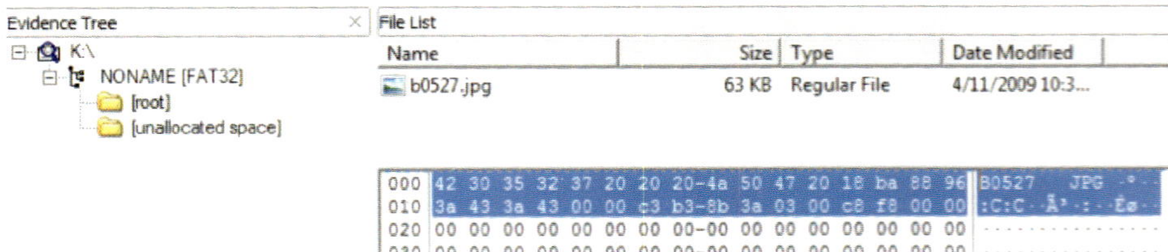

Offsets 0-7 are the filename: BO527 (0x42 30 35 32 37); notice the 3 bytes of 0x20 20 20, these are spaces making up the remainder of the 8 bytes.

Offsets 8-10 are the extension: JPG; this is not required and will be filled with spaces is not present.

For both the name and the extension, there are limitations as to the characters that are allowed. Some of these disallowed are (/ \ . ? * ^ < > + :).

These characters are not allowed because they are used in command line arguments.

Offset 11 is the attributes: 0x20. This is a bitwise value meaning that the bits making up the value have different meanings. Below is the table of attribute bits[3].

0000 0001	Read-Only File
0000 0010	Hidden File
0000 0100	System File
0000 1000	Volume Label
0000 1111	Long Filename
0001 0000	Directory
0010 0000	Archive

From the example above, the file has the attribute of Archive. This attribute was originally used for backup purpose[4]. When a file was backed up, this attribute was turned off. If the file then was modified, the archive bit would be flipped back on and this would indicate to the backup software that it needed to be backed up again.

Some of these attributes can be combined. For example, a file could have the attributes of Read-Only, Hidden, System, and Archive. This would result in a byte of 00100111 or 0x27.

Operating system files have been set to Hidden, System and Read-Only so that users did not modify or delete these needed files by accident. Years ago, there were cases of suspects setting the Hidden attribute to keep their child pornography a secret, but this was not a very effective method of securing files.

Offset 12 is for upper case: 0x18 indicates that the file name needs to be converted to uppercase[5]. Note that in the display listing the name is b0527, and the hex/ASCII view is B0527. This is due to the fact that in FAT the names are to be in all upper case. If the original name was written in all uppercase then offset 12 would be 0x00 and if it is in all lower case then the value would be greater than 0. In the situation where there is mixed case in the name, the value will be 0 but there will be additional data added that will be discussed later in this chapter.

Offset 13 is for the Created Time tenths of a second: 0xBA or 186, which is not used in FAT12/16.

Offset 14-15 is the Created Time: 0x88 96 (0x96 88 in little endian); the method of calculation is done at the bit level. This is not used in FAT 12/16.

In this case, 10010110 10001000 for 0x9688

10010 hours 110100 for minutes and 01000 for seconds

18 hours 52 minutes and 16 (8x2) seconds

Using the FTK Imager Hex Interpreter, if the two bytes are highlighted then the DOS time is converted. There are other date decoders where you can type in the values and have them converted. One such free tool is DCode (Date Decoder) from ***www.digital-detective.co.uk***.

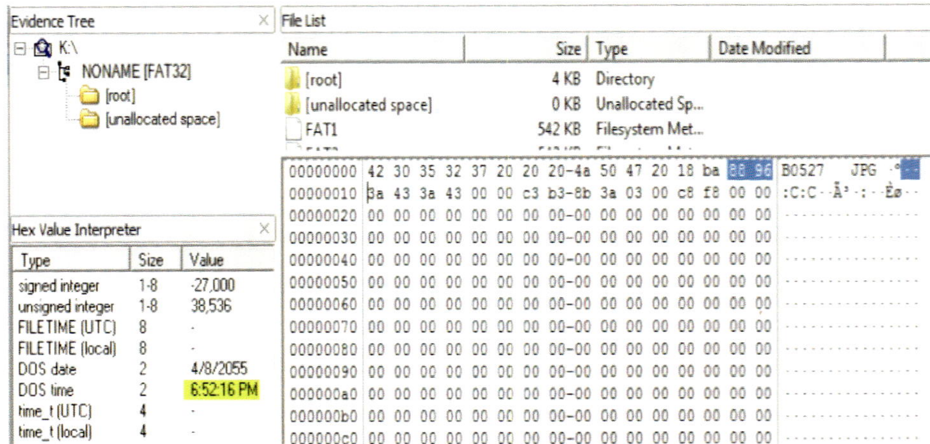

Offsets 16-17 are for the Created Date: 0x3A 43 (0x433A in little endian). This is the date the file was first added to the volume, not necessarily when it was first created. The date is also a bitwise calculated value. This not used in FAT12/16.

15 14 13 12 11 10 9	8 7 6 5	4 3 2 1 0
(0 – 127 Years+1980)	(1-12 Months)	(1-31 Days)

In this case, 01000011 00111010 for 0x433A

0100001 for the year, 1001 for the month, and 11010 for the day

2013 (33+1980), 9th month, 26th day

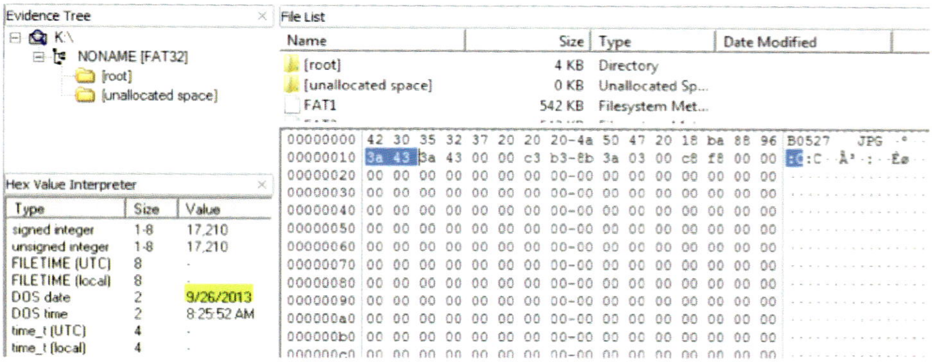

Evidence Tree

K:\
NONAME [FAT32]
[root]
[unallocated space]

File List

Name	Size	Type	Date Modified
[root]	4 KB	Directory	
[unallocated space]	0 KB	Unallocated Sp...	
FAT1	542 KB	Filesystem Met...	

```
00000000 42 30 35 32 37 20 20 20-4a 50 47 20 18 ba 88 96 B0527   JPG  
00000010 3a 43 3a 43 00 00 c3 b3-8b 3a 03 00 c8 f8 00 00 :C:C  Å³ :  Èø
00000020 00 00 00 00 00 00 00 00-00 00 00 00 00 00 00 00
00000030 00 00 00 00 00 00 00 00-00 00 00 00 00 00 00 00
00000040 00 00 00 00 00 00 00 00-00 00 00 00 00 00 00 00
00000050 00 00 00 00 00 00 00 00-00 00 00 00 00 00 00 00
00000060 00 00 00 00 00 00 00 00-00 00 00 00 00 00 00 00
00000070 00 00 00 00 00 00 00 00-00 00 00 00 00 00 00 00
00000080 00 00 00 00 00 00 00 00-00 00 00 00 00 00 00 00
00000090 00 00 00 00 00 00 00 00-00 00 00 00 00 00 00 00
000000a0 00 00 00 00 00 00 00 00-00 00 00 00 00 00 00 00
000000b0 00 00 00 00 00 00 00 00-00 00 00 00 00 00 00 00
000000c0 00 00 00 00 00 00 00 00-00 00 00 00 00 00 00 00
```

Hex Value Interpreter

Type	Size	Value
signed integer	1-8	17,210
unsigned integer	1-8	17,210
FILETIME (UTC)	8	-
FILETIME (local)	8	-
DOS date	2	9/26/2013
DOS time	2	8:25:52 AM
time_t (UTC)	4	-
time_t (local)	4	-

Offsets 18-19 are for the Last Accessed Date: 0x3A43 (0x433A in Little Endian). The last accessed time is when the file was last touched by some process, either user initiated or system initiated. In this case, the file was not accessed after it was created so it has the same date. There is no Last Accessed Time recorded in the FAT directory structure.

Offsets 20-21 are the two high-byte values for the starting cluster location: 0x00 00 (or 0x00 00 in Little Endian :). In FAT32 there are 4 bytes used for the starting cluster location. These are at offsets 20-21 and 26-27. Offsets 26-27 are the two lower byte values. The byte order would be read as offset 21 20 27 26. This would be the beginning cluster for the file.

Offsets 22-23 are the Last Modified Time for the file: 0xC3B3 (0xB3C3 in Little Endian). This is the time the file was last saved, not necessarily modified. It is calculated in the same bitwise manner as the Created Time.

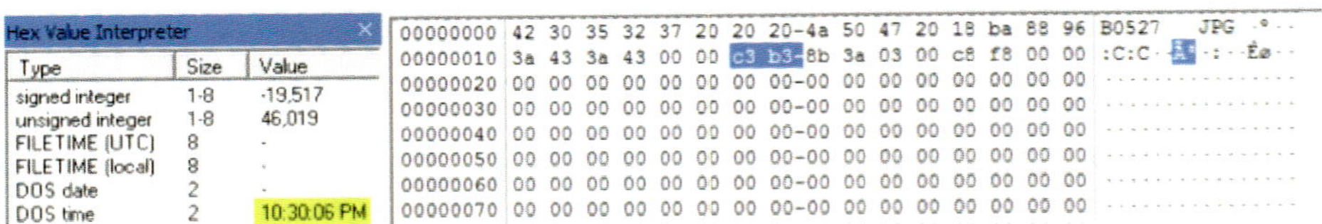

Offsets 24-25 are the Last Modified Date for the file: 0x8B3A (0x3A8B in Little Endian). It is calculated in the same bitwise manner as the Created Time. Note that the file was saved before the creation date; this indicated that the file was copied from another location to this volume as the Last Modified date travels with a file during a normal Windows copy procedure.

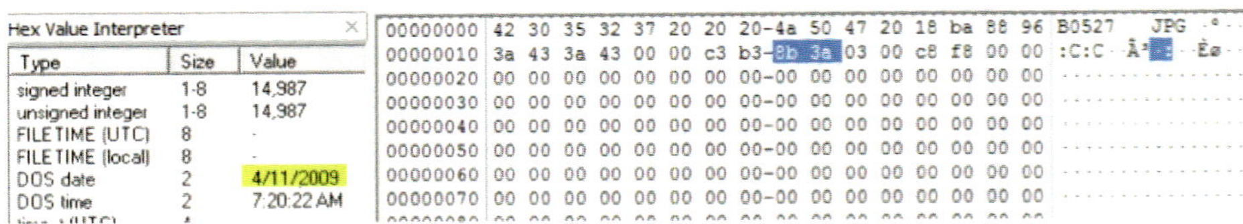

Offsets 26-27 are the lower bytes to the starting cluster location as mentioned above: 0x03 00 (0x0003 in Little Endian). Combined with bytes 20 and 21 gives 0x00 00 00 03 or Cluster 3. Because the offsets are split, they cannot all be highlighted and interpreted by FTK Imager's Hex Interpreter.

Offset 28-31 is the file size: 0x C8 F8 00 00 (0x00 00 F8 C8 in little endian). This is the number of bytes in the file. When interpreting the file size, it can never be a negative value so we always use the unsigned number. Also note that there is a file size limitation because there are only 4 bytes (32-bit value) to accommodate the number of bytes. The largest hex value for 4 bytes would be 0x FF FF FF FF, which works out to be 4 gigabytes. So if you have a large video file that you want to copy to a flash drive (not a pirated copy, of course, that would never happen!), it would have to be split up in to 4 gigabyte pieces in order to be placed on a FAT formatted flash drive.

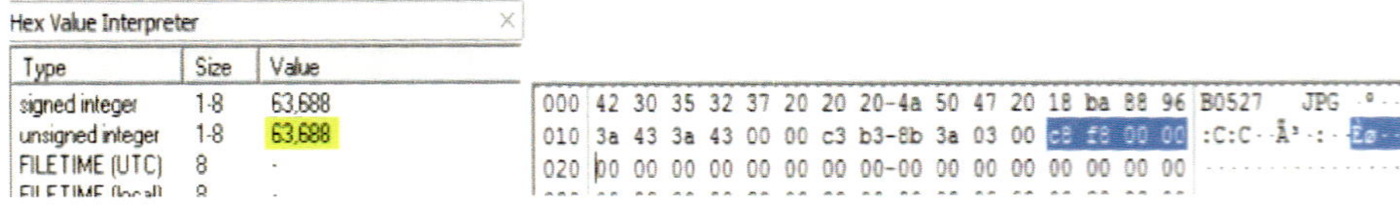

PRACTICAL EXERCISE 1

Interpret the following 32-byte FAT32 directory entries, **showing your work** for date and time calculations.

Entry 1 (32 bytes)
48 41 52 56 45 59 20 20 48 54 4D 03 18 B8 CE A5
3A 43 3A 43 00 00 41 AC CD 40 1A 00 66 0E 00 00

What is the file name?

What is the extension?

List the attributes this file has:

Was the name originally in all upper or lower case?

How many tenths of a second are there in the Creation Time?

What is the Creation Time?

What is the Creation Date?

What is the Last Accessed Date?

What is the Last Modified Time?

What is the Last Modified Date?

What is the starting Cluster? (show the proper byte order for calculation)

How many bytes are there in the file? (provide the hex and decimal values):

Entry 2 (32 bytes)

4E 54 55 53 45 52 20 20 44 41 54 20 00 5A 10 A6
32 43 34 43 00 00 73 65 70 40 92 32 00 00 08 00

What is the file name?

What is the extension?

List the attributes this file has?

Was the name originally in all upper or lower case?

How many tenths of a second are there in the Creation Time?

What is the Creation Time?

What is the Creation Date?

What is the Last Accessed Date?

What is the Last Modified Time?

What is the Last Modified Date?

What is the starting Cluster? (show the proper byte order for calculation)

How many bytes are there in the file? (provide the hex and decimal values)

Determining the sector location of the Root Directory

Finding the Root Directory can be done by obtaining information from the VBR.

```
000 eb 58 90 4d 53 44 4f 53-35 2e 30 00 02 08 8a 17 ëX·MSDOS5.0·····
010 02 00 00 00 00 f8 00 00-3f 00 ff 00 80 e0 2e 00 ·····ø··?·ÿ··à.·
020 00 08 11 00 3b 04 00 00-00 00 00 00 02 00 00 00 ····;···········
030 01 00 06 00 00 00 00 00-00 00 00 00 00 00 00 00 ················
040 80 00 29 0f dc 4c a4 4e-4f 20 4e 41 4d 45 20 20 ··)·ÜL¤NO NAME
050 20 20 46 41 54 33 32 20-20 20 33 c9 8e d1 bc f4   FAT32   3É·Ñ¼ô
```

Offsets 14-15 in the VBR are the number of reserved sectors, this includes the VBR and large number unused sectors. In this case it is (0x8A17 or 6026 sectors).

Offset 16 is the number of copies of the File Allocation Table, which follows the reserved sectors, this should always be 2.

Offsets 36-39 are the number of sectors in the File Allocation Table (Offset 22-23 for FAT12/16). This is 0x3B040000 or 1083 sectors.

The location of the Root Directory will be at
6026 + (1083 x 2) = 8192.

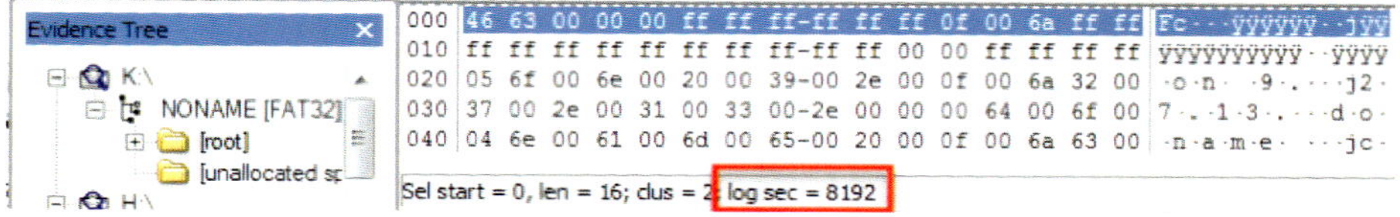

Subdirectories

Subdirectories or subfolders can be created and have the same structure as the Root Directory. They hold 32-byte entries for the files and subdirectories. One unique factor to subdirectories is that they all have the same first two entries.

Entry 1 is referred to as Dot "." and entry 2 is referred to as Dot Dot ".." in the structure. The Dot entry is a pointer to the current location and the Dot Dot entry is a pointer to the parent directory. This is a remnant of the Unix origins.

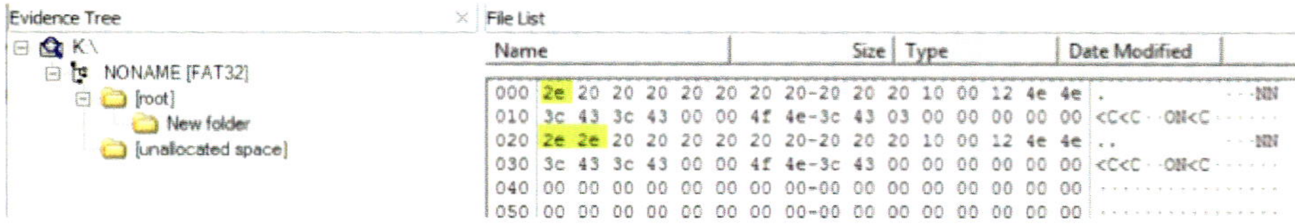

Note that for each entry there are dates of creation and that the size is 0.

The subdirectory itself has an entry in the Root Directory and has the Created, Modified and Accessed dates. The attribute is set to Directory but could also be Hidden and Read-Only. The file size of a directory is always 0 even if there are files listed in it.

Long File Names

As was just shown, the file name length in a FAT directory is limited to up to eight characters and three characters for the extension. This limitation greatly hindered the user in trying to be descriptive in their naming conventions. It can be difficult to be creative in coming up with names for the files that describe its contents in eight characters, especially when you may have several documents that are similar.

With the introduction of Windows 1995, the ability to have files with up to 255 characters was introduced[6]. This ability had to conform and fit into the FAT directory structure. A compatibility with older systems such as DOS had been included with this new process as well. Through Windows 8 the ability to add 255 character file names is still in effect.

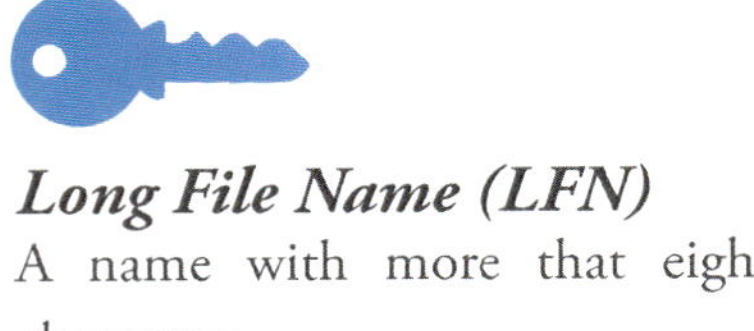

Long File Name (LFN)
A name with more that eight characters.

Let's explore the process of including ***Long File Names (LFN)*** to a FAT directory structure. Below is the 32-byte structure for the LFN. The names are stored in Unicode, which means that there will be 2 bytes for each character.

Long File Names			
0	00	1	Sequence Number
1	01	10	Unicode characters 1-5
11	0B	1	Attribute: 0x0F
12	0C	1	Type: 0
13	0D	1	Checksum of short name
14	0E	12	Unicode characters 6-11
26	1A	2	Starting cluster: 0
28	1C	4	Unicode characters 12-13

Note that at offset 1 there are five characters, at offset 14 there are six characters, and at offset 28 there are two characters, making a total of 13 characters. This is a far cry from 255, so multiple 32-byte entries are used. There are also characters that are valid for LFN that were not valid for an 8.3 ***Short File Name (SFN)***; such as, <space> or a period.

Short File Name (SFN)
An 8.3-compatible name generated from the LFN.

It should also be noted that nowhere in this structure are the dates associated with the file or the size or starting cluster. This structure is also not compatible with older systems such as DOS. To include this information and be compatible, an SFN name is created for the LFN. The first six valid SFN characters are taken, and a tilde (~) and a number are added. The three characters after the right most period are used for the extension and all the characters are converted to uppercase. For example:

LFN
Really Long File Name.txt

SFN
REALLY~1.TXT

If we add a second LFN:

LFN
Really Really Long File Name.txt

SFN
REALLY~2.TXT

If the number of identical SFN exceeds four then the naming scheme is slightly different. Starting with the fifth file, the first two characters of the name are used followed by four characters generated from a hash of the LFN and then a tilde (~)5[7]. So if we had four REALLY files, the fifth file would be RE4AD3~5.TXT with the 4AD3 a being hash-generated characters.

Another example of a LFN would be:

LFN
This is an example of a very long file name created on 9.27.13.doc

SFN
THISIS~1.DOC

Note that the <space> between "This" and "is" is ignored and the right most period is before "doc"

The SFN will be created for any file with more than eight characters or if there is a mixed case name. For example: TeSt.Txt would require a LFN and a SFN. The SFN entry will include the dates, the size and the starting cluster.

The LFN and SFN are kept in sync by way of a checksum value that is calculated based on the characters in the SFN. This single-byte checksum value is included in each 32-byte LFN entry.

What can be challenging in reviewing inside of a hex viewer is that the directory displays text upwardly instead of writing the entries in a downward fashion.

Long File Name Entry X
..
..
..
Long File Name Entry 2
Long File Name Entry 1
Short File Name Entry

From our example above: This is an example of a very long file name created on 9.27.13.doc

c
on 9.27.13.do
name created
ry long file
ample of a ve
This is an ex
THISIS~1.DOC

It takes some experience to learn to read LFN entries as the hex viewers typically displays only 16 bytes per row so each entry is two rows in length. As shown in the structure table above, there are also additional bytes of information that are included in the entries that split up the characters in the name. This includes the sequence number, checksum, attribute, and starting cluster.

Below is the hex view of the directory structure with a long file name that we will walk through.

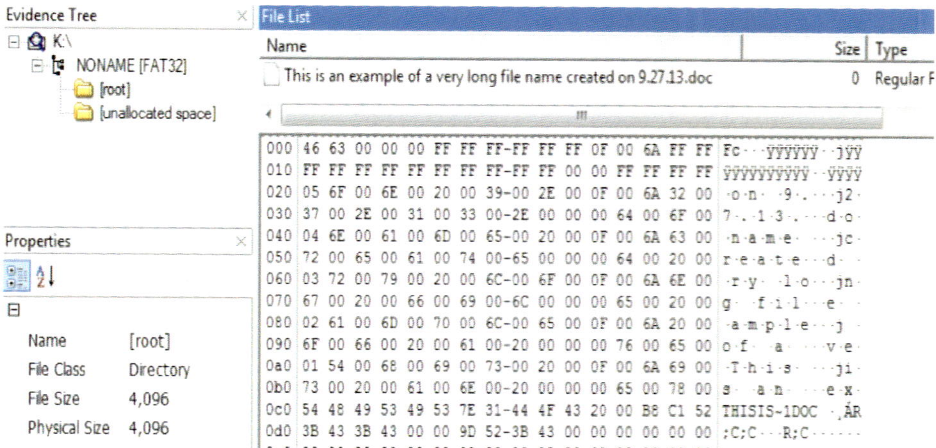

First, note the SFN that is created. It can be parsed just as we did earlier in this chapter with regards to the dates and times, starting cluster number and file size.

```
000 46 63 00 00 00 FF FF FF-FF FF FF 0F 00 6A FF FF  Fc···ÿÿÿÿÿÿ··jÿÿ
010 FF FF FF FF FF FF FF FF-FF FF 00 00 FF FF FF FF  ÿÿÿÿÿÿÿÿÿÿ··ÿÿÿÿ
020 05 6F 00 6E 00 20 00 39-00 2E 00 0F 00 6A 32 00  ·o·n· ·9·.···j2·
030 37 00 2E 00 31 00 33 00-2E 00 00 00 64 00 6F 00  7·.·1·3·.···d·o·
040 04 6E 00 61 00 6D 00 65-00 20 00 0F 00 6A 63 00  ·n·a·m·e· ···jc·
050 72 00 65 00 61 00 74 00-65 00 00 00 64 00 20 00  r·e·a·t·e···d· ·
060 03 72 00 79 00 20 00 6C-00 6F 00 0F 00 6A 6E 00  ·r·y· ·l·o···jn·
070 67 00 20 00 66 00 69 00-6C 00 00 00 65 00 20 00  g· ·f·i·l···e· ·
080 02 61 00 6D 00 70 00 6C-00 65 00 0F 00 6A 20 00  ·a·m·p·l·e···j ·
090 6F 00 66 00 20 00 61 00-20 00 00 00 76 00 65 00  o·f· ·a· ···v·e·
0a0 01 54 00 68 00 69 00 73-00 20 00 0F 00 6A 69 00  ·T·h·i·s· ···ji·
0b0 73 00 20 00 61 00 6E 00-20 00 00 00 65 00 78 00  s· ·a·n· ···e·x·
0c0 54 48 49 53 49 53 7E 31-44 4F 43 20 00 B8 C1 52  THISIS~1DOC ·¸ÁR
0d0 3B 43 3B 43 00 00 9D 52-3B 43 00 00 00 00 00 00  ;C;C···R;C······
```

The LFN is then added going up. The next entry going up will contain the beginning 12 characters of the name including spaces.

```
000 46 63 00 00 00 FF FF FF-FF FF FF 0F 00 6A FF FF Fc···ÿÿÿÿÿÿ··jÿÿ
010 FF FF FF FF FF FF FF FF-FF FF 00 00 FF FF FF FF ÿÿÿÿÿÿÿÿÿÿ··ÿÿÿÿ
020 05 6F 00 6E 00 20 00 39-00 2E 00 0F 00 6A 32 00 ·o·n· ·9·.···j2·
030 37 00 2E 00 31 00 33 00-2E 00 00 00 64 00 6F 00 7·.·1·3·.···d·o·
040 04 6E 00 61 00 6D 00 65-00 20 00 0F 00 6A 63 00 ·n·a·m·e· ···jc·
050 72 00 65 00 61 00 74 00-65 00 00 00 64 00 20 00 r·e·a·t·e···d· ·
060 03 72 00 79 00 20 00 6C-00 6F 00 0F 00 6A 6E 00 ·r·y· ·l·o···jn·
070 67 00 20 00 66 00 69 00-6C 00 00 00 65 00 20 00 g· ·f·i·l···e· ·
080 02 61 00 6D 00 70 00 6C-00 65 00 0F 00 6A 20 00 ·a·m·p·l·e···j ·
090 6F 00 66 00 20 00 61 00-20 00 00 00 76 00 65 00 o·f· ·a· ···v·e·
0a0 01 54 00 68 00 69 00 73-00 20 00 0F 00 6A 69 00 ·T·h·i·s· ···ji·
0b0 73 00 20 00 61 00 6E 00-20 00 00 00 65 00 78 00 s· ·a·n· ···e·x·
0c0 54 48 49 53 49 53 7E 31-44 4F 43 20 00 B8 C1 52 THISIS~1DOC ·¸ÁR
0d0 3B 43 3B 43 00 00 9D 52-3B 43 00 00 00 00 00 00 ;C;C··R;C······
```

Offset 0 – Sequence number: 0x01. This is a number assigned to each entry of the LFN. The sequence number will count up for each entry until the last entry for the name. This last entry will be 0x4X, X being the next entry number. If there are more than 15 entries the last sequence number will begin with 0x5X, more than 30 it will be 0x6X and so forth.

Offsets 1-10 – First five Unicode characters: 0x54 00 68 00 69 00 73 00 20 00. (This) Note the 0x00 padding between each character.

Offset 11 – Attribute: 0x0F. This will be the case for all LFN.
Offset 12 – Type: 0x00. This will be the case for all LFN.

Offset 13 – Checksum: 0x6A. This is the calculated value from the characters THISIS~1TXT.

Offset 14-25 – Characters 6-11: 0x69 00 73 00 20 00 61 00 6E 00 20 00 (is an).

Offset 26-27 – Starting Cluster: 0x00 00, this is not used and will be zero.

Offset 28-31 – Characters 12 & 13: 0x65 00 78 00 (ex)

```
000  46 63 00 00 00 FF FF FF-FF FF FF 0F 00 6A FF FF  Fc···ÿÿÿÿÿÿ··jÿÿ
010  FF FF FF FF FF FF FF FF-FF FF 00 00 FF FF FF FF  ÿÿÿÿÿÿÿÿÿÿ··ÿÿÿÿ
020  05 6F 00 6E 00 20 00 39-00 2E 00 0F 00 6A 32 00  ·o·n· ·9·.···j2·
030  37 00 2E 00 31 00 33 00-2E 00 00 00 64 00 6F 00  7·.·1·3·.···d·o·
040  04 6E 00 61 00 6D 00 65-00 20 00 0F 00 6A 63 00  ·n·a·m·e· ···jc·
050  72 00 65 00 61 00 74 00-65 00 00 00 64 00 20 00  r·e·a·t·e···d· ·
060  03 72 00 79 00 20 00 6C-00 6F 00 0F 00 6A 6E 00  ·r·y· ·l·o···jn·
070  67 00 20 00 66 00 69 00-6C 00 00 00 65 00 20 00  g· ·f·i·l···e· ·
080  02 61 00 6D 00 70 00 6C-00 65 00 0F 00 6A 20 00  ·a·m·p·l·e···j ·
090  6F 00 66 00 20 00 61 00-20 00 00 00 76 00 65 00  o·f· ·a· ···v·e·
0a0  01 54 00 68 00 69 00 73-00 20 00 0F 00 6A 69 00  ·T·h·i·s· ···ji·
0b0  73 00 20 00 61 00 6E 00-20 00 00 00 65 00 78 00  s· ·a·n· ···e·x·
0c0  54 48 49 53 49 53 7E 31-44 4F 43 20 00 B8 C1 52  THISIS~1DOC ·¸ÁR
0d0  3B 43 3B 43 00 00 9D 52-3B 43 00 00 00 00 00 00  ;C;C··R;C······
```

Note that at offset 0 of each entry the sequence number in red counts up, ending with a 0x46 , with 6 indicating the sixth entry. The checksum values in blue are calculated based upon THISISDOC and is the same for each entry in the LFN.

Also note that the last entry, which is only needed for the letter "c" is then filled with padding of 0xFF.

PRACTICAL EXERCISE 2

```
000 45 58 41 4d 50 4c 45 20-54 58 54 08 00 00 00 00 EXAMPLE TXT·····
010 00 00 00 00 00 00 27 6e-3c 43 00 00 00 00 00 00 ······'n<C······
020 42 74 00 78 00 74 00 00-00 ff ff 0f 00 4f ff ff Bt·x·t···ÿÿ··Oÿÿ
030 ff ff ff ff ff ff ff ff-ff ff 00 00 ff ff ff ff ÿÿÿÿÿÿÿÿÿÿ··ÿÿÿÿ
040 01 45 00 78 00 61 00 6d-00 70 00 0f 00 4f 6c 00 ·E·x·a·m·p···Ol·
050 65 00 20 00 46 00 69 00-6c 00 00 00 65 00 2e 00 e· ·F·i·l···e·.·
060 45 58 41 4d 50 4c 7e 31-54 58 54 20 00 bf 2d 6e EXAMPL~1TXT ·¿-n
070 3c 43 3c 43 00 00 a0 6a-3c 43 00 00 00 00 00 00 <C<C·· j<C······
080 41 45 00 78 00 61 00 6d-00 70 00 0f 00 5a 6c 00 AE·x·a·m·p···Zl·
090 45 00 2e 00 74 00 78 00-74 00 00 00 00 00 ff ff E·.·t·x·t·····ÿÿ
0a0 45 58 41 4d 50 4c 45 20-54 58 54 20 00 3c 31 6e EXAMPLE TXT ·<1n
0b0 3c 43 3c 43 00 00 d3 6a-3c 43 00 00 00 00 00 00 <C<C··Ój<C······
0c0 4b 2e 00 74 00 78 00 74-00 00 00 0f 00 b0 ff ff K.·t·x·t·····°ÿÿ
0d0 ff ff ff ff ff ff ff ff-ff ff 00 00 ff ff ff ff ÿÿÿÿÿÿÿÿÿÿ··ÿÿÿÿ
0e0 0a 73 00 20 00 63 00 61-00 72 00 0f 00 b0 72 00 ·s· ·c·a·r···°r·
0f0 69 00 65 00 64 00 20 00-6f 00 00 00 75 00 74 00 i·e·d· ·o···u·t·
100 09 20 00 63 00 6f 00 6e-00 76 00 0f 00 b0 65 00 · ·c·o·n·v···°e·
110 6e 00 74 00 69 00 6f 00-6e 00 00 00 20 00 69 00 n·t·i·o·n··· ·i·
120 08 6f 00 77 00 20 00 74-00 68 00 0f 00 b0 65 00 ·o·w· ·t·h···°e·
130 20 00 6e 00 61 00 6d 00-69 00 00 00 6e 00 67 00  ·n·a·m·i···n·g·
140 07 6d 00 6f 00 6e 00 73-00 74 00 0f 00 b0 72 00 ·m·o·n·s·t···°r·
150 61 00 74 00 69 00 6f 00-6e 00 00 00 20 00 68 00 a·t·i·o·n··· ·h·
160 06 65 00 6e 00 74 00 72-00 69 00 0f 00 b0 65 00 ·e·n·t·r·i···°e·
170 73 00 20 00 74 00 6f 00-20 00 00 00 64 00 65 00 s· ·t·o· ···d·e·
180 05 6c 00 65 00 20 00 64-00 69 00 0f 00 b0 72 00 ·l·e· ·d·i···°r·
190 65 00 63 00 74 00 6f 00-72 00 00 00 79 00 20 00 e·c·t·o·r···y· ·
1a0 04 65 00 71 00 75 00 69-00 72 00 0f 00 b0 65 00 ·e·q·u·i·r···°e·
1b0 20 00 6d 00 75 00 6c 00-74 00 00 00 69 00 70 00  ·m·u·l·t···i·p·
1c0 03 67 00 20 00 65 00 6e-00 6f 00 0f 00 b0 75 00 ·g· ·e·n·o···°u·
1d0 67 00 68 00 20 00 74 00-6f 00 00 00 20 00 72 00 g·h· ·t·o··· ·r·
1e0 02 66 00 69 00 6c 00 65-00 20 00 0f 00 b0 6e 00 ·f·i·l·e· ···°n·
1f0 61 00 6d 00 65 00 20 00-6c 00 00 00 6f 00 6e 00 a·m·e· ·l···o·n·
200 01 45 00 78 00 61 00 6d-00 70 00 0f 00 b0 6c 00 ·E·x·a·m·p···°l·
210 65 00 20 00 6f 00 66 00-20 00 00 00 61 00 20 00 e· ·o·f· ···a· ·
220 45 58 41 4d 50 4c 7e 32-54 58 54 20 00 7b 33 6e EXAMPL~2TXT ·{3n
230 3c 43 3c 43 00 00 3b 6b-3c 43 00 00 00 00 00 00 <C<C··;k<C······

240 42 72 00 2e 00 74 00 78-00 74 00 0f 00 90 00 00 Br·.·t·x·t······
250 ff ff ff ff ff ff ff ff-ff ff 00 00 ff ff ff ff ÿÿÿÿÿÿÿÿÿÿ··ÿÿÿÿ
260 01 45 00 78 00 61 00 6d-00 70 00 0f 00 90 6c 00 ·E·x·a·m·p····l·
270 65 00 20 00 66 00 6f 00-6c 00 00 00 64 00 65 00 e· ·f·o·l···d·e·
280 45 58 41 4d 50 4c 7e 33-54 58 54 10 00 3e 36 6e EXAMPL~3TXT··>6n
290 3c 43 3c 43 00 00 c7 6d-3c 43 03 00 00 00 00 00 <C<C··Çm<C······
2a0 42 65 00 2e 00 74 00 78-00 74 00 0f 00 70 00 00 Be·.·t·x·t···p··
2b0 ff ff ff ff ff ff ff ff-ff ff 00 00 ff ff ff ff ÿÿÿÿÿÿÿÿÿÿ··ÿÿÿÿ
2c0 01 65 00 78 00 2e 00 61-00 6d 00 0f 00 70 70 00 ·e·x·.·a·m···pp·
2d0 6c 00 65 00 2e 00 20 00-66 00 00 00 69 00 6c 00 l·e·.· ·f···i·l·
2e0 45 58 41 4d 50 4c 7e 34-54 58 54 20 00 24 40 6e EXAMPL~4TXT ·$@n
2f0 3c 43 3c 43 00 00 e2 6a-3c 43 00 00 00 00 00 00 <C<C··âj<C······
300 41 45 00 78 00 61 00 6d-00 70 00 0f 00 d1 31 00 AE·x·a·m·p···Ñ1·
310 65 00 2e 00 74 00 78 00-74 00 00 00 00 00 ff ff e·.·t·x·t·····ÿÿ
320 45 58 41 4d 50 31 45 20-54 58 54 20 00 bd 43 6e EXAMP1E TXT ·½Cn
330 3c 43 3c 43 00 00 d4 6d-3c 43 00 00 00 00 00 00 <C<C··Ôm<C······
340 42 72 00 65 00 61 00 64-00 2e 00 0f 00 74 74 00 Br·e·a·d·.···tt·
350 78 00 74 00 00 00 ff ff-ff ff 00 00 ff ff ff ff x·t···ÿÿÿÿ··ÿÿÿÿ
360 01 45 00 78 00 61 00 6d-00 5f 00 0f 00 74 70 00 ·E·x·a·m·_···tp·
370 6c 00 65 00 61 00 73 00-65 00 00 00 20 00 5f 00 l·e·a·s·e··· ·_·
380 45 58 41 4d 5f 50 7e 31-54 58 54 20 00 a6 4f 6e EXAM_P~1TXT ·¦On
390 3c 43 3c 43 00 00 e9 6d-3c 43 00 00 00 00 00 00 <C<C··ém<C······
```

List each LFN, its associated SFN, the checksum value, and all the sequence values.

CHAPTER SUMMARY

In this chapter we covered the process of formatting drives. Formatting sets up the System Area of a volume, which includes the Volume Boot Record and File Allocation Table. The System Area of FAT12/16 volumes also include the Root Directory. The Root Directory of a FAT32 is included as part of the Data Area. The Data Area is where the content of files and subdirectories. Formatting writes out the Volume Boot Record, zeroes out the File Allocation Table and the entire Root Directory of a FAT12/16 volume or the first sector of a FAT32 volume. The Data Area is not overwritten during a quick format process, but may be overwritten on a full format under certain operating systems.

The Root Directory is the primary location for file names and starting location. The directory structure is 32 bytes and has the dates associated with the files along with the file size. The starting cluster of the file is included in the entry along with file attributes. The standard directory entry accommodates filenames with up to eight characters and up to three characters for the extension.

For files with names longer than eight characters, a system was developed to handle up to 255 characters and still remain within the 32-byte directory structure. For each file that is over eight characters or has a mixed case name, there will a Short File Name entry created with the dates and times and a Long File Name entry, using as many 32-byte entries as needed to complete the name in Unicode.

KEY TERMS

Formatting: Process of setting the System Area and Data Area of a partition by writing a Volume Boot Record and zeroing out the File Allocation Table and all or part of the Root Directory.

System Area: Area of the partition containing file system information.

Data Area: Area of the partition where the content of files and folders is written.

Root Directory: Primary folder for filenames and metadata about the files.

Long File Name (LFN): A name with more that eight characters.

Short File Name (SFN): An 8.3-compatible name generated from the LFN.

AT HOME EXERCISE

Open image file LFN.E01 in FTK Imager.

What version of FAT was this volume formatted in?

According to the VBR, how many reserved sectors are there?

How many copies of the FAT are there?

How many sectors are there per FAT?

What sector is the Root Directory in?

What is the Volume Label?

For each file provide the following:

	Long File Name	**Checksum**	**Short File Name**
1.			
2.			
3.			
4.			
5.			
6.			

Provide the Creation Time for each file (**show your work**)

1.

2.

3.

4.

5.

6.

Provide the Modified Time for each file (**show your work**)

1.

2.

3.

4.

5.

6.

REFERENCES

1. Formatting disks and drives: frequently asked questions. (2013). Retrieved from http://windows.microsoft.com/en-us/windows7/formatting-disks-and-drives-frequently-asked-questions

2. Differences between a quick format and a regular format during a "clean" installation of windows xp. (n.d.). Retrieved from http://support.microsoft.com/kb/302686

3. Carrier, B. (2005). File system forensic analysis. (pp. 265). Upper Saddle River:
Addison-Wesley

4. Yabumoto, K. (2000, January 17). Xxcopy technical bulletin. Retrieved from http://www.xxcopy.com/xxcopy06.htm

5. Verstak, A. (1999, April 10). directory structure. Retrieved from http://averstak.tripod.com/fatdox/dir.htm

6. Information about long file names. (n.d.). Retrieved from http://www.computerhope.com/issues/ch000209.htm

7. Bunting, S. (2012). Ence computer forensics: The official encase certified examiner study guide. (3rd ed., p. 51). Indianapolis: Sybex.

CASE STUDY 4: TIME TRAVEL

A large national insurance company was suing a psychiatrist/attorney for fraudulent conduct. The individual was negotiating insurance payment for accident victims and was getting twice the normal payout. He was apparently working or conspiring with someone on the inside of the insurance company who was also investigated. The case files for the victims represented by the defendant had inconsistent documents or missing documents.

I was appointed by the federal court to act as an independent examiner. I conducted an examination of the defendant's computer and found evidence that another hard drive existed that was never turned over. During the trial, this fact came out (it was put in the report months prior but no action was taken at that time) and the judge ordered that the drive was to be turned over to me for examination. Several days later, the drive appeared.

The drive turned out to be an external USB drive formatted with the FAT file system. During the examination, several deleted files were found that had creation dates that were just days old and during the trial. These files were WordPerfect temporary files associated with word processing documents. When WordPerfect is run and existing files are opened, it creates temporary versions of the document. Most users are unaware of this fact because the temporary files are immediately deleted when the file is closed. Examining the file further revealed that they were associated with a document that was of particular importance in the trial. The document had a creation date going back several years. One other document in the same folder had creation and last written dates that were a few years old but the last accessed date was years older and match that of the critical evidentiary file.

There is no way for a file to have a last accessed date before the creation or last written date without the clock being manipulated. Based upon the testing and the available facts, it was apparent that the defendant backdated the computer clock to several years back and created the evidentiary file, but during the process he accidently accessed another document while the date was set back. The last accessed date typically is not displayed for files, so he would not see this change. Typically, only the last written date is provided when viewing a folder in Windows Explorer.

I was called back to testify on these new results and the jury ended up finding for the plaintiff (the insurance company) and awarded payment of several millions of dollars.

07 FILE SYSTEMS: FAT PART III

To this point, we have covered two of the three components of the System Area. The third area is the File Allocation Table, which tracks the usage of each of the clusters in the Data Area.

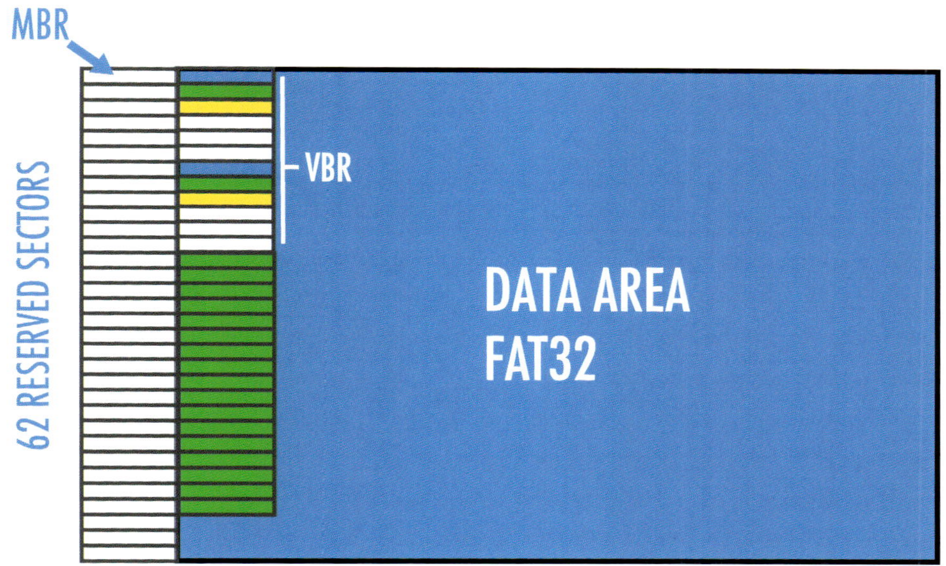

As a reminder from the previous chapters, there are two copies of the VBR in a FAT32 file system and there are two copies of the FAT in all versions of FAT. The Root Directory is in the Data Area in FAT32 and part of the System Area in FAT12/16. The location of the FAT can be found by determining the number of reserved sectors listed in the VBR offset 14-15. The number of sectors in the FAT is also contained within the VBR.

We will now explore how the FAT tracks clusters and what occurs when files are created. This is valuable in understanding what occurs when a suspect or subject is copying off files to a flash drive, whether they are corporate trade secret files or a child porn library. Knowing what occurs during the process is forensically important.

The File Allocated Table tracks each cluster's usage. It also has pointers to all the clusters used in a file.

Let's go back and review clusters.

Clusters are the smallest unit of data that the File System will read or write. Clusters are made up of one or more sectors (if not one then an even number).

Analogy
Drive = Book
Partition = Story
Cluster = Page
Sector = Paragraph

Here is a page.

In this case, there are 8 sectors per cluster.

This information is in the Volume Boot Record.

8 * 512 byte per sector = 4096

4K cluster

In the FAT file system, the cluster sizes vary depending upon the size of the volume. The table below shows the variations in the number of sectors per clusters[1].

Volume Size Range	Sectors per Cluster
32MB – 64MB	1
64MB – 128MB	2
128MB – 256MB	4
256MB – 8GB	8
8GB – 16GB	16
16GB – 32GB	32
32GB – 2TB	64

Only one file can occupy a cluster. So even if the file is only 100 bytes in length and the cluster is 4K, the entire cluster will be reserved for that file.

The remainder of the cluster not used by the file is usually referred to as File Slack[2].

There are two types of slack: RAM and Residual[3].

RAM Slack is the space from the end of the file (black) to the end of the sector the file ends in (red). When saving a file, the system wants to file entire sectors, so it will take data from Random Access Memory (RAM) and fill the sector. In past days, there could be useful data found in this space; however, Microsoft made a change that will overwrite the RAM slack with zeros.

The Residual Slack, also known as Disk Slack (in green) is the remaining sectors in the cluster with no file data. This space can potentially contain data from a previous file. We saw in the last chapter that formatting a drive typically does not overwrite the data area, so after formatting and adding a new shorter file, this may result in old data associated with a new file.

-> Format Drive

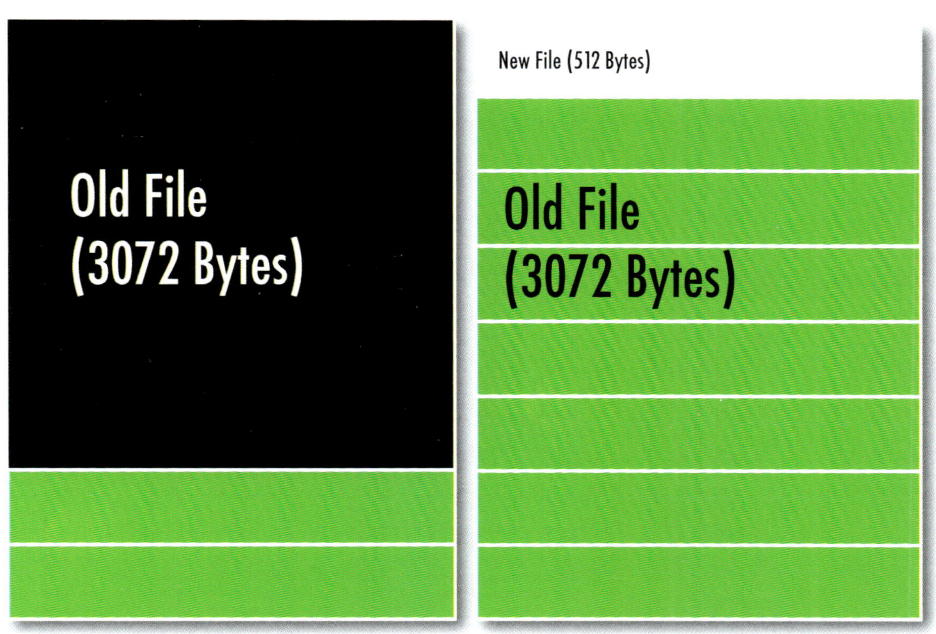

FOLLOW ALONG EXERCISE

Format a USB drive with a FAT32 file system (make sure it has no files you want to keep) and copy Conny.txt to the drive.

Open up the drive in FTK Imager by Add Evidence Item > Logical Drive, and then choose the volume letter you just formatted.

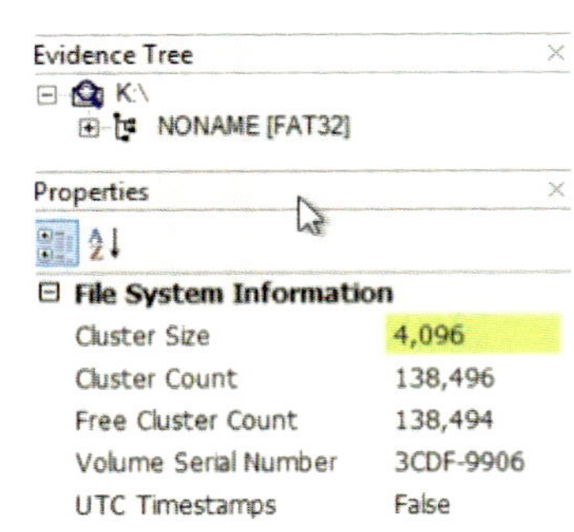

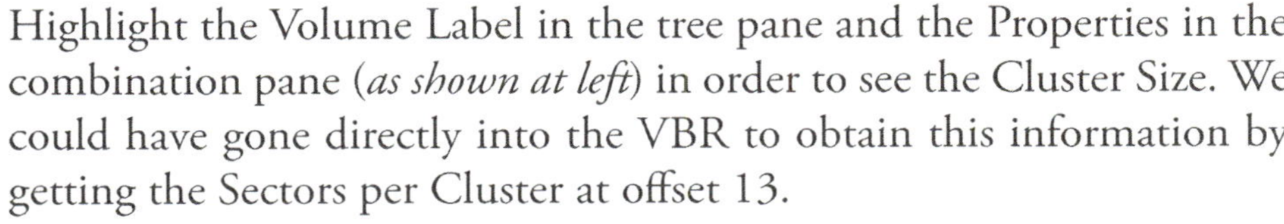

Highlight the Volume Label in the tree pane and the Properties in the combination pane (*as shown at left*) in order to see the Cluster Size. We could have gone directly into the VBR to obtain this information by getting the Sectors per Cluster at offset 13.

Note the number of byte per cluster is 4096. If you divide by 512 bytes per sector, then you know you have 8 sectors per cluster.

See the VBR below, offset 13.

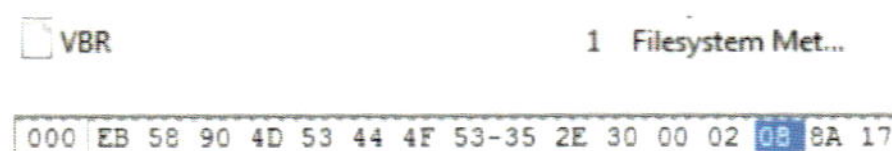

Next view the Root Directory and highlight the Conny.txt file.

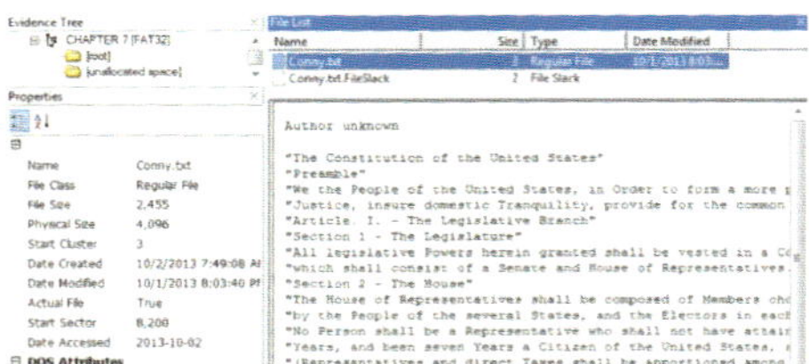

Under the properties pane, the File Size is listed as 2455 bytes.
Take the File Size / Cluster Size or 2455 / 4096 = 0.599 clusters, then round up to a full cluster.

Rounding up gives 1 cluster needed for Conny.txt

Take the Cluster Size – File Size or 4096 – 2455 = 1641 bytes in File Slack (RAM and Residual).

FTK Imager breaks down the File Slack as well. Since this previous data on the drives will vary, everyone will have different data.

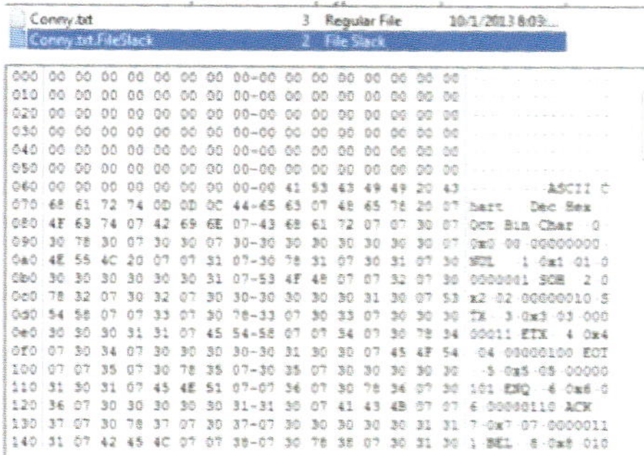

Going back up to the properties pane, the starting cluster (from the directory entry) is Cluster 3. This is where the data is stored.

In FTK Imager, highlight the volume label again, then in the view pane, right click and select Goto Sector/Cluster and enter 3.

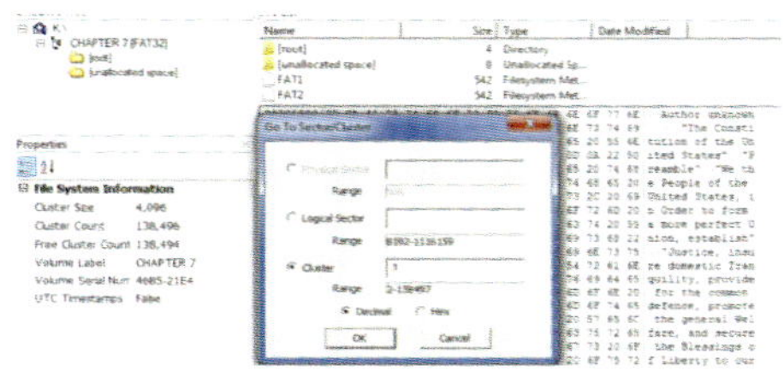

This will redirect your location to Cluster 3 and display the contents.

```
00001000 0D 0A 41 75 74 68 6F 72-20 75 6E 6B 6E 6F 77 6E ··Author unknown
00001010 20 0D 0A 0D 0A 22 54 68-65 20 43 6F 6E 73 74 69  ····"The Consti
00001020 74 75 74 69 6F 6E 20 6F-66 20 74 68 65 20 55 6E tution of the Un
00001030 69 74 65 64 20 53 74 61-74 65 73 22 0D 0A 22 50 ited States"··"P
00001040 72 65 61 6D 62 6C 65 22-0D 0A 22 57 65 20 74 68 reamble"··"We th
00001050 65 20 50 65 6F 70 6C 65-20 6F 66 20 74 68 65 20 e People of the 
00001060 55 6E 69 74 65 64 20 53-74 61 74 65 73 2C 20 69 United States, i
00001070 6E 20 4F 72 64 65 72 20-74 6F 20 66 6F 72 6D 20 n Order to form 
00001080 61 20 6D 6F 72 65 20 70-65 72 66 65 63 74 20 55 a more perfect U
00001090 6E 69 6F 6E 2C 20 65 73-74 61 62 6C 69 73 68 22 nion, establish"
000010a0 0D 0A 22 4A 75 73 74 69-63 65 2C 20 69 6E 73 75 ··"Justice, insu
000010b0 72 65 20 64 6F 6D 65 73-74 69 63 20 54 72 61 6E re domestic Tran
000010c0 71 75 69 6C 69 74 79 2C-20 70 72 6F 76 69 64 65 quility, provide
000010d0 20 66 6F 72 20 74 68 65-20 63 6F 6D 6D 6F 6E 20  for the common 
000010e0 64 65 66 65 6E 63 65 2C-20 70 72 6F 6D 6F 74 65 defence, promote
000010f0 20 74 68 65 20 67 65 6E-65 72 61 6C 20 57 65 6C  the general Wel
00001100 66 61 72 65 2C 20 61 6E-64 20 73 65 63 75 72 65 fare, and secure
00001110 20 74 68 65 20 42 6C 65-73 73 69 6E 67 73 20 6F  the Blessings o
00001120 66 20 4C 69 62 65 72 74-79 20 74 6F 20 6F 75 72 f Liberty to our
00001130 73 65 6C 76 65 73 20 61-6E 64 20 6F 75 72 20 50 selves and our P
00001140 6F 73 74 65 72 69 74 79-2C 20 64 6F 20 6F 72 64 osterity, do ord
00001150 61 69 6E 20 61 6E 64 20-65 73 74 61 62 6C 69 73 ain and establis
00001160 68 20 74 68 69 73 20 43-6F 6E 73 74 69 74 75 74 h this Constitut
00001170 69 6F 6E 20 66 6F 72 20-74 68 65 20 55 6E 69 74 ion for the Unit
00001180 65 64 20 53 74 61 74 65-73 20 6F 66 20 41 6D 65 ed States of Ame
00001190 72 69 63 61 2E 22 0D 0A-22 41 72 74 69 63 6C 65 rica."··"Article
000011a0 2E 20 49 2E 20 2D 20 54-68 65 20 4C 65 67 69 73 . I. - The Legis
000011b0 6C 61 74 69 76 65 20 42-72 61 6E 63 68 22 0D 0A lative Branch"··
000011c0 22 53 65 63 74 69 6F 6E-20 31 20 2D 20 54 68 65 "Section 1 - The
000011d0 20 4C 65 67 69 73 6C 61-74 75 72 65 22 0D 0A 22  Legislature"··"
000011e0 41 6C 6C 20 6C 65 67 69-73 6C 61 74 69 76 65 20 All legislative 
000011f0 50 6F 77 65 72 73 20 68-65 72 65 69 6E 20 67 72 Powers herein gr
00001200 61 6E 74 65 64 20 73 68-61 6C 6C 20 62 65 20 76 anted shall be v
00001210 65 73 74 65 64 20 69 6E-20 61 20 43 6F 6E 67 72 ested in a Congr
00001220 65 73 73 20 6F 66 20 74-68 65 20 55 6E 69 74 65 ess of the Unite
00001230 64 20 53 74 61 74 65 73-2C 22 0D 0A 22 77 68 69 d States,"··"whi
00001240 63 68 20 73 68 61 6C 6C-20 63 6F 6E 73 69 73 74 ch shall consist
00001250 20 6F 66 20 61 20 53 65-6E 61 74 65 20 61 6E 64  of a Senate and
Cursor pos = 4096; clus = 3; log sec = 8200
```

Make a mental note of this data as we will now re-format the drive and see the changes that occur.

Format your USB flash drive again (if using Windows Vista/7/8, do not uncheck the Quick Format). Copy File2.txt to the drive.

Add the logical drive into FTK Imager again. Click on the Root Directory in the tree pane and on File2.txt in the table pane to view the properties.

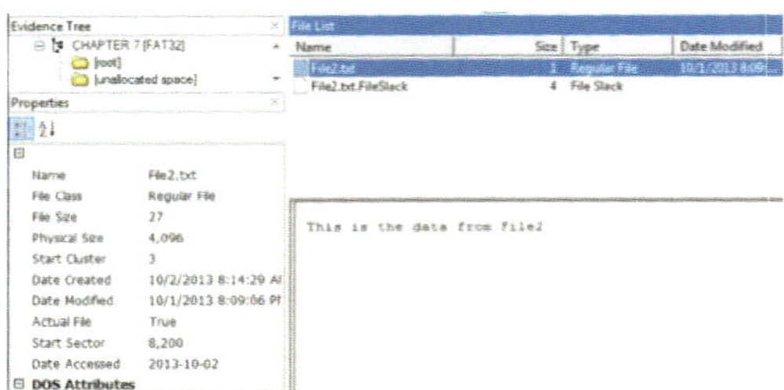

File2.txt is only 27 bytes but still needs a full cluster. This leaves 4069 bytes of slack.

Click on the volume label in the tree pane, and then in the lower right pane, right click and go to Sector/Cluster, and enter cluster 3.

Note that the RAM slack is all zeroes, and the Residual slack has data from the previous US Constitution file.

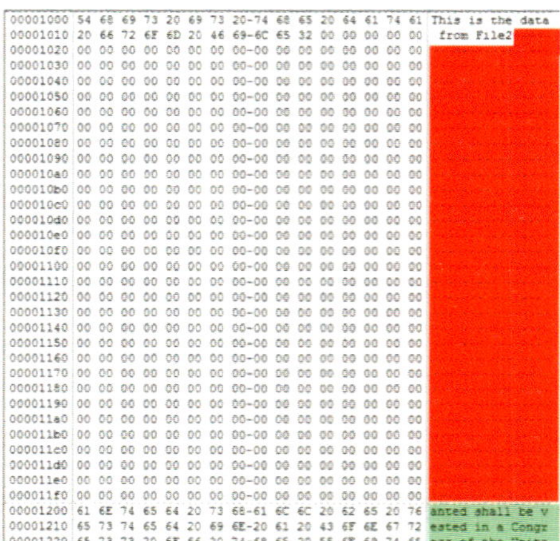

You can continue down through the remainder of the cluster.

Go to the eighth sector of the cluster and you may note data that was present before Conny.txt was placed on the drive. This shows that the Residual Slack may contain data from numerous files going back in history.

Slack in a Directory

Calculating the slack on a directory is a little more complicated because there is no file size. You must go to the end of the last 32-byte entry to determine the number of bytes in the folder. Use this value to determine the RAM and Residual slack.

File Tracking in FAT

Let's now look to see how the files are tracked. In FAT32, there are 4 bytes used in the File Allocation Table referencing each cluster. In FAT12/16, there are only 2 bytes. In these 4 bytes, there are only a few types of available options[4].

0x00 00 00 00	Cluster is unused
0x00 00 00 01	Reserved
0x00 00 00 02 – 0x0F FF FF F6	Cluster number
0x0F FF FF F7	Bad Cluster
0x0F FF FF FF	End of File

The first 4 bytes of the FAT Allocation Table is the Media Descriptor, which you may remember from Chapter 5 in the VBR. The descriptor is either for a floppy disk or hard disk; this will typically be 0xF8 FF FF 0F. The next 4 bytes are reserved and typically contain 0xFF FF FF 0F. Starting at offset 8 will be the cluster references. Below is what we will see after formatting a disk.

Media Descriptor	Reserved	Cluster 2	Cluster 3
0XF8FFFF0F	**0XFFFFFFFF**	**0XFFFFFF0F**	**0X00000000**
Cluster 4	Cluster 5	Cluster 6	Cluster 7
0X00000000	**0X00000000**	**0X00000000**	**0X00000000**
Cluster 8	Cluster 9	Cluster 10	Cluster 11
0X00000000	**0X00000000**	**0X00000000**	**0X00000000**

This will continue on until all the clusters on the drive are referenced. Note that the first cluster number is 2[5]. **This is important to remember!** There is no cluster 0 or cluster 1, as the reference spaces for these are used for the media descriptor and reserved bytes.

Cluster 2 under FAT32 will always be the Root Directory, so these reference bytes will be filled with either an End of File Marker (0xFFFFFF0F) or a number. This means that the files and folders we add will begin with cluster 3. Look back up to the Conny.txt properties and the File2.txt properties and see that these files were placed in cluster 3.

In those cases we saw we only needed one cluster (cluster 3), so in the File Allocation Table under cluster reference there would be an End of File Marker (0xFFFFFF0F).

If we had a directory of files as below, we will see half of the File Allocation Table is filled out. Assume from the VBR that there are 8 sectors per cluster.

Root Directory

Name	**Size**	**Starting Cluster**
Letter to Mom.doc	5000	3
My vacation pics.jpg	13525	5
To Do List.txt	786	8
BUDGET.XLS	8193	9

We must determine how many clusters are needed for each file. This is done as we did previously by dividing the file size by the number of bytes per cluster and rounding up.

Root Directory

Name	**Size**	**Starting Cluster**	**# of Clusters**
Letter to Mom.doc	5000	3	5000/4096 = 1.22 (2)
My vacation pics.jpg	11525	5	11525/4096 = 2.81 (3)
To Do List.txt	786	8	786/4096 = 0.19 (1)
BUDGET.XLS	8193	9	8193/4096 = 2.01 (3)

Media Descriptor	Reserved	Cluster 2	Cluster 3
0XF8FFFF0F	**0XFFFFFFFF**	**0XFFFFFF0F**	**0X04000000**
Cluster 4	Cluster 5	Cluster 6	Cluster 7
0XFFFFFF0F	**0X06000000**	**0X07000000**	**0XFFFFFF0F**
Cluster 8	Cluster 9	Cluster 10	Cluster 11
0XFFFFFF0F	**0X0A000000**	**0X0B000000**	**0XFFFFFF0F**

In Letter to Mom.doc, there were two clusters needed and the first cluster is 3. In the File Allocation Table under the reference bytes for cluster 3, we see that the number 4 (0x00000004 Little Endian) is placed there. This is a pointer to the next cluster for the file. When we look at the cluster 4 reference bytes, we note that there is an End of File Marker (0xFFFFFF0F) meaning that this is the last cluster for this file.

In My vacation pics.jpg, there are three clusters needed and the first cluster is 5. In the cluster 5 reference there is a pointer to cluster 6, in the cluster 6 reference there is a pointer to 7, and in the cluster 7 reference there is an End of File Marker.
In To Do List.txt, there is only one cluster needed and it is cluster 8. There is just the End of File Marker in the cluster 8 reference.

In BUDGET.XLS there are three clusters needed, starting in cluster 9. The cluster 9 reference has a pointer to cluster 10 (0x0000000A Little Endian). The cluster 10 reference points to cluster 11 and the cluster 11 reference has an End of File Marker.

When clusters associated with a file are next to each in sequence, they are referred to as ***contiguous***. However, it is possible the clusters will not be next to each other; this is referred to as ***fragmented***. You have heard the phrase "defragging the drive." This is a process where fragmented file data is moved around to make the file contiguous. This makes accessing the file more efficient.

Contiguous Clusters
File clusters that are next to each other on the volume

Fragmented
Files whose clusters are not next to each other on the volume

An example of fragmented files:

Root Directory

Name	**Size**	**Starting Cluster**	**# of Clusters**
Letter to Mom.doc	5000	3	5000/4096 = 1.22 (2)
To Do List.txt	786	4	786/4096 = 0.19 (1)
My vacation pics.jpg	11525	5	11525/4096 = 2.81 (3)
BUDGET.XLS	8193	7	8193/4096 = 2.01 (3)

Media Descriptor	Reserved	Cluster 2	Cluster 3
0XF8FFFF0F	**0XFFFFFFFF**	**0XFFFFFF0F**	**0X06000000**
Cluster 4	Cluster 5	Cluster 6	Cluster 7
0XFFFFFF0F	**0X08000000**	**0XFFFFFF0F**	**0X09000000**
Cluster 8	Cluster 9	Cluster 10	Cluster 11
0X0A000000	**0X0B000000**	**0XFFFFFF0F**	**0XFFFFFF0F**

In this case we have the same file, but instead of copying them all at once as is to the drive, they have grown and changed over time. Letter to Mom.doc probably only needed one cluster to begin with and To Do List.txt was added. Letter to Mom.doc grew and needed an additional cluster. The file system will not move one file to fit another when saving, that is what defragging does.

PRACTICAL EXERCISE 1

Fill out the File Allocation Table based upon the file information below, using EOF for End of File Marker.

VBR
EB 58 90 4D 53 44 4F 53 35 2E 30 00 02 02 8A 17
02 00 00 00 00 F8 00 00 3F 00 FF 00 80 E0 2E 00
00 08 11 00 3B 04 00 00 00 00 00 00 02 00 00 00
01 00 06 00 00 00 00 00 00 00 00 00 00 00 00 00
80 00 29 DE FB 98 64 4E 4F 20 4E 41 4D 45 20 20
20 20 46 41 54 33 32 20 20 20
How many sectors per cluster?

How many bytes per cluster?

FileName	Size	Starting Cluster
FILE1.DOC	8211	3
FILE2.XLS	2049	12
FILE3.MP3	511	17
FILE4.PDF	18743	18

2	3	4	5	6	7
8	9	10	11	12	13
14	15	16	17	18	19
20	21	22	23	24	25
26	27	28	29	30	31
32	33	34	35	36	37
38	39	40	41	42	43
44	45	46	47	48	49

VBR
EB 58 90 4D 53 44 4F 53 35 2E 30 00 02 04 8A 17
02 00 00 00 00 F8 00 00 3F 00 FF 00 80 E0 2E 00
00 08 11 00 3B 04 00 00 00 00 00 00 02 00 00 00
01 00 06 00 00 00 00 00 00 00 00 00 00 00 00 00
80 00 29 DE FB 98 64 4E 4F 20 4E 41 4D 45 20 20
20 20 46 41 54 33 32 20 20 20

How many sectors per cluster?

How many bytes per cluster?

Fill out the File Allocation Table based upon the file information below.

FileName	Size	Starting Cluster
TEST1.TXT	5365	3
TEST2.TXT	4095	7
TEST3.TXT	13423	9
TEST4.TXT	16001	16
TEST5.TXT	15	17

2	3	4	5	6	7
			BAD		
8	**9**	**10**	**11**	**12**	**13**
14	**15**	**16**	**17**	**18**	**19**
					BAD
20	**21**	**22**	**23**	**24**	**25**
BAD					
26	**27**	**28**	**29**	**30**	**31**

As shown at the beginning of this chapter, there is a backup copy of the File Allocation Table. The backup copy is synchronized immediately as the data is written.

When a file is created, data is written to four areas[6]:

A. The directory entry is created.
B. The data is written to the assigned clusters.
C. File Allocation Table copy 1 is filled in.
D. File Allocation Table copy 2 is filled in.

PRACTICAL EXERCISE 2

Using FTK Imager or HxD, open FAT_FILE.001.

How many sectors per cluster are there?

How many bytes per cluster are there?

Complete the table below based upon your examination for each entry in the image. Ignore folders but not their content.

Filename	Size	Starting Cluster	List Clusters

Determining RAM Slack and Residual Slack size

Understanding where you may find keyword hits or other potentially valuable data of evidentiary value can very useful.

RAM Slack
The space from the end of the file to the end of the sector the file ends in.

Residual Slack
The remaining sectors after the RAM slack in the cluster with no file data.

RAM Slack – Data from the end of the file to the end of the sector.

Starting with the file size, determine how many sectors this file will occupy by dividing by 512 and then rounding up to the nearest sector. Multiply this rounded up number by 512 and subtract the file size. Example 1: File Size = 1547 / 512 = 3.02 (rounded to 4)

4 x 512 = 2048 -1547 = 501 bytes of RAM slack

Example 2: File Size = 16383 / 512 = 31.99 (rounded to 32)

32 x 512 = 16384 - 16383 = 1 byte of RAM slack

Note that the largest size RAM slack can be is 511 bytes.

Residual Slack – Data from the end of the RAM Slack to the end of the last cluster associated with the file.

Start with determining the cluster size. Then determine how many clusters are needed for the file. Multiply the cluster size by the number of clusters; this is known as the physical size of the file versus the logical size of the file, which is the same as the file size. Subtract the logical file size and the bytes in the RAM Slack from the physical size.

Example 1: Cluster size = 4096, File Size = 1547, Cluster needed = 1

Physical size = 4096 – 1547 – 501(RAM Slack) = 2048 Residual Slack

Example 2: Cluster size=4096, File Size=16385,
Clusters needed=16385/4096 =4.01

5 Clusters x 4096 = 20480 – 16385 – 511 (RAM Slack) = 3584 bytes (7 sectors)

The File slack is the combination of the RAM and Residual Slack values.

PRACTICAL EXERCISE 3

Using the FAT_FILE.001 from Practical 2, complete the table below for each entry (file and folder) in the image.

Filename	File Slack	RAM Slack	Residual Slack

CHAPTER SUMMARY

The File Allocation Table (FAT) is a system for tracking cluster usage by files and folders. The table uses a series of pointers to indicate and track which clusters are used by which files.

A cluster is a grouping of contiguous sectors. The number of sectors per cluster is established in the Volume Boot Record and is constant across the entire volume. The size varies depending upon the size of the volume, the larger the volume the more sectors per cluster.

Only one file can be stored in a cluster. Any space from the end of the file data and the end of the cluster is referred to as slack. There are two types of slack, RAM and Residual.

In FAT32 the Root Directory is part of the Data Area and always begins in cluster 2. There is no cluster 0 or cluster 1. The files and subdirectories added will begin in cluster three.

Files that have all their clusters next to each on the volume are considered contiguous; however, if the clusters are separated from each other, then the file is fragmented. Defragging a drive puts the data into contiguous clusters.

There is a backup copy of the FAT immediately following the first copy in the volume.

The steps in writing a file are:

- Making the directory entry
- Writing the data to the appropriate clusters
- Assigning the clusters in the 1st copy of the FAT
- Assigning the clusters in the 2nd copy of the FAT

KEY TERMS

RAM Slack - the space from the end of the file to the end of the sector the file ends in.
Residual Slack - is the remaining sectors after the RAM slack in the cluster with no file data.
Fragmented – files whose clusters are not next to each other on the volume
Contiguous Clusters – file clusters that are next to each other on the volume

AT HOME EXERCISE

1. Using FTK Imager, open FAT_HW1.E01 – contiguous clusters.

How many sectors per cluster are there?

How many bytes per cluster are there?

Complete the table below based upon your examination for each entry (file and folder) in the image.

Filename	Size	Starting Cluster	List Clusters	RAM Slack Size	Residual Slack Size

2. Using FTK Imager, open FAT_HW2.E01 – fragmented clusters (verify the contents to see if there consistent).

How many sectors per cluster are there?

How many bytes per cluster are there?

Complete the table below based upon your examination for each entry (file and folder) in the image.

Filename	Size	Starting Cluster	List Clusters	RAM Slack Size	Residual Slack Size

ADVANCED EXERCISE

3. Using FTK Imager, open FAT_HW3.E01 – advanced fragmented clusters.
A tool named Defrag from Dave Whitey, **www.flexomizer.com,** was used. It pseudo-randomly assigns the cluster location for the files so that they are highly fragmented.

How many sectors per cluster are there?

How many bytes per cluster are there?

Complete the table below based upon your examination for each entry (file and folder) in the image.

Filename	Size	Starting Cluster	List Clusters	RAM Slack Size	Residual Slack Size

REFERENCES

1. (n.d.). Retrieved from http://support.microsoft.com/kb/140365

2. Slack space. (n.d.). Retrieved from http://encyclopedia2.thefreedictionary.com/File Slack

3. Carrier, B. (2005). File system forensic analysis. (pp. 188). Upper Saddle River: Addison-Wesley

4. Bunting, S. (2012). Ence computer forensics: The official encase certified examiner study guide. (3rd ed., p. 63). Indianapolis: Sybex.

5. Sammes, T., & Jenkinson, B. (2007). Forensic computing, a practitioner's guide. (2nd ed., pp. 191). London: Springer Publishing.

6. (2003, February 13), FAT Logical File Structure, Powerpoint presentation, IACIS

08 FILE SYSTEMS: FAT PART IV

Recovering Deleted Files

From a forensic standpoint, it is important to understand how files are saved and stored, but it is also very important to understand how to recover any deleted data if possible.

In Chapter 7, we covered the steps involved in saving a file on a FAT volume.

1. Making the directory entry.
2. Writing the data to the appropriate clusters.
3. Assigning the clusters in the 1st copy of the FAT.
4. Assigning the clusters in the 2nd copy of the FAT.

Chapter 8 will cover the steps that occur when a file is deleted and how to go about reversing the process.

We will start off with the directory structure, similar to what we used in Chapter 7, and start the deletion process.

Root Directory

Name	**Size**	**Starting Cluster**	**# of Clusters**
FILE1.TXT	5000	3	5000/4096 = 1.22 (2)
TODO.DOC	786	4	786/4096 = 0.19 (1)
PICS.JPG	11525	5	11525/4096 = 2.81 (3)
BUDGET.XLS	8193	7	8193/4096 = 2.01 (3)

Media Descriptor	Reserved	Cluster 2	Cluster 3
0XF8FFFF0F	**0XFFFFFFFF**	**0XFFFFFF0F**	**0X06000000**
Cluster 4	Cluster 5	Cluster 6	Cluster 7
0XFFFFFF0F	**0X08000000**	**0XFFFFFF0F**	**0X09000000**
Cluster 8	Cluster 9	Cluster 10	Cluster 11
0X0A000000	**0X0B000000**	**0XFFFFFF0F**	**0XFFFFFF0F**

Begin by deleting FILE1.TXT

When a file is deleted in the FAT File System, the cluster references in both copies of the File Allocation Table are set to 0x00000000. In the Root Directory or in the subdirectory, the first character of the file name is changed to 0xE5, which in ASCII is the Sigma character (σ).[1] This is done so that if this character is encountered by the operating system, it is directed to skip over this entry for display purposes. This also marks the directory entry as one that can be overwritten.

Root Directory

Name	**Size**	**Starting Cluster**	**# of Clusters**
σILE1.TXT	5000	3	5000/4096 = 1.22 (2)
TODO.DOC	786	4	786/4096 = 0.19 (1)
PICS.JPG	11525	5	11525/4096 = 2.81 (3)
BUDGET.XLS	8193	7	8193/4096 = 2.01 (3)

Media Descriptor	Reserved	Cluster 2	Cluster 3
0XF8FFFF0F	**0XFFFFFFFF**	**0XFFFFFF0F**	**0X06000000**
Cluster 4	Cluster 5	Cluster 6	Cluster 7
0XFFFFFF0F	**0X08000000**	**0XFFFFFF0F**	**0X09000000**
Cluster 8	Cluster 9	Cluster 10	Cluster 11
0X0A000000	**0X0B000000**	**0XFFFFFF0F**	**0XFFFFFF0F**

During the deletion process, nothing happens to the contents in the data area, clusters 3 and 6. However, since the references to clusters 3 and 6 are zeroed, this indicates that these clusters are available when a new file is created or copied. The file system has a pointer system for selecting the next available cluster. This pointer continues to work down through the FAT finding available clusters, and will cycle back around to the beginning of the FAT once it reaches the end.[2] Predicting which cluster is to be used next or how long a cluster will remain available is a very difficult task. A common question asked of forensic examiners is "how long before a deleted file gets overwritten?" The answer is dependent on so many factors, such as frequency of computer usage and type of usage. If someone deletes a file and never adds any data, then the file may never get overwritten; however, if the drive is nearly full and the person actively surfs the web on a daily basis, then the file could get overwritten almost instantaneously. If we continue the process of deleting all the files, then the result would be:

Root Directory

Name	**Size**	**Starting Cluster**	**# of Clusters**
σILE1.TXT	5000	3	5000/4096 = 1.22 (2)
σODO.DOC	786	4	786/4096 = 0.19 (1)
σICS.JPG	11525	5	11525/4096 = 2.81 (3)
σUDGET.XLS	8193	7	8193/4096 = 2.01 (3)

Media Descriptor	Reserved	Cluster 2	Cluster 3
0XF8FFFF0F	**0XFFFFFFFF**	**0XFFFFFF0F**	**0X06000000**
Cluster 4	Cluster 5	Cluster 6	Cluster 7
0X00000000	**0X00000000**	**0X00000000**	**0X00000000**
Cluster 8	Cluster 9	Cluster 10	Cluster 11
0X00000000	**0X00000000**	**0X00000000**	**0X00000000**

Deleting all the files has an effect similar to re-formatting the drive, except the directory entries are still mostly intact when a file is deleted. This is what makes the recovery possible.

FOLLOW ALONG EXERCISE

Plug in a USB flash drive, preferably into a Windows 7 system.

Format the drive with a FAT32 file system and uncheck the Quick Format (using a small USB drive will make this go faster). The intent is to wipe the contents of the drive so we are starting with known data (zeroes). Set the allocation unit size to 2048 before starting the format process. An allocation unit is the same as the cluster size.

From the Chapter 8 Files folder, check the properties of LITTLE.TXT to determine the file size.

Using the allocation size set when formatting the USB drive, determine how many clusters are needed for each file.

LITTLE.TXT	4095 Bytes	2 Clusters

Copy LITTLE.TXT to the USB drive.

Open FTK Imager and add the USB drive as evidence. Highlight FAT1 and view in hex. Note that references for clusters 3 and 4 are allocated.

Click on the Root directory and note the LITTLE.TXT file name.

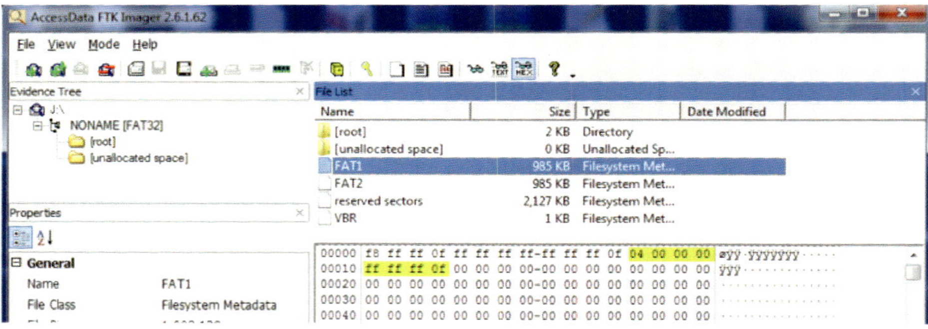

Next open the USB drive in Windows Explorer and delete LITTLE.TXT (hold the shift key while selecting delete).

Go back to FTK Imager and re-add the USB drive. Go to the Root directory and view the name. Notice the first character is changed to a hex 0xE5. FTK Imager displays an exclamation point, but in ASCII it is a sigma character.

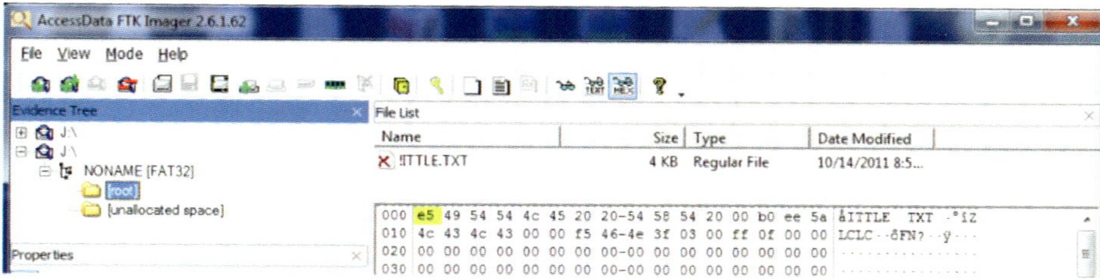

View FAT1 and note that the references for clusters 3 and 4 are now all zeroes.

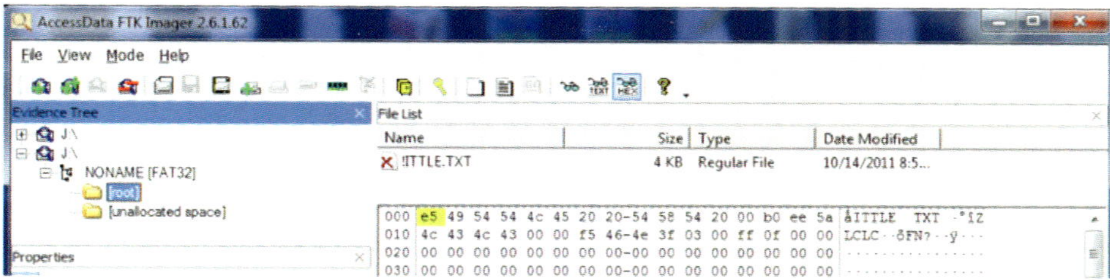

Now let's reverse the process and recover the deleted files. Since FTK Imager does not allow hex editing, we have to use a hex editor. We have used HxD in the past for making changes; however, this tool does have a current limitation if using it under Windows Vista or above (7/8). For these versions of Windows, there is a protection against direct access to media that HxD, cannot overcome.[3] Windows XP does not have this protection and we can use HxD to edit to recover the file in place. Due to this limitation of HxD a new hex editor will be introduced. This tool is named Active@ Disk Editor and will allow direct access to the drives. This tool also has some advanced features that will be useful when we explore the NTFS file system. The editor can be downloaded at ***www.disk-editor.org***. Another great advantage of this tool is that it is free.

This tool will work in a similar manner to the other hex editors/viewers we have used. Start by opening the drive; in this case we will open the USB flash drive volume.

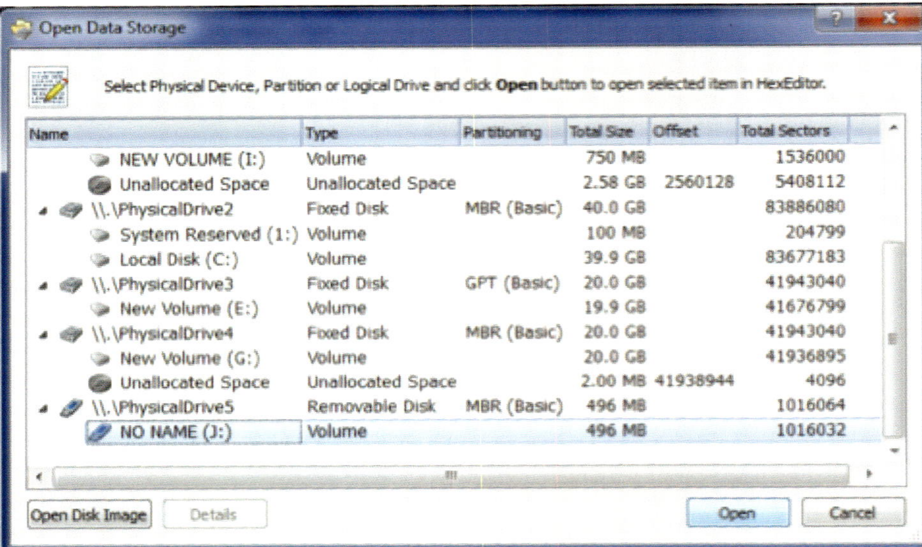

This will take you to the VBR. If this were an actual case, you would want to start here to determine how many sectors per cluster from offset 13. In our case, we already know our cluster size is 2048 bytes and that LITTLE.TXT needs 2 clusters. Again, if this were a real forensic analysis, we would go to the directory listing for the deleted file and note the file size. From the size, we determine how many clusters are needed.

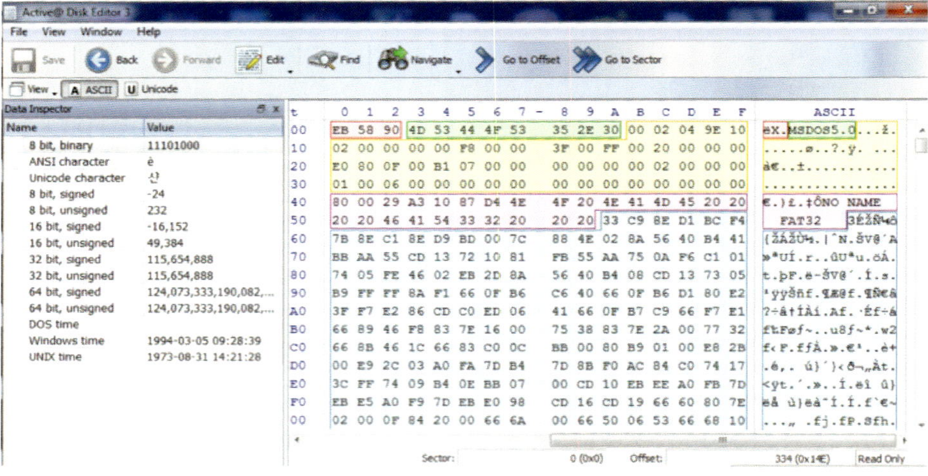

Notice the color-coding automatically added by the editor. It recognizes that the VBR is being displayed and breaks down some of the features. In order to recover our delete file we need to go to the Root Directory to begin so we can get the starting cluster number.

As we saw in Chapter 6, we can get the Root Directory location from the VBR by adding the reserved sectors from offsets 14-15 plus (number of sectors per FAT X 2) from offsets 36-39. These values can be obtained from Active@ Disk Editor directly as there is a built-in hex interpreter like with FTK Imager. With this tool, you will highlight the first byte in the group and use the interpreted value that is appropriate. For example, for the reserved sectors at offsets 14-15, highlight byte 14. Since this is a two-byte value that makes it 16 bits.

Use the 16-bit, unsigned value in the interpreter pane because there cannot be a negative number of sectors.

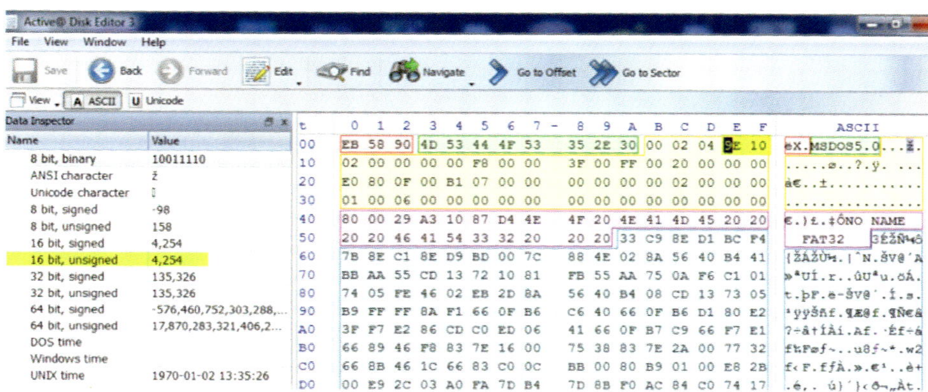

0x9E10 or 0x109E Little Endian equals 4254

Offsets 36-39 are a 32-bit, unsigned value 0x000007B1 in Little Endian equaling 1969

4254 + (1969x2) = sector 8192

You can also add the drive to FTK Imager, highlight the [Root], and note the sector number, but that would not be half as fun.

In the upper right, click on Go to Sector and enter 8192.

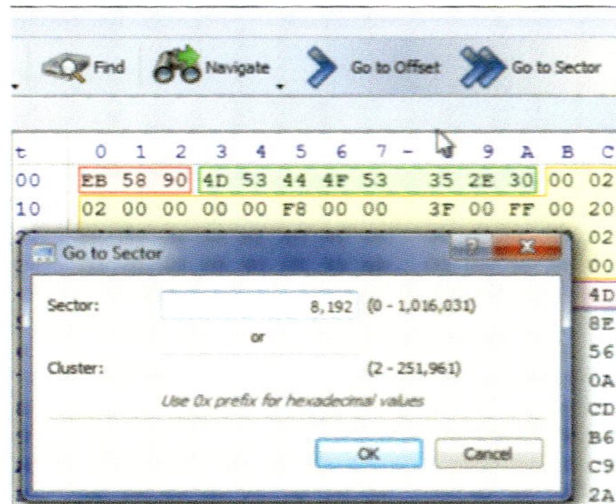

t	0	1	2	3	4	5	6	7	8	9	A	B	C	D	E	F	ASCII
00	E5	49	54	54	4C	45	20	20	54	58	54	20	00	80	DA	51	åITTLE TXT .€ÚQ
10	4F	43	4F	43	00	00	F5	46	4E	3F	03	00	FF	0F	00	00	OCOC..õFN?..ÿ...

We will obtain the starting cluster from offsets 26-27 of the directory entry. In this case, it is as we saw when copying the file, cluster 3. The first character has been changed to 0xE5. This is the first change that is needed. We know that the first character was "L", but in real cases, you will not know on short filenames what the original character was and it is best not to guess. For example, in a murder case you find a file σill.doc, it would be nice to change the character to K, but that might be considered prejudicial. You can change it to any valid character, but the forensic standard is to use an underscore "_." This character is typically not found in filenames and months after the case is worked, you will be able to look at it and see that this is a file you recovered.

To make the change, right click and select the Allow Edit Content option at the bottom. In the ASCII pane, change the first character to "_" and click on save in the upper left.

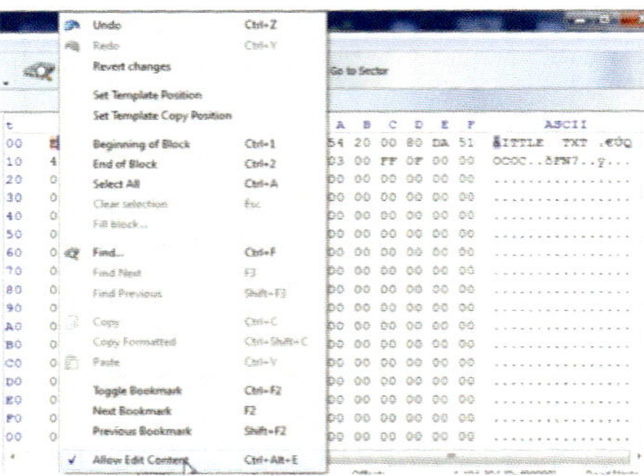

The File Allocation Table must now be altered to link the clusters. From above we already have the number of reserved sectors needed to find the beginning of the FAT, in this case it is 4254. Go to sector 4254.

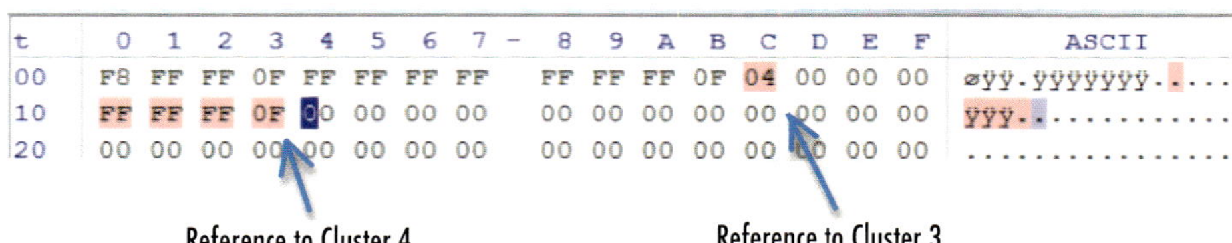

t	0	1	2	3	4	5	6	7	8	9	A	B	C	D	E	F	ASCII
00	F8	FF	FF	0F	FF	FF	FF	FF	FF	FF	FF	0F	04	00	00	00	øÿÿ.ÿÿÿÿÿÿÿ.....
10	FF	FF	FF	0F	00	00	00	00	00	00	00	00	00	00	00	00	ÿÿÿ.............
20	00	00	00	00	00	00	00	00	00	00	00	00	00	00	00	00	....

Change the Reference to cluster 3 to point to cluster 4 (0x04 00 00 00).

Change the Reference to cluster 4 to an End of File Marker (0xFF FF FF 0F).

These changes need to be repeated in the second copy of the FAT. Add reserved sectors to the number of sectors per FAT (4254+1969 = 6223). Make sure to save your changes. Exit Active@ Disk Editor.

You should now be able to open the recovered file from Windows Explorer.

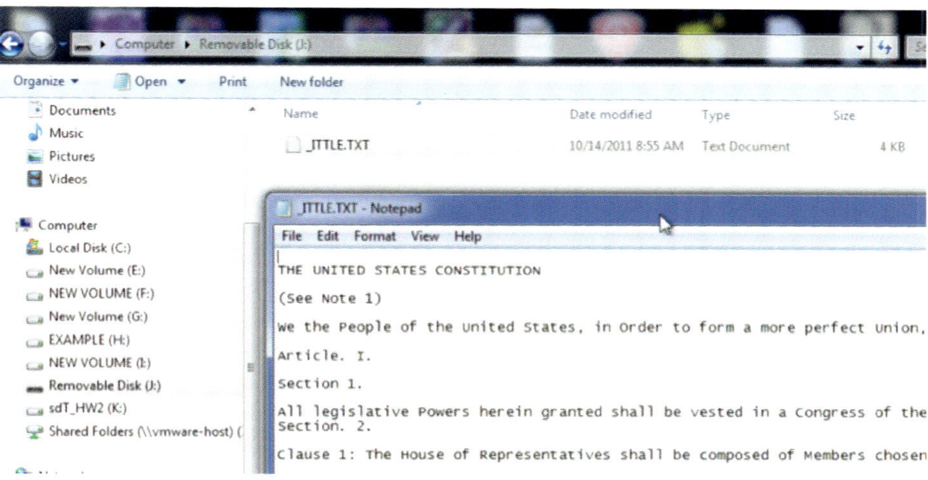

PRACTICAL EXERCISE 1

In the Chapter 8 Files folder check the properties on MEDIUM.TXT and BIGFILE.TXT.

What is the file size of MEDIUM.TXT?

Using the value of 2048 bytes per cluster, how many clusters will MEDIUM.TXT need?

What is the file size of BIGFILE.TXT?

Using the value of 2048 bytes per cluster, how many clusters will BIGFILE.TXT need?

Copy MEDIUM.TXT and BIGFILE.TXT to your USB flash drive.

Delete _ITTLE.TXT, MEDIUM.TXT and BIGFILE.TXT

Use Active@ Disk Editor to recover the three files.

List the clusters utilized for each file:

LITTLE.TXT

MEDIUM.TXT

BIGFILE.TXT

Recovering Fragmented Files

Recovering contiguous files is fairly straightforward and automated tools can easily restore these, but fragmented files can be more of a challenge because only the first cluster is known for sure. Analyzing the content will be necessary in order to determine which clusters go with which files.

For example, let's use a cluster size of 20 bytes.

File1.txt	35 bytes	Starting cluster of 3
File2.txt	3 bytes	Starting cluster of 4

Contents of cluster 3

12345678901234567890

Contents of cluster 4

ABC

Contents of cluster 5

ABCDEFGHIJKLMNO

Contents of cluster 6

123456789012345

Viewing the contents will show that most likely File1.txt uses clusters 3 and 6, but we cannot say absolutely in this case. In files such as pictures where the contents are dependent on each other to properly display, then it can be determined exactly which clusters go together.

PRACTICAL EXERCISE 2

UnZip and Open FRAGMENT.001 in a hex editor (HxD or Active@ Disk Editor)

How many sectors per cluster are there?

How many bytes per cluster are there?

How many reserved sectors are there?

How many sectors are there per FAT?

What sector does the Root Directory start in?

Recover the 10 files and list the clusters needed.

Filename **List the clusters**

Recovering Long Filenames

Previously, we looked at the recovery of short filenames and the issue with not knowing the first character of the name. With long filenames this issue does not exist. The first character of each entry in the directory is still replaced with 0xE5 but the first character is not a letter.

Name	Size	Type	Date Modified
Criminal-Defense-Cha...	78 KB	Regular File	9/26/2012 1:38:...

```
000 e5 66 00 00 00 ff ff ff-ff ff ff 0f 00 5e ff ff åf···ÿÿÿÿÿÿ··^ÿÿ
010 ff ff ff ff ff ff ff ff-ff ff 00 00 ff ff ff ff ÿÿÿÿÿÿÿÿÿÿ··ÿÿÿÿ
020 e5 2d 00 46 00 6f 00 72-00 65 00 0f 00 5e 6e 00 å-·F·o·r·e···^n·
030 73 00 69 00 63 00 73 00-2e 00 00 00 70 00 64 00 s·i·c·s·.···p·d·
040 e5 73 00 2d 00 69 00 6e-00 2d 00 0f 00 5e 43 00 ås·-·i·n·-···^C·
050 6f 00 6d 00 70 00 75 00-74 00 00 00 65 00 72 00 o·m·p·u·t···e·r·
060 e5 6e 00 73 00 65 00 2d-00 43 00 0f 00 5e 68 00 ån·s·e·-·C···^h·
070 61 00 6c 00 6c 00 65 00-6e 00 00 00 67 00 65 00 a·l·l·e·n···g·e·
080 e5 43 00 72 00 69 00 6d-00 69 00 0f 00 5e 6e 00 åC·r·i·m·i···^n·
090 61 00 6c 00 2d 00 44 00-65 00 00 00 66 00 65 00 a·l·-·D·e···f·e·
0a0 e5 52 49 4d 49 4e 7e 31-50 44 46 20 00 33 f0 9a åRIMIN~1PDF ·3ð·
0b0 4f 43 4f 43 00 00 c6 6c-3a 41 03 00 15 35 01 00 OCOC··Æl:A···5··
```

As a reminder of Chapter 6 and the Long Filename, the first character of the LFN entry is the sequence number (01, 02, 03, 04, 45). The full name is preserved in the LFN. For recovery purposes, the SFN can be fully recovered. The LFN sequence numbers can be replaced.

Name	Size	Type	Date Modified
Criminal-Defense-Cha...	78 KB	Regular File	9/26/2012 1:38:...

```
000 45 66 00 00 00 ff ff ff-ff ff ff 0f 00 5e ff ff Ef···ÿÿÿÿÿÿ··^ÿÿ
010 ff ff ff ff ff ff ff ff-ff ff 00 00 ff ff ff ff ÿÿÿÿÿÿÿÿÿÿ··ÿÿÿÿ
020 04 2d 00 46 00 6f 00 72-00 65 00 0f 00 5e 6e 00 ·-·F·o·r·e···^n·
030 73 00 69 00 63 00 73 00-2e 00 00 00 70 00 64 00 s·i·c·s·.···p·d·
040 03 73 00 2d 00 69 00 6e-00 2d 00 0f 00 5e 43 00 ·s·-·i·n·-···^C·
050 6f 00 6d 00 70 00 75 00-74 00 00 00 65 00 72 00 o·m·p·u·t···e·r·
060 02 6e 00 73 00 65 00 2d-00 43 00 0f 00 5e 68 00 ·n·s·e·-·C···^h·
070 61 00 6c 00 6c 00 65 00-6e 00 00 00 67 00 65 00 a·l·l·e·n···g·e·
080 01 43 00 72 00 69 00 6d-00 69 00 0f 00 5e 6e 00 ·C·r·i·m·i···^n·
090 61 00 6c 00 2d 00 44 00-65 00 00 00 66 00 65 00 a·l·-·D·e···f·e·
0a0 43 52 49 4d 49 4e 7e 31-50 44 46 20 00 33 f0 9a CRIMIN~1PDF ·3ð·
0b0 4f 43 4f 43 00 00 c6 6c-3a 41 03 00 15 35 01 00 OCOC··Æl:A···5··
```

PRACTICAL EXERCISE 3

UnZip and Open DEL_LFN.001 in a hex editor (HxD or Active@ Editor)

How many sectors per cluster are there?

How many bytes per cluster are there?

How many reserved sectors are there?

How many sectors are there per FAT?

What sector does the Root Directory start in?

Recover the 10 files and list the sequence numbers needed. Save your changes to the Root Directory, FAT1 and FAT2

Filename	**List sequence numbers**

Exit out of your hex editor and open the image in FTK Imager.

Select File>Image Mounting

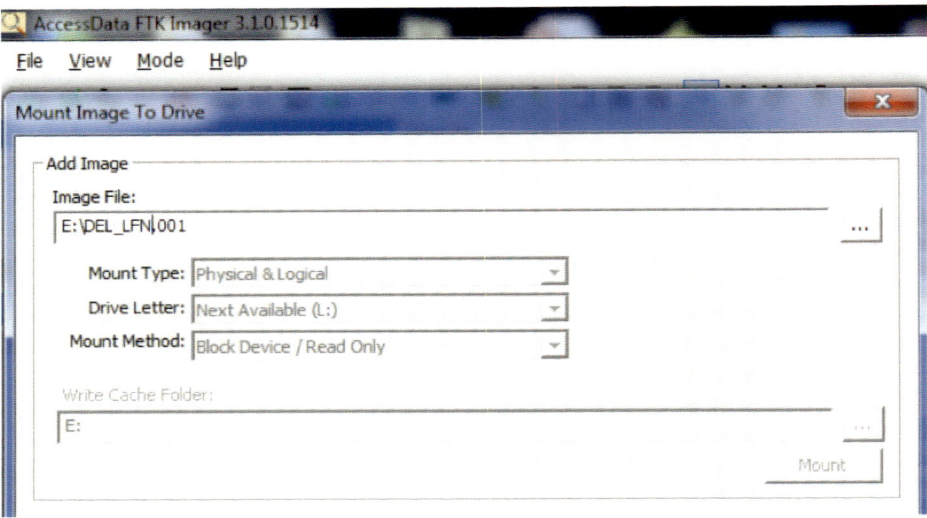

This will mount the image in such a way that you can access the files from Windows Explorer. Open each of the recovered files and describe the contents.

RECOVERING FILES FROM A FORMATTED DRIVE

As presented earlier, when the disk is formatted the Root Directory and the File Allocation Table are zeroed out. The data is still available, but there is no longer a filename, file size and/or starting cluster, unless there is a recoverable subfolder that lists the files. This makes recovery more challenging. The process will require identifying file headers; remember this from Chapter 2. Below is a list of a few common file headers from ***www.filesignatures.net:***

Extension	Header (signature) (Hex)	Associated Program
DOC	D0 CF 11 E0 A1 B1 1A E1 00	Microsoft Office
EML	46 72 6F 6D	Generic Email
EXE	4D 5A	Windows Executable
GIF	47 49 46 38	Graphic Interchange Format
JPG	FF D8 FF E0	JPEG Graphics Format
MOV	73 6B 69 70	Quicktime Movie
PDF	25 50 44 46	Adobe Acrobat
ZIP	50 4B 07 08	PK Zip File

You can use the hex editor to search for either the ASCII or Hex values. This will provide the starting cluster; however, the size of the file is still unknown. This will require examining the cluster data and matching up the data. As noted previously, contiguous files are fairly easy to recover, but fragmented files may not be fully identified.

Some files, such as JPG images, have end of file markers at the end, 0xFF D9.

Besides identifying the clusters, the directory structure needs to be recreated as well. The entire 32 bytes do not need to be entered, but a name with extension (offsets 0-10), starting cluster (offsets 26-27) and size (offsets 28-31).

PRACTICAL EXERCISE 4

Open the image file Format.001 and recover six contiguous files.

Mount the image in FTK Imager and open each recovered file and provide the following information on each file.

Filename and extension	Clusters used	File Size	Description

PRACTICAL EXERCISE 5 – Recovering pictures

FATtleship - Go around the room and have each student select a cluster to recover five files that may or may not be contiguous. The files are 6, 5, 4, 3, and 2 clusters in length.

The instructor will call out "Hit!" or "Miss!"

		2	3	4	5	6	7	8	9	A	B
C	D	E	F	10	11	12	13	14	15	16	17
18	19	1A	1B	1C	1D	1E	1F	20	21	22	23
24	25	26	27	28	29	2A	2B	2C	2D	2E	2F
30	31	32	33	34	35	36	37	38	39	3A	3B
3C	3D	3E	3F	40	41	42	43	44	45	46	47
48	49	4A	4B	4C	4D	4E	4F	50	51	52	53
54	55	56	57	58	59	5A	5B	5C	5D	5E	5F
60	61	62	63	64	65	66	67	68	69	6A	6B
6C	6D	6E	6F	70	71	72	73	74	75	76	77
78	79	7A	7B	7C	7D	7E	7F	80	81	82	83

Once all five files have been identified, open FATSHIP.001, recover each picture, mount the image, and describe the contents of each picture.

File 1 (6 clusters)

File 2 (5 clusters)

File 3 (4 clusters)

File 4 (3 clusters)

File 5 (2 clusters)

CHAPTER SUMMARY

When files are deleted the first character of the short file name is replaced with 0xE5 and the cluster references in both copies of the FAT are zeroed. The data area is not altered. This allows files to be recovered.

The recovery process:

1. Change the first character of each of the directory entries (SFN and LFN).

2. Change the FAT cluster references to point to the required numbers and an End of File Marker in the last reference. Make the changes in both copies of the FAT.

If there is only a short filename, then the original first character is unknown and the convention is to use "_." If there is a long filename, then the first character can be identified. The sequence numbers need to be replaced in the LFN.

The starting cluster is available in the directory entry.

The VBR has the number of sectors per cluster, which can be used to calculate the bytes per cluster. Using the file size from the directory entry, the number of needed clusters can be determined.

If the file originally had contiguous clusters, then the recovery can be straightforward. Fragmented files can be difficult to recover, as only the starting cluster is known.

If the volume has been formatted, then the Root Directory and the FAT are zeroed out. The recovery process involves identifying file signatures and the related clusters.

AT HOME EXERCISE

1. Open Del_HW1.001 – contiguous clusters

How many sectors per cluster are there?

How many bytes per cluster are there?

Recover the deleted files, then mount the image in FTK Imager.

Filename	Size	Clusters	Describe the contents

2. Open Del_HW2.001 – fragmented clusters (verify the contents to see if there consistent)

How many sectors per cluster are there?

How many bytes per cluster are there?

Recover the deleted files, then mount the image in FTK Imager.

Filename	**Size**	**Clusters**	**Describe the contents**

ADVANCED EXERCISE

3. Open Del_HW3.001 – advanced formatting and fragmented clusters.

Recover the five photos from the FATTLESHIP game.
(hint: only focus on clusters 2-35)

How many sectors per cluster are there?

How many bytes per cluster are there?

Recover the deleted files, then mount the image in FTK Imager.

Filename	**Size**	**Clusters**	**Describe the contents**

REFERENCES

1. Sammes, T., & Jenkinson, B. (2007). *Forensic Computing, a Practitioner's Guide.* (2nd ed., pp. 198-199). London: Springer Publishing.

2. Munegowda, K., Rugal, G., & Manikandan, V. (2013). *Cluster Allocation Strategies of the exFAT and FAT File System: a Comparative Study in Embedded Storage Systems.*

3. *Changes to the File System and to the Storage Stack to Restrict Direct Disk Access and Direct Volume Access in Windows Vista and in Windows Server 2008.* (n.d.). Retrieved from http://support.microsoft.com/kb/942448.

4. *Detect EOF for JPG Images.* (n.d.). Retrieved from http://stackoverflow.com/questions/4585527/detect-eof-for-jpg-images.

09 FILE SYSTEMS: NTFS PART I

New Technology File System

NTFS
New Technology File System introduced by Microsoft in 1993.

POSIX
Portable Operating System Interface is a standard for operating systems to be compatible with Unix.

In 1993, Microsoft released a new file system utilized by Windows NT[1]. This operating system provided many features not available in DOS and was intended to comply with the POSIX (Portable Operating System Interface for Unix) standard, which is accepted by ISO and ANSI[2]. The POSIX standard is designed for operating systems, but in order to incorporate some of the features, the file system must allow for them. For example, one of the features is the ability to differentiate between file names of the same letters but opposite cases[3] , such as:

TEST.TXT versus test.txt

In FAT, these would be considered the same filename and could not both exist in the same directory.

Another feature in the standard is to allow one file to have more than one filename[3]. These multiple names are referred to as Hard Links and will be discussed in more detail in the next chapter.

The current version of NTFS is 3.1, which was introduced with Windows XP and has remained the same throughout the iterations of Windows since that time[4]. At the time of this writing, Windows 8 is still running on NTFS 3.1. This file system is extremely complex with respect to the FAT File System and cannot be fully covered in a few chapters; however, we will cover the fundamentals of file creation and tracking.

Comparison between FAT and NTFS

As a reminder, under the FAT File System there are two areas: the system area and the data area. Files are stored in the data area. The system area has the Volume Boot Record and two copies of the File Allocation Table.

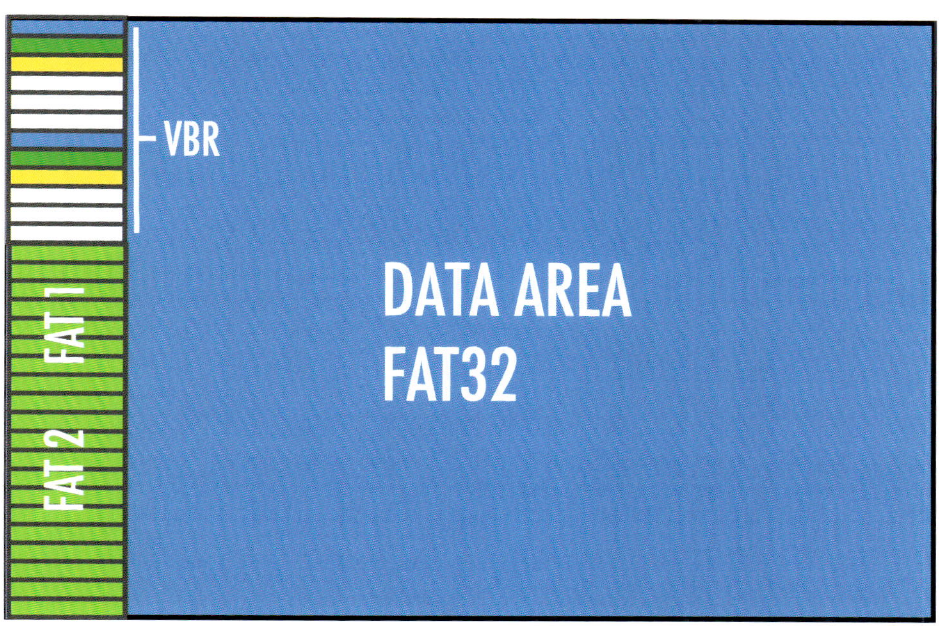

Under NTFS, there is only a data area and no system area. The system-related information is stored in files. Information such as that found in the Volume Boot Record is contained in a file.

Additional Comparison of NTFS and FAT32[5]

	NTFS	FAT32
Maximum Files	Unlimited	4194304
Maximum File Size	Size of Volume	Approx. 4 GB
Starting Cluster	0	2
Boot Record Location/Backup	0, last sector in the volume	0, 6
Cluster Size 32-64MB drive	4K	512 bytes
Cluster Size 64-128MB drive	4K	1K
Cluster Size 128-256MB drive	4K	2K
Cluster Size 256MB-8GB drive	4K	4K
Cluster Size 8-16GB Drive	4K	8K
Cluster Size 16-32GB Drive	4K	16K
Cluster Size 32-2TB Drive	4K	32K

Metadata Files
A set of NTFS system files, most of which start with $.

$MFT
The Master File Table is a system metadata file, which is considered to be the center of the file system.

Attribute – In relation to NTFS file system, an attribute is a description of a feature of a file, such as its name or content.

System Information

As stated, the system information is stored in files instead of specific areas on the volume. These files are created when the volume is formatted and are referred to as ***metadata files.*** These special files are hidden from view of the user, but are present in the root of every NTFS volume.

There are at least 15 metadata files that are created[6].

Note a newly-formatted NTFS volume as displayed by Windows Explorer.

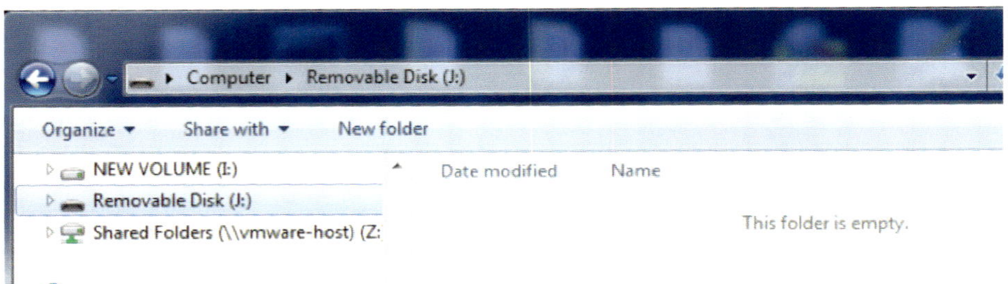

The same volume below using FTK Imager.

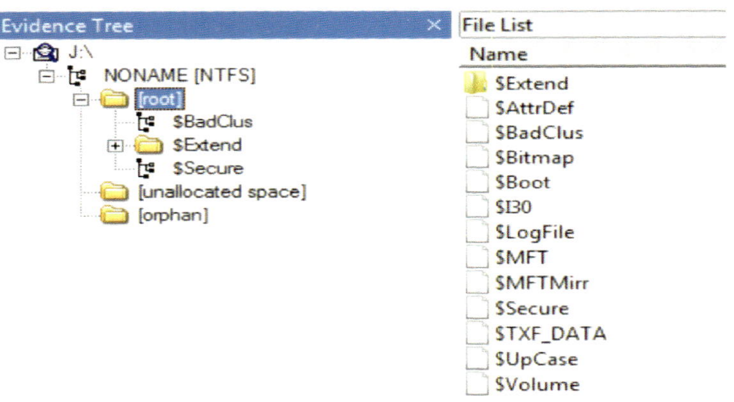

The $Extend folder also contains metadata files.

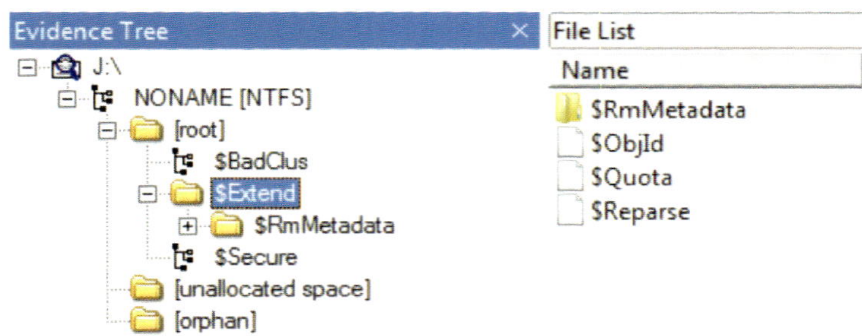

$MFT – This is the Master File Table and the essential file of the NTFS file system.

The $MFT is a relational database that has data on every file on the volume, including the $MFT itself[7]. The database is made up of 1024-byte records and there is at least one record for each file and folder. The first twelve records are reserved for metadata files (records 0-11) and records 12-15 are reserved for some future metadata files. The first record (record 0) is for the $MFT itself. The $MFT is set as 12.5% of the volume and the clusters assigned to file are near the middle of the volume and not the beginning of the volume[8]. The next three chapters will go into more detail about $MFT records.

$MFTMIRR – This is a backup of the first four records of the $MFT[9].

These four records are always for the following files:

Record 0 - $MFT
Record 1 - $MFTMIRR
Record 2 - $LOGFILE
Record 3 - $VOLUME

$LOGFILE – The $Logfile is a transactional database that records changes to a file system and can be utilized if a "rollback" is needed. Essentially, this provides an "Undo" feature to the file system. The $Logfile can provide forensic evidence of the test creation, renaming, and moving of files[10].

Below is a view inside the $Logfile after the creation of the file TEST.TXT. While all this information surrounding the file may seem undecipherable, it should become clear after the next two chapters.

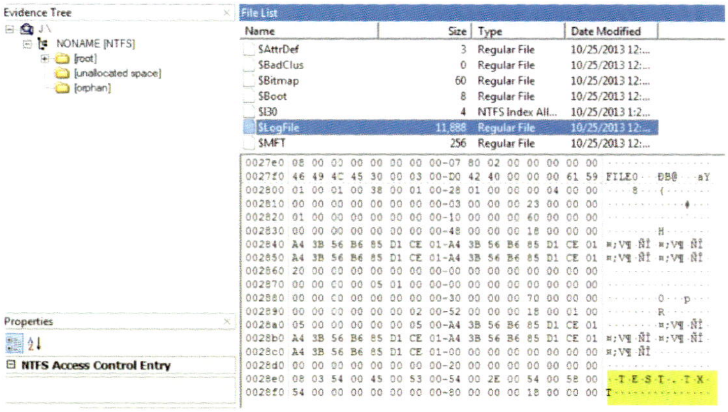

$VOLUME – This file not only has the volume name, but also has the version of the file system. This is where it is verified that Windows 8 is still running the same version as Windows XP. This file contains a setting for the state of the volume. If there was an application problem during shutdown or a hardware problem requiring Checkdisk to be run on startup, there is a setting referred to as a "Dirty Bit" set in $Volume[11]. When the system starts up, it checks this bit and will run corrective action is needed.

Attribute
In relation to NTFS file system, an attribute is a description of a feature of a file, such as its name or content.

$ATTRDEF – Files are made of a series of ***attributes***, which will be discussed in greater detail in the next chapter. These attributes are not like those discussed with the FAT Directory structure. This metadata file contains the definitions of each of the available attributes[12]. The definitions can change with different versions of NTFS.

Below is a listing of the current definitions in NTFS version 3.1[13].

Attribute Header (Hex)	Description
10 00 00 00	Standard Information
20 00 00 00	Attribute List
30 00 00 00	Filename
40 00 00 00	Object Identifier
50 00 00 00	Security Descriptor
60 00 00 00	Volume Name
70 00 00 00	Volume Information
80 00 00 00	Data
90 00 00 00	Index Root
a0 00 00 00	Index Allocation
b0 00 00 00	Bitmap
c0 00 00 00	SymbolicLink/Reparse Point
d0 00 00 00	EA Information
e0 00 00 00	EA
00 01 00 00	Logged Utility Stream

The . is the Root Directory. As stated above, everything on the volume is a file, including the Root Directory.

$Bitmap – This file tracks the cluster usage of the volume. Each bit in the file (not bytes) represents a cluster. A "0" represents an unused cluster and a "1" represents an allocated cluster. This is somewhat similar to the File Allocation Table with the exception that there is no linkage between the clusters. The $Bitmap only tracks allocation. When a file is deleted the bit is flipped from a 1 to a 0.

Example:

File1.txt	clusters 0 - 4
File2.txt	clusters 6 - 7
File3.txt	clusters 8 - 15
File4.txt	cluster 16

$Bitmap Contents

```
7 6 5 4 3 2 1 0 15 14 13 12 11 10 9 8  23 22 21 20 19 18 17 16
1 1 0 1 1 1 1 1  1  1  1  1  1  1 1 1   0  0  0  0  0  0  0  1
      DF                 FF                       01
```

In order to identify a specific cluster in the $Bitmap, take the offset byte and multiply by 8.

FF FF FF FF FF FF FF AC FF FF FF FF FF

Notice AC is at offset 7. This byte covers clusters 56-63 (10101100). Clusters 56, 58, 60 and 61 are allocated.

$Boot – This is the Volume Boot Record information and can be up to 16 sectors in length[14]. This information is located in sector 0 as we saw in the FAT file system. There is a backup copy of the first sector of the $Boot located in the last sector of the volume. This means the first and last sectors of the volume are identical.

The information contained in the $Boot can be used to recover deleted partitions in the same manner that we saw in FAT. For MBR partitions, the partition type for NTFS is 0x07.

Below is the breakdown of the $Boot[14].

DEC OFFSET	HEX OFFSET	SIZE (BYTES)	DESCRIPTION
0	0x00	3	Jump Instruction
3	0x03	8	OEM ID
11	0x0B	2	Bytes Per Sector – normally 512 bytes (0x00 02)
13	0x0D	1	Sectors Per Cluster
14	0x0E	2	Reserved sectors – always zero in NTFS
16	0x10	5	Values must be 0x00
21	0x15	1	Media Descriptor
22	0x16	2	Values must be 0x00
24	0x18	8	Not used and not checked by NTFS
32	0x20	4	Values must be 0x00
36	0x24	4	Not used by NTFS
40	0x28	8	Total Sectors in the Volume
48	0x30	8	Logical Starting Cluster # for the $MFT
56	0x38	8	Logical Starting Cluster # for the $MFTMirr
64	0x40	1	Clusters Per $MFT Record
65	0x41	3	Not used by NTFS
68	0x44	1	Clusters Per Index Buffer
69	0x45	3	Not used by NTFS
72	0x48	8	Volume Serial Number
80	0x50	4	Not used by NTFS
84	0x54	426	Bootstrap Code
510	0x01FE	42	End of Sector marker (0x55 AA)

We will parse through the $Boot as we did with the FAT VBR.

```
0000 EB 52 90 4E 54 46 53 20-20 20 20 00 02 08 00 00 ëR·NTFS    ·····
0010 00 00 00 00 00 F8 00 00-3F 00 FF 00 01 00 00 00 ·····ø··?·ÿ·····
0020 00 00 00 00 80 00 00 00-FE FF 3B 00 00 00 00 00 ········þÿ;·····
0030 FF 7F 02 00 00 00 00 00-02 00 00 00 00 00 00 00 ÿ···············
0040 F6 00 00 00 01 00 00 00-7F 07 C4 34 0E C4 34 C2 ö·········Ä4·Ä4Â
0050 00 00 00 00 FA 33 C0 8E-D0 BC 00 7C FB 68 C0 07 ····ú3À·Ð¼·|ûhÀ·
0060 1F 1E 68 66 00 CB 88 16-0E 00 66 81 3E 03 00 4E ··hf·Ë····f·>··N
0070 54 46 53 75 15 B4 41 BB-AA 55 CD 13 72 0C 81 FB TFSu·´A»ªUÍ·r··û
0080 55 AA 75 06 F7 C1 01 00-75 03 E9 DD 00 1E 83 EC Uªu·÷Á··u·éÝ···ì
0090 18 68 1A 00 B4 48 8A 16-0E 00 8B F4 16 1F CD 13 ·h··´H·····ô··Í·
00a0 9F 83 C4 18 9E 58 1F 72-E1 3B 06 0B 00 75 DB A3 ··Ä··X·rá;···uÛ£
00b0 0F 00 C1 2E 0F 00 04 1E-5A 33 DB B9 00 20 2B C8 ··Á.····Z3Û¹· +È
00c0 66 FF 06 11 00 03 16 0F-00 8E C2 FF 06 16 00 E8 fÿ·······Âÿ···è
00d0 4B 00 2B C8 77 EF B8 00-BB CD 1A 66 23 C0 75 2D K·+Èwï¸·»Í·f#Àu-
00e0 66 81 FB 54 43 50 41 75-24 81 F9 02 01 72 1E 16 f·ûTCPAu$·ù··r··
00f0 68 07 BB 16 68 70 0E 16-68 09 00 66 53 66 53 66 h·»·hp··h··fSfSf
0100 55 16 16 16 68 B8 01 66-61 0E 07 CD 1A 33 C0 BF U···h¸·fa··Í·3À¿
0110 28 10 B9 D8 0F FC F3 AA-E9 5F 01 90 90 66 60 1E (·¹Ø·üóªé_···f`·
0120 06 66 A1 11 00 66 03 06-1C 00 1E 66 68 00 00 00 ·f¡··f·····fh···
0130 00 66 50 06 53 68 01 00-68 10 00 B4 42 8A 16 0E ·fP·Sh··h··´B···
0140 00 16 1F 8B F4 CD 13 66-59 5B 5A 66 59 66 59 1F ····ôÍ·fY[ZfYfY·
0150 0F 82 16 00 66 FF 06 11-00 03 16 0F 00 8E C2 FF ····fÿ········Âÿ
0160 0E 16 00 75 BC 07 1F 66-61 C3 A0 F8 01 E8 09 00 ···u¼··faÃ ø·è··
0170 A0 FB 01 E8 03 00 F4 EB-FD B4 01 8B F0 AC 3C 00  û·è··ôëý´··ð¬<·
0180 74 09 B4 0E BB 07 00 CD-10 EB F2 C3 0D 0A 41 20 t·´·»··Í·ëòÃ··A 
0190 64 69 73 6B 20 72 65 61-64 20 65 72 72 6F 72 20 disk read error 
01a0 6F 63 63 75 72 72 65 64-00 0D 0A 42 4F 4F 54 4D occurred···BOOTM
01b0 47 52 20 69 73 20 6D 69-73 73 69 6E 67 00 0D 0A GR is missing···
01c0 42 4F 4F 54 4D 47 52 20-69 73 20 63 6F 6D 70 72 BOOTMGR is compr
01d0 65 73 73 65 64 00 0D 0A-50 72 65 73 73 20 43 74 essed···Press Ct
01e0 72 6C 2B 41 6C 74 2B 44-65 6C 20 74 6F 20 72 65 rl+Alt+Del to re
01f0 73 74 61 72 74 0D 0A 00-8C A9 BE D6 00 00 55 AA start···©¾Ö··Uª
```

The first three bytes (decimal offsets 0-2) are jump code to directing the system pointer to bootstrap code.

```
0000 EB 52 90 4E 54 46 53 20-20 20 20 00 02 08 00 00 ëR·NTFS    ·····
0010 00 00 00 00 00 F8 00 00-3F 00 FF 00 01 00 00 00 ·····ø··?·ÿ·····
0020 00 00 00 00 80 00 00 00-FE FF 3B 00 00 00 00 00 ········þÿ;·····
0030 FF 7F 02 00 00 00 00 00-02 00 00 00 00 00 00 00 ÿ···············
0040 F6 00 00 00 01 00 00 00-7F 07 C4 34 0E C4 34 C2 ö·········Ä4·Ä4Â
```

Decimal Offsets 3 – 10 contain the Original Equipment Manufacturer (OEM) id and version.

```
0000 EB 52 90 4E 54 46 53 20-20 20 20 00 02 08 00 00 ëR·NTFS    ·····
0010 00 00 00 00 00 F8 00 00-3F 00 FF 00 01 00 00 00 ·····ø··?·ÿ·····
0020 00 00 00 00 80 00 00 00-FE FF 3B 00 00 00 00 00 ········þÿ;·····
0030 FF 7F 02 00 00 00 00 00-02 00 00 00 00 00 00 00 ÿ···············
0040 F6 00 00 00 01 00 00 00-7F 07 C4 34 0E C4 34 C2 ö·········Ä4·Ä4Â
```

Decimal Offsets 11-12 contain the number of bytes per sector. 0x0200 = 512

```
0000 EB 52 90 4E 54 46 53 20-20 20 20 00 02 08 00 00 ëR·NTFS     ·····
0010 00 00 00 00 00 F8 00 00-3F 00 FF 00 01 00 00 00 ·····ø··?·ÿ·····
0020 00 00 00 00 80 00 00 00-FE FF 3B 00 00 00 00 00 ········þÿ;·····
0030 FF 7F 02 00 00 00 00 00-02 00 00 00 00 00 00 00 ÿ···············
0040 F6 00 00 00 01 00 00 00-7F 07 C4 34 0E C4 34 C2 ö·········Ä4·Ä4Â
```

Decimal Offset 13 is the number of sectors per cluster.

```
0000 EB 52 90 4E 54 46 53 20-20 20 20 00 02 08 00 00 ëR·NTFS     ·····
0010 00 00 00 00 00 F8 00 00-3F 00 FF 00 01 00 00 00 ·····ø··?·ÿ·····
0020 00 00 00 00 80 00 00 00-FE FF 3B 00 00 00 00 00 ········þÿ;·····
0030 FF 7F 02 00 00 00 00 00-02 00 00 00 00 00 00 00 ÿ···············
0040 F6 00 00 00 01 00 00 00-7F 07 C4 34 0E C4 34 C2 ö·········Ä4·Ä4Â
```

Decimal Offsets 14 - 20 will be 0's

```
0000 EB 52 90 4E 54 46 53 20-20 20 20 00 02 08 00 00 ëR·NTFS     ·····
0010 00 00 00 00 00 F8 00 00-3F 00 FF 00 01 00 00 00 ·····ø··?·ÿ·····
0020 00 00 00 00 80 00 00 00-FE FF 3B 00 00 00 00 00 ········þÿ;·····
0030 FF 7F 02 00 00 00 00 00-02 00 00 00 00 00 00 00 ÿ···············
0040 F6 00 00 00 01 00 00 00-7F 07 C4 34 0E C4 34 C2 ö·········Ä4·Ä4Â
```

Decimal Offset 21 will be the media descriptor, typically F8.

```
0000 EB 52 90 4E 54 46 53 20-20 20 20 00 02 08 00 00 ëR·NTFS     ·····
0010 00 00 00 00 00 F8 00 00-3F 00 FF 00 01 00 00 00 ·····ø··?·ÿ·····
0020 00 00 00 00 80 00 00 00-FE FF 3B 00 00 00 00 00 ········þÿ;·····
0030 FF 7F 02 00 00 00 00 00-02 00 00 00 00 00 00 00 ÿ···············
0040 F6 00 00 00 01 00 00 00-7F 07 C4 34 0E C4 34 C2 ö·········Ä4·Ä4Â
```

Decimal Offsets 22-39 are either reserved (0's) or the data is not checked and utilized by the file system.

```
0000 EB 52 90 4E 54 46 53 20-20 20 20 00 02 08 00 00 ëR·NTFS     ·····
0010 00 00 00 00 00 F8 00 00-3F 00 FF 00 01 00 00 00 ·····ø··?·ÿ·····
0020 00 00 00 00 80 00 00 00-FE FF 3B 00 00 00 00 00 ········þÿ;·····
0030 FF 7F 02 00 00 00 00 00-02 00 00 00 00 00 00 00 ÿ···············
0040 F6 00 00 00 01 00 00 00-7F 07 C4 34 0E C4 34 C2 ö·········Ä4·Ä4Â
```

Decimal Offsets 40-47 are the total number of sectors in the volume. (0x00 00 00 00 00 3B FF FE = 3932158)

```
0000 EB 52 90 4E 54 46 53 20-20 20 20 00 02 08 00 00 ëR·NTFS     ·····
0010 00 00 00 00 00 F8 00 00-3F 00 FF 00 01 00 00 00 ·····ø··?·ÿ·····
0020 00 00 00 00 80 00 00 00-FE FF 3B 00 00 00 00 00 ········þÿ;·····
0030 FF 7F 02 00 00 00 00 00-02 00 00 00 00 00 00 00 ÿ···············
0040 F6 00 00 00 01 00 00 00-7F 07 C4 34 0E C4 34 C2 ö·········Ä4·Ä4Â
```

v

Decimal Offsets 48-55 are the starting cluster of the $MFT (0x 00 00 00 00 00 02 7F FF = 163839)

```
0000 EB 52 90 4E 54 46 53 20-20 20 20 00 02 08 00 00 ëR·NTFS     ·····
0010 00 00 00 00 00 F8 00 00-3F 00 FF 00 01 00 00 00 ·····ø··?·ÿ·····
0020 00 00 00 00 80 00 00 00-FE FF 3B 00 00 00 00 00 ········þÿ;·····
0030 FF 7F 02 00 00 00 00 00-02 00 00 00 00 00 00 00 ÿ···············
0040 F6 00 00 00 01 00 00 00-7F 07 C4 34 0E C4 34 C2 ö·········Ä4·Ä4Â
```

Decimal Offsets 56-63 are the starting cluster of the $MFTMIRR (0x00 00 00 00 00 00 00 02 = 2)

```
0000 EB 52 90 4E 54 46 53 20-20 20 20 00 02 08 00 00 ëR·NTFS     ·····
0010 00 00 00 00 00 F8 00 00-3F 00 FF 00 01 00 00 00 ·····ø··?·ÿ·····
0020 00 00 00 00 80 00 00 00-FE FF 3B 00 00 00 00 00 ········þÿ;·····
0030 FF 7F 02 00 00 00 00 00-02 00 00 00 00 00 00 00 ÿ···············
0040 F6 00 00 00 01 00 00 00-7F 07 C4 34 0E C4 34 C2 ö·········Ä4·Ä4Â
```

Decimal Offset 64 is the number of clusters or bytes per $MFT record. If the value is positive, then it is the number of clusters value; if the number is negative, then it is 2 raised to the value and the number of bytes. F6 = -10. The value is 2^{10} or 1024 bytes.

```
0000 EB 52 90 4E 54 46 53 20-20 20 20 00 02 08 00 00 ëR·NTFS     ·····
0010 00 00 00 00 00 F8 00 00-3F 00 FF 00 01 00 00 00 ·····ø··?·ÿ·····
0020 00 00 00 00 80 00 00 00-FE FF 3B 00 00 00 00 00 ········þÿ;·····
0030 FF 7F 02 00 00 00 00 00-02 00 00 00 00 00 00 00 ÿ···············
0040 F6 00 00 00 01 00 00 00-7F 07 C4 34 0E C4 34 C2 ö·········Ä4·Ä4Â
```

Decimal Offsets 65-67 are not used

Decimal Offset 68 is the number of clusters or bytes per Index record (directory). If the value is positive, then it is the number of clusters' value; if the number is negative, then it is 2 raised to the value and the number of bytes. In this case there is 1 Cluster, since it is positive.

```
0000 EB 52 90 4E 54 46 53 20-20 20 20 00 02 08 00 00 ëR·NTFS     ·····
0010 00 00 00 00 00 F8 00 00-3F 00 FF 00 01 00 00 00 ·····ø··?·ÿ·····
0020 00 00 00 00 80 00 00 00-FE FF 3B 00 00 00 00 00 ········þÿ;·····
0030 FF 7F 02 00 00 00 00 00-02 00 00 00 00 00 00 00 ÿ···············
0040 F6 00 00 00 01 00 00 00-7F 07 C4 34 0E C4 34 C2 ö·········Ä4·Ä4Â
```

Decimal Offsets 69-71 are not used

Decimal Offsets 72-79 are for the serial number

```
0000 EB 52 90 4E 54 46 53 20-20 20 20 00 02 08 00 00 ëR·NTFS     ·····
0010 00 00 00 00 00 F8 00 00-3F 00 FF 00 01 00 00 00 ·····ø··?·ÿ·····
0020 00 00 00 00 80 00 00 00-FE FF 3B 00 00 00 00 00 ········þÿ;·····
0030 FF 7F 02 00 00 00 00 00-02 00 00 00 00 00 00 00 ÿ···············
0040 F6 00 00 00 01 00 00 00-7F 07 C4 34 0E C4 34 C2 ö·········Ä4·Ä4Â
```

Decimal Offsets 80-82 are unused.

Decimal Offsets 83-509 are boot code.

Decimal Offsets 510-511 are the signature bytes.

```
01b0 47 52 20 69 73 20 6D 69-73 73 69 6E 67 00 0D 0A GR is missing···
01c0 42 4F 4F 54 4D 47 52 20-69 73 20 63 6F 6D 70 72 BOOTMGR is compr
01d0 65 73 73 65 64 00 0D 0A-50 72 65 73 73 20 43 74 essed···Press Ct
01e0 72 6C 2B 41 6C 74 2B 44-65 6C 20 74 6F 20 72 65 rl+Alt+Del to re
01f0 73 74 61 72 74 0D 0A 00-8C A9 BE D6 00 00 55 AA start····©¾Ö··Uª
```

PRACTICAL EXERCISE 1

Viewing the first sector of the $Boot, answer the questions below.

```
000000000 EB 52 90 4E 54 46 53 20-20 20 20 00 02 08 00 00 ëR·NTFS     ·····
000000010 00 00 00 00 00 F8 00 00-3F 00 FF 00 00 08 04 00 ·····ø··?·ÿ·····
000000020 00 00 00 00 80 00 80 00-FF EF 7B 02 00 00 00 00 ········ÿï{·····
000000030 00 00 0C 00 00 00 00 00-02 00 00 00 00 00 00 00 ················
000000040 F6 00 00 00 01 00 00 00-88 86 60 FA C6 60 FA B4 ö·········`úÆ`ú´
000000050 00 00 00 00 FA 33 C0 8E-D0 BC 00 7C FB 68 C0 07 ····ú3À·Ð¼·|ûhÀ·
000000060 1F 1E 68 66 00 CB 88 16-0E 00 66 81 3E 03 00 4E ··hf·Ë····f·>··N
000000070 54 46 53 75 15 B4 41 BB-AA 55 CD 13 72 0C 81 FB TFSu·´A»ªUÍ·r··û
000000080 55 AA 75 06 F7 C1 01 00-75 03 E9 DD 00 1E 83 EC Uªu·÷Á··u·éÝ···ì
000000090 18 68 1A 00 B4 48 8A 16-0E 00 8B F4 16 1F CD 13 ·h··´H·····ô··Í·
0000000a0 9F 83 C4 18 9E 58 1F 72-E1 3B 06 0B 00 75 DB A3 ··Ä··X·rá;···uÛ£
0000000b0 0F 00 C1 2E 0F 00 04 1E-5A 33 DB B9 00 20 2B C8 ··Á.····Z3Û¹· +È
0000000c0 66 FF 06 11 00 03 16 0F-00 8E C2 FF 06 16 00 E8 fÿ········Âÿ···è
0000000d0 4B 00 2B C8 77 EF B8 00-BB CD 1A 66 23 C0 75 2D K·+Èwï¸·»Í·f#Àu-
0000000e0 66 81 FB 54 43 50 41 75-24 81 F9 02 01 72 1E 16 f·ûTCPAu$·ù··r··
0000000f0 68 07 BB 16 68 70 0E 16-68 09 00 66 53 66 53 66 h·»·hp··h··fSfSf
000000100 55 16 16 16 68 B8 01 66-61 0E 07 CD 1A 33 C0 BF U···h¸·fa··Í·3À¿
000000110 28 10 B9 D8 0F FC F3 AA-E9 5F 01 90 90 66 60 1E (·¹Ø·üóªé_···f`·
000000120 06 66 A1 11 00 66 03 06-1C 00 1E 66 68 00 00 00 ·f¡··f·····fh···
000000130 00 66 50 06 53 68 01 00-68 10 00 B4 42 8A 16 0E ·fP·Sh··h··´B···
000000140 00 16 1F 8B F4 CD 13 66-59 5B 5A 66 59 66 59 1F ····ôÍ·fY[ZfYfY·
000000150 0F 82 16 00 66 FF 06 11-00 03 16 0F 00 8E C2 FF ····fÿ········Âÿ
000000160 0E 16 00 75 BC 07 1F 66-61 C3 A0 F8 01 E8 09 00 ···u¼··faà ø·è··
000000170 A0 FB 01 E8 03 00 F4 EB-FD B4 01 8B F0 AC 3C 00  û·è··ôëý´··ð¬<·
000000180 74 09 B4 0E BB 07 00 CD-10 EB F2 C3 0D 0A 41 20 t·´·»··Í·ëòÃ··A 
000000190 64 69 73 6B 20 72 65 61-64 20 65 72 72 6F 72 20 disk read error 
0000001a0 6F 63 63 75 72 72 65 64-00 0D 0A 42 4F 4F 54 4D occurred···BOOTM
0000001b0 47 52 20 69 73 20 6D 69-73 73 69 6E 67 00 0D 0A GR is missing···
0000001c0 42 4F 4F 54 4D 47 52 20-69 73 20 63 6F 6D 70 72 BOOTMGR is compr
0000001d0 65 73 73 65 64 00 0D 0A-50 72 65 73 73 20 43 74 essed···Press Ct
0000001e0 72 6C 2B 41 6C 74 2B 44-65 6C 20 74 6F 20 72 65 rl+Alt+Del to re
0000001f0 73 74 61 72 74 0D 0A 00-8C A9 BE D6 00 00 55 AA start····©¾Ö··Uª
```

What is the OEM version that was used to set up this volume?

How many bytes are there per sector?

How many sectors are there per cluster?

Based upon the previous answer, how many bytes per cluster?

How many sectors are there in the partition?

What cluster does the $MFT start in?

What cluster does the $MFTMIRR start in?

What is the volume serial number?

What is the VBR signature?

PRACTICAL EXERCISE 2

Open 9_Pract2.E01 with FTK Imager and answer the following questions.

How many bytes are there per sector?

How many sectors are there per cluster?

Based upon the previous answer, how many bytes per cluster?

How many sectors are there in the partition?

What cluster does the $MFT start in?

What cluster does the $MFTMIRR start in?

What is the volume serial number?

What is the VBR signature?

What sector is the Backup Boot Record in?

Examine the $Bitmap and list which clusters out of the first 300 are not allocated.

Metadata Files

$Badclus – This file tracks the bad clusters in the same manner as allocated clusters are tracked. The $Badclus is another bitmap that uses 1's for bad clusters. With today's drives, bad clusters are rare, but it only take one sector in the cluster to go bad for the entire cluster to be marked.

$Quota – A feature was added to limit the amount of space on the volume that a user could save data to. The $Quota file has the per-user space limitation. These limitations are applied on a per-volume basis. This feature is off by default and rarely used.

$Secure – This file has the security descriptors for all the files and is tied to the MFT entry with a security ID.

$Upcase – The file handles the system ability to recognize a file independent on whether it is uppercase or lowercase. Searching for readme.doc can return README.DOC and Readme.doc. This is also used for sorting purposes.

$Extend – This is a folder that contains several metadata files, such as the $Quota, $Reparse, $ObjId, and $UsnJrnl.

$ObjId – The file has the GUIDs associated with shortcuts to files. This is part of the link tracking system. If a shortcut is created for a file (such as in the Recent Folder), a GUID is created and used to track and change location on the volume.

$Reparse – Reparse points are managed by this file. A more in=depth discussion on reparse points will be conducted in Chapter 12.

$UsnJrnl – This is the Update Sequence application journal that logs changes to files. The time of the change and the filenames will be located in this log.

These metadata files should be present on all NTFS volumes. Each file will be tracked in the $MFT and will be recorded in the same order. Files are referenced in the $MFT by their record number.

FTK Imager will provide that $MFT record number as part of the properties of any file on a NTFS volume.

Since each record in the $MFT is 1024 bytes, if you know the record number, then multiply that value by 1024 to find the offset within the $MFT. FTK Imager does, however, provide this offset as well.

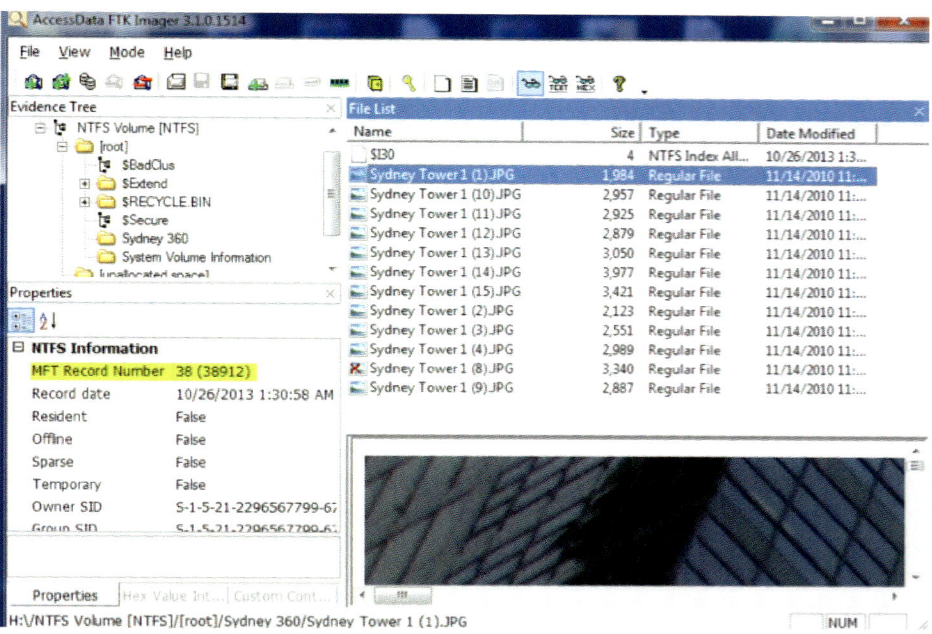

Go to offset 38912 in the $MFT.

```
09800 46 49 4C 45 30 00 03 00-DA 5C 40 00 00 00 00 00 FILE0···Ú\@·····
09810 01 00 02 00 38 00 01 00-E8 01 00 00 04 00 00 ····8···è·······
09820 00 00 00 00 00 00 00 00-04 00 00 00 26 00 00 00 ············&···
09830 03 00 00 00 00 00 00 00-10 00 00 00 60 00 00 00 ············`···
09840 00 00 00 00 00 00 00 00-48 00 00 00 18 00 00 00 ········H·······
09850 43 A0 60 05 EB D1 CE 01-5F C6 18 B1 51 84 CB 01 C `·ëÑÎ·_Æ·±Q·Ë·
09860 06 6E 84 05 EB D1 CE 01-43 A0 60 05 EB D1 CE 01 ·n··ëÑÎ·C `·ëÑÎ·
09870 20 00 00 00 00 00 00 00-00 00 00 00 00 00 00 00  ···············
09880 00 00 00 00 09 01 00 00-00 00 00 00 00 00 00 00 ················
09890 00 00 00 00 00 00 00 00-30 00 00 00 78 00 00 00 ········0···x···
098a0 00 00 00 00 00 00 03 00-5A 00 00 00 18 00 01 00 ········Z·······
098b0 25 00 00 00 00 00 01 00-43 A0 60 05 EB D1 CE 01 %·······C `·ëÑÎ·
098c0 43 A0 60 05 EB D1 CE 01-43 A0 60 05 EB D1 CE 01 C `·ëÑÎ·C `·ëÑÎ·
098d0 43 A0 60 05 EB D1 CE 01-00 00 1F 00 00 00 00 00 C `·ëÑÎ·········
098e0 00 00 00 00 00 00 00 00-20 00 00 00 00 00 00 00 ········ ·······
098f0 0C 02 53 00 59 00 44 00-4E 00 45 00 59 00 7E 00 ··S·Y·D·N·E·Y·~·
09900 31 00 2E 00 4A 00 50 00-47 00 20 00 31 00 20 00 1·.·J·P·G· ·1· ·
09910 30 00 00 00 88 00 00 00-00 00 00 00 00 00 02 00 0···············
09920 6E 00 00 00 18 00 01 00-25 00 00 00 00 00 01 00 n·······%·······
09930 43 A0 60 05 EB D1 CE 01-43 A0 60 05 EB D1 CE 01 C `·ëÑÎ·C `·ëÑÎ·
09940 43 A0 60 05 EB D1 CE 01-43 A0 60 05 EB D1 CE 01 C `·ëÑÎ·C `·ëÑÎ·
09950 00 00 1F 00 00 00 00 00-00 00 00 00 00 00 00 00 ················
09960 20 00 00 00 00 00 00 00-16 01 53 00 79 00 64 00  ·········S·y·d·
09970 6E 00 65 00 79 00 20 00-54 00 6F 00 77 00 65 00 n·e·y· ·T·o·w·e·
09980 72 00 20 00 31 00 20 00-28 00 31 00 29 00 2E 00 r· ·1· ·(·1·)·.·
09990 4A 00 50 00 47 00 00 00-80 00 00 00 48 00 00 00 J·P·G·······H···
099a0 01 00 00 00 00 00 01 00-00 00 00 00 00 00 00 00 ················
099b0 EF 01 00 00 00 00 00 00-40 00 00 00 00 00 00 00 ï·······@·······
099c0 00 00 1F 00 00 00 00 00-79 FD 1E 00 00 00 00 00 ········yý······
099d0 79 FD 1E 00 00 00 00 00-22 F0 01 2D 0A 00 00 00 yý······"ð·-····
099e0 FF FF FF FF 82 79 47 11-00 00 00 00 00 00 00 00 ÿÿÿÿ·yG·········
```

Cursor pos = 38912; clus = 174515; log sec = 1396124

Note that the beginning of the record starts with FILE. We will see this in more detail in the next chapter. The filename Sydney Tower 1 (1).JPG is highlighted to show this is the record we were looking for.

PRACTICAL EXERCISE 3

Use the image file from Practical Exercise 2 and view in FTK Imager.

Provide the filename, $MFT number and $MFT Offset for each file and folder in the image. Remember to go into each folder as well.

CHAPTER SUMMARY

NTFS is much more complex than the FAT file system examined earlier. Everything on the NTFS volume is treated as a file. There is no system area on the volume.

The Master File Table is a relational database that maintains information about every file on the volume. Each file has at least one record in the Master File Table and these records are 1024 bytes in length.

When formatting a NTFS volume, a series of metadata files are created that contain the system information. Most of these metadata files begin with a $. The exception is the Root Directory.

The $Boot file contains the volume boot record information and contains the cluster size and the number of sectors on the volume. This information can be used to recover deleted partitions.

KEY TERMS

NTFS – New Technology File System introduced by Microsoft in 1993.

POSIX – Portable Operating System Interface is a standard for operating systems to be compatible with Unix.

Metadata Files – A set of NTFS system files, most of which start with $.

$MFT – The Master File Table is a system metadata file, which is considered to be the center of the file system.

Attribute – In relation to NTFS file system, an attribute is a description of a feature of a file, such as its name or content.

AT HOME EXERCISE 1

From the $Bitmap:

Starting at offset 400, list the clusters that are not allocated.

FF FF FF FF FF FF FF FF 35 02 FF FF FF FF FF FF FF FE 0F FF FF
FF FF FF FF FF FF FF 46 FF FF FF FF FF FF FF FF FF FF FF 00
FF FF D1 FF FF FF FF FF FF EF

AT HOME EXERCISE 2

Examine image file 9_HW2.001 with HxD or Active@ Disk Editor.

Run a search for NTFS boot record information.

How many valid hits do you get for the beginning of a partition?

Recover any deleted partitions.

For any recovered partition list the following:

Beginning sector of the partitions:

Total sectors in the partitions:

Starting cluster of each $MFT:

List the $MFT number for each file below from each partition:

$MFTMIRR

$BOOT

.

$Bitmap

$Badclus

$Reparse

AT HOME ADVANCED EXERCISE

Examine image file 9_HW3.001 with HxD or Active@ Disk Editor. This drive formerly was set up as an MBR drive.

Run a search for NTFS boot record information.

How many valid hits do you get for the beginning of a partition?

Recover any deleted partitions.

For any recovered NTFS partition, list the following:

Beginning sector of the partitions:

Total sectors in the partitions:

Starting cluster of each $MFT:

List the $MFT number for each file below from each partition:

$MFTMIRR

$BOOT

.

$Bitmap

$Badclus

$Reparse

Each NTFS partition has a file that has an obvious code in it; list the code from each partition.

REFERENCES

1. Bunting, S. (2012). *ENCE EnCase Computer Forensics: The Official EnCase Certified Examiner Study Guide.* (3rd ed., p. 73). Indianapolis: Sybex.

2. *What is Posix Compliance?.* (n.d.). Retrieved from http://www.lynuxworks.com/products/posix/posix.php3

3. *Posix Compliance.* (n.d.). Retrieved from http://technet.microsoft.com/en-us/library/cc976809.aspx

4. Medeiros, J. (2008). *NTFS Forensics: A Programmer's View of Raw Filesystem Data Extraction* . Retrieved from http://grayscale-research.org/new/pdfs/NTFS forensics.pdf

5. *Default Cluster Size for NTFS, FAT, and exFAT.* (n.d.). Retrieved from http://support.microsoft.com/kb/140365

6. Sammes, T., & Jenkinson, B. (2007). *Forensic Computing, a Practitioner's Guide.* (2nd ed., pp. 216). London: Springer Publishing.

7. Carrier, B. (2005). *File System Forensic Analysis.* (pp. 302). Upper Saddle River: Addison-Wesley

8. Sammes, T., & Jenkinson, B. (2007). *Forensic Computing, a Practitioner's Guide.* (2nd ed., pp. 218). London: Springer Publishing.

9. Carrier, B. (2005). *File System Forensic Analysis.* (pp. 303). Upper Saddle River: Addison-Wesley

10. Cowen, D. (2013, January 7). [Web log message]. Retrieved from http://hackingexposedcomputerforensicsblog.blogspot.com/2013/01/ntfs-triforce-deeper-look-inside.html

11. *A Hard Drive's Dirty Bit is Set for Two Main Reasons.* (2011, September 8). Retrieved from http://www.qbs-pchelp.co.uk/blog/2011/09/a-hard-drives-dirty-bit-is-set-for-two-main-reasons/

12. Carrier, B. (2005). *File System Forensic Analysis.* (pp. 305-306). Upper Saddle River: Addison-Wesley

13. Sammes, T., & Jenkinson, B. (2007). *Forensic Computing, a Practitioner's Guide.* (2nd ed., pp. 223-224). London: Springer Publishing.

14. Attoe, R. (2010). NTFS (new technology file system). In *IACIS Advanced Windows Forensic Examiner's Manual* (p. 17-18).

10 FILE SYSTEMS: NTFS PART II

Master File Table

In the last chapter, the Master File Table ($MFT) was introduced briefly during the review of the metadata files created during formatting. As a reminder of what was covered in the last chapter, the $MFT is a relational database that has data on every file on the volume, including the $MFT itself[1]. The database is made up of 1024-byte records and there is at least one record for each file and folder. The first 12 records are reserved for metadata files (records 0-11), and records 12-15 are reserved for some future metadata files. The first record (record 0) is for the $MFT itself. The $MFT is set as 12.5% of the volume and the clusters assigned to the file are near the middle of the volume, not the beginning of the volume[2].

The 1024-byte record in the $MFT is made up of attributes[3]. NTFS attributes are like the attributes of people, name, birthdate, etc. These attributes are defined in the $ATTRDEF metadata reviewed in the last chapter. The current list of attributes is below[4].

Attribute Type Identifier (Hex)	Description
10 00 00 00	Standard Information
20 00 00 00	Attribute List
30 00 00 00	Filename
40 00 00 00	Object Identifier
50 00 00 00	Security Descriptor
60 00 00 00	Volume Name
70 00 00 00	Volume Information
80 00 00 00	Data
90 00 00 00	Index Root
a0 00 00 00	Index Allocation
b0 00 00 00	Bitmap
c0 00 00 00	SymbolicLink/Reparse Point
d0 00 00 00	EA Information
e0 00 00 00	EA
00 01 00 00	Logged Utility Stream

A definition for a ***file*** can be: A series of attributes.

Each file will have a Standard Information Attribute (SIA), a Filename Attribute (FNA), and a Data Attribute (DATA)[5]. They may also have several other attributes such as an Object Identifier and a Logged Utility Stream or multiple Filename Attributes and Data Attributes.

Each record in the $MFT begins with a 56-byte header followed by the attributes[6]. You will note that in the attribute table above, there is an attribute identifier that is a hexadecimal value. The order of the attributes will be in numerical order in the record.

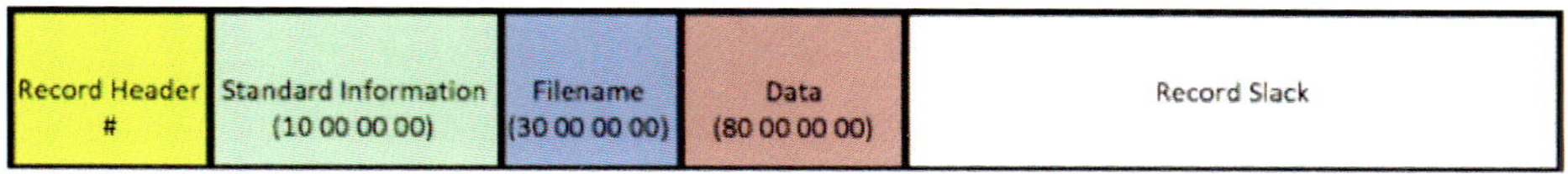

If additional attributes are added they will be reordered based upon the attribute identifier number.

Folders have $MFT records as well. The difference in folder records is that they typically do not have a DATA attribute, but have an Index Root attribute instead[7]. This attribute is a listing of files in the folder.

To start, we will examine the Record Header information[8].

MFT RECORD HEADER			
DEC OFFSET	HEX OFFSET	SIZE (BYTES)	DESCRIPTION
0	0	4	"FILE" SIGNATURE
4	4	2	Offset to update sequence (fixup array)
6	6	2	Number of entries in the update sequence (fixup array)
8	8	8	$Log File Sequence Number
16	10	2	Sequence Count (number times the record has been used)
18	12	2	Hard Link Count (file names)
20	14	2	Offset to Start of Attributes
22	16	2	Flags (Deleted Files – 00 00; Allocated Files – 01 00; Deleted Directory – 02 00; Allocated Directory – 03 00)
24	18	4	Amount of space used by $MFT records (bytes)
28	1C	4	Amount of space allocated for $MFT records
32	20	8	Base File Reference
40	28	2	Next Attribute ID
42	2A	2	Reserved
44	2C	4	$MFT Record Number
48	30	>0	Update Sequence Number (WinXP/Vista/Win7)

We will walk thru the header, but first we must cover the Update Sequence Array so it is understandable when we get into the header. The Update Sequence Array, also known as a Fixup Array, is a method designed to link sectors together[9]. Microsoft uses Update Sequence Arrays in the $Logfile and in folder structures as well.

The Update Sequence Array places two bytes of data at the end of reach sector in the group. In terms of the $MFT record, which is 1024 bytes, this means there are two sectors. The sequence values go into offsets 510 and 511 of each of these two sectors.

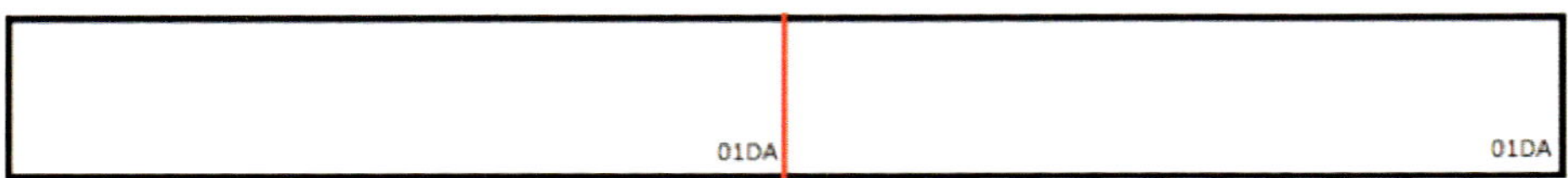

The sequence values are not written until after the attributes are in place. Adding these bytes can overwrite existing data.

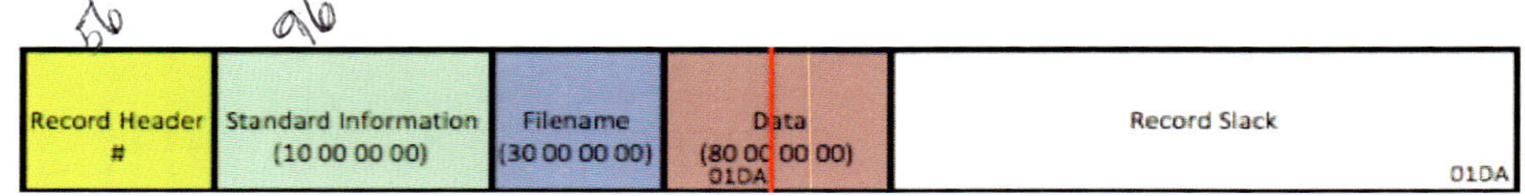

Notice that our sector boundary is in the middle of the data attribute in our example record. For the sake of our example, let's say that we had ABCD written at the end of the first sector and continuing into the second sector. The last bytes of the first sector are AB (0x65 66). The Update Sequence values (0x01 DA) will overwrite the A and B. To prevent the loss of this information, the A and B are placed into the Update Sequence Array along with the last two bytes of the second sector (most likely 0x00 00) since we do not have an attribute in this space. The array is simply another word for table. So we have a table the looks like this:

Update Sequence Value	1st Sector Bytes (Offsets 510 & 511)	2nd Sector Bytes (Offsets 510 & 511)
0x01DA	0x6566	0x0000

The original data is replaced when called upon to read the Data Attribute by a program that is interprets NTFS and is aware of the Update Sequence Array.

We will look at a file named HEADER.TXT.

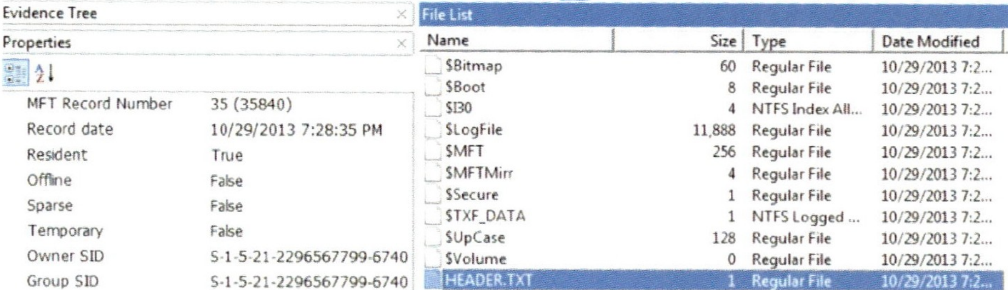

Note that it has a MFT record number of 35 and offset of 35840 in the $MFT (35x1024). We will go to that offset in the $MFT.

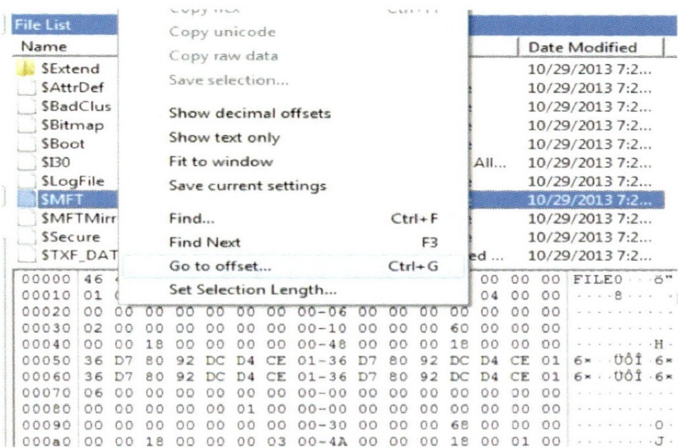

The Record Header is highlighted below. We will parse through the 56 bytes.

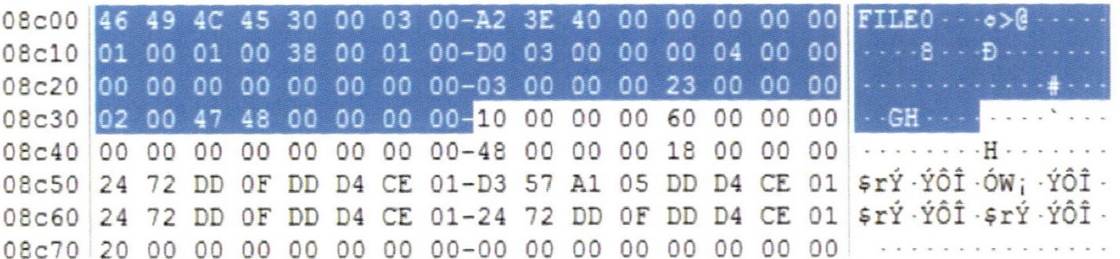

The first four bytes are the record signature. Each record always starts with FILE, making them easily recognizable.

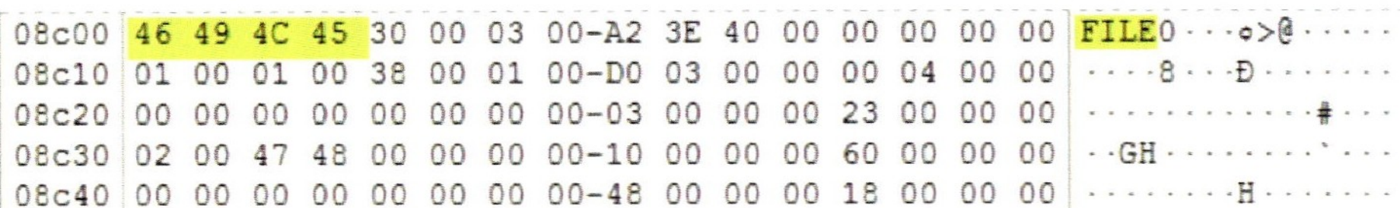

Offsets 4-5 are the offset to the Update Sequence Array. Starting at the beginning of the header, there are 48 bytes to the table (0x0030 – 48 bytes).

```
08c00 46 49 4C 45 30 00 03 00-A2 3E 40 00 00 00 00 00  FILE0···⟐>@·····
08c10 01 00 01 00 38 00 01 00-D0 03 00 00 00 04 00 00  ····8···Đ·······
08c20 00 00 00 00 00 00 00 00-03 00 00 00 23 00 00 00  ············#···
08c30 02 00 47 48 00 00 00 00-10 00 00 00 60 00 00 00  ··GH········`···
08c40 00 00 00 00 00 00 00 00-48 00 00 00 18 00 00 00  ········H·······
```

Offsets 6-7 are the number of entries in the Update Sequence Array. This is will include the Update Sequence values, the first sector values and the second sector values.

```
08c00 46 49 4C 45 30 00 03 00-A2 3E 40 00 00 00 00 00  FILE0···⟐>@·····
08c10 01 00 01 00 38 00 01 00-D0 03 00 00 00 04 00 00  ····8···Đ·······
08c20 00 00 00 00 00 00 00 00-03 00 00 00 23 00 00 00  ············#···
08c30 02 00 47 48 00 00 00 00-10 00 00 00 60 00 00 00  ··GH········`···
08c40 00 00 00 00 00 00 00 00-48 00 00 00 18 00 00 00  ········H·······
```

Offsets 8-15 are the $Logfile Sequence Number. This is used to track the file activity in the log.

```
08c00 46 49 4C 45 30 00 03 00-A2 3E 40 00 00 00 00 00  FILE0···⟐>@·····
08c10 01 00 01 00 38 00 01 00-D0 03 00 00 00 04 00 00  ····8···Đ·······
08c20 00 00 00 00 00 00 00 00-03 00 00 00 23 00 00 00  ············#···
08c30 02 00 47 48 00 00 00 00-10 00 00 00 60 00 00 00  ··GH········`···
08c40 00 00 00 00 00 00 00 00-48 00 00 00 18 00 00 00  ········H·······
```

Here is the same sequence number found in the $Logfile.

```
$LogFile     11,888  Regular File  10/29/2013 7:2...
$MFT            256  Regular File  10/29/2013 7:2...

002500 00 00 00 00 00 00 00 00-98 09 70 84 22 00 00 00  ··········p·"···
002510 A2 3E 40 00 00 00 00 00-00 00 00 00 00 00 00 00  ⟐>@·············
002520 00 00 00 00 00 00 00 00-A8 00 00 00 00 00 00 00  ········¨·······
002530 01 00 00 00 18 00 00 00-00 00 00 00 00 00 00 00  ················
```

Offsets 16-17 are referred to as the sequence count. This sequence is unrelated to the Update Sequence and the $Logfile Sequence Number. In this case, the sequence count is the number of times this $MFT record has been used[10]. When a file is deleted, the $MFT record can be reused. In this case, the record has only been used once.

```
08c00 46 49 4C 45 30 00 03 00-A2 3E 40 00 00 00 00 00  FILE0···⟐>@·····
08c10 01 00 01 00 38 00 01 00-D0 03 00 00 00 04 00 00  ····8···Đ·······
08c20 00 00 00 00 00 00 00 00-03 00 00 00 23 00 00 00  ············#···
08c30 02 00 47 48 00 00 00 00-10 00 00 00 60 00 00 00  ··GH········`···
08c40 00 00 00 00 00 00 00 00-48 00 00 00 18 00 00 00  ········H·······
```

Offsets 18-19 have the number of hard links. Hard links are filenames and the file may have several names all pointing to the same data[11]. This value tracks the number of these names; in this example, this is just one.

```
08c00 46 49 4C 45 30 00 03 00-A2 3E 40 00 00 00 00 00 FILE0···o>@·····
08c10 01 00 01 00 38 00 01 00-D0 03 00 00 00 04 00 00 ····8···Ð·······
08c20 00 00 00 00 00 00 00 00-03 00 00 00 23 00 00 00 ············#···
08c30 02 00 47 48 00 00 00 00-10 00 00 00 60 00 00 00 ··GH········`···
08c40 00 00 00 00 00 00 00 00-48 00 00 00 18 00 00 00 ········H·······
```

Offsets 20-21 have the offset to the beginning of the attributes. The attributes begin immediately after the header, and since the header is 56 bytes, then the offset will be 56.

```
08c00 46 49 4C 45 30 00 03 00-A2 3E 40 00 00 00 00 00 FILE0···o>@·····
08c10 01 00 01 00 38 00 01 00-D0 03 00 00 00 04 00 00 ····8···Ð·······
08c20 00 00 00 00 00 00 00 00-03 00 00 00 23 00 00 00 ············#···
08c30 02 00 47 48 00 00 00 00-10 00 00 00 60 00 00 00 ··GH········`···
08c40 00 00 00 00 00 00 00 00-48 00 00 00 18 00 00 00 ········H·······
```

Offsets 22-23 have a flag on the state of the file or folder. The values are 0x00 00 for a deleted file, 0x01 00 for an active (allocated) file, 0x02 00 for a deleted folder, and 0x03 00 for an active folder. The value below shows this is an active file.

```
08c00 46 49 4C 45 30 00 03 00-A2 3E 40 00 00 00 00 00 FILE0···o>@·····
08c10 01 00 01 00 38 00 01 00-D0 03 00 00 00 04 00 00 ····8···Ð·······
08c20 00 00 00 00 00 00 00 00-03 00 00 00 23 00 00 00 ············#···
08c30 02 00 47 48 00 00 00 00-10 00 00 00 60 00 00 00 ··GH········`···
08c40 00 00 00 00 00 00 00 00-48 00 00 00 18 00 00 00 ········H·······
```

Offsets 24-27 are the number of bytes used in the $MFT record (0x D0 03 00 00 = 973 bytes).

```
08c00 46 49 4C 45 30 00 03 00-A2 3E 40 00 00 00 00 00 FILE0···o>@·····
08c10 01 00 01 00 38 00 01 00-D0 03 00 00 00 04 00 00 ····8···Ð·······
08c20 00 00 00 00 00 00 00 00-03 00 00 00 23 00 00 00 ············#···
08c30 02 00 47 48 00 00 00 00-10 00 00 00 60 00 00 00 ··GH········`···
08c40 00 00 00 00 00 00 00 00-48 00 00 00 18 00 00 00 ········H·······
```

Offsets 28–31 are the maximum size of a record (0x00 04 00 00 = 1024 bytes).

```
08c00 46 49 4C 45 30 00 03 00-A2 3E 40 00 00 00 00 00 FILE0···o>@·····
08c10 01 00 01 00 38 00 01 00-D0 03 00 00 00 04 00 00 ····8···Ð·······
08c20 00 00 00 00 00 00 00 00-03 00 00 00 23 00 00 00 ············#···
08c30 02 00 47 48 00 00 00 00-10 00 00 00 60 00 00 00 ··GH········`···
08c40 00 00 00 00 00 00 00 00-48 00 00 00 18 00 00 00 ········H·······
```

Offsets 32-39 are the base record number. If a file requires more than one record because all the attribute information cannot fit into one 1024-byte record, then additional records are added and they will point back to the first (base) record number for the file. In this case, this is the base record, so the value is 0.

```
08c00 46 49 4C 45 30 00 03 00-A2 3E 40 00 00 00 00 00 FILE0···ⴰ>@·····
08c10 01 00 01 00 38 00 01 00-D0 03 00 00 00 04 00 00 ····8···Ð·······
08c20 00 00 00 00 00 00 00 00-03 00 00 00 23 00 00 00 ············#···
08c30 02 00 47 48 00 00 00 00-10 00 00 00 60 00 00 00 ··GH········`···
08c40 00 00 00 00 00 00 00 00-48 00 00 00 18 00 00 00 ········H·······
```

Offsets 40-41 are for the next attribute number. This is to be a count of the attributes in the record and what the next number would be. The example below shows a value of 3, counting 0, 1, 2, 3, etc. This file has three attributes (0-2), so the next attribute would be the third attribute (we will cover this in more detail later). Testing shows that this value only counts up and will never be reduced even if attributes are removed.

```
08c00 46 49 4C 45 30 00 03 00-A2 3E 40 00 00 00 00 00 FILE0···ⴰ>@·····
08c10 01 00 01 00 38 00 01 00-D0 03 00 00 00 04 00 00 ····8···Ð·······
08c20 00 00 00 00 00 00 00 00-03 00 00 00 23 00 00 00 ············#···
08c30 02 00 47 48 00 00 00 00-10 00 00 00 60 00 00 00 ··GH········`···
08c40 00 00 00 00 00 00 00 00-48 00 00 00 18 00 00 00 ········H·······
```

Offsets 42-43 are reserved bytes.

```
08c00 46 49 4C 45 30 00 03 00-A2 3E 40 00 00 00 00 00 FILE0···ⴰ>@·····
08c10 01 00 01 00 38 00 01 00-D0 03 00 00 00 04 00 00 ····8···Ð·······
08c20 00 00 00 00 00 00 00 00-03 00 00 00 23 00 00 00 ············#···
08c30 02 00 47 48 00 00 00 00-10 00 00 00 60 00 00 00 ··GH········`···
08c40 00 00 00 00 00 00 00 00-48 00 00 00 18 00 00 00 ········H·······
```

Offsets 44-47 are the $MFT record number. This record is 0x23 00 00 00 = 35.

```
08c00 46 49 4C 45 30 00 03 00-A2 3E 40 00 00 00 00 00 FILE0···ⴰ>@·····
08c10 01 00 01 00 38 00 01 00-D0 03 00 00 00 04 00 00 ····8···Ð·······
08c20 00 00 00 00 00 00 00 00-03 00 00 00 23 00 00 00 ············#···
08c30 02 00 47 48 00 00 00 00-10 00 00 00 60 00 00 00 ··GH········`···
08c40 00 00 00 00 00 00 00 00-48 00 00 00 18 00 00 00 ········H·······
```

Offsets 48-56 are the Update Sequence Array. This is the table discussed above. The table will contained the sequence values (0x02 00), the values copied from the end of the first sector (0x47 48), and from the end of the second sector (0x00 00) from the record. The last two bytes in the table are unused.

```
08c00  46 49 4C 45 30 00 03 00-A2 3E 40 00 00 00 00 00  FILE0···¢>@·····
08c10  01 00 01 00 38 00 01 00-D0 03 00 00 00 04 00 00  ····8···Ð·······
08c20  00 00 00 00 00 00 00 00-03 00 00 00 23 00 00 00  ············#···
08c30  02 00 47 48 00 00 00 00-10 00 00 00 60 00 00 00  ··GH········`···
08c40  00 00 00 00 00 00 00 00-48 00 00 00 18 00 00 00  ········H·······
```

Below is a view of the end of the first sector showing the sequence values replacing the GH (0x47 48).

```
08dd0  50 51 52 53 54 55 56 57-58 59 5A 0D 0A 41 42 43  PQRSTUVWXYZ··ABC
08de0  44 45 46 47 48 49 4A 4B-4C 4D 4F 50 51 52 53 54  DEFGHIJKLMOPQRST
08df0  55 56 57 58 59 5A 0D 0A-41 42 43 44 45 46 02 00  UVWXYZ··ABCDEF··
08e00  49 4A 4B 4C 4D 4F 50 51-52 53 54 55 56 57 58 59  IJKLMOPQRSTUVWXY
08e10  5A 0D 0A 41 42 43 44 45-46 47 48 49 4A 4B 4C 4D  Z··ABCDEFGHIJKLM
```

Below is a view of the end of the second sector showing the sequence values replacing the 0 0 (0x00 00).

```
091d0  00 00 00 00 00 00 00 00-00 00 00 00 00 00 00 00  ················
091e0  00 00 00 00 00 00 00 00-00 00 00 00 00 00 00 00  ················
091f0  00 00 00 00 00 00 00 00-00 00 00 00 00 00 02 00  ················
09200  00 00 00 00 00 00 00 00-00 00 00 00 00 00 00 00  ················
09210  00 00 00 00 00 00 00 00-00 00 00 00 00 00 00 00  ················
```

Below is the text file showing the contents. Note that the GH is displayed and not 0x02 00.

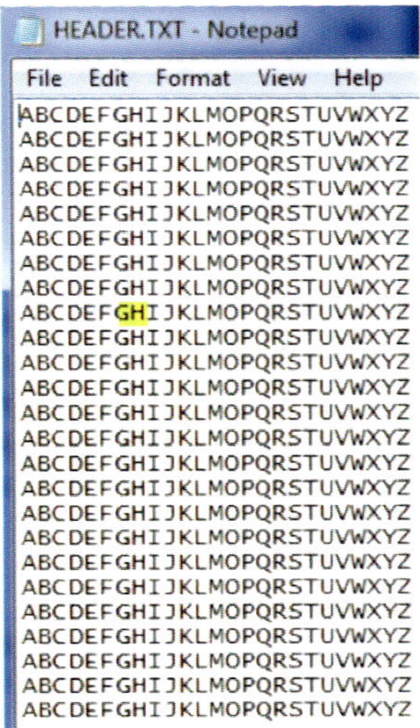

PRACTICAL EXERCISE 1

Open 10_Pract1.001 in FTK Imager and complete the table for the three files (record numbers 35, 37, and 39).

RECORD HEADER	Record #35	Record #37	Record#39
ASCII File Signature Identifier is:			
Offset to Update Sequence Array:			
Number of entries in the Update Array:			
$Logfile sequence number (Hex):			
Sequence count:			
Hard Link count:			
Offset to the first attribute:			
Is the file/folder deleted:			
Logical size of the record:			
Physical size of the record:			
Next attribute identification:			
$MFT Record Number:			
Update Sequence Array values:			
Open $Logfile and enter the first offset to the $Logfile Sequence Number for this file:			

Attributes

The remainder of the record will have three or more attributes. Attributes are either Resident or Non-Resident, meaning the content is either in the $MFT Record or stored on an available cluster. The first 16 bytes of each attribute will have the same types of data. If the attribute is resident, the next eight bytes will also be the same for all resident attributes, for a total of 24. These first 16 or 24 bytes are known as the attribute header, not to be confused with the Record header.

The header will begin with the attribute type ID followed by the size of the attribute, then whether or not the attribute is resident or non-resident. Some attributes are named by the user, but most are not.

Standard Information Attribute (SIA)

Every file and folder has a SIA and the beginning of the attribute always starts with 0x10 00 00 00[12]. The primary contents of this attribute are the dates and times associated with the file or folder. Attributes all have a similar structure, so we will walk through this for the SIA[13].

Standard Information Attribute (10 00 00 00)			
DEC OFFSET	**HEX OFFSET**	**SIZE (BYTES)**	**DESCRIPTION**
0	0	4	Attribute Type Identifier
4	4	4	Length of the Attribute
8	8	1	Resident (0x00) or Non-Resident Flag (0x01)
9	9	1	Length of Stream Name in Unicode characters
10	0A	2	Offset to the stream name
12	0C	2	Flags
14	0E	2	Attribute Identifier
16	10	4	Size of Resident Data
20	14	2	Offset to Resident Data
22	16	1	Indexing (00=no, 01=yes)
23	17	1	Padding
24	18	8	Creation Time
32	20	8	Modified Time
40	28	8	$MFT Modified Time
48	30	8	Last Access Time
56	38	4	DOS Flags (See table below)
60	3C	4	Maximum number of versions
64	40	4	Version number
68	44	4	Class ID
72	48	4	Owner ID
76	4C	4	Security ID
80	50	8	Quota Charged
88	58	8	Update Sequence Number

Note the attribute type identifier in the first four bytes at the beginning; this is at offset 56 of the record. Recall from above that in the record header, we saw the attributes begin at offset 56. All offsets in the SIA table are referenced from the beginning of the attribute, not from the beginning of the record.

```
08c00 46 49 4C 45 30 00 03 00-0B 42 40 00 00 00 00 00 FILE0···B@·····
08c10 01 00 01 00 38 00 01 00-F8 03 00 00 00 04 00 00 ····8···ø·······
08c20 00 00 00 00 00 00 00 00-04 00 00 00 23 00 00 00 ············#···
08c30 03 00 56 57 00 00 00 00-10 00 00 00 60 00 00 00 ··VW········`···
08c40 00 00 00 00 00 00 00 00-48 00 00 00 18 00 00 00 ········H·······
08c50 24 72 DD 0F DD D4 CE 01-D3 57 A1 05 DD D4 CE 01 $rÝ·ÝÔÎ·ÓW¡·ÝÔÎ·
08c60 BE A5 4E 38 8C D5 CE 01-24 72 DD 0F DD D4 CE 01 ¾¥N8·ÕÎ·$rÝ·ÝÔÎ·
08c70 20 00 00 00 00 00 00 00-00 00 00 00 00 00 00 00  ···············
08c80 00 00 00 00 05 01 00 00-00 00 00 00 00 00 00 00 ················
08c90 00 00 00 00 00 00 00 00-30 00 00 00 70 00 00 00 ········0···p···
```

Offsets 4-7 provide the length of the attribute starting at the identifier (0x60 00 00 00 = 96 bytes). The SIA has always been 96 bytes[14]. Note that is what is highlighted in yellow above.

```
08c30 03 00 56 57 00 00 00 00-10 00 00 00 60 00 00 00 ··VW········`···
08c40 00 00 00 00 00 00 00 00-48 00 00 00 18 00 00 00 ········H·······
08c50 24 72 DD 0F DD D4 CE 01-D3 57 A1 05 DD D4 CE 01 $rÝ·ÝÔÎ·ÓW¡·ÝÔÎ·
08c60 BE A5 4E 38 8C D5 CE 01-24 72 DD 0F DD D4 CE 01 ¾¥N8·ÕÎ·$rÝ·ÝÔÎ·
08c70 20 00 00 00 00 00 00 00-00 00 00 00 00 00 00 00 ················
08c80 00 00 00 00 05 01 00 00-00 00 00 00 00 00 00 00 ················
08c90 00 00 00 00 00 00 00 00-30 00 00 00 70 00 00 00 ········0···p···
```

Offset 8 determines whether the content of the attribute is contained in the $MFT (0x00) or whether is stored in another cluster on the drive (0x01). If the data is stored in the $MFT record, it is referred to as "resident." If the data is stored on another cluster, it is referred to as "non-resident." The contents of the SIA are always resident, but when we get to the DATA attribute there will be an example of non-resident content.

```
08c30 03 00 56 57 00 00 00 00-10 00 00 00 60 00 00 00 ··VW········`···
08c40 00 00 00 00 00 00 00 00-48 00 00 00 18 00 00 00 ········H·······
08c50 24 72 DD 0F DD D4 CE 01-D3 57 A1 05 DD D4 CE 01 $rÝ·ÝÔÎ·ÓW¡·ÝÔÎ·
08c60 BE A5 4E 38 8C D5 CE 01-24 72 DD 0F DD D4 CE 01 ¾¥N8·ÕÎ·$rÝ·ÝÔÎ·
08c70 20 00 00 00 00 00 00 00-00 00 00 00 00 00 00 00 ················
08c80 00 00 00 00 05 01 00 00-00 00 00 00 00 00 00 00 ················
08c90 00 00 00 00 00 00 00 00-30 00 00 00 70 00 00 00 ········0···p···
```

Offsets 9-13 represent the length of the stream name (the contents of the attributes can be named and are referred to as a stream), offset to the name (stream), and any flags. The SIA does not have a named stream, so these bytes will always be zero.

```
08c30 03 00 56 57 00 00 00 00-10 00 00 00 60 00 00 00 ··VW········`···
08c40 00 00 00 00 00 00 00 00-48 00 00 00 18 00 00 00 ········H·······
08c50 24 72 DD 0F DD D4 CE 01-D3 57 A1 05 DD D4 CE 01 $rÝ·ÝÔÎ·ÓW¡·ÝÔÎ·
08c60 BE A5 4E 38 8C D5 CE 01-24 72 DD 0F DD D4 CE 01 ¾¥N8·ÕÎ·$rÝ·ÝÔÎ·
08c70 20 00 00 00 00 00 00 00-00 00 00 00 00 00 00 00 ················
08c80 00 00 00 00 05 01 00 00-00 00 00 00 00 00 00 00 ················
08c90 00 00 00 00 00 00 00 00-30 00 00 00 70 00 00 00 ········0···p···
```

Offsets 14-15 are for the Attribute Identifier. This is not the same as the Attribute Type Identifier. The Attribute Type Attribute (i.e., 0x10 00 00 00) is the same for each record. The Attribute Identifier, however, can change between records. This identifier is assigned when the attribute is added. Since the SIA is always added first, it is identified as 0x00 00[15]. The DATA attribute may be 0x01 00 and the Filename Attribute may be 0x02 00. These numbers will vary as the attributes are added.

```
08c30  03 00 56 57 00 00 00 00-10 00 00 00 60 00 00 00  ··VW········`···
08c40  00 00 00 00 00 00 00 00-48 00 00 00 18 00 00 00  ········H·······
08c50  24 72 DD 0F DD D4 CE 01-D3 57 A1 05 DD D4 CE 01  $rÝ·ÝÔÎ·ÓW¡·ÝÔÎ·
08c60  BE A5 4E 38 8C D5 CE 01-24 72 DD 0F DD D4 CE 01  ¾¥N8·ÕÎ·$rÝ·ÝÔÎ·
08c70  20 00 00 00 00 00 00 00-00 00 00 00 00 00 00 00   ···············
08c80  00 00 00 00 05 01 00 00-00 00 00 00 00 00 00 00  ················
08c90  00 00 00 00 00 00 00 00-30 00 00 00 70 00 00 00  ········0···p···
```

Offsets 16-19 are for the size of the content of the attribute. The previous 16 bytes and the next 8 bytes are part of the attribute header. The contents will follow after the attribute header. The size of the contents of the SIA is always 72 bytes (0x48 00).

```
08c30  03 00 56 57 00 00 00 00-10 00 00 00 60 00 00 00  ··VW········`···
08c40  00 00 00 00 00 00 00 00-48 00 00 00 18 00 00 00  ········H·······
08c50  24 72 DD 0F DD D4 CE 01-D3 57 A1 05 DD D4 CE 01  $rÝ·ÝÔÎ·ÓW¡·ÝÔÎ·
08c60  BE A5 4E 38 8C D5 CE 01-24 72 DD 0F DD D4 CE 01  ¾¥N8·ÕÎ·$rÝ·ÝÔÎ·
08c70  20 00 00 00 00 00 00 00-00 00 00 00 00 00 00 00   ···············
08c80  00 00 00 00 05 01 00 00-00 00 00 00 00 00 00 00  ················
08c90  00 00 00 00 00 00 00 00-30 00 00 00 70 00 00 00  ········0···p···
```

Offsets 20-21 are for the offset to the attribute content. The attribute header is 24 bytes (0x18 00 = 24) and the contents start right after. Offset 22 is for indexing and offset 23 is padding with 00.

```
08c30  03 00 56 57 00 00 00 00-10 00 00 00 60 00 00 00  ··VW········`···
08c40  00 00 00 00 00 00 00 00-48 00 00 00 18 00 00 00  ········H·······
08c50  24 72 DD 0F DD D4 CE 01-D3 57 A1 05 DD D4 CE 01  $rÝ·ÝÔÎ·ÓW¡·ÝÔÎ·
08c60  BE A5 4E 38 8C D5 CE 01-24 72 DD 0F DD D4 CE 01  ¾¥N8·ÕÎ·$rÝ·ÝÔÎ·
08c70  20 00 00 00 00 00 00 00-00 00 00 00 00 00 00 00   ···············
08c80  00 00 00 00 05 01 00 00-00 00 00 00 00 00 00 00  ················
08c90  00 00 00 00 00 00 00 00-30 00 00 00 70 00 00 00  ········0···p···
```

Offsets 24-31 have the file's creation date and time in Windows date/time format. The times are stored in Universal Time Coordinate (UTC) format. Note that FTK Imager also interprets the local time, but this is based upon the examiner's computer settings and not necessarily from what the subject's setting are. The file creation date/time is when the file was first copied or created on this volume. If a file exists on a different volume and is copied to this volume, the file creation date/time will likely be the date of copying.

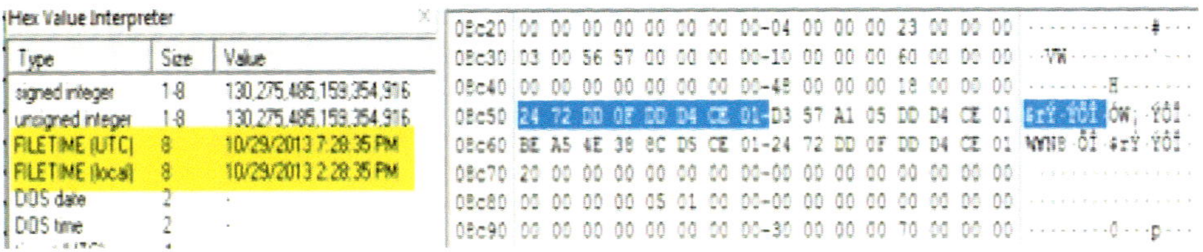

Offsets 32-39 have the file's last modified date and time in Windows date/time format. This time is also stored in Universal Time Coordinate (UTC) format. The last modified date/time is when the file was last saved, not necessarily changed. This date/time may travel with the file if it is copied from another volume. So a file copied now would have today's file creation date/time, but the last modified date/time could be from three years ago.

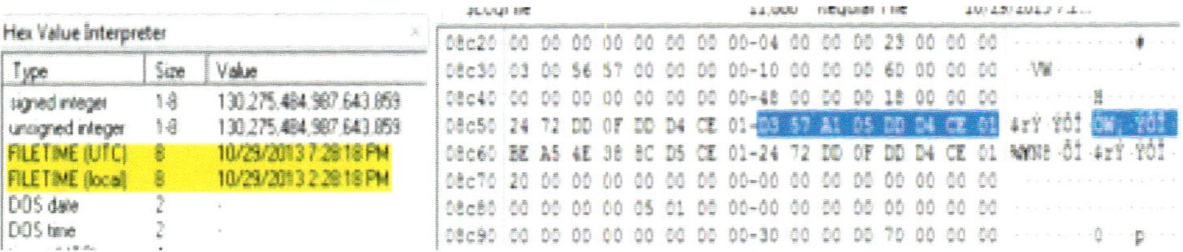

Offsets 40-47 are for the $MFT record last modified date/time. Whenever the $MFT record for this particular file gets updated, then this date/time is updated[16]. For example, if the file name is changed, this does not impact the other dates and times and they are not changed. However, this would affect the record as the filename attribute would change.

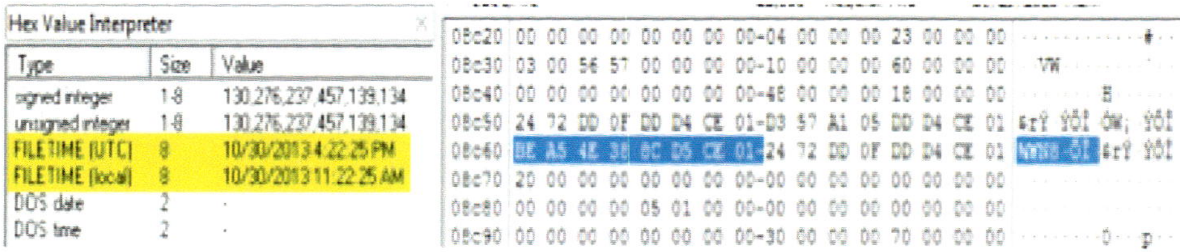

Offsets 48-55 are for the file's last accessed date/time. This can be updated when the file is clicked on, opened, viewed, or scanned. Starting with Microsoft Vista, the operating system no longer updates this date/time upon access alone[17]. The field gets filled in when the file is created on the volume and then typically only gets updated when the file is saved, reducing the number of writes to the drive.

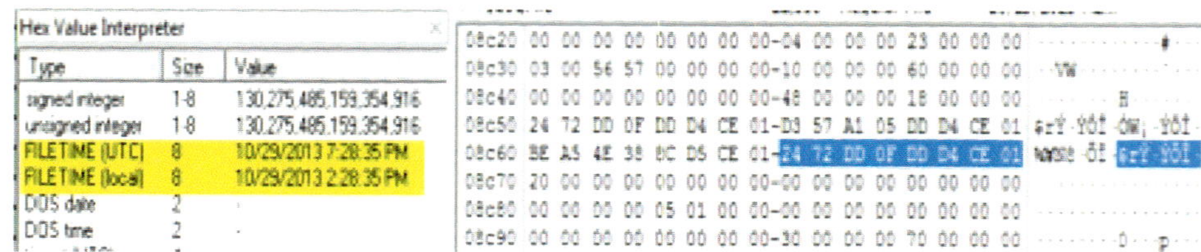

Offsets 56-59 are for the DOS attributes, similar to what we covered in the FAT directory structures.

Below is a table with the attributes[18].

DOS ATTRIBUTES		
Hex	**Binary**	**Description**
0x0001	0000 0000 0000 0001	Read Only
0x0002	0000 0000 0000 0010	Hidden
0x0004	0000 0000 0000 0100	System
0x0010	0000 0000 0001 0000	Directory
0x0020	0000 0000 0010 0000	Archive
0x0040	0000 0000 0100 0000	Device
0x0080	0000 0000 1000 0000	Normal
0x0100	0000 0001 0000 0000	Temporary
0x0200	0000 0010 0000 0000	Sparse File
0x0400	0000 0100 0000 0000	Reparse Point
0x0800	0000 1000 0000 0000	Compressed
0x1000	0001 0000 0000 0000	Offline
0x2000	0010 0000 0000 0000	Not Content Indexed
0x4000	0100 0000 0000 0000	Encrypted

Some of the bits can be combined, like Read Only, Hidden, and System. In the example below, only the Archive attribute is selected.

```
08c30 03 00 56 57 00 00 00 00-10 00 00 00 60 00 00 00  ··VW········`···
08c40 00 00 00 00 00 00 00 00-48 00 00 00 18 00 00 00  ········H·······
08c50 24 72 DD 0F DD D4 CE 01-D3 57 A1 05 DD D4 CE 01  $rÝ·ÝÔÎ·ÓW¡·ÝÔÎ·
08c60 BE A5 4E 38 8C D5 CE 01-24 72 DD 0F DD D4 CE 01  ¾¥N8·ÕÎ·$rÝ·ÝÔÎ·
08c70 20 00 00 00 00 00 00 00-00 00 00 00 00 00 00 00  ················
08c80 00 00 00 00 05 01 00 00-00 00 00 00 00 00 00 00  ················
08c90 00 00 00 00 00 00 00 00-30 00 00 00 70 00 00 00  ········0···p···
```

Offsets 60-63 are for Maximum version number and offsets 64-67 are for the version number. These values may be more relevant for networked systems as opposed to stand-alone systems. Offsets 68-71 are for the class ID and offsets 72-75 are for the owner ID. These values are not typically used.

```
08c30 03 00 56 57 00 00 00 00-10 00 00 00 60 00 00 00  ··VW········`···
08c40 00 00 00 00 00 00 00 00-48 00 00 00 18 00 00 00  ········H·······
08c50 24 72 DD 0F DD D4 CE 01-D3 57 A1 05 DD D4 CE 01  $rÝ·ÝÔÎ·ÓW¡·ÝÔÎ·
08c60 BE A5 4E 38 8C D5 CE 01-24 72 DD 0F DD D4 CE 01  ¾¥N8·ÕÎ·$rÝ·ÝÔÎ·
08c70 20 00 00 00 00 00 00 00-00 00 00 00 00 00 00 00  ················
08c80 00 00 00 00 05 01 00 00-00 00 00 00 00 00 00 00  ················
08c90 00 00 00 00 00 00 00 00-30 00 00 00 70 00 00 00  ········0···p···
```

Offsets 76-79 are for the security descriptors and associate with the $Secure metadata file.

```
08c30  03 00 56 57 00 00 00 00-10 00 00 00 60 00 00 00  ··VW········`···
08c40  00 00 00 00 00 00 00 00-48 00 00 00 18 00 00 00  ········H·······
08c50  24 72 DD 0F DD D4 CE 01-D3 57 A1 05 DD D4 CE 01  $rÝ·ÝÔÎ·ÓW¡·ÝÔÎ·
08c60  BE A5 4E 38 8C D5 CE 01-24 72 DD 0F DD D4 CE 01  ¾¥N8·ÕÎ·$rÝ·ÝÔÎ·
08c70  20 00 00 00 00 00 00 00-00 00 00 00 00 00 00 00  ················
08c80  00 00 00 00 05 01 00 00-00 00 00 00 00 00 00 00  ················
08c90  00 00 00 00 00 00 00 00-30 00 00 00 70 00 00 00  ········0···p···
```

Offsets 80-87 are for drive quotas, which are no longer used, so these values are typically zero.

```
08c30  03 00 56 57 00 00 00 00-10 00 00 00 60 00 00 00  ··VW········`···
08c40  00 00 00 00 00 00 00 00-48 00 00 00 18 00 00 00  ········H·······
08c50  24 72 DD 0F DD D4 CE 01-D3 57 A1 05 DD D4 CE 01  $rÝ·ÝÔÎ·ÓW¡·ÝÔÎ·
08c60  BE A5 4E 38 8C D5 CE 01-24 72 DD 0F DD D4 CE 01  ¾¥N8·ÕÎ·$rÝ·ÝÔÎ·
08c70  20 00 00 00 00 00 00 00-00 00 00 00 00 00 00 00  ················
08c80  00 00 00 00 05 01 00 00-00 00 00 00 00 00 00 00  ················
08c90  00 00 00 00 00 00 00 00-30 00 00 00 70 00 00 00  ········0···p···
```

Offsets 88-95 are for the sequence number for the $UsnJrnl. Recall that this is the application journaling metadata file. If journaling is turned on, then there will be values in these offsets. Windows 7 utilizes journaling, but apparently not on a removable drive as seen below.

```
08c30  03 00 56 57 00 00 00 00-10 00 00 00 60 00 00 00  ··VW········`···
08c40  00 00 00 00 00 00 00 00-48 00 00 00 18 00 00 00  ········H·······
08c50  24 72 DD 0F DD D4 CE 01-D3 57 A1 05 DD D4 CE 01  $rÝ·ÝÔÎ·ÓW¡·ÝÔÎ·
08c60  BE A5 4E 38 8C D5 CE 01-24 72 DD 0F DD D4 CE 01  ¾¥N8·ÕÎ·$rÝ·ÝÔÎ·
08c70  20 00 00 00 00 00 00 00-00 00 00 00 00 00 00 00  ················
08c80  00 00 00 00 05 01 00 00-00 00 00 00 00 00 00 00  ················
08c90  00 00 00 00 00 00 00 00-30 00 00 00 70 00 00 00  ········0···p···
```

Examining a $MFT record off a hard drive on a Windows 7 system did reveal the sequence numbers.

```
0008c30  19 02 00 00 00 00 00 00-10 00 00 00 60 00 00 00  ············`···
0008c40  00 00 00 00 00 00 00 00-48 00 00 00 18 00 00 00  ········H·······
0008c50  B2 1B C4 57 A4 46 CA 01-10 53 B7 54 BD 30 CE 01  ²·ÄW¤FÊ··S·T½0Î·
0008c60  10 53 B7 54 BD 30 CE 01-B2 1B C4 57 A4 46 CA 01  ·S·T½0Î·²·ÄW¤FÊ·
0008c70  20 20 00 00 00 00 00 00-00 00 00 00 00 00 00 00  ················
0008c80  00 00 00 00 48 02 00 00-00 00 00 00 00 00 00 00  ····H···········
0008c90  98 7B FC 27 00 00 00 00-30 00 00 00 78 00 00 00  ·{ü'····0···x···
```

PRACTICAL EXERCISE 2

Open 10_Pract1.E01 in FTK Imager and complete the table for the three files (record numbers 35, 37, and 39).

STANDARD INFORMATION ATTRIBUTE	Record #35	Record #37	Record#39
The length of this attribute is:			
Size of the Resident data is:			
Offset to the Resident data is:			
The date the file was created is:			
The date the file was modified is:			
What is the Last Access Date/Time (UTC):			
The last access time of the file is:			
The file name type is:			
The DOS attributes are:			
The Security ID is:			

Filename Attribute (FNA)

As mentioned in the last chapter, every file and folder has a ***Filename Attribute***. The same is true for the Standard Information Attribute[19]. The Attribute Type Identifier for the FNA is 0x30 00 00 00 (30).

Record Header #	Standard Information (10 00 00 00)	Filename (30 00 00 00)	Data (80 00 00 00)	Record Slack

Below is the breakdown of FNA[20]. The first 24 bytes are the standard resident attribute header, the same as we saw in the SIA[21].

File Name Attribute (30 00 00 00)			
DEC OFFSET	**HEX OFFSET**	**SIZE (BYTES)**	**DESCRIPTION**
0	0	4	Attribute Type Identifier
4	4	4	Length of the Attribute
8	8	1	Resident (0x00) or Non-Resident Flag (0x01)
9	9	1	Length of Stream Name in Unicode characters
10	0A	2	Offset to the stream name
12	0C	2	Flags
14	0E	2	Attribute Identifier
16	10	4	Size of Resident Data
20	14	2	Offset to Resident Data
22	16	1	Indexing (00=no, 01=yes)
23	17	1	Padding of 00
24	18	6	$MFT Record Number of the Parent Directory
30	1E	2	Sequence number of the Parent Directory
32	20	8	Creation Time
40	28	8	Modification Time
48	30	8	$MFT Modification Time
56	38	8	Last Access Time
64	40	8	Allocated size of index (if record is an index)
72	48	8	Actual size of index (if record is an index)
80	50	4	File Type Flags
84	54	4	Reparse Value
88	58	1	File name length in Unicode
89	59	1	File name type: 00-Posix 01-Win32 02-DOS Short Name 03-Win32/DOS
90	5A	varies	File name

We will again look at a file named HEADER.TXT.

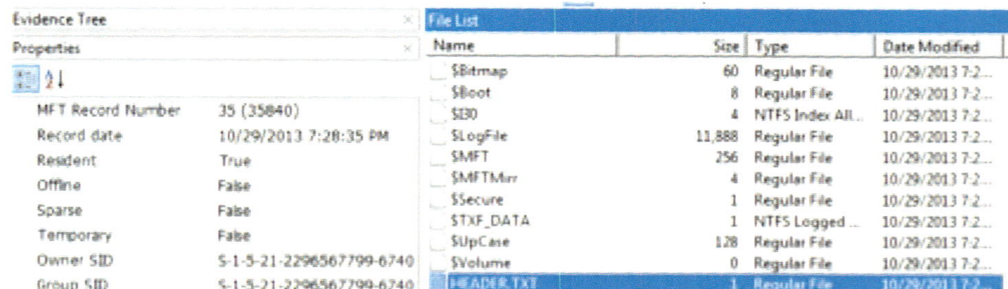

Note that it has a MFT record number of 35 and offset of 35840 in the $MFT (35x1024). We will go to that offset in the $MFT.

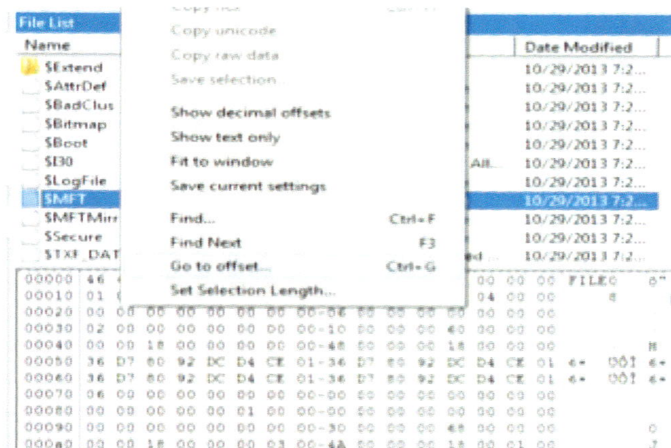

The FNA is highlighted in blue below. Note that the first four bytes are the type identifier (0x30 00 00 00).

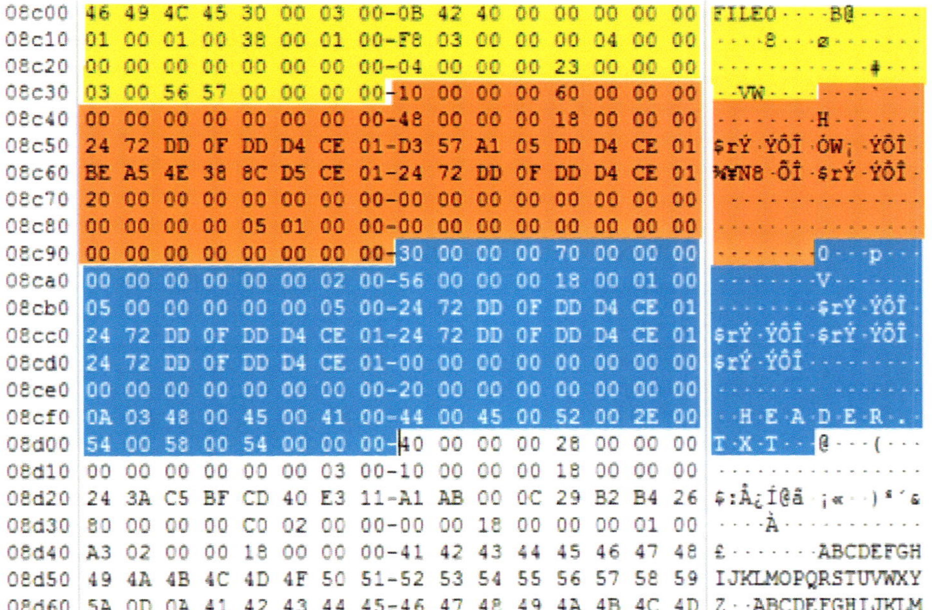

Offsets 4-7 provide the length of the attribute starting at the identifier (0x70 00 00 00 = 112 bytes). The FNA size is variable as the length of the filename can vary. A filename can be up to 255 characters in length[22].

```
08c90 00 00 00 00 00 00 00 00-30 00 00 00 70 00 00 00 ········0···p···
08ca0 00 00 00 00 00 00 02 00-56 00 00 00 18 00 01 00 ········V·······
08cb0 05 00 00 00 00 00 05 00-24 72 DD 0F DD D4 CE 01 ········$rÝ·ÝÔÎ·
08cc0 24 72 DD 0F DD D4 CE 01-24 72 DD 0F DD D4 CE 01 $rÝ·ÝÔÎ·$rÝ·ÝÔÎ·
08cd0 24 72 DD 0F DD D4 CE 01-00 00 00 00 00 00 00 00 $rÝ·ÝÔÎ·········
08ce0 00 00 00 00 00 00 00 00-20 00 00 00 00 00 00 00 ········ ·······
08cf0 0A 03 48 00 45 00 41 00-44 00 45 00 52 00 2E 00 ··H·E·A·D·E·R·.·
08d00 54 00 58 00 54 00 00 00-40 00 00 00 28 00 00 00 T·X·T···@···(···
```

Offset 8 represents whether the content of the attribute is contained in the $MFT (0x00) or whether is stored out in another cluster on the drive (0x01). If the data is stored in the $MFT record, it is referred to as "resident." If the data is stored on another cluster, is it referred to as "non-resident." It is possible for the filename to be non-resident, but highly unlikely.

```
08c90 00 00 00 00 00 00 00 00-30 00 00 00 70 00 00 00 ········0···p···
08ca0 00 00 00 00 00 00 02 00-56 00 00 00 18 00 01 00 ········V·······
08cb0 05 00 00 00 00 00 05 00-24 72 DD 0F DD D4 CE 01 ········$rÝ·ÝÔÎ·
08cc0 24 72 DD 0F DD D4 CE 01-24 72 DD 0F DD D4 CE 01 $rÝ·ÝÔÎ·$rÝ·ÝÔÎ·
08cd0 24 72 DD 0F DD D4 CE 01-00 00 00 00 00 00 00 00 $rÝ·ÝÔÎ·········
08ce0 00 00 00 00 00 00 00 00-20 00 00 00 00 00 00 00 ········ ·······
08cf0 0A 03 48 00 45 00 41 00-44 00 45 00 52 00 2E 00 ··H·E·A·D·E·R·.·
08d00 54 00 58 00 54 00 00 00-40 00 00 00 28 00 00 00 T·X·T···@···(···
08d10 00 00 00 00 00 00 03 00-10 00 00 00 18 00 00 00 ················
```

Offsets 9-13 represent the length of the stream name (the contents of the attributes can be named and is referred to as a stream), offset to the name (stream), and any flags. The FNA does not have a named stream, so these bytes will always be zero.

```
08c90 00 00 00 00 00 00 00 00-30 00 00 00 70 00 00 00 ········0···p···
08ca0 00 00 00 00 00 00 02 00-56 00 00 00 18 00 01 00 ········V·······
08cb0 05 00 00 00 00 00 05 00-24 72 DD 0F DD D4 CE 01 ········$rÝ·ÝÔÎ·
08cc0 24 72 DD 0F DD D4 CE 01-24 72 DD 0F DD D4 CE 01 $rÝ·ÝÔÎ·$rÝ·ÝÔÎ·
08cd0 24 72 DD 0F DD D4 CE 01-00 00 00 00 00 00 00 00 $rÝ·ÝÔÎ·········
08ce0 00 00 00 00 00 00 00 00-20 00 00 00 00 00 00 00 ········ ·······
08cf0 0A 03 48 00 45 00 41 00-44 00 45 00 52 00 2E 00 ··H·E·A·D·E·R·.·
08d00 54 00 58 00 54 00 00 00-40 00 00 00 28 00 00 00 T·X·T···@···(···
```

Offsets 14-15 are for the Attribute Identifier. This identifier is assigned when the attribute is added. The FNA is often the third attribute, 0x02 00, with SIA being 0x00 00 and DATA Attribute 0x03 00.

```
08c90 00 00 00 00 00 00 00 00-30 00 00 00 70 00 00 00 ········0···p···
08ca0 00 00 00 00 00 00 02 00-56 00 00 00 18 00 01 00 ········V·······
08cb0 05 00 00 00 00 00 05 00-24 72 DD 0F DD D4 CE 01 ········$rÝ·ÝÔÎ·
08cc0 24 72 DD 0F DD D4 CE 01-24 72 DD 0F DD D4 CE 01 $rÝ·ÝÔÎ·$rÝ·ÝÔÎ·
08cd0 24 72 DD 0F DD D4 CE 01-00 00 00 00 00 00 00 00 $rÝ·ÝÔÎ·········
08ce0 00 00 00 00 00 00 00 00-20 00 00 00 00 00 00 00 ········ ·······
08cf0 0A 03 48 00 45 00 41 00-44 00 45 00 52 00 2E 00 ··H·E·A·D·E·R·.·
08d00 54 00 58 00 54 00 00 00-40 00 00 00 28 00 00 00 T·X·T···@···(···
```

Offsets 16-19 are for the size of the content of the attribute. The previous 16 bytes and the next 8 bytes are part of the attribute header. As mentioned above, the size of the contents will vary.

```
08c90 00 00 00 00 00 00 00 00-30 00 00 00 70 00 00 00 ········0···p···
08ca0 00 00 00 00 00 00 02 00-56 00 00 00 18 00 01 00 ········V·······
08cb0 05 00 00 00 00 00 05 00-24 72 DD 0F DD D4 CE 01 ········$rÝ·ÝÔÎ·
08cc0 24 72 DD 0F DD D4 CE 01-24 72 DD 0F DD D4 CE 01 $rÝ·ÝÔÎ·$rÝ·ÝÔÎ·
08cd0 24 72 DD 0F DD D4 CE 01-00 00 00 00 00 00 00 00 $rÝ·ÝÔÎ·········
08ce0 00 00 00 00 00 00 00 00-20 00 00 00 00 00 00 00 ········ ·······
08cf0 0A 03 48 00 45 00 41 00-44 00 45 00 52 00 2E 00 ··H·E·A·D·E·R·.·
08d00 54 00 58 00 54 00 00 00-40 00 00 00 28 00 00 00 T·X·T···@···(···
```

Offsets 20-21 are for the offset to the attribute content. The attribute header is 24 bytes and the contents start right after (0x18 00 = 24). Offset 22 is for indexing, which is on in this case. Offset 23 is for padding.

```
08c90 00 00 00 00 00 00 00 00-30 00 00 00 70 00 00 00 ········0···p···
08ca0 00 00 00 00 00 00 02 00-56 00 00 00 18 00 01 00 ········V·······
08cb0 05 00 00 00 00 00 05 00-24 72 DD 0F DD D4 CE 01 ········$rÝ·ÝÔÎ·
08cc0 24 72 DD 0F DD D4 CE 01-24 72 DD 0F DD D4 CE 01 $rÝ·ÝÔÎ·$rÝ·ÝÔÎ·
08cd0 24 72 DD 0F DD D4 CE 01-00 00 00 00 00 00 00 00 $rÝ·ÝÔÎ·········
08ce0 00 00 00 00 00 00 00 00-20 00 00 00 00 00 00 00 ········ ·······
08cf0 0A 03 48 00 45 00 41 00-44 00 45 00 52 00 2E 00 ··H·E·A·D·E·R·.·
08d00 54 00 58 00 54 00 00 00-40 00 00 00 28 00 00 00 T·X·T···@···(···
```

Offsets 24-29 are the $MFT record number of the parent to this file. The parent will be a folder. The parent may also have a parent if it is a subfolder. Tracing the parentage can demonstrate the full path of the file. In this case, the parent's $MFT record is 5. Looking back to Chapter 9, record number 5 is the Root Directory, so the path would be \HEADER.TXT. Offsets 30-31 are listed as the sequence number of the parent, but it is unclear how this is utilized.

```
08c90 00 00 00 00 00 00 00 00-30 00 00 00 70 00 00 00  ········0···p···
08ca0 00 00 00 00 00 00 02 00-56 00 00 00 18 00 01 00  ········V·······
08cb0 05 00 00 00 00 00 05 00-24 72 DD 0F DD D4 CE 01  ········$rÝ·ÝÔÎ·
08cc0 24 72 DD 0F DD D4 CE 01-24 72 DD 0F DD D4 CE 01  $rÝ·ÝÔÎ·$rÝ·ÝÔÎ·
08cd0 24 72 DD 0F DD D4 CE 01-00 00 00 00 00 00 00 00  $rÝ·ÝÔÎ·········
08ce0 00 00 00 00 00 00 00 00-20 00 00 00 00 00 00 00  ········ ·······
08cf0 0A 03 48 00 45 00 41 00-44 00 45 00 52 00 2E 00  ··H·E·A·D·E·R·.·
08d00 54 00 58 00 54 00 00 00-40 00 00 00 28 00 00 00  T·X·T···@···(···
```

Offsets 32-39 have the file's creation date and time in Windows format.
Offsets 40-47 have the file's last modified date and time in Windows format.
Offsets 48-55 have the $MFT records last modified date and time in Windows format.
Offsets 56-63 have the file's last accessed date and time in Windows.

These dates and time are created with the filename attribute, but may not get updated at the same frequency as those in the SIA[23].

```
08c90 00 00 00 00 00 00 00 00-30 00 00 00 70 00 00 00  ········0···p···
08ca0 00 00 00 00 00 00 02 00-56 00 00 00 18 00 01 00  ········V·······
08cb0 05 00 00 00 00 00 05 00-24 72 DD 0F DD D4 CE 01  ········$rÝ·ÝÔÎ·
08cc0 24 72 DD 0F DD D4 CE 01-24 72 DD 0F DD D4 CE 01  $rÝ·ÝÔÎ·$rÝ·ÝÔÎ·
08cd0 24 72 DD 0F DD D4 CE 01-00 00 00 00 00 00 00 00  $rÝ·ÝÔÎ·········
08ce0 00 00 00 00 00 00 00 00-20 00 00 00 00 00 00 00  ········ ·······
08cf0 0A 03 48 00 45 00 41 00-44 00 45 00 52 00 2E 00  ··H·E·A·D·E·R·.·
08d00 54 00 58 00 54 00 00 00-40 00 00 00 28 00 00 00  T·X·T···@···(···
```

In this example, all four dates and times are the same.

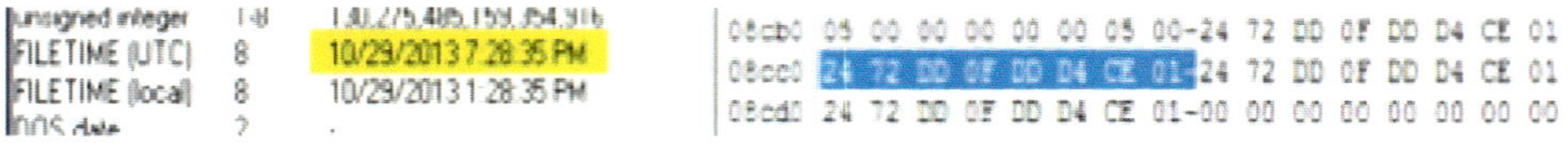

```
FILETIME (UTC)    8   10/29/2013 7:28:35 PM      08cb0 05 00 00 00 00 00 05 00-24 72 DD 0F DD D4 CE 01
FILETIME (local)  8   10/29/2013 1:28:35 PM      08cc0 24 72 DD 0F DD D4 CE 01-24 72 DD 0F DD D4 CE 01
                                                 08cd0 24 72 DD 0F DD D4 CE 01-00 00 00 00 00 00 00 00
```

A comparison to the dates and time of the SIA shows these dates/times.

Created:	10/29/2013 7:28:35PM (UTC)
Last Modified:	10/29/2013 7:18:35PM (UTC)
Record Modified:	10/30/2013 4:22:35PM (UTC)
Last Accessed:	10/29/2013 7:28:35PM (UTC)

The SIA dates and times are what are reported by Windows and forensic tools; the FNA dates and time are not as reliable.

Offsets 64-71 are used for the allocated size of a folder index – these bytes will not be used for a file. Offsets 72-79 are used for the actual size of a folder and are also not used for a file.

```
08c90 00 00 00 00 00 00 00 00-30 00 00 00 70 00 00 00 ········0···p···
08ca0 00 00 00 00 00 00 02 00-56 00 00 00 18 00 01 00 ········V·······
08cb0 05 00 00 00 00 00 05 00-24 72 DD 0F DD D4 CE 01 ········$rÝ·ÝÔÎ·
08cc0 24 72 DD 0F DD D4 CE 01-24 72 DD 0F DD D4 CE 01 $rÝ·ÝÔÎ·$rÝ·ÝÔÎ·
08cd0 24 72 DD 0F DD D4 CE 01-00 00 00 00 00 00 00 00 $rÝ·ÝÔÎ·········
08ce0 00 00 00 00 00 00 00 00-20 00 00 00 00 00 00 00 ················
08cf0 0A 03 48 00 45 00 41 00-44 00 45 00 52 00 2E 00 ··H·E·A·D·E·R·.·
08d00 54 00 58 00 54 00 00 00-40 00 00 00 28 00 00 00 T·X·T···@···(···
```

Offsets 80-83 are for the File attributes, similar to the FAT Directory attributes and the same as discussed in the SIA. See the DOS attribute table in Chapter 10.

```
08c90 00 00 00 00 00 00 00 00-30 00 00 00 70 00 00 00 ········0···p···
08ca0 00 00 00 00 00 00 02 00-56 00 00 00 18 00 01 00 ········V·······
08cb0 05 00 00 00 00 00 05 00-24 72 DD 0F DD D4 CE 01 ········$rÝ·ÝÔÎ·
08cc0 24 72 DD 0F DD D4 CE 01-24 72 DD 0F DD D4 CE 01 $rÝ·ÝÔÎ·$rÝ·ÝÔÎ·
08cd0 24 72 DD 0F DD D4 CE 01-00 00 00 00 00 00 00 00 $rÝ·ÝÔÎ·········
08ce0 00 00 00 00 00 00 00 00-20 00 00 00 00 00 00 00 ················
08cf0 0A 03 48 00 45 00 41 00-44 00 45 00 52 00 2E 00 ··H·E·A·D·E·R·.·
08d00 54 00 58 00 54 00 00 00-40 00 00 00 28 00 00 00 T·X·T···@···(···
```

Offsets 84-87 are designated for Reparse values. Reparse points will be discussed in the next chapter and the usage in the FNA is unclear.

```
08c90 00 00 00 00 00 00 00 00-30 00 00 00 70 00 00 00 ········0···p···
08ca0 00 00 00 00 00 00 02 00-56 00 00 00 18 00 01 00 ········V·······
08cb0 05 00 00 00 00 00 05 00-24 72 DD 0F DD D4 CE 01 ········$rÝ·ÝÔÎ·
08cc0 24 72 DD 0F DD D4 CE 01-24 72 DD 0F DD D4 CE 01 $rÝ·ÝÔÎ·$rÝ·ÝÔÎ·
08cd0 24 72 DD 0F DD D4 CE 01-00 00 00 00 00 00 00 00 $rÝ·ÝÔÎ·········
08ce0 00 00 00 00 00 00 00 00-20 00 00 00 00 00 00 00 ················
08cf0 0A 03 48 00 45 00 41 00-44 00 45 00 52 00 2E 00 ··H·E·A·D·E·R·.·
08d00 54 00 58 00 54 00 00 00-30 00 00 00 70 00 00 00 T·X·T···0···p···
```

Offset 88 is for the number of bytes in the filename in Unicode. 0x0A equals 10 characters, HEADER.TXT

```
08c90 00 00 00 00 00 00 00 00-30 00 00 00 70 00 00 00 ········0···p···
08ca0 00 00 00 00 00 00 02 00-56 00 00 00 18 00 01 00 ········V·······
08cb0 05 00 00 00 00 00 05 00-24 72 DD 0F DD D4 CE 01 ········$rÝ·ÝÔÎ·
08cc0 24 72 DD 0F DD D4 CE 01-24 72 DD 0F DD D4 CE 01 $rÝ·ÝÔÎ·$rÝ·ÝÔÎ·
08cd0 24 72 DD 0F DD D4 CE 01-00 00 00 00 00 00 00 00 $rÝ·ÝÔÎ·········
08ce0 00 00 00 00 00 00 00 00-20 00 00 00 00 00 00 00 ················
08cf0 0A 03 48 00 45 00 41 00-44 00 45 00 52 00 2E 00 ··H·E·A·D·E·R·.·
08d00 54 00 58 00 54 00 00 00-30 00 00 00 70 00 00 00 T·X·T···0···p···
```

Offset 89 is for the filename type. 00 is for a POSIX name, which fully allows 255 Unicode characters. 01 is for Win32 names, which is a subset of Unicode characters, but still allows 255 characters. 02 is DOS compliant, meaning it fits the 8.3 rule and is typically the Short Filename that is created from the Long Filename. 03 is a DOS compatible filename. This is a name that originally meets the 8.3 rule, such as HEADER.TXT and no long filename is needed.

```
08c90  00 00 00 00 00 00 00 00-30 00 00 00 70 00 00 00  ········0···p···
08ca0  00 00 00 00 00 00 02 00-56 00 00 00 18 00 01 00  ········V·······
08cb0  05 00 00 00 00 00 05 00-24 72 DD 0F DD D4 CE 01  ········$rÝ·ÝÔÎ·
08cc0  24 72 DD 0F DD D4 CE 01-24 72 DD 0F DD D4 CE 01  $rÝ·ÝÔÎ·$rÝ·ÝÔÎ·
08cd0  24 72 DD 0F DD D4 CE 01-00 00 00 00 00 00 00 00  $rÝ·ÝÔÎ·········
08ce0  00 00 00 00 00 00 00 00-20 00 00 00 00 00 00 00
08cf0  0A 03 48 00 45 00 41 00-44 00 45 00 52 00 2E 00  ··H·E·A·D·E·R·.·
08d00  54 00 58 00 54 00 00 00-30 00 00 00 70 00 00 00  T·X·T···0···p···
```

Offset 90 is the beginning of the filename and the size varies to fit the name up to 255 characters.

```
08c90  00 00 00 00 00 00 00 00-30 00 00 00 70 00 00 00  ········0···p···
08ca0  00 00 00 00 00 00 02 00-56 00 00 00 18 00 01 00  ········V·······
08cb0  05 00 00 00 00 00 05 00-24 72 DD 0F DD D4 CE 01  ········$rÝ·ÝÔÎ·
08cc0  24 72 DD 0F DD D4 CE 01-24 72 DD 0F DD D4 CE 01  $rÝ·ÝÔÎ·$rÝ·ÝÔÎ·
08cd0  24 72 DD 0F DD D4 CE 01-00 00 00 00 00 00 00 00  $rÝ·ÝÔÎ·········
08ce0  00 00 00 00 00 00 00 00-20 00 00 00 00 00 00 00
08cf0  0A 03 48 00 45 00 41 00-44 00 45 00 52 00 2E 00  ··H·E·A·D·E·R·.·
08d00  54 00 58 00 54 00 00 00-30 00 00 00 70 00 00 00  T·X·T···0···p···
```

A file may have multiple names, meaning multiple Filename attributes, one right after the other. An example would be a Long Filename and a Short Filename.

```
0a000  46 49 4C 45 30 00 03 00-9D 62 40 00 00 00 00 00  FILE0···b@·····
0a010  01 00 02 00 38 00 01 00-D0 01 00 00 00 04 00 00  ····8···Ð·······
0a020  00 00 00 00 00 00 00 00-04 00 00 00 28 00 00 00  ············(···
0a030  03 00 00 00 00 00 00 00-10 00 00 00 60 00 00 00  ············`···
0a040  00 00 00 00 00 00 00 00-48 00 00 00 18 00 00 00  ········H·······
0a050  9C A8 D8 9F 52 DB CE 01-00 27 78 61 4F F3 C9 01  ·Ø·RÛÎ··'xaOóÉ·
0a060  C4 D0 74 A4 52 DB CE 01-9C A8 D8 9F 52 DB CE 01  ÄÐt¤RÛÎ··Ø·RÛÎ·
0a070  20 00 00 00 00 00 00 00-00 00 00 00 00 00 00 00
0a080  00 00 00 00 05 01 00 00-00 00 00 00 00 00 00 00
0a090  00 00 00 00 00 00 00 00-30 00 00 00 70 00 00 00  ········0···p···
0a0a0  00 00 00 00 00 00 03 00-52 00 00 00 18 00 01 00  ········R·······
0a0b0  24 00 00 00 00 00 01 00-9C A8 D8 9F 52 DB CE 01  $·········Ø·RÛÎ·
0a0c0  9C A8 D8 9F 52 DB CE 01-9C A8 D8 9F 52 DB CE 01  ··Ø·RÛÎ···Ø·RÛÎ·
0a0d0  9C A8 D8 9F 52 DB CE 01-00 00 9C 02 00 00 00 00  ··Ø·RÛÎ·········
0a0e0  00 00 00 00 00 00 00 00-20 00 00 00 00 00 00 00
0a0f0  08 02 24 00 4D 00 46 00-54 00 5F 00 57 00 7E 00  ··$·M·F·T·_·W·~·
0a100  31 00 68 00 20 00 46 00-30 00 00 00 78 00 00 00  1·h· ·F·0···x···
0a110  00 00 00 00 00 00 02 00-60 00 00 00 18 00 01 00
0a120  24 00 00 00 00 00 01 00-9C A8 D8 9F 52 DB CE 01  $·········Ø·RÛÎ·
0a130  9C A8 D8 9F 52 DB CE 01-9C A8 D8 9F 52 DB CE 01  ··Ø·RÛÎ···Ø·RÛÎ·
0a140  9C A8 D8 9F 52 DB CE 01-00 00 9C 02 00 00 00 00  ··Ø·RÛÎ·········
0a150  00 00 00 00 00 00 00 00-20 00 00 00 00 00 00 00
0a160  0F 01 24 00 4D 00 46 00-54 00 5F 00 77 00 69 00  ··$·M·F·T·_·w·i·
0a170  74 00 68 00 20 00 46 00-69 00 6C 00 65 00 73 00  t·h· ·F·i·l·e·s·
```

PRACTICAL EXERCISE 3

Open 10_Pract1.E01 in FTK Imager and complete the table for the three files (record numbers 35, 37, and 39). Note that number 37 has two filename attributes.

FILENAME ATTRIBUTE	FILE #35	FILE #37-1	FILE #37-2	FILE #39
What is the size of the attribute:				
The $MFT Record number of the parent is:				
What is the Creation Date/Time (UTC):				
What is the Modification Date/Time (UTC):				
What is the Record Modification Date/Time (UTC):				
What is the Last Access Date/Time (UTC):				
The file name length in Unicode is:				
The file name type is:				
The actual file name itself is:				

Write out the full path for each of the three files up to the Root Directory (i.e., \FilePath Folder1\File1.txt).

35:
37:
39:

PRACTICAL EXERCISE 4

1. Format a USB Flash Drive with NTFS.

2. Open the drive in Windows Explorer.

3. Create a New Text Document.

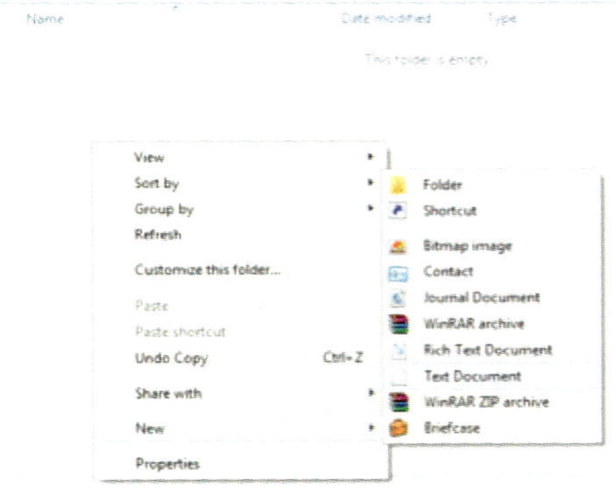

4. Leave the name as New Text Document.txt.

5. Open FTK Imager and click add evidence. Select Logical Drive and the drive letter of the USB.

6. Select the $MFT and go to offset 35840, the New Text Document.txt should be record number 35 (35x1024=35840).

7. How many Filename Attributes are there? ___________

8. Open a command prompt window by running CMD.

9. Change to the USB drive: <drive letter>:

10. Type the following: fsutil hardlink create TESTFILE.TXT NEWTEX~1.TXT

11. Go back and re-add the USB drive to FTK Imager and view record # 35 again.

12. How many Filename Attributes are there now? __________

CHAPTER SUMMARY

The ***Master File Table*** is set up in 1024 byte records with each file and folder having at least one record in the table. Each record will begin with a 56-byte header for volumes formatted with Windows XP or later.

The ***record header*** always begins with a signature of ***FILE*** and has the record number near the end. This record is useful in tracking parentage of a file.

The record header utilizes an Update Sequence Array in order to link the two sectors that make up the record's 1024 bytes.

There is a flag in the header indicating whether or not the file or folder is deleted.

The header is the offset to the beginning of the file attributes. The first attribute in the file record is the Standard Information Attribute (SIA).

The ***Standard Information Attribute*** will be present in every file and folder and is 96 bytes in length, starting with the Attribute Type Identifier 0x10 00 00 00.

The SIA begins with standard header information like all attributes. The header is 24 bytes in length and has an indicator that the attribute is resident, meaning the content of the attribute is present in the record.
The content of the SIA is the four dates/times associates with the file:

Creation Date/Time
Last Modified Date/Time
Record Modification Date/Time
Last Accessed Date/Time

Every file and folder will have a ***Filename Attribute (FNA).*** This attribute will vary in size as the file name can be between 1 and 255 characters in length.

The FNA includes the file's parent $MFT record number. This number can be used to trace the full path of the file. This can be helpful if $MFT records are recovered in unallocated space.

There can be multiple Filename Attributes associated with a single file. These multiple attributes are known as ***Hard Links***. The names can be used for long or short filenames or to names in different folders, which all point to the same data.

There are dates and times included in the FNA, but these are not updated at the same frequency as the dates and times in the SIA. It is advised not to rely on the FNA dates and times.

On the following page, read the contents of the nine files containing $MFT records in a hex editor and parse the information.

AT HOME EXERCISE

RECORD HEADER	File 1	File 2	File 3
ASCII File Signature Identifier is:			
Offset to Update Sequence Array:			
Number of entries in the Update Array:			
$Logfile sequence number (Hex):			
Sequence count:			
Hard Link count:			
Offset to the first attribute:			
Is the file/folder deleted:			
Logical size of the record:			
Physical size of the record:			
Next attribute identification:			
$MFT Record Number:			
Update Sequence array values:			
STANDARD INFORMATION ATTRIBUTE			
The length of this attribute is:			
Size of the Resident data is:			
Offset to the Resident data is:			
The date/time (Local) the file was created is:			
The date/time (UTC) the file was modified is:			
The last $MFT modified date/time (Local) is:			
The last access date/time (UTC) of the file is:			
The DOS attributes are:			
The Security ID is:			
FILENAME ATTRIBUTE			
What is the size of the attribute:			
The $MFT Record number of the parent is:			
What is the Creation Date/Time (UTC):			
What is the Modification Date/Time (UTC):			
What is the Record Modification Date/Time (UTC)			
What is the Last Access Date/Time (UTC):			
The file name length in Unicode is:			
The file name type is:			
The actual file name itself is:			
FILENAME ATTRIBUTE			
What is the size of the attribute:			
The $MFT Record number of the parent is:			
What is the Creation Date/Time (UTC):			
What is the Modification Date/Time (UTC):			
What is the Record Modification Date/Time (UTC):			
What is the Last Access Date/Time (UTC):			
The file name length in Unicode is:			
The file name type is:			
The actual file name itself is:			

Complete the table for the nine (9) $MFT record files.

RECORD HEADER	File 4	File 5	File 6
ASCII File Signature Identifier is:			
Offset to Update Sequence Array:			
Number of entries in the Update Array:			
$Logfile sequence number (Hex):			
Sequence count:			
Hard Link count:			
Offset to the first attribute:			
Is the file/folder deleted:			
Logical size of the record:			
Physical size of the record:			
Next attribute identification:			
$MFT Record Number:			
Update Sequence array values:			
STANDARD INFORMATION ATTRIBUTE			
The length of this attribute is:			
Size of the Resident data is:			
Offset to the Resident data is:			
The date/time (Local) the file was created is:			
The date/time (UTC) the file was modified is:			
The last $MFT modified date/time (Local) is:			
The last access date/time (UTC) of the file is:			
The DOS attributes are:			
The Security ID is:			
FILENAME ATTRIBUTE			
What is the size of the attribute:			
The $MFT Record number of the parent is:			
What is the Creation Date/Time (UTC):			
What is the Modification Date/Time (UTC):			
What is the Record Modification Date/Time (UTC)			
What is the Last Access Date/Time (UTC):			
The file name length in Unicode is:			
The file name type is:			
The actual file name itself is:			
FILENAME ATTRIBUTE			
What is the size of the attribute:			
The $MFT Record number of the parent is:			
What is the Creation Date/Time (UTC):			
What is the Modification Date/Time (UTC):			
What is the Record Modification Date/Time (UTC):			
What is the Last Access Date/Time (UTC):			
The file name length in Unicode is:			
The file name type is:			
The actual file name itself is:			

Complete the table for the nine (9) $MFT record files.

RECORD HEADER	File 7	File 8	File 9
ASCII File Signature Identifier is:			
Offset to Update Sequence Array:			
Number of entries in the Update Array:			
$Logfile sequence number (Hex):			
Sequence count:			
Hard Link count:			
Offset to the first attribute:			
Is the file/folder deleted:			
Logical size of the record:			
Physical size of the record:			
Next attribute identification:			
$MFT Record Number:			
Update Sequence array values:			
STANDARD INFORMATION ATTRIBUTE			
The length of this attribute is:			
Size of the Resident data is:			
Offset to the Resident data is:			
The date/time (Local) the file was created is:			
The date/time (UTC) the file was modified is:			
The last $MFT modified date/time (Local) is:			
The last access date/time (UTC) of the file is:			
The DOS attributes are:			
The Security ID is:			
FILENAME ATTRIBUTE			
What is the size of the attribute:			
The $MFT Record number of the parent is:			
What is the Creation Date/Time (UTC):			
What is the Modification Date/Time (UTC):			
What is the Record Modification Date/Time (UTC)			
What is the Last Access Date/Time (UTC):			
The file name length in Unicode is:			
The file name type is:			
The actual file name itself is:			
FILENAME ATTRIBUTE			
What is the size of the attribute:			
The $MFT Record number of the parent is:			
What is the Creation Date/Time (UTC):			
What is the Modification Date/Time (UTC):			
What is the Record Modification Date/Time (UTC):			
What is the Last Access Date/Time (UTC):			
The file name length in Unicode is:			
The file name type is:			
The actual file name itself is:			

REFERENCES

1. Carrier, B. (2005). File System Forensic Analysis. (pp. 302). Upper Saddle River: Addison-Wesley.
2. Sammes, T., & Jenkinson, B. (2007). Forensic Computing, a Practitioner's Guide. (2nd ed., pp. 218). London: Springer Publishing.
3. Master File Table. (2013, October 1). Retrieved from http://msdn.microsoft.com/en-us/library/bb470206(v=vs.85).aspx.
4. Attribute - $attribute_list. (n.d.). Retrieved from http://inform.pucp.edu.pe/~inf232/Ntfs/ntfs_doc_v0.5/attributes/attribute_list.html.
5. Carrier, B. (2005). File System Forensic Analysis. (pp. 303). Upper Saddle River: Addison-Wesley.
6. Sammes, T., & Jenkinson, B. (2007). Forensic Computing, a Practitioner's Guide. (2nd ed., pp. 226). London: Springer Publishing.
7. (2010). Encase advanced computer forensics. (v6.15pvi ed., p. 19). Pasadena: Guidance Software, Inc.
8. Carrier, B. (2005). File System Forensic Analysis. (pp. 353). Upper Saddle River: Addison-Wesley.
9. Concept - fixup. (2001, July 11). Retrieved from http://www.reddragonfly.org/ntfs/concepts/fixup.html.
10. Concept – file record. (2001, July 11). Retrieved from http://www.reddragonfly.org/ntfs/concepts/fixup.html.
11. Attoe, R. (2010). Ntfs (new technology file system). In IACIS Advanced Windows Forensic Examiner's Manual (p. 125).
12. Carrier, B. (2005). File System Forensic Analysis. (pp. 355-356). Upper Saddle River: Addison-Wesley.
13. Master file table. (2013, October 1). Retrieved from http://msdn.microsoft.com/en-us/library/bb470206(v=vs.85).aspx.
14. Sammes, T., & Jenkinson, B. (2007). Forensic Computing, a Practitioner's Guide. (2nd ed., pp. 251). London: Springer Publishing.
15. Russon, R., & Fledel, Y. (n.d.). NTFS Documentation. Retrieved from http://ftp.kolibrios.org/users/Asper/docs/NTFS/ntfsdoc.html.
16. Mueller, L. (2009, February 1). [Web log message]. Retrieved from http://www.forensickb.com/2009/02/detecting-timestamp-changing-utlities.html.
17. [Web log message]. (2006, November 7). Retrieved from http://blogs.technet.com/b/filecab/archive/2006/11/07/disabling-last-access-time-in-windows-vista-to-improve-ntfs-performance.asp.
18. Carrier, B. (2005). File System Forensic Analysis. (pp. 360-361). Upper Saddle River: Addison-Wesley.
19. Carrier, B. (2005). File System Forensic Analysis. (pp. 303). Upper Saddle River: Addison-Wesley.
20. Carrier, B. (2005). File System Forensic Analysis. (pp. 362). Upper Saddle River: Addison-Wesley.
21. Master file table. (2013, October 1). Retrieved from http://msdn.microsoft.com/en-us/library/bb470206(v=vs.85).aspx.
22. NTFS vs FAT vs exFAT. (n.d.). Retrieved from http://www.ntfs.com/ntfs_vs_fat.htm.
23. Carrier, B. (2005). File System Forensic Analysis. (pp. 364-365). Upper Saddle River: Addison-Wesley.

CASE STUDY 5: CD BURNING

A salesman for a company left employment and went to work for a competitor. The original company was concerned about the former employee taking sensitive files and made a request to have his work computer examined. During the analysis, it was noted that numerous files under his My Documents folder and subfolders had last accessed dates just prior to his resignation. Most, but not all the files were affected.

In the past, many anti-virus scans would trip the last accessed date of files being examined but this will affect all the files on the drive, not selective ones under one folder. It was possible that these selective files could have been copied onto another drive, but analysis of the register did not show any other drive previous connected. The number and size of the files also would have prevented them from being emailed out.

Further examination revealed that the $MFT Last Written date/time for each of the files was approximately 20-30 seconds AFTER the Last Accessed date/time. This meant that whatever operation was occurring was changing the $MFT record of the file. Examination of the $MFT records showed the Next Attribute ID value was incremented higher than what should have been expected for the number of attributes present. For the most part, there were five attributes found, SIA, FNA, FNA, OBJID, and DATA. The Next Attribute ID would typically be 6; however this value was also higher. This would indicate that another attribute had been added and then removed. The record slack also contained data consistent with another attribute being added before the OBJID attribute.

Another possibility for copying data from a drive is by burning them to CD. No third-party burning software was found, but Windows has a built-in burning program. Files are simply dropped onto the drive letter of the CD drive and then they can be written. Testing this possibility was done by taking several files and copying their $MFT records. The names were then dropped onto the CD drive letter and another copy of the $MFT records were made. Finally, the files were burned to a CD in the manner described and then their $MFT records would be compared.

When the files were dragged to the CD drive letter, a Hardlink (a Filename Attribute) was created in the CD burning folder. The Next Atribute ID was incremented because there were not seven attributes. This also shifted the OBJID and DATA attributes down in the record. Once the burning was complete, the hardlink was deleted from the record and the OBJID and DATA attributes were copied back to their original location, leaving data in the record slack space. The Next Attribute ID is not reduced, so it remained at seven.

When confronted, the former employee admitted to burning the files to disc.

11 FILE SYSTEMS: NTFS PART III

In the past chapter, we looked at the $MFT record and the required attributes for each file and folder. The Standard Information Attribute and the Filename Attributes are present in every file and folder. These attributes contain the metadata about the files, dates, names, and parents. The next attribute to be examined actually contains the content of the file.

Data Attribute

Each file (non-folder) will have a Data Attribute[1]. This is the content of the file, the picture, document, programing, etc. The Data Attribute can be either Resident or Non-Resident[2]. This means the content of the file is either stored in the $MFT record or out in a cluster. The Attribute Type Identifier for the Data Attribute is 0x80 00 00 00 (80). Below is the breakdown of the Resident Data Attribute[3].

DATA ATTRIBUTE-RESIDENT (80 00 00 00)			
DEC OFFSET	**HEX OFFSET**	**SIZE (BYTES)**	**DESCRIPTION**
0	0	4	Attribute Type Identifier
4	4	4	Length of the Attribute
8	8	1	Resident (0x00) or Non-Resident Flag (0x01)
9	9	1	Length of Stream Name in Unicode characters
10	0A	2	Offset to the stream name
12	0C	2	Flags
14	0E	2	Attribute Identifier
16	10	4	Size of Resident Data
20	14	2	Offset to Resident Data
22	16	1	Indexing (00=no, 01=yes)
23	17	1	Padding
24	18	varies	Data

Note that the first 24 bytes contain the same types of information, as does the Filename Attribute; this is because all Resident attributes use the same attribute header information. The content of the attribute begins at offset 24.

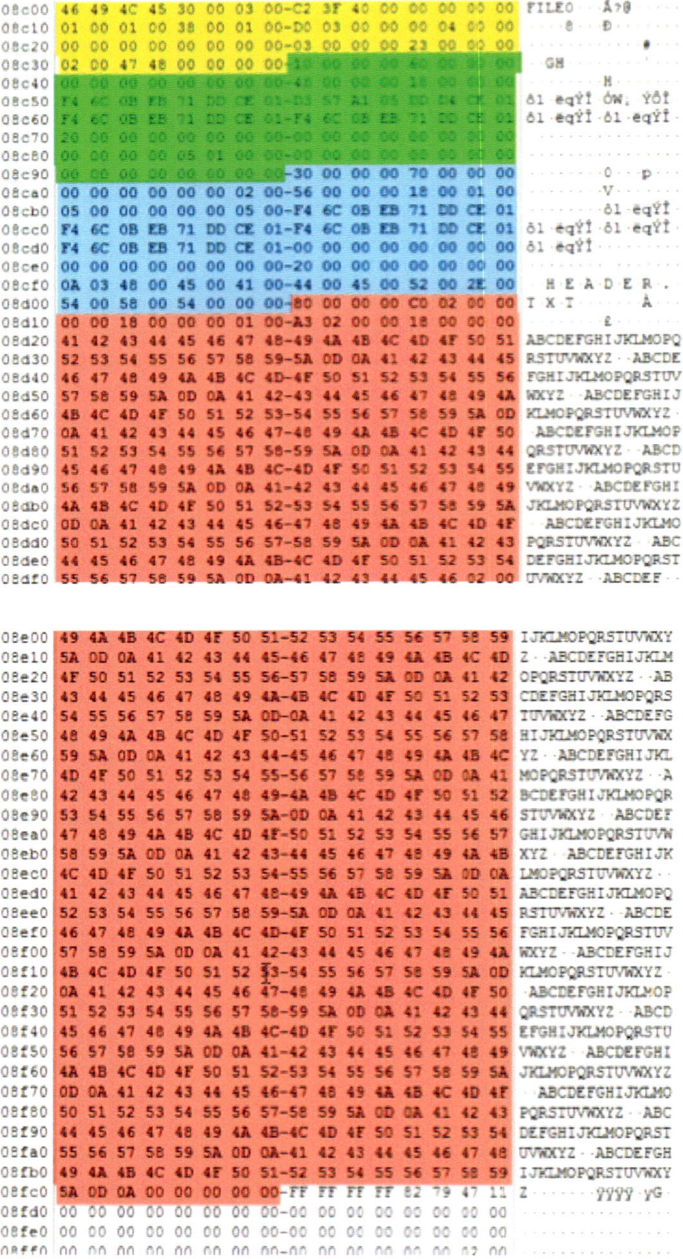

Note the Attribute Type Identifier of 0x80 00 00 00 and the attribute size of 704 bytes (0xC0 02 00 00).

```
08d00 54 00 58 00 54 00 00 00-80 00 00 00 C0 02 00 00 T·X·T·······À···
08d10 00 00 18 00 00 00 01 00-A3 02 00 00 18 00 00 00 ········£·······
08d20 41 42 43 44 45 46 47 48-49 4A 4B 4C 4D 4F 50 51 ABCDEFGHIJKLMOPQ
```

The size of the attribute content is (0xA3 02 00 00) or 675 bytes. This indicates that the content of Header.txt is stored in this record. A record can hold up to approximately 750 bytes of content, depending the number of attributes present. Once the attribute fills the record it becomes Non-Resident.

```
08d00 54 00 58 00 54 00 00 00-80 00 00 00 C0 02 00 00 T·X·T·······À···
08d10 00 00 18 00 00 00 01 00-A3 02 00 00 18 00 00 00 ········£·······
08d20 41 42 43 44 45 46 47 48-49 4A 4B 4C 4D 4F 50 51 ABCDEFGHIJKLMOPQ
```

End of Record Marker

After the last attribute, there is a marker for the end of the record (0xFF FF FF FF 82 79 47 11). Any data after the marker to the end of the sector is RECORD SLACK[4].

```
08fd0 51 52 53 54 55 56 57 58-59 5A 0D 0A 41 42 43 44 QRSTUVWXYZ··ABCD
08fe0 45 46 47 48 49 4A 4B 4C-4D 4E 4F 50 51 52 0D 0A EFGHIJKLMNOPQR··
08ff0 FF FF FF FF 82 79 47 11-00 00 00 00 00 00 02 00 ÿÿÿÿ·yG·········
```

PRACTICAL EXERCISE 1

Open 11_Pract1.E01 in FTK Imager and complete the table for the five files (record numbers 35-39).

DATA ATTRIBUTE	#35	#36	#37	#38	#39
Size of Attribute					
Attribute Identifier					
Size of the Content					

PRACTICAL EXERCISE 2

1. Format a USB flash drive with NTFS.

2. Open the drive in Windows Explorer.

3. Copy the file HEADER.TXT from the Chapter 11 files to the flash drive.

4. Open FTK Imager and click add evidence. Select Logical Drive and the drive letter of the USB flash drive.

5. Select the $MFT and go to offset 35840; the HEADER.TXT should be record number 35 (35x1024=35840).

6. Provide the following information for the Data Attribute:
Size of the Attribute:
Size of the Content:
Describe the Content:
Offset to the End of Record Marker from the beginning of the record:
What is data is in the Record Slack:

7. Reformat the flash drive with NTFS.

8. Open the HEADER.TXT file from the Chapter 11 folder with Notepad. Do not skip step 7 and open the file from the flash drive. Once open, add the letters STUVWXYZ to the end of the file and save.

9. Copy the file to the flash drive.

10. Open FTK Imager and click add evidence. Select Logical Drive and the drive letter of the USB flash drive.

11. Select the $MFT and go to offset 35840; the HEADER.TXT should be record number 35 (35x1024=35840).

12. Provide the following information for the Data Attribute:
Size of the Attribute:
What data is in the Record Slack:

Note the data is now Non-Resident.

13. Open the HEADER.TXT file from the flash drive with Notepad. Once open, remove the letters STUVWXYZ from the end of the file and save.

14. Open FTK Imager and click add evidence. Select Logical Drive and the drive letter of the USB flash drive.

15. Select the $MFT and go to offset 35840; the HEADER.TXT should be record number 35 (35x1024=35840).

16. Provide the following information for the Data Attribute:
Size of the Attribute:
What data is in the Record Slack:

Note that once a file is Non-Resident, it will remain Non-Resident.

Non-Resident Data Attribute

If the content of the file is too large to fit within the confines of the $MFT record, it is stored outside the $MFT in an available cluster or clusters. Since the content is not contained in the Data Attribute, what is stored there is the listing of the clusters needed for the file.

Below is the breakdown of a Non-Resident Data Attribute[5].

Data Attribute-Non Resident (80 00 00 00)			
DEC OFFSET	HEX OFFSET	SIZE (BYTES)	DESCRIPTION
0	0	4	Attribute Type Identifier
4	4	4	Length of the Attribute
8	8	1	Resident (0x00) or Non-Resident Flag (0x01)
9	9	1	Length of Stream Name in Unicode characters
10	0A	2	Offset to the stream name
12	0C	2	Flags
14	0E	2	Attribute Identifier
16	10	8	Starting VCN of runlist
24	18	8	Ending VCN of runlist
32	20	2	Offset to runlist in bytes
34	22	2	Used for compression
36	24	4	Unused
40	28	8	Allocated size for content in bytes (physical size)
48	30	8	Actual size of content in bytes (logical size)
56	38	8	Initialized size of content in bytes
64	40	varies	Data runs

Note that the first 16 bytes are the same as the other attributes we have looked at. The Attribute Type Identifier remains as 0x80 00 00 00.

```
4a64900  2E 00 50 00 4E 00 47 00-80 00 00 00 58 00 00 00  .·P·N·G·····X···
4a64910  01 00 00 00 00 00 03 00-00 00 00 00 00 00 00 00  ················
4a64920  22 00 00 00 00 00 00 00-40 00 00 00 00 00 00 00  "·······@·······
4a64930  00 30 02 00 00 00 00 00-CD 23 02 00 00 00 00 00  ·0······Í#······
4a64940  CD 23 02 00 00 00 00 00-31 07 01 4B 54 21 07 55  Í#······1··KT!·U
4a64950  5F 31 10 EA D6 FB 21 05-7C 16 00 8A EF D8 EC 86  _1·êÖû!·|···ïØi·
4a64960  FF FF FF FF 82 79 47 11-00 00 00 00 00 00 00 00  ÿÿÿÿ·yG·········
```

Note that at offset 8, the Resident flag is set to 0x01.

```
4a64900  2E 00 50 00 4E 00 47 00-80 00 00 00 58 00 00 00  .·P·N·G·····X···
4a64910  01 00 00 00 00 00 03 00-00 00 00 00 00 00 00 00  ················
4a64920  22 00 00 00 00 00 00 00-40 00 00 00 00 00 00 00  "·······@·······
4a64930  00 30 02 00 00 00 00 00-CD 23 02 00 00 00 00 00  ·0······Í#······
4a64940  CD 23 02 00 00 00 00 00-31 07 01 4B 54 21 07 55  Í#······1··KT!·U
4a64950  5F 31 10 EA D6 FB 21 05-7C 16 00 8A EF D8 EC 86  _1·êÖû!·|···ïØi·
4a64960  FF FF FF FF 82 79 47 11-00 00 00 00 00 00 00 00  ÿÿÿÿ·yG·········
```

Starting at offsets 16 through 23 is the beginning of the Virtual Cluster Number (VCN) listing and offsets 24 through 31 is the ending Virtual Cluster Number (VCN). The Virtual Cluster Numbers are the counts of the clusters in the file starting with 0[6]. Offsets 16-23 are the start with 0x00 00 00 00 00 00 00 00. I have not come across any starting VCNs other than 0. The ending VCN is this case is 0x22 00 00 00 00 00 00 00, equaling 34. This means there are 35 clusters associated with this file (0-34).

```
4a64900  2E 00 50 00 4E 00 47 00-80 00 00 00 58 00 00 00  .·P·N·G·····X···
4a64910  01 00 00 00 00 00 03 00-00 00 00 00 00 00 00 00  ················
4a64920  22 00 00 00 00 00 00 00-40 00 00 00 00 00 00 00  "·······@·······
4a64930  00 30 02 00 00 00 00 00-CD 23 02 00 00 00 00 00  ·0······Í#······
4a64940  CD 23 02 00 00 00 00 00-31 07 01 4B 54 21 07 55  Í#······1··KT!·U
4a64950  5F 31 10 EA D6 FB 21 05-7C 16 00 8A EF D8 EC 86  _1·êÖû!·|···ïØi·
4a64960  FF FF FF FF 82 79 47 11-00 00 00 00 00 00 00 00  ÿÿÿÿ·yG·········
```

Offsets 32-33 have the offset to the runlist. One advantage to NTFS over FAT is the fact that all the clusters are identified for a file. Recall that in FAT, only the first cluster is identified. The clusters are identified in what are classed runlists[7]. The list begins at offset 64 in all Non-Resident Data Attributes.

```
4a64900  2E 00 50 00 4E 00 47 00-80 00 00 00 58 00 00 00  .·P·N·G·····X···
4a64910  01 00 00 00 00 00 03 00-00 00 00 00 00 00 00 00  ················
4a64920  22 00 00 00 00 00 00 00-40 00 00 00 00 00 00 00  "·······@·······
4a64930  00 30 02 00 00 00 00 00-CD 23 02 00 00 00 00 00  ·0······Í#······
4a64940  CD 23 02 00 00 00 00 00-31 07 01 4B 54 21 07 55  Í#······1··KT!·U
4a64950  5F 31 10 EA D6 FB 21 05-7C 16 00 8A EF D8 EC 86  _1·êÖû!·|···ïØi·
4a64960  FF FF FF FF 82 79 47 11-00 00 00 00 00 00 00 00  ÿÿÿÿ·yG·········
```

Offsets 34-35 are for compression values if used. The file system allows for file compression; however, this feature is not utilized often. Offsets 36-39 are unused.

```
4a64900 2E 00 50 00 4E 00 47 00-80 00 00 00 58 00 00 00 ..P.N.G.....X...
4a64910 01 00 00 00 00 00 03 00-00 00 00 00 00 00 00 00 ................
4a64920 22 00 00 00 00 00 00 00-40 00 00 00 00 00 00 00 ".......@.......
4a64930 00 30 02 00 00 00 00 00-CD 23 02 00 00 00 00 00 .0......Í#......
4a64940 CD 23 02 00 00 00 00 00-31 07 01 4B 54 21 07 55 Í#......1..KT!.U
4a64950 5F 31 10 EA D6 FB 21 05-7C 16 00 8A EF D8 EC 86 _1.êÖû!.|...ïØi.
4a64960 FF FF FF FF 82 79 47 11-00 00 00 00 00 00 00 00 ÿÿÿÿ.yG.........
```

Offsets 40-47 are for the allocated size for the content of the file. This is also known as the Physical Size. This is the total size of all the clusters assigned to the file. Like what we saw in FAT, only one file can be assigned to a cluster and even if only one byte were used in the file, the entire cluster would be allocated. In our example, we have seen that there are 35 clusters. This particular drive has a cluster size of 4096 byes (8 sectors) (35x4096=143,360).

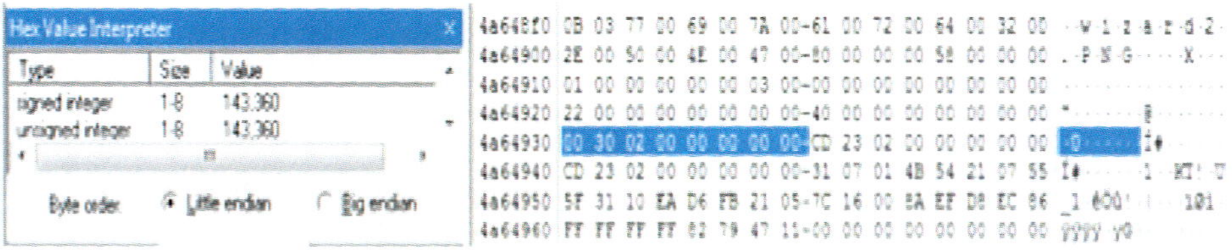

Offsets 48-55 are for the actual size of the file content. In this case, the file size is 140,237 bytes. The file slack would be 3,123 bytes.

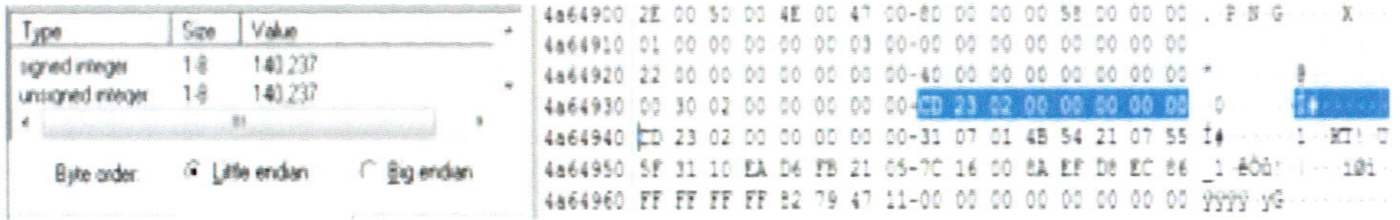

Offsets 56-63 are for the Initialized Size of the file. There is a special type of file known as a Sparse file where a large amount of data may be allocated to the file for future use, but the contents are very small[8]. The Initialized size is what is actually used in the large space. There are typically very few sparse files, so the Initialized and Actual sizes are the same in most files.

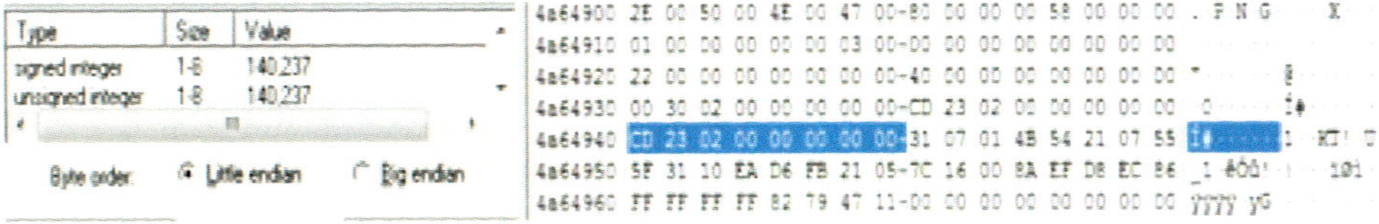

At offset 64 is the beginning of the data runlist. The size of the runlist will vary depending upon the number of clusters needed. The runlist is not a list of every cluster number that is used as this could be lengthy if there are a lot of clusters. Instead, the runlist is the number of clusters needed and a starting location.

For example:

FILE1.TXT size: 16,300 bytes
cluster size: 4,096 clusters needed: 4 starting cluster: 100

The runlist has the number of clusters needed (0x04=4) and the starting location (0x64=100). This runlist can be entered in 2 bytes (04 64). The way in which NTFS will provide this data is as follows:

11 04 64 and is interpreted as: byte one – 1+1=2 bytes needed for the runlist (the left 1 for the location and right 1 for the length). 4 is the length and 100 is the starting location. The file uses clusters 100, 101, 102, and 103.

Let's expand on this and say that the file needs 300 clusters and starts in cluster 75,255. Clusters 75,255 through 75,554 will be used.

The length is 300 (0x012C) with a Starting Cluster of 75,255 (0x0125F7).

Two bytes are needed for the length and three bytes are needed for the starting cluster.

The runlist would be: 32 2C 01 F7 25 01.

Five bytes (3 + 2 = 5) are needed by the runlist.

Three bytes for the location stored in Little Endian.
32 2C 01 F7 25 01

Two bytes for the length stored in Little Endian.
32 2C 01 F7 25 01

If this is a contiguous file, then this is the only list needed. Most files on an NTFS volume will be contiguous, as Windows Vista/7/8 will automatically run Defrag once a week[9]. If the file is fragmented, then multiple runlists are needed. Our file from the above screen captures is moderately fragmented with four runlists needed.

```
4a64900 2E 00 50 00 4E 00 47 00-80 00 00 00 58 00 00 00 ..P.N.G.....X...
4a64910 01 00 00 00 00 00 03 00-00 00 00 00 00 00 00 00 ................
4a64920 22 00 00 00 00 00 00 00-40 00 00 00 00 00 00 00 ".......@.......
4a64930 00 30 02 00 00 00 00 00-CD 23 02 00 00 00 00 00 .0......Í#......
4a64940 CD 23 02 00 00 00 00 00-31 07 01 4B 54 21 07 55 Í#......1..KT!.U
4a64950 5F 31 10 EA D6 FB 21 05-7C 16 00 8A EF D8 EC 86 _1.êÖû!.|...ïØì.
4a64960 FF FF FF FF 82 79 47 11-00 00 00 00 00 00 00 00 ÿÿÿÿ.yG.........
```

First, let's identify the runlists.

31 07 01 4B 54 21 07 55 5F 31 10 EA D6 FB
21 05 7C 16

Since the next byte after the fourth runlist is 0x00, this indicates the end of the runs. We will breakdown the runlists.

First Run

31 07 01 4B 54: 3 + 1 = next 4 bytes (3 for the location and 1 for the length)

Length = 0x07 or 7 clusters

Location = 0x01 4B 54 or 5524225 (remember data is in Little Endian 0x 54 4B 01)

Run: 5524225, 5524226, 5524227, 5524228, 5524229, 5524230 & 5524230

Next Run

21 07 55 5F: 2 + 1 = next 3 bytes (2 for the location and 1 for the length)

Length = 0x07 or 7 clusters

Location = 0x55 5F or 24405; starting with the second run, the location is added or subtracted to the previous location. The location is a signed integer, meaning it can be positive or negative values. To determine if the value is positive or negative, check the left-most nibble. Any nibble value in the left-most location greater than 7 will be negative[10].

Nibble Values

Hex	Bin		Hex	Bin
0	0000		8	1000
1	0001		9	1001
2	0010		A	1010
3	0011		B	1011
4	0100		C	1100
5	0101		D	1101
6	0110		E	1110
7	0111		F	1111

Note that every hex value greater than 7 has a binary value starting with 1. This indicates a negative value. The location above is 0x5F 55 and the left most nibble is 5, indicating it is a positive value.

Previous starting location was 5524225 + 24405 = 5548630

Run: 5548630, 5548631, 5548632, 5548633, 5548634, 5548635, 5548637

Next Run

31 10 EA D6 FB: 3 + 1 = next 4 bytes (3 for the location and 1 for the length)

Length = 0x010 or 16 clusters

Location = 0xEA D6 FB, in Little Endian this is 0xFB D6 EA

Note the left-most nibble is F, indicating this is a negative value = -272,662

Previous starting location was 5548630 – 272662 = 5275968

Run: 5275968, 5275969, 5275970, 5275971, 5275972, 5275973, 5275974, 5275975, 5275976, 5275977, 5275978, 5275979, 5275980, 5275981, 5275982, 5275983

Last Run

21 05 7C 16: 2 + 1 = next 3 bytes (2 for the location and 1 for the length)

Length = 0x05 or 5 clusters.

Location = 0x7C 16, in Little Endian this is 0x167C

Note the left-most nibble is 1, indicating this is a positive value = 5756
Previous location was 5275968 + 5756 = 5281724

Run: 5281724, 5281725, 5281726, 5281727, 5281728

This file has a total of 35 clusters.

VCN	Cluster Number	Location	Run
0	5524225		1
1	5524226		1
2	5524227		1
3	5524228		1
4	5524229		1
5	5524230		1
6	5524231		1
7	5548630	5524225 + 24405	2
8	5548631		2
9	5548632		2
10	5548633		2
11	5548634		2
12	5548635		2
13	5548636		2
14	5275968	5548630 - 272662	3
15	5275969		3
16	5275970		3
17	5275971		3
18	5275972		3
19	5275973		3
20	5275974		3

21	5275975		3
22	5275976		3
23	5275977		3
24	5275978		3
25	5275979		3
26	5275980		3
27	5275981		3
28	5275982		3
29	5275983		3
30	5281784	5275968 + 5756	4
31	5281785		4
32	5281726		4
33	5281727		4
34	5281728		4

PRACTICAL EXERCISE 3

Decode the following file runlists. Provide the cluster location and lengths for each run.

File1: 31 01 D0 0F 2A

File2: 31 04 55 A1 5B 21 01 E3 03 31 04 AD 44 3C

File3: 21 04 BC 1F 31 01 A7 D4 14 21 02 8A 72 21 06 00 8D 31 02 97 B2 F9 31 06 E6 1A FB

Alternate Data Streams

Like with the Filename Attribute, there can be multiple Data Attributes. The primary Data Attribute is known as the Default Unnamed Data Stream, or DUDS[11]. There is no name assigned to this attribute. Any additional Data Attributes will be named and thus are Named Data Streams or Alternate Data Streams (ADS)[12].

These additional attributes have the same structure as the primary Data Attribute and can be either Resident or Non-Resident.

These additional attributes are added by applications or can be added by users.

The DUDS is in red and the ADS is in yellow.

```
08cf0 0A 03 48 00 45 00 41 00-44 00 45 00 52 00 2E 00  ··H·E·A·D·E·R·.·
08d00 54 00 58 00 54 00 00 00-80 00 00 00 48 00 00 00  T·X·T·······H···
08d10 01 00 00 00 00 00 03 00-00 00 00 00 00 00 00 00  ················
08d20 00 00 00 00 00 00 00 00-40 00 00 00 00 00 00 00  ········@·······
08d30 00 10 00 00 00 00 00 00-D0 02 00 00 00 00 00 00  ········Ð·······
08d40 D0 02 00 00 00 00 00 00-11 01 24 00 01 00 00 00  Ð·········$·····
08d50 80 00 00 00 58 00 00 00-00 09 18 00 00 00 04 00  ····X···········
08d60 22 00 00 00 30 00 00 00-45 00 78 00 74 00 72 00  "···0···E·x·t·r·
08d70 61 00 2E 00 74 00 78 00-74 00 47 48 49 4A 4B 4C  a·.·t·x·t·GHIJKL
08d80 54 68 69 73 20 69 73 20-61 6E 20 65 78 61 6D 70  This is an examp
08d90 6C 65 20 6F 66 20 61 6E-20 41 44 53 0D 0A 0D 0A  le of an ADS····
08da0 0D 0A FF FF 82 79 47 11-FF FF FF FF 82 79 47 11  ··ÿÿ·yG·ÿÿÿÿ·yG·
```

Examining this ADS Data Attribute will be like walking through a Resident Attribute. The Attribute Type Identifier will be 0x80 00 00 00. The length is 88 bytes (0x58 00 00 00).

```
08cf0 0A 03 48 00 45 00 41 00-44 00 45 00 52 00 2E 00  ··H·E·A·D·E·R·.·
08d00 54 00 58 00 54 00 00 00-80 00 00 00 48 00 00 00  T·X·T·······H···
08d10 01 00 00 00 00 00 03 00-00 00 00 00 00 00 00 00  ················
08d20 00 00 00 00 00 00 00 00-40 00 00 00 00 00 00 00  ········@·······
08d30 00 10 00 00 00 00 00 00-D0 02 00 00 00 00 00 00  ········Ð·······
08d40 D0 02 00 00 00 00 00 00-11 01 24 00 01 00 00 00  Ð·········$·····
08d50 80 00 00 00 58 00 00 00-00 09 18 00 00 00 04 00  ····X···········
08d60 22 00 00 00 30 00 00 00-45 00 78 00 74 00 72 00  "···0···E·x·t·r·
08d70 61 00 2E 00 74 00 78 00-74 00 00 00 00 00 00 00  a·.·t·x·t·······
08d80 54 68 69 73 20 69 73 20-61 6E 20 65 78 61 6D 70  This is an examp
08d90 6C 65 20 6F 66 20 61 6E-20 41 44 53 0D 0A 0D 0A  le of an ADS····
08da0 0D 0A FF FF 82 79 47 11-FF FF FF FF 82 79 47 11  ··ÿÿ·yG·ÿÿÿÿ·yG·
```

The attribute is identified as Resident based upon offset 8 (0x00). At offset 9 is the number Unicode character in the stream name (0x09), 9 characters. At offsets 10-11 are the offset to the stream name (0x18 00), 24 bytes.

```
08d50 80 00 00 00 58 00 00 00-00 09 18 00 00 00 04 00  ····X···········
08d60 22 00 00 00 30 00 00 00-45 00 78 00 74 00 72 00  "···0···E·x·t·r·
08d70 61 00 2E 00 74 00 78 00-74 00 00 00 00 00 00 00  a·.·t·x·t·······
08d80 54 68 69 73 20 69 73 20-61 6E 20 65 78 61 6D 70  This is an examp
08d90 6C 65 20 6F 66 20 61 6E-20 41 44 53 0D 0A 0D 0A  le of an ADS····
08da0 0D 0A FF FF 82 79 47 11-FF FF FF FF 82 79 47 11  ··ÿÿ·yG·ÿÿÿÿ·yG·
```

Going to offset 24 is the name of the stream, in this case it is Extra.txt (9 Unicode characters). This is followed by the content of the stream.

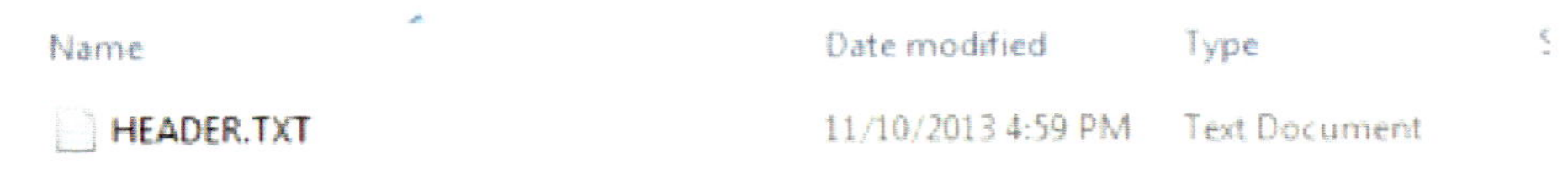

Note that if the folder contents are viewed in Windows Explorer, this data stream cannot be seen.

Name	Date modified	Type
HEADER.TXT	11/10/2013 4:59 PM	Text Document

Looking at the content of the file does not show the ADS either.

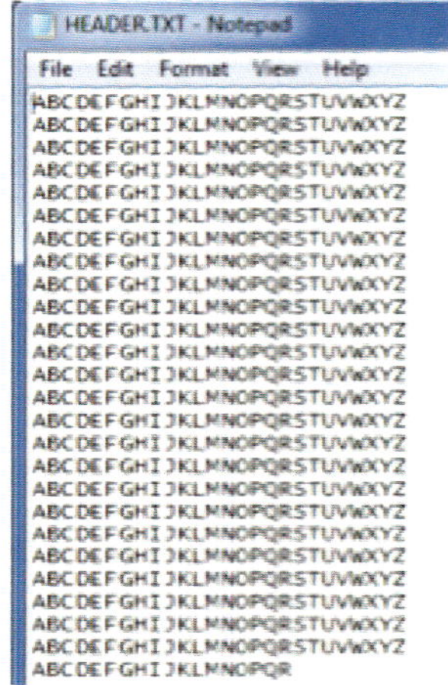

The ADS can be identified in forensic tools such as EnCase, FTK, XWays, and many others.

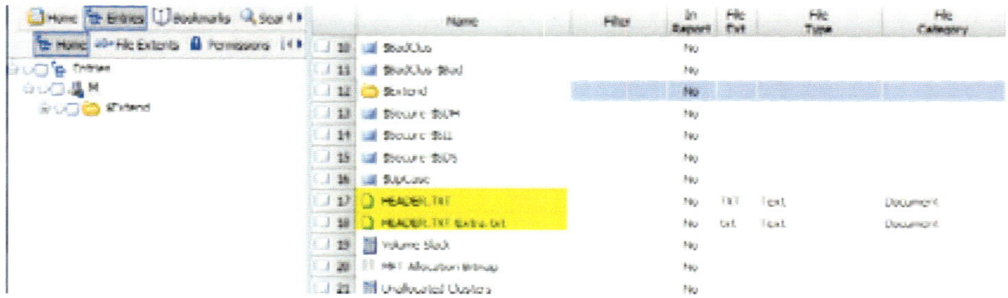

A user can create an ADS simply by using a program like Notepad.

Follow Along Exercise

1. Use the flash drive from Practical #2.

2. Open a command prompt by going to the start menu and typing <CMD><enter>

3. Change the prompt to the USB drive letter <drive letter>:

4. Type: notepad header.txt:New ADS<enter>

5. You will be prompted to create the document, select Yes.

6. Type: Good way to hide data from friends.

7. Save and close Notepad.

8. Open FTK Imager and add the flash drive as evidence.

9. Select the $MFT record and go to offset 35840 and examine the ADS you just created.

Object Identifier Attribute (ObjID)

This attribute is not complex and has little content, but its presence can have forensic significance. The attribute is between 40 and 88 bytes in length and is always Resident. The attribute has a 24-byte header and up to four 16-byte GUIDs for the file. The attribute identifier is 0x40 00 00 00 (40) and the breakdown is below[13].

Object ID Attribute (40 00 00 00)			
DEC OFFSET	**HEX OFFSET**	**SIZE (BYTES)**	**DESCRIPTION**
0	0	4	Attribute Type Identifier
4	4	4	Length of the Attribute
8	8	1	Resident-00 or Non-Resident-01
9	9	1	Length of Stream Name
10	0A	2	Offset to the Stream Name
12	0C	2	Flags
14	0E	2	Attribute Identifier
16	10	4	Size of Resident Data
20	14	4	Offset to Resident Data
24	18	16	GUID Object ID
40	28	16	GUID Birth Volume ID
56	38	16	GUID Birth Object ID
72	48	16	GUID Domain ID

The forensic significance of this attribute is that its presence may indicate that the file was opened[14]. There is a common claim by the subject that the file was only copied or downloaded, but never opened.

The Object ID is part of the Distributed Link Tracking Service of Windows[15]. If a shortcut is generated for the file, then the attribute will be added. When many files are opened, there is a shortcut link file created in the user's Recent folder.

Below is a $MFT record of a file that has not been opened with just the three attributes (SIA, FNA, and Data).

```
08c00 46 49 4C 45 30 00 03 00-66 36 20 00 00 00 00 00 FILE0···f6 ·····
08c10 01 00 01 00 38 00 01 00-90 01 00 00 00 04 00 00 ····8···········
08c20 00 00 00 00 00 00 00 00-03 00 00 00 23 00 00 00 ············#···
08c30 02 00 00 00 00 00 00 00-10 00 00 00 60 00 00 00 ············`···
08c40 00 00 00 00 00 00 00 00-48 00 00 00 18 00 00 00 ········H·······
08c50 AE FF 4D 5F 27 E3 CE 01-67 7F BA 8D 1A 9E CE 01 ®ÿM_'ãÎ·g·º···Î·
08c60 AE FF 4D 5F 27 E3 CE 01-AE FF 4D 5F 27 E3 CE 01 ®ÿM_'ãÎ·®ÿM_'ãÎ·
08c70 20 00 00 00 00 00 00 00-00 00 00 00 00 00 00 00  ···············
08c80 00 00 00 00 05 01 00 00-00 00 00 00 00 00 00 00 ················
08c90 00 00 00 00 00 00 00 00-30 00 00 00 70 00 00 00 ········0···p···
08ca0 00 00 00 00 00 00 02 00-54 00 00 00 18 00 01 00 ········T·······
08cb0 05 00 00 00 00 00 05 00-AE FF 4D 5F 27 E3 CE 01 ········®ÿM_'ãÎ·
08cc0 AE FF 4D 5F 27 E3 CE 01-AE FF 4D 5F 27 E3 CE 01 ®ÿM_'ãÎ·®ÿM_'ãÎ·
08cd0 AE FF 4D 5F 27 E3 CE 01-00 00 00 00 00 00 00 00 ®ÿM_'ãÎ·········
08ce0 00 00 00 00 00 00 00 00-20 00 00 00 00 00 00 00 ········ ·······
08cf0 09 03 41 00 53 00 43 00-49 00 49 00 2E 00 74 00 ··A·S·C·I·I·.·t·
08d00 78 00 74 00 00 00 00 00-80 00 00 00 80 00 00 00 x·t·············
08d10 00 00 18 00 00 00 01 00-68 00 00 00 18 00 00 00 ········h·······
08d20 5F 75 74 73 69 64 65 20-6F 66 20 61 20 64 6F 67 _utside of a dog
08d30 2C 20 61 20 62 6F 6F 6B-20 69 73 20 6D 61 6E 27 , a book is man'
08d40 73 20 62 65 73 74 20 66-72 69 65 6E 64 2E 0D 0A s best friend.··
08d50 49 6E 73 69 64 65 20 6F-66 20 61 20 64 6F 67 2C Inside of a dog,
08d60 20 69 74 27 73 20 74 6F-6F 20 64 61 72 6B 20 74  it's too dark t
08d70 6F 20 72 65 61 64 2E 20-2D 20 47 72 6F 75 63 68 o read. - Grouch
08d80 6F 20 4D 61 72 78 0D 0A-FF FF FF FF 82 79 47 11 o Marx··ÿÿÿÿ·yG·
08d90 00 00 00 00 00 00 00 00-00 00 00 00 00 00 00 00 ················
08da0 00 00 00 00 00 00 00 00-00 00 00 00 00 00 00 00 ················
08db0 00 00 00 00 00 00 00 00-00 00 00 00 00 00 00 00 ················
08dc0 00 00 00 00 00 00 00 00-00 00 00 00 00 00 00 00 ················
08dd0 00 00 00 00 00 00 00 00-00 00 00 00 00 00 00 00 ················
08de0 00 00 00 00 00 00 00 00-00 00 00 00 00 00 00 00 ················
08df0 00 00 00 00 00 00 00 00-00 00 00 00 00 00 02 00 ················
```

After the file has been opened once, note how the record has changed. The file is not saved or modified, just simply opened.

```
08c00 46 49 4C 45 30 00 03 00-DF 3E 20 00 00 00 00 00 FILE0···ß> ·····
08c10 01 00 01 00 38 00 01 00-B8 01 00 00 00 04 00 00 ····8···¸·······
08c20 00 00 00 00 00 00 00 00-04 00 00 00 23 00 00 00 ············#···
08c30 03 00 00 00 00 00 00 00-10 00 00 00 60 00 00 00 ············`···
08c40 00 00 00 00 00 00 00 00-48 00 00 00 18 00 00 00 ········H·······
08c50 AE FF 4D 5F 27 E3 CE 01-67 7F BA 8D 1A 9E CE 01 ®ÿM_'ãÎ·g·º···Î·
08c60 22 6A 4F 01 28 E3 CE 01-AE FF 4D 5F 27 E3 CE 01 "jO·(ãÎ·®ÿM_'ãÎ·
08c70 20 00 00 00 00 00 00 00-00 00 00 00 00 00 00 00  ···············
08c80 00 00 00 00 05 01 00 00-00 00 00 00 00 00 00 00 ················
08c90 00 00 00 00 00 00 00 00-30 00 00 00 70 00 00 00 ········0···p···
08ca0 00 00 00 00 00 00 02 00-54 00 00 00 18 00 01 00 ········T·······
08cb0 05 00 00 00 00 00 05 00-AE FF 4D 5F 27 E3 CE 01 ········®ÿM_'ãÎ·
08cc0 AE FF 4D 5F 27 E3 CE 01-AE FF 4D 5F 27 E3 CE 01 ®ÿM_'ãÎ·®ÿM_'ãÎ·
08cd0 AE FF 4D 5F 27 E3 CE 01-00 00 00 00 00 00 00 00 ®ÿM_'ãÎ·········
08ce0 00 00 00 00 00 00 00 00-20 00 00 00 00 00 00 00 ········ ·······
08cf0 09 03 41 00 53 00 43 00-49 00 49 00 2E 00 74 00 ··A·S·C·I·I·.·t·
08d00 78 00 74 00 00 00 00 00-40 00 00 00 28 00 00 00 x·t·····@···(···
08d10 00 00 00 00 00 00 03 00-10 00 00 00 18 00 00 00 ················
08d20 20 19 94 AF D3 4E E3 11-B1 10 00 0C 29 B2 B4 30  ··¯ÓNã·±···)²´0
08d30 80 00 00 00 80 00 00 00-00 00 18 00 00 00 01 00 ················
08d40 68 00 00 00 18 00 00 00-5F 75 74 73 69 64 65 20 h·······_utside 
08d50 6F 66 20 61 20 64 6F 67-2C 20 61 20 62 6F 6F 6B of a dog, a book
08d60 20 69 73 20 6D 61 6E 27-73 20 62 65 73 74 20 66  is man's best f
08d70 72 69 65 6E 64 2E 0D 0A-49 6E 73 69 64 65 20 6F riend.··Inside o
08d80 66 20 61 20 64 6F 67 2C-20 69 74 27 73 20 74 6F f a dog, it's to
08d90 6F 20 64 61 72 6B 20 74-6F 20 72 65 61 64 2E 20 o dark to read. 
08da0 2D 20 47 72 6F 75 63 68-6F 20 4D 61 72 78 0D 0A - Groucho Marx··
08db0 FF FF FF FF 82 79 47 11-00 00 00 00 00 00 00 00 ÿÿÿÿ·yG·········
08dc0 00 00 00 00 00 00 00 00-00 00 00 00 00 00 00 00 ················
08dd0 00 00 00 00 00 00 00 00-00 00 00 00 00 00 00 00 ················
08de0 00 00 00 00 00 00 00 00-00 00 00 00 00 00 00 00 ················
08df0 00 00 00 00 00 00 00 00-00 00 00 00 00 00 03 00 ················
```

As stated above, this is always a Resident attribute so the first 24 bytes will be the standard header. Offset 24 of the attribute will be the Object ID GUID. The other GUIDs are not added nearly as often and some require the computer to be on a Windows domain.

```
08cf0 09 03 41 00 53 00 43 00-49 00 49 00 2E 00 74 00 ··A·S·C·I·I·.·t·
08d00 78 00 74 00 00 00 00 00-40 00 00 00 28 00 00 00 x·t·····@···(···
08d10 00 00 00 00 00 00 03 00-10 00 00 00 18 00 00 00 ················
08d20 20 19 94 AF D3 4E E3 11-B1 10 00 0C 29 B2 B4 30  ··¯ÓNã·±···)²´0
08d30 80 00 00 00 80 00 00 00-00 00 18 00 00 00 01 00 ················
08d40 68 00 00 00 18 00 00 00-5F 75 74 73 69 64 65 20 h·······_utside 
08d50 6F 66 20 61 20 64 6F 67-2C 20 61 20 62 6F 6F 6B of a dog, a book
08d60 20 69 73 20 6D 61 6E 27-73 20 62 65 73 74 20 66  is man's best f
08d70 72 69 65 6E 64 2E 0D 0A-49 6E 73 69 64 65 20 6F riend.··Inside o
```

This translates to {AF941920-4ED3-11E3-B110-000C29B2B430} as a File GUID.

PRACTICAL EXERCISE 4

Open 11_Pract2.E01 in FTK Imager and identify the files that you can show were opened. List the GUID for each in proper notation.

Reparse Attribute

Reparse points are methods of redirecting references to files and folders. Reparse points act like shortcut files (.lnk) for files, folders, and volumes, but are accomplished at the file system level and not the operating system level[16]. These have been available in Microsoft Windows since version 2000, but have only been routinely utilized since Vista[17]. The directory junctions work in a similar way as hard links do for filenames.

A folder such as \Documents and Settings is an example of a Reparse point[18].

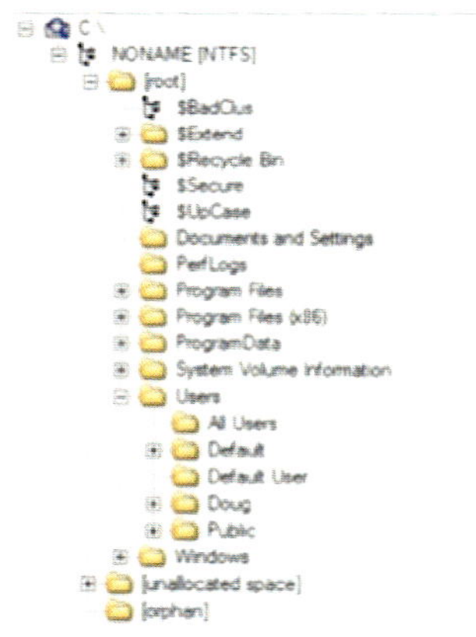

There are a number of additional examples:

C:\Users\<Profilename>\My Documents points to
C:\Users\<Profilename>\Documents

C:\Users\<Profilename>\Application Data points to
C:\Users\<Profilename>\Appdata

C:\Users\<Profilename>\Recent
points to C:\Users\<Profilename>\AppData\
Roaming\Microsoft\Windows\Recent

Below is the breakdown of the Reparse Point Attribute[19].

Reparse Point Attribute (C0 00 00 00)			
DEC OFFSET	**HEX OFFSET**	**SIZE (BYTES)**	**DESCRIPTION**
0	0	4	Attribute Type Identifier
4	4	4	Length of the Attribute
8	8	1	Resident-00 or Non-Resident-01
9	9	1	Length of Stream Name
10	0A	2	Offset to the stream name
12	0C	2	Flags
14	0E	2	Attribute Identifier
16	10	4	Size of Resident Data
20	14	4	Offset to Resident Data
24	18	4	Reparse Point Type 0x68000008 DFS 0x88000003 Mount point 0xA0000003 Junction 0xA8000004 HSM 0xE8000000 Symbolic link
28	1C	2	Data Length
30	1E	2	Unused
32	20	2	Offset to target's name starting 16 bytes into the content
34	22	2	Length of target's name
36	24	2	Offset to target's print name starting 16 bytes into the content
38	26	2	Length of target's print name
40	22	varied	Folder Path

We are focusing on Directory Junction Reparse Points because you will run into them in every Windows case and it is important to understand why there are these empty folders in each user's profile folder. Microsoft chose to make the folder name change with Vista, but many older programs still looked for folders such as Documents and Settings and would fail without it being present. Making the directory junction would allow a legacy program to send data to Documents and Settings*Profilename* and it would get redirected to Users*Profilename*.

The directory junction folder \Documents and Settings has its own $MFT Record.

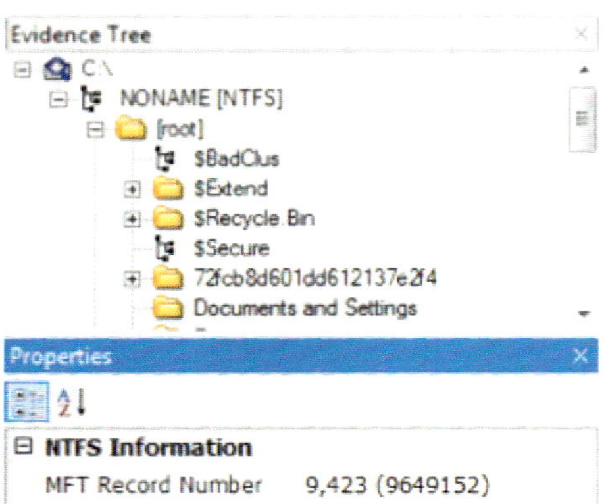

Parsing through the $MFT record for this entry will show how the redirection takes place.

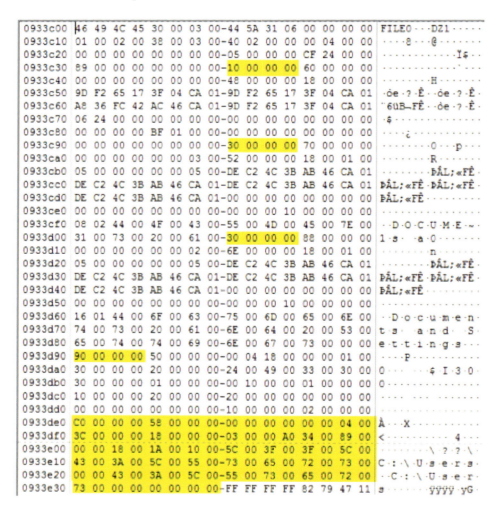

```
0933c00 46 49 4C 45 30 00 03 00-44 5A 31 06 00 00 00 00 FILE0···DZ1·····
0933c10 01 00 02 00 38 00 03 00-40 02 00 00 00 04 00 00 ····8···@·······
0933c20 00 00 00 00 00 00 00 00-05 00 00 00 CF 24 00 00 ············Ï$··
0933c30 89 00 00 00 00 00 00 00-10 00 00 00 60 00 00 00 ············`···
0933c40 00 00 00 00 00 00 00 00-48 00 00 00 18 00 00 00 ········H·······
0933c50 9D F2 65 17 3F 04 CA 01-9D F2 65 17 3F 04 CA 01 ·òe·?·Ê··òe·?·Ê·
0933c60 A8 36 FC 42 AC 46 CA 01-9D F2 65 17 3F 04 CA 01 ¨6üB¬FÊ··òe·?·Ê·
0933c70 06 24 00 00 00 00 00 00-00 00 00 00 00 00 00 00 ·$··············
0933c80 00 00 00 00 BF 01 00 00-00 00 00 00 00 00 00 00 ····¿···········
0933c90 00 00 00 00 00 00 00 00-30 00 00 00 70 00 00 00 ········0···p···
0933ca0 00 00 00 00 00 00 03 00-52 00 00 00 18 00 01 00 ········R·······
0933cb0 05 00 00 00 00 00 05 00-DE C2 4C 3B AB 46 CA 01 ········ÞÂL;«FÊ·
0933cc0 DE C2 4C 3B AB 46 CA 01-DE C2 4C 3B AB 46 CA 01 ÞÂL;«FÊ·ÞÂL;«FÊ·
0933cd0 DE C2 4C 3B AB 46 CA 01-00 00 00 00 00 00 00 00 ÞÂL;«FÊ·········
0933ce0 00 00 00 00 00 00 00 00-00 00 10 00 00 00 00 00 ················
0933cf0 08 02 44 00 4F 00 43 00-55 00 4D 00 45 00 7E 00 ··D·O·C·U·M·E·~·
0933d00 31 00 73 00 20 00 61 00-30 00 00 00 88 00 00 00 1·s· ·a·0·······
0933d10 00 00 00 00 00 00 02 00-6E 00 00 00 18 00 01 00 ········n·······
0933d20 05 00 00 00 00 00 05 00-DE C2 4C 3B AB 46 CA 01 ········ÞÂL;«FÊ·
0933d30 DE C2 4C 3B AB 46 CA 01-DE C2 4C 3B AB 46 CA 01 ÞÂL;«FÊ·ÞÂL;«FÊ·
0933d40 DE C2 4C 3B AB 46 CA 01-00 00 00 00 00 00 00 00 ÞÂL;«FÊ·········
0933d50 00 00 00 00 00 00 00 00-00 00 10 00 00 00 00 00 ················
0933d60 16 01 44 00 6F 00 63 00-75 00 6D 00 65 00 6E 00 ··D·o·c·u·m·e·n·
0933d70 74 00 73 00 20 00 61 00-6E 00 64 00 20 00 53 00 t·s· ·a·n·d· ·S·
0933d80 65 00 74 00 74 00 69 00-6E 00 67 00 73 00 00 00 e·t·t·i·n·g·s···
0933d90 90 00 00 00 50 00 00 00-00 04 18 00 00 00 01 00 ····P···········
0933da0 30 00 00 00 20 00 00 00-24 00 49 00 33 00 30 00 0··· ···$·I·3·0·
0933db0 30 00 00 00 01 00 00 00-00 10 00 00 01 00 00 00 0···············
0933dc0 10 00 00 00 20 00 00 00-20 00 00 00 00 00 00 00 ···· ··· ·······
0933dd0 00 00 00 00 00 00 00 00-10 00 00 00 02 00 00 00 ················
0933de0 C0 00 00 00 58 00 00 00-00 00 00 00 00 00 04 00 À···X···········
0933df0 3C 00 00 00 18 00 00 00-03 00 00 A0 34 00 89 00 <··········4···
0933e00 00 00 18 00 1A 00 10 00-5C 00 3F 00 3F 00 5C 00 ········\·?·?·\·
0933e10 43 00 3A 00 5C 00 55 00-73 00 65 00 72 00 73 00 C·:·\·U·s·e·r·s·
0933e20 00 00 43 00 3A 00 5C 00-55 00 73 00 65 00 72 00 ··C·:·\·U·s·e·r·
0933e30 73 00 00 00 00 00 00 00-FF FF FF FF 82 79 47 11 s·······ÿÿÿÿ·yG·
```

This is a Standard Information Attribute, two Filename Attributes, an Index Root Attribute (we will examine these next), and the Reparse Point Attribute.

The Reparse Point Attribute is Resident and will have the same 24-byte Resident attribute header as other Resident attributes. The attribute type identifier is 0xC0 00 00 00. Starting at offset 24, there is a 4-byte reparse type flag. This will indicate what type of reparse point it was for. For directory junctions, the flag is (0xA0 00 00 03).

```
0933de0  C0 00 00 00 58 00 00 00-00 00 00 00 00 00 04 00  À···X···········
0933df0  3C 00 00 00 18 00 00 00-03 00 00 A0 34 00 89 00  <·········· 4···
0933e00  00 00 18 00 1A 00 10 00-5C 00 3F 00 3F 00 5C 00  ········\·?·?·\·
0933e10  43 00 3A 00 5C 00 55 00-73 00 65 00 72 00 73 00  C·:·\·U·s·e·r·s·
0933e20  00 00 43 00 3A 00 5C 00-55 00 73 00 65 00 72 00  ··C·:·\·U·s·e·r·
0933e30  73 00 00 00 00 00 00 00-FF FF FF FF 82 79 47 11  s·······ÿÿÿÿ·yG·
```

Offsets 28-29 are for the size of the reparse data. In this instance, it is 0x00 34 or 52 bytes.

```
0933de0  C0 00 00 00 58 00 00 00-00 00 00 00 00 00 04 00  À···X···········
0933df0  3C 00 00 00 18 00 00 00-03 00 00 A0 34 00 89 00  <·········· 4···
0933e00  00 00 18 00 1A 00 10 00-5C 00 3F 00 3F 00 5C 00  ········\·?·?·\·
0933e10  43 00 3A 00 5C 00 55 00-73 00 65 00 72 00 73 00  C·:·\·U·s·e·r·s·
0933e20  00 00 43 00 3A 00 5C 00-55 00 73 00 65 00 72 00  ··C·:·\·U·s·e·r·
0933e30  73 00 00 00 00 00 00 00-FF FF FF FF 82 79 47 11  s·······ÿÿÿÿ·yG·
```

Offsets 30-31 are apparently unused and may be padding.

Offsets 32-33 are for the offset to the target's name. This offset starts 16 bytes into the content, so since the value is 0x00 00, this means that the target's name is 16 bytes into the content after the header. The header is 24 bytes plus the 16 bytes of the content, equaling 40 bytes from the beginning of the attribute.

```
0933de0  C0 00 00 00 58 00 00 00-00 00 00 00 00 00 04 00  À···X···········
0933df0  3C 00 00 00 18 00 00 00-03 00 00 A0 34 00 89 00  <·········· 4···
0933e00  00 00 18 00 1A 00 10 00-5C 00 3F 00 3F 00 5C 00  ········\·?·?·\·
0933e10  43 00 3A 00 5C 00 55 00-73 00 65 00 72 00 73 00  C·:·\·U·s·e·r·s·
0933e20  00 00 43 00 3A 00 5C 00-55 00 73 00 65 00 72 00  ··C·:·\·U·s·e·r·
0933e30  73 00 00 00 00 00 00 00-FF FF FF FF 82 79 47 11  s·······ÿÿÿÿ·yG·
```

Offsets 34-35 are for the length of the target's name. Here the length is 0x00 18 or 24 bytes.

```
0933de0  C0 00 00 00 58 00 00 00-00 00 00 00 00 00 04 00  À···X···········
0933df0  3C 00 00 00 18 00 00 00-03 00 00 A0 34 00 89 00  <·········· 4···
0933e00  00 00 18 00 1A 00 10 00-5C 00 3F 00 3F 00 5C 00  ········\·?·?·\·
0933e10  43 00 3A 00 5C 00 55 00-73 00 65 00 72 00 73 00  C·:·\·U·s·e·r·s·
0933e20  00 00 43 00 3A 00 5C 00-55 00 73 00 65 00 72 00  ··C·:·\·U·s·e·r·
0933e30  73 00 00 00 00 00 00 00-FF FF FF FF 82 79 47 11  s·······ÿÿÿÿ·yG·
```

Offsets 36-37 are for the offset to the print name of the target; this is a second copy of the folder name. 0x00 1A (26) is the number of bytes starting 16 bytes into the content. This means starting with a 24-byte header and 16 bytes into the content, and 26 bytes from that point equals 66 bytes from the beginning of the attribute.

```
0933de0 C0 00 00 00 58 00 00 00-00 00 00 00 00 00 04 00 À···X···········
0933df0 3C 00 00 00 18 00 00 00-03 00 00 A0 34 00 89 00 <·········· 4···
0933e00 00 00 18 00 1A 00 10 00-5C 00 3F 00 3F 00 5C 00 ········\·?·?·\·
0933e10 43 00 3A 00 5C 00 55 00-73 00 65 00 72 00 73 00 C·:·\·U·s·e·r·s·
0933e20 00 00 43 00 3A 00 5C 00-55 00 73 00 65 00 72 00 ··C·:·\·U·s·e·r·
0933e30 73 00 00 00 00 00 00 00-FF FF FF FF 82 79 47 11 s·······ÿÿÿÿ·yG·
```

Offsets 38-39 are for the length of the print name. In this case it is 0x00 10 or 16 bytes.

```
0933de0 C0 00 00 00 58 00 00 00-00 00 00 00 00 00 04 00 À···X···········
0933df0 3C 00 00 00 18 00 00 00-03 00 00 A0 34 00 89 00 <·········· 4···
0933e00 00 00 18 00 1A 00 10 00-5C 00 3F 00 3F 00 5C 00 ········\·?·?·\·
0933e10 43 00 3A 00 5C 00 55 00-73 00 65 00 72 00 73 00 C·:·\·U·s·e·r·s·
0933e20 00 00 43 00 3A 00 5C 00-55 00 73 00 65 00 72 00 ··C·:·\·U·s·e·r·
0933e30 73 00 00 00 00 00 00 00-FF FF FF FF 82 79 47 11 s·······ÿÿÿÿ·yG·
```

Starting at offset 40 (16 bytes into the content) is the target's name and target's print name. This size will vary depending upon the name. In this case, \Documents and Settings points to the target \Users.

```
0933de0 C0 00 00 00 58 00 00 00-00 00 00 00 00 00 04 00 À···X···········
0933df0 3C 00 00 00 18 00 00 00-03 00 00 A0 34 00 89 00 <·········· 4···
0933e00 00 00 18 00 1A 00 10 00-5C 00 3F 00 3F 00 5C 00 ········\·?·?·\·
0933e10 43 00 3A 00 5C 00 55 00-73 00 65 00 72 00 73 00 C·:·\·U·s·e·r·s·
0933e20 00 00 43 00 3A 00 5C 00-55 00 73 00 65 00 72 00 ··C·:·\·U·s·e·r·
0933e30 73 00 00 00 00 00 00 00-FF FF FF FF 82 79 47 11 s·······ÿÿÿÿ·yG·
```

Directory junctions can be created in Windows Vista/7/8 using the mklink command.

Mklink /J Link Target

Example: mklink /J \Accounts \Users
This will create a directory junction named Accounts redirecting to Users.

PRACTICAL EXERCISE 5

Open 11_Pract2.E01 in FTK Imager and identify the directory junctions, their $MFT number, and names of the folders they point to.

CHAPTER SUMMARY

Files will have a Data Attribute and this attribute can be either Resident or Non-Resident, meaning the data is either stored in the $MFT record or on an available cluster. If the content is Non-Resident, then the cluster references are stored in the attribute. The references are in a runlist.

A runlist has the number of contiguous clusters and the starting location. If the file is fragmented, then there will be multiple runlists.

A file can have multiple Data Attributes. The primary attribute is the Default Unnamed Data Stream (DUDS), and any subsequent attribute will be a named or Alternate Data Stream (ADS). These additional attributes can be Resident or Non-Resident.

The Object ID attribute contains one or more GUID values as part of the Distributive Link Tracking service of Windows. The presence of the GUID means that a Link File (Shortcut File) was created for the target. This is indicative of the file being opened as a large number of link files are in the \Recent folder.

The next attribute examined is the Reparse Point Attribute. Reparse points are redirectors for files, folders, and volumes. There are several types of the reparse points; directory junction, mount points, and symbolic links. Starting with Windows Vista, a number of Directory Junctions and some Symbolic Links are automatically created for legacy purposes.

AT HOME EXERCISE

1. Examine file 11_MFT with FTK Imager and complete the table below.

RECORD HEADER	File 122	File 142	File 297
ASCII File Signature Identifier is:			
Offset to Update Sequence Array:			
Number of entries in the Update Array:			
$Logfile sequence number (Hex):			
Sequence count:			
Hard Link count:			
Offset to the first attribute:			
Is the file/folder deleted:			
Logical size of the record:			
Physical size of the record:			
Next attribute identification:			
$MFT Record Number:			
Update Sequence array values:			
STANDARD INFORMATION ATTRIBUTE			
The length of this attribute is:			
Size of the Resident data is:			
Offset to the Resident data is:			
The date/time (Local) the file was created is:			
The date/time (UTC) the file was modified is:			
The last $MFT modified date/time (Local) is:			
The last access date/time (UTC) of the file is:			
The DOS attributes are:			
The Security ID is:			
FILENAME ATTRIBUTE			
What is the size of the attribute:			
The $MFT Record number of the parent is:			
What is the Creation Date/Time (UTC):			
What is the Modification Date/Time (UTC):			
What is the Record Modification Date/Time (UTC)			
What is the Last Access Date/Time (UTC):			
The file name length in Unicode is:			
The file name type is:			
The actual file name itself is:			
FILENAME ATTRIBUTE			
What is the size of the attribute:			
The $MFT Record number of the parent is:			
What is the Creation Date/Time (UTC):			
What is the Modification Date/Time (UTC):			
What is the Record Modification Date/Time (UTC):			
What is the Last Access Date/Time (UTC):			
The file name length in Unicode is:			
The file name type is:			
The actual file name itself is:			

DATA ATTRIBUTE (if present)	Record 122	Record 142	Record 297
Resident or Non-Resident:			
If Resident, # of Bytes of Data:			
What is the name of the ADS:			
If Non-Resident, Provide the length and location of the clusters:			
2nd DATA Attribute			
Resident or-Non-Resident,			
Size of Content			
Name of Stream			

2. Open 11_HW1.E01 in FTK Imager and identify the files (not folders) that you can show were opened. List the GUID for each in proper notation.

3. Open 11_HW1.E01 in FTK Imager and identify the directory junctions, their $MFT number, and names of the folders they point to.

ADVANCED HOMEWORK 1

1. Format a USB flash drive with NTFS.
2. Create a text file in the root of the drive and add the text 12345; save the file.
3. Create a folder named Files.
4. Create a hard link for your text file in the Files folder.
5. Create an Alternate Data Stream for your text file named HIDDEN and add 678910.
6. View the $MFT record for the text file in FTK Imager and copy

the contents or a screen capture below to show the hard link and ADS.

ADVANCED HOMEWORK 2[20]

Open 11_HW2.E01 in FTK Imager.

Run a search across the Unallocated Space only for deleted $MFT records (use data from the header to carve).

For each of the recovered records (less than 15), list the Record ID and the Parent ID.

Record ID	**Parent ID**

For the record with an ID number of 334, identify the full path of this file from the deleted records and from the $MFT from the root to the file. (For example: \myfiles\pictures\home\pic.jpg).

Examine record ID number 334 and identify the ADS.

Export the contents and describe what it displays.

REFERENCES

1. Ntfs file attributes. (n.d.). Retrieved from http://www.active-undelete.com/ntfs_file_types.htm.
2. Sammes, T., & Jenkinson, B. (2007). Forensic computing, a practitioner's guide. (2nd ed., pp. 240). London: Springer Publishing.
3. Sammes, T., & Jenkinson, B. (2007). Forensic computing, a practitioner's guide. (2nd ed., pp. 239-240). London: Springer Publishing.
4. Forensics: Mft slack. (2009, March 29). Retrieved from http://whereismydata.wordpress.com/2009/03/29/mft-slack/.
5. Sammes, T., & Jenkinson, B. (2007). Forensic computing, a practitioner's guide. (2nd ed., pp. 241-242). London: Springer Publishing.
6. Stanek, W. (2009). windows server® 2008 inside out. Newton: O'Reilly Media, Inc.
7. Sammes, T., & Jenkinson, B. (2007). Forensic computing, a practitioner's guide. (2nd ed., pp. 246-247). London: Springer Publishing.
8. Sparse files. (n.d.). Retrieved from http://msdn.microsoft.com/en-us/library/windows/desktop/aa365564(v=vs.85).aspx.
9. What is disk defragmentation?. (n.d.). Retrieved from http://windows.microsoft.com/en-us/windows-vista/what-is-disk-defragmentation.
10. Sammes, T., & Jenkinson, B. (2007). Forensic computing, a practitioner's guide. (2nd ed., pp. 20). London: Springer Publishing.
11. File streams. (n.d.). Retrieved from http://msdn.microsoft.com/en-us/library/windows/desktop/aa364404(v=vs.85).aspx.
12. Marlin, J. (2013, March 24). [Web log message]. Retrieved from http://blogs.technet.com/b/askcore/archive/2013/03/24/alternate-data-streams-in-ntfs.aspx.
13. Carrier, B. (2005). File system forensic analysis. (pp. 367). Upper Saddle River: Addison-Wesley.
14. Parsonage, H. (2010, July). © Harry Parsonage, September 2008, updated November 2009, July 2010. The meaning of linkfiles in forensic examinations. Retrieved from computerforensics.parsonage.co.uk/downloads/TheMeaningofLIFE.pdf.
15. Distributed link tracking and object identifiers. (n.d.). Retrieved from http://msdn.microsoft.com/en-us/library/windows/desktop/aa363997(v=vs.85).aspx.
16. Reparse points. (n.d.). Retrieved from http://msdn.microsoft.com/en-us/library/windows/desktop/aa365503(v=vs.85).aspx.
17. (2009, December 30). Retrieved from http://www.xxcopy.com/xxtb_050.htm.
18. Cannot open "documents and settings" folder. (n.d.). Retrieved from http://social.technet.microsoft.com/Forums/windows/en-US/5fef6787-7d4a-421d-afb4-4b77740b330c/cannot-open-documents-and-settings-folder?forum=w7itprogeneral.
19. Attribute - $reparse_point (0xc0). (n.d.). Retrieved from http://inform.pucp.edu.pe/~inf232/Ntfs/ntfs_doc_v0.5/attributes/reparse_point.html.
20. Based upon the teaching of Dan Purcell from Operating System and File System Forensics (CIS 6386).

12 FILE SYSTEMS: NTFS PART IV

As stated in Chapter 9, in the beginning of the analysis of NTFS, this file system is extremely complex and it is not possible to cover all the intricacies. The majority of facets of file management and the attributes containing potential forensic significance have been covered; the exception is the management of the folder structures.

NTFS Folder Structure

The last attribute to be examined deals with the NTFS directories. There are many additional attributes and NTFS features that could be examined, but this will be the last dealt with in this textbook.

The directory structure in NTFS is vastly more complex than the 32-byte FAT directories. As stated several times, files will each have a Standard Information Attribute, one or more Filename Attributes, and one or more Data Attributes. Folders, on the other hand, will have a Standard Information Attribute, one or more Filename Attributes, and an Index Root Attribute. This attribute is always Resident. However, if the directory entries will not fit in the $MFT record, then an additional attribute is added named $Index_Allocation Attribute, which will handle Non-Resident information.

The Index Root Attribute is more complex than some other attributes we have examined and is broken down as follows[1]:

Attribute Header
Attribute Name
Attribute Content
Index Node Header
Index Node Entries

Attribute Header	Attribute Name	Attribute Content	Index Node	Header	Index Node Entry 1	Index Node Entry 2	Index Node Entry 3

The breakdown of the Attribute is also much longer than the other attributes studied[2].

Index Root Attribute (90 00 00 00)			
DEC OFFSET	**HEX OFFSET**	**SIZE (BYTES)**	**DESCRIPTION**
0	0	4	Attribute Type Identifier
4	4	4	Length of the Attribute
8	8	1	Resident (0x00) or Non-Resident Flag (0x01)
9	9	1	Length of Stream Name in Unicode characters
10	0A	2	Offset to the stream name
12	0C	2	Flags (Compressed, Sparse, Encrypted)
14	0E	2	Attribute Identifier
16	10	4	Size of Resident data
20	14	2	Offset to Resident data
22	16	2	Padding
24	18	8	Stream Name in Unicode
Index Header			
32	20	4	Type of attribute stored in index
36	24	4	Collation sorting rule
40	28	4	Size of each index record in bytes
44	2C	1	Size of each index record in clusters
45	2D	3	Padding
Node Header			
48	30	4	Offset to the index node
52	34	4	Node length
56	38	4	Node allocated length
60	3C	4	Flags - Small 0x00 or Large 0x01 plus padding
Index (Directory) Entry			
64	40	8	MFT Record of Entry (6 bytes)
72	48	2	Length of the Entire Entry
74	4A	2	Length of the Content of the Entry
76	4C	4	Flags - 0x00 Resident Only 0x01 Resident and Non-Residen 0x01 No entries 0x02 Last entry 0x03 All Non-Resident
80	50	8	MFT Record of the Parent (6 bytes)
88	58	8	Creation Date/Time

96	60	8	Last Modified Date/Time
104	68	8	MFT Record Modified Date/Time
112	70	8	Last Accessed Date/Time
120	78	8	Allocated Size of the File
128	80	8	Actual Size of the File
136	88	8	File Attributes (System, Hidden, etc.)
144	90	1	Length of the Filename
145	91	1	Filename Type
146	92	varies	Filename
Entries will be repeated for each filename, even LFN and SFN			

We will now walk through an example of a small directory and parse the Index Root Attribute.

The attribute has the same 24-byte header as other resident attributes; the type identifier is 0x90 00 00 00. We will start with offset 24, which has an 8-byte stream name. The name is always $I30.

```
08d70  31 00 00 00 00 00 00 00-90 00 00 00 B8 00 00 00  1···········¸···
08d80  00 04 18 00 00 00 01 00-98 00 00 00 20 00 00 00  ················
08d90  24 00 49 00 33 00 30 00-30 00 00 00 01 00 00 00  $·I·3·0·0·······
08da0  00 10 00 00 01 00 00 00-10 00 00 00 88 00 00 00  ················
08db0  88 00 00 00 00 00 00 00-24 00 00 00 00 00 01 00  ········$·······
08dc0  68 00 52 00 00 00 00 00-23 00 00 00 00 00 01 00  h·R·····#·······
08dd0  1E 7D 41 05 88 E8 CE 01-76 E6 46 FF 87 E8 CE 01  ·}A··èÎ·væFÿ·èÎ·
08de0  1E 7D 41 05 88 E8 CE 01-1E 7D 41 05 88 E8 CE 01  ·}A··èÎ··}A··èÎ·
08df0  08 00 00 00 00 00 00 00-05 00 00 00 00 00 02 00  ················
08e00  20 00 00 00 00 00 00 00-08 03 74 00 65 00 73 00   ·········t·e·s·
08e10  74 00 2E 00 74 00 78 00-74 00 00 00 00 00 00 00  t·.·t·x·t·······
08e20  00 00 00 00 00 00 00 00-10 00 00 00 02 00 00 00  ················
08e30  FF FF FF FF 82 79 47 11-00 00 00 00 00 00 00 00  ÿÿÿÿ·yG·········
```

Offsets 32-35 are for the attribute identifier that is included in the index, which is a Filename (0x30 00 00 00).

```
08d70  31 00 00 00 00 00 00 00-90 00 00 00 B8 00 00 00  1···········¸···
08d80  00 04 18 00 00 00 01 00-98 00 00 00 20 00 00 00  ················
08d90  24 00 49 00 33 00 30 00-30 00 00 00 01 00 00 00  $·I·3·0·0·······
08da0  00 10 00 00 01 00 00 00-10 00 00 00 88 00 00 00  ················
08db0  88 00 00 00 00 00 00 00-24 00 00 00 00 00 01 00  ········$·······
08dc0  68 00 52 00 00 00 00 00-23 00 00 00 00 00 01 00  h·R·····#·······
08dd0  1E 7D 41 05 88 E8 CE 01-76 E6 46 FF 87 E8 CE 01  ·}A··èÎ·væFÿ·èÎ·
08de0  1E 7D 41 05 88 E8 CE 01-1E 7D 41 05 88 E8 CE 01  ·}A··èÎ··}A··èÎ·
08df0  08 00 00 00 00 00 00 00-05 00 00 00 00 00 02 00  ················
08e00  20 00 00 00 00 00 00 00-08 03 74 00 65 00 73 00   ·········t·e·s·
08e10  74 00 2E 00 74 00 78 00-74 00 00 00 00 00 00 00  t·.·t·x·t·······
08e20  00 00 00 00 00 00 00 00-10 00 00 00 02 00 00 00  ················
08e30  FF FF FF FF 82 79 47 11-00 00 00 00 00 00 00 00  ÿÿÿÿ·yG·········
```

Offsets 36-39 are for the sorting correlation rule. NTFS uses a type of balanced tree for sorting filenames[3]. This value relates to the rules utilized for sorting. This rule is beyond understanding of the subject.

```
08d70  31 00 00 00 00 00 00 00-90 00 00 00 B8 00 00 00  1···········¸···
08d80  00 04 18 00 00 00 01 00-98 00 00 00 20 00 00 00  ················
08d90  24 00 49 00 33 00 30 00-30 00 00 00 01 00 00 00  $·I·3·0·0·······
08da0  00 10 00 00 01 00 00 00-10 00 00 00 88 00 00 00  ················
08db0  88 00 00 00 00 00 00 00-24 00 00 00 00 00 01 00  ········$·······
08dc0  68 00 52 00 00 00 00 00-23 00 00 00 00 00 01 00  h·R·····#·······
08dd0  1E 7D 41 05 88 E8 CE 01-76 E6 46 FF 87 E8 CE 01  ·}A··èÎ·væFÿ·èÎ·
08de0  1E 7D 41 05 88 E8 CE 01-1E 7D 41 05 88 E8 CE 01  ·}A··èÎ··}A··èÎ·
08df0  08 00 00 00 00 00 00 00-05 00 00 00 00 00 02 00  ················
08e00  20 00 00 00 00 00 00 00-08 03 74 00 65 00 73 00   ·········t·e·s·
08e10  74 00 2E 00 74 00 78 00-74 00 00 00 00 00 00 00  t·.·t·x·t·······
08e20  00 00 00 00 00 00 00 00-10 00 00 00 02 00 00 00  ················
08e30  FF FF FF FF 82 79 47 11-00 00 00 00 00 00 00 00  ÿÿÿÿ·yG·········
```

Offsets 40-43 have the number of bytes for an index node if stored outside the $MFT (0x00 10 00 00 = 4096 bytes). Offsets 44-47 have the number of clusters used (0x01 00 00 00 = 1 cluster).

```
08d70  31 00 00 00 00 00 00 00-90 00 00 00 B8 00 00 00  1···········¸···
08d80  00 04 18 00 00 00 01 00-98 00 00 00 20 00 00 00  ················
08d90  24 00 49 00 33 00 30 00-30 00 00 00 01 00 00 00  $·I·3·0·0·······
08da0  00 10 00 00 01 00 00 00-10 00 00 00 88 00 00 00  ················
08db0  88 00 00 00 00 00 00 00-24 00 00 00 00 00 01 00  ········$·······
08dc0  68 00 52 00 00 00 00 00-23 00 00 00 00 00 01 00  h·R·····#·······
08dd0  1E 7D 41 05 88 E8 CE 01-76 E6 46 FF 87 E8 CE 01  ·}A··èÎ·væFÿ·èÎ·
08de0  1E 7D 41 05 88 E8 CE 01-1E 7D 41 05 88 E8 CE 01  ·}A··èÎ··}A··èÎ·
08df0  08 00 00 00 00 00 00 00-05 00 00 00 00 00 02 00  ················
08e00  20 00 00 00 00 00 00 00-08 03 74 00 65 00 73 00   ·········t·e·s·
08e10  74 00 2E 00 74 00 78 00-74 00 00 00 00 00 00 00  t·.·t·x·t·······
08e20  00 00 00 00 00 00 00 00-10 00 00 00 02 00 00 00  ················
08e30  FF FF FF FF 82 79 47 11-00 00 00 00 00 00 00 00  ÿÿÿÿ·yG·········
```

Offsets 48-51 are the offset to the Index Node. In this case, the offset is 16 bytes (0x10 00 00 00) from attribute offset 48. This is where the index node begins.

```
08d70  31 00 00 00 00 00 00 00-90 00 00 00 B8 00 00 00  1···········¸···
08d80  00 04 18 00 00 00 01 00-98 00 00 00 20 00 00 00  ················
08d90  24 00 49 00 33 00 30 00-30 00 00 00 01 00 00 00  $·I·3·0·0·······
08da0  00 10 00 00 01 00 00 00-10 00 00 00 88 00 00 00  ················
08db0  88 00 00 00 00 00 00 00-24 00 00 00 00 00 01 00  ········$·······
08dc0  68 00 52 00 00 00 00 00-23 00 00 00 00 00 01 00  h·R·····#·······
08dd0  1E 7D 41 05 88 E8 CE 01-76 E6 46 FF 87 E8 CE 01  ·}A··èÎ·væFÿ·èÎ·
08de0  1E 7D 41 05 88 E8 CE 01-1E 7D 41 05 88 E8 CE 01  ·}A··èÎ··}A··èÎ·
08df0  08 00 00 00 00 00 00 00-05 00 00 00 00 00 02 00  ················
08e00  20 00 00 00 00 00 00 00-08 03 74 00 65 00 73 00   ·········t·e·s·
08e10  74 00 2E 00 74 00 78 00-74 00 00 00 00 00 00 00  t·.·t·x·t·······
08e20  00 00 00 00 00 00 00 00-10 00 00 00 02 00 00 00  ················
08e30  FF FF FF FF 82 79 47 11-00 00 00 00 00 00 00 00  ÿÿÿÿ·yG·········
```

Offsets 52-55 are the node length, starting at offset 48 through the end of the attribute. (0x88 00 00 00 = 136 bytes)

```
08d70 31 00 00 00 00 00 00 00-90 00 00 00 B8 00 00 00 1···········,···
08d80 00 04 18 00 00 00 01 00-98 00 00 00 20 00 00 00 ················
08d90 24 00 49 00 33 00 30 00-30 00 00 00 01 00 00 00 $·I·3·0·0·······
08da0 00 10 00 00 01 00 00 00-10 00 00 00 88 00 00 00 ················
08db0 88 00 00 00 00 00 00 00-24 00 00 00 00 00 01 00 ········$·······
08dc0 68 00 52 00 00 00 00 00-23 00 00 00 00 00 01 00 h·R·····#·······
08dd0 1E 7D 41 05 88 E8 CE 01-76 E6 46 FF 87 E8 CE 01 ·}A··èÎ·væFÿ·èÎ·
08de0 1E 7D 41 05 88 E8 CE 01-1E 7D 41 05 88 E8 CE 01 ·}A··èÎ··}A··èÎ·
08df0 08 00 00 00 00 00 00 00-05 00 00 00 00 00 02 00 ················
08e00 20 00 00 00 00 00 00 00-08 03 74 00 65 00 73 00  ·········t·e·s·
08e10 74 00 2E 00 74 00 78 00-74 00 00 00 00 00 00 00 t·.·t·x·t·······
08e20 00 00 00 00 00 00 00 00-10 00 00 00 02 00 00 00 ················
08e30 FF FF FF FF 82 79 47 11-00 00 00 00 00 00 00 00 ÿÿÿÿ·yG·········
```

Offsets 56-59 are for the located length, which is the same as the node length in this case. Offsets 60-63 are for flags and padding. The flag is 0x00 for a small index or 0x01 for a large index. This is similar a Resident, Non-Resident flag.

```
08d70 31 00 00 00 00 00 00 00-90 00 00 00 B8 00 00 00 1···········,···
08d80 00 04 18 00 00 00 01 00-98 00 00 00 20 00 00 00 ················
08d90 24 00 49 00 33 00 30 00-30 00 00 00 01 00 00 00 $·I·3·0·0·······
08da0 00 10 00 00 01 00 00 00-10 00 00 00 88 00 00 00 ················
08db0 88 00 00 00 00 00 00 00-24 00 00 00 00 00 01 00 ········$·······
08dc0 68 00 52 00 00 00 00 00-23 00 00 00 00 00 01 00 h·R·····#·······
08dd0 1E 7D 41 05 88 E8 CE 01-76 E6 46 FF 87 E8 CE 01 ·}A··èÎ·væFÿ·èÎ·
08de0 1E 7D 41 05 88 E8 CE 01-1E 7D 41 05 88 E8 CE 01 ·}A··èÎ··}A··èÎ·
08df0 08 00 00 00 00 00 00 00-05 00 00 00 00 00 02 00 ················
08e00 20 00 00 00 00 00 00 00-08 03 74 00 65 00 73 00  ·········t·e·s·
08e10 74 00 2E 00 74 00 78 00-74 00 00 00 00 00 00 00 t·.·t·x·t·······
08e20 00 00 00 00 00 00 00 00-10 00 00 00 02 00 00 00 ················
08e30 FF FF FF FF 82 79 47 11-00 00 00 00 00 00 00 00 ÿÿÿÿ·yG·········
```

Offsets 64-71 are the $MFT record number for the entry and sequence number. The first 6 bytes are the record number and the last 2 bytes are the sequence number. This is same format as was used in the Filename Attribute for the parent number. (0x24 00 00 00 00 00 01 00 = record number 36).

```
08d70 31 00 00 00 00 00 00 00-90 00 00 00 B8 00 00 00 1···········,···
08d80 00 04 18 00 00 00 01 00-98 00 00 00 20 00 00 00 ················
08d90 24 00 49 00 33 00 30 00-30 00 00 00 01 00 00 00 $·I·3·0·0·······
08da0 00 10 00 00 01 00 00 00-10 00 00 00 88 00 00 00 ················
08db0 88 00 00 00 00 00 00 00-24 00 00 00 00 00 01 00 ········$·······
08dc0 68 00 52 00 00 00 00 00-23 00 00 00 00 00 01 00 h·R·····#·······
08dd0 1E 7D 41 05 88 E8 CE 01-76 E6 46 FF 87 E8 CE 01 ·}A··èÎ·væFÿ·èÎ·
08de0 1E 7D 41 05 88 E8 CE 01-1E 7D 41 05 88 E8 CE 01 ·}A··èÎ··}A··èÎ·
08df0 08 00 00 00 00 00 00 00-05 00 00 00 00 00 02 00 ················
08e00 20 00 00 00 00 00 00 00-08 03 74 00 65 00 73 00  ·········t·e·s·
08e10 74 00 2E 00 74 00 78 00-74 00 00 00 00 00 00 00 t·.·t·x·t·······
08e20 00 00 00 00 00 00 00 00-10 00 00 00 02 00 00 00 ················
08e30 FF FF FF FF 82 79 47 11-00 00 00 00 00 00 00 00 ÿÿÿÿ·yG·········
```

Offsets 72-73 are for the entire length of the entry starting from the $MFT record number (0x68 00 = 104 bytes).

```
08d70  31 00 00 00 00 00 00 00-90 00 00 00 B8 00 00 00  1···········¸···
08d80  00 04 18 00 00 00 01 00-98 00 00 00 20 00 00 00  ················
08d90  24 00 49 00 33 00 30 00-30 00 00 00 01 00 00 00  $·I·3·0·0·······
08da0  00 10 00 00 01 00 00 00-10 00 00 00 88 00 00 00  ················
08db0  88 00 00 00 00 00 00 00-24 00 00 00 00 00 01 00  ········$·······
08dc0  68 00 52 00 00 00 00 00-23 00 00 00 00 00 01 00  h·R·····#·······
08dd0  1E 7D 41 05 88 E8 CE 01-76 E6 46 FF 87 E8 CE 01  ·}A··èÎ·væFÿ·èÎ·
08de0  1E 7D 41 05 88 E8 CE 01-1E 7D 41 05 88 E8 CE 01  ·}A··èÎ··}A··èÎ·
08df0  08 00 00 00 00 00 00 00-05 00 00 00 00 00 02 00  ················
08e00  20 00 00 00 00 00 00 00-08 03 74 00 65 00 73 00   ·········t·e·s·
08e10  74 00 2E 00 74 00 78 00-74 00 00 00 00 00 00 00  t·.·t·x·t·······
08e20  00 00 00 00 00 00 00 00-10 00 00 00 02 00 00 00  ················
08e30  FF FF FF FF 82 79 47 11-00 00 00 00 00 00 00 00  ÿÿÿÿ·yG·········
```

Offsets 74-75 are for the number of bytes of content in the entry (0x52 00 = 82 bytes). This content begins 6 bytes from this offset.

```
08d70  31 00 00 00 00 00 00 00-90 00 00 00 B8 00 00 00  1···········¸···
08d80  00 04 18 00 00 00 01 00-98 00 00 00 20 00 00 00  ················
08d90  24 00 49 00 33 00 30 00-30 00 00 00 01 00 00 00  $·I·3·0·0·······
08da0  00 10 00 00 01 00 00 00-10 00 00 00 88 00 00 00  ················
08db0  88 00 00 00 00 00 00 00-24 00 00 00 00 00 01 00  ········$·······
08dc0  68 00 52 00 00 00 00 00-23 00 00 00 00 00 01 00  h·R·····#·······
08dd0  1E 7D 41 05 88 E8 CE 01-76 E6 46 FF 87 E8 CE 01  ·}A··èÎ·væFÿ·èÎ·
08de0  1E 7D 41 05 88 E8 CE 01-1E 7D 41 05 88 E8 CE 01  ·}A··èÎ··}A··èÎ·
08df0  08 00 00 00 00 00 00 00-05 00 00 00 00 00 02 00  ················
08e00  20 00 00 00 00 00 00 00-08 03 74 00 65 00 73 00   ·········t·e·s·
08e10  74 00 2E 00 74 00 78 00-74 00 00 00 00 00 00 00  t·.·t·x·t·······
08e20  00 00 00 00 00 00 00 00-10 00 00 00 02 00 00 00  ················
08e30  FF FF FF FF 82 79 47 11-00 00 00 00 00 00 00 00  ÿÿÿÿ·yG·········
```

Offsets 76-79 are for flags indicating whether the entries are Resident or not.

```
08d70  31 00 00 00 00 00 00 00-90 00 00 00 B8 00 00 00  1···········¸···
08d80  00 04 18 00 00 00 01 00-98 00 00 00 20 00 00 00  ················
08d90  24 00 49 00 33 00 30 00-30 00 00 00 01 00 00 00  $·I·3·0·0·······
08da0  00 10 00 00 01 00 00 00-10 00 00 00 88 00 00 00  ················
08db0  88 00 00 00 00 00 00 00-24 00 00 00 00 00 01 00  ········$·······
08dc0  68 00 52 00 00 00 00 00-23 00 00 00 00 00 01 00  h·R·····#·······
08dd0  1E 7D 41 05 88 E8 CE 01-76 E6 46 FF 87 E8 CE 01  ·}A··èÎ·væFÿ·èÎ·
08de0  1E 7D 41 05 88 E8 CE 01-1E 7D 41 05 88 E8 CE 01  ·}A··èÎ··}A··èÎ·
08df0  08 00 00 00 00 00 00 00-05 00 00 00 00 00 02 00  ················
08e00  20 00 00 00 00 00 00 00-08 03 74 00 65 00 73 00   ·········t·e·s·
08e10  74 00 2E 00 74 00 78 00-74 00 00 00 00 00 00 00  t·.·t·x·t·······
08e20  00 00 00 00 00 00 00 00-10 00 00 00 02 00 00 00  ················
08e30  FF FF FF FF 82 79 47 11-00 00 00 00 00 00 00 00  ÿÿÿÿ·yG·········
```

Offsets 80-87 are for the $MFT record of the file's parent with sequence number. (0x23 00 00 00 00 00 = record number 35).

```
08d70  31 00 00 00 00 00 00 00-90 00 00 00 B8 00 00 00  1···········¸···
08d80  00 04 18 00 00 00 01 00-98 00 00 00 20 00 00 00  ················
08d90  24 00 49 00 33 00 30 00-30 00 00 00 01 00 00 00  $·I·3·0·0·······
08da0  00 10 00 00 01 00 00 00-10 00 00 00 88 00 00 00  ················
08db0  88 00 00 00 00 00 00 00-24 00 00 00 00 00 01 00  ········$·······
08dc0  68 00 52 00 00 00 00 00-23 00 00 00 00 00 01 00  h·R·····#·······
08dd0  1E 7D 41 05 88 E8 CE 01-76 E6 46 FF 87 E8 CE 01  ·}A··èÎ·væFÿ·èÎ·
08de0  1E 7D 41 05 88 E8 CE 01-1E 7D 41 05 88 E8 CE 01  ·}A··èÎ··}A··èÎ·
08df0  08 00 00 00 00 00 00 00-05 00 00 00 00 00 02 00  ················
08e00  20 00 00 00 00 00 00 00-08 03 74 00 65 00 73 00  ··········t·e·s·
08e10  74 00 2E 00 74 00 78 00-74 00 00 00 00 00 00 00  t·.·t·x·t·······
08e20  00 00 00 00 00 00 00 00-10 00 00 00 02 00 00 00  ················
08e30  FF FF FF FF 82 79 47 11-00 00 00 00 00 00 00 00  ÿÿÿÿ·yG·········
```

Offsets 88-119 are for the Created, Modified, Record Modified, and Last Accessed dates, like the filename attribute.

```
08d70  31 00 00 00 00 00 00 00-90 00 00 00 B8 00 00 00  1···········¸···
08d80  00 04 18 00 00 00 01 00-98 00 00 00 20 00 00 00  ················
08d90  24 00 49 00 33 00 30 00-30 00 00 00 01 00 00 00  $·I·3·0·0·······
08da0  00 10 00 00 01 00 00 00-10 00 00 00 88 00 00 00  ················
08db0  88 00 00 00 00 00 00 00-24 00 00 00 00 00 01 00  ········$·······
08dc0  68 00 52 00 00 00 00 00-23 00 00 00 00 00 01 00  h·R·····#·······
08dd0  1E 7D 41 05 88 E8 CE 01-76 E6 46 FF 87 E8 CE 01  ·}A··èÎ·væFÿ·èÎ·
08de0  1E 7D 41 05 88 E8 CE 01-1E 7D 41 05 88 E8 CE 01  ·}A··èÎ··}A··èÎ·
08df0  08 00 00 00 00 00 00 00-05 00 00 00 00 00 02 00  ················
08e00  20 00 00 00 00 00 00 00-08 03 74 00 65 00 73 00  ··········t·e·s·
08e10  74 00 2E 00 74 00 78 00-74 00 00 00 00 00 00 00  t·.·t·x·t·······
08e20  00 00 00 00 00 00 00 00-10 00 00 00 02 00 00 00  ················
08e30  FF FF FF FF 82 79 47 11-00 00 00 00 00 00 00 00  ÿÿÿÿ·yG·········
```

Offsets 120-127 are for the allocated size of the file (0x08 00 00 00 00 00 00 00 = 8 bytes). Offsets 128-133 are for the actual file size (0x05 00 00 00 00 00 00 00 = 5 bytes). Note the last 2 bytes actually list as 0x02 00, but these are the fixup codes from the record header (remember this from Chapter 10 – we must replace these bytes with 0x00 00 from the Update Sequence Array at offset 50 in the Record Header).

```
08d70  31 00 00 00 00 00 00 00-90 00 00 00 B8 00 00 00  1···········¸···
08d80  00 04 18 00 00 00 01 00-98 00 00 00 20 00 00 00  ················
08d90  24 00 49 00 33 00 30 00-30 00 00 00 01 00 00 00  $·I·3·0·0·······
08da0  00 10 00 00 01 00 00 00-10 00 00 00 88 00 00 00  ················
08db0  88 00 00 00 00 00 00 00-24 00 00 00 00 00 01 00  ········$·······
08dc0  68 00 52 00 00 00 00 00-23 00 00 00 00 00 01 00  h·R·····#·······
08dd0  1E 7D 41 05 88 E8 CE 01-76 E6 46 FF 87 E8 CE 01  ·}A··èÎ·væFÿ·èÎ·
08de0  1E 7D 41 05 88 E8 CE 01-1E 7D 41 05 88 E8 CE 01  ·}A··èÎ··}A··èÎ·
08df0  08 00 00 00 00 00 00 00-05 00 00 00 00 00 02 00  ················
08e00  20 00 00 00 00 00 00 00-08 03 74 00 65 00 73 00  ··········t·e·s·
08e10  74 00 2E 00 74 00 78 00-74 00 00 00 00 00 00 00  t·.·t·x·t·······
08e20  00 00 00 00 00 00 00 00-10 00 00 00 02 00 00 00  ················
08e30  FF FF FF FF 82 79 47 11-00 00 00 00 00 00 00 00  ÿÿÿÿ·yG·········
```

Offsets 136-143 are for the file flags for System, Hidden, Read-Only, Archive, etc.) (0x20 00 00 00 00 00 00 00 = 20 for Archive).

```
08d70  31 00 00 00 00 00 00 00-90 00 00 00 B8 00 00 00  1···········¸···
08d80  00 04 18 00 00 00 01 00-98 00 00 00 20 00 00 00  ················
08d90  24 00 49 00 33 00 30 00-30 00 00 00 01 00 00 00  $·I·3·0·0·······
08da0  00 10 00 00 01 00 00 00-10 00 00 00 88 00 00 00  ················
08db0  88 00 00 00 00 00 00 00-24 00 00 00 00 00 01 00  ········$·······
08dc0  68 00 52 00 00 00 00 00-23 00 00 00 00 00 01 00  h·R·····#·······
08dd0  1E 7D 41 05 88 E8 CE 01-76 E6 46 FF 87 E8 CE 01  ·}A··èÎ·væFÿ·èÎ·
08de0  1E 7D 41 05 88 E8 CE 01-1E 7D 41 05 88 E8 CE 01  ·}A··èÎ··}A··èÎ·
08df0  08 00 00 00 00 00 00 00-05 00 00 00 00 00 02 00  ················
08e00  20 00 00 00 00 00 00 00-08 03 74 00 65 00 73 00  ··········t·e·s·
08e10  74 00 2E 00 74 00 78 00-74 00 00 00 00 00 00 00  t·.·t·x·t·······
08e20  00 00 00 00 00 00 00 00-10 00 00 00 02 00 00 00  ················
08e30  FF FF FF FF 82 79 47 11-00 00 00 00 00 00 00 00  ÿÿÿÿ·yG·········
```

Offset 144 is the number of bytes in the filename (0x08 test.txt).

```
08d70  31 00 00 00 00 00 00 00-90 00 00 00 B8 00 00 00  1···········¸···
08d80  00 04 18 00 00 00 01 00-98 00 00 00 20 00 00 00  ················
08d90  24 00 49 00 33 00 30 00-30 00 00 00 01 00 00 00  $·I·3·0·0·······
08da0  00 10 00 00 01 00 00 00-10 00 00 00 88 00 00 00  ················
08db0  88 00 00 00 00 00 00 00-24 00 00 00 00 00 01 00  ········$·······
08dc0  68 00 52 00 00 00 00 00-23 00 00 00 00 00 01 00  h·R·····#·······
08dd0  1E 7D 41 05 88 E8 CE 01-76 E6 46 FF 87 E8 CE 01  ·}A··èÎ·væFÿ·èÎ·
08de0  1E 7D 41 05 88 E8 CE 01-1E 7D 41 05 88 E8 CE 01  ·}A··èÎ··}A··èÎ·
08df0  08 00 00 00 00 00 00 00-05 00 00 00 00 00 02 00  ················
08e00  20 00 00 00 00 00 00 00-08 03 74 00 65 00 73 00  ··········t·e·s·
08e10  74 00 2E 00 74 00 78 00-74 00 00 00 00 00 00 00  t·.·t·x·t·······
08e20  00 00 00 00 00 00 00 00-10 00 00 00 02 00 00 00  ················
08e30  FF FF FF FF 82 79 47 11-00 00 00 00 00 00 00 00  ÿÿÿÿ·yG·········
```

Offset 145 is for the filename type (0x03).
00-Posix
01-Win32
02-DOS Short Name
03-Win32/DOS

```
08d70  31 00 00 00 00 00 00 00-90 00 00 00 B8 00 00 00  1···········¸···
08d80  00 04 18 00 00 00 01 00-98 00 00 00 20 00 00 00  ················
08d90  24 00 49 00 33 00 30 00-30 00 00 00 01 00 00 00  $·I·3·0·0·······
08da0  00 10 00 00 01 00 00 00-10 00 00 00 88 00 00 00  ················
08db0  88 00 00 00 00 00 00 00-24 00 00 00 00 00 01 00  ········$·······
08dc0  68 00 52 00 00 00 00 00-23 00 00 00 00 00 01 00  h·R·····#·······
08dd0  1E 7D 41 05 88 E8 CE 01-76 E6 46 FF 87 E8 CE 01  ·}A··èÎ·væFÿ·èÎ·
08de0  1E 7D 41 05 88 E8 CE 01-1E 7D 41 05 88 E8 CE 01  ·}A··èÎ··}A··èÎ·
08df0  08 00 00 00 00 00 00 00-05 00 00 00 00 00 02 00  ················
08e00  20 00 00 00 00 00 00 00-08 03 74 00 65 00 73 00  ··········t·e·s·
08e10  74 00 2E 00 74 00 78 00-74 00 00 00 00 00 00 00  t·.·t·x·t·······
08e20  00 00 00 00 00 00 00 00-10 00 00 00 02 00 00 00  ················
08e30  FF FF FF FF 82 79 47 11-00 00 00 00 00 00 00 00  ÿÿÿÿ·yG·········
```

Offset 146 is the beginning of the filename.

```
08d70 31 00 00 00 00 00 00 00-90 00 00 00 B8 00 00 00 1···········¸···
08d80 00 04 18 00 00 00 01 00-98 00 00 00 20 00 00 00 ················
08d90 24 00 49 00 33 00 30 00-30 00 00 00 01 00 00 00 $·I·3·0·0·······
08da0 00 10 00 00 01 00 00 00-10 00 00 00 88 00 00 00 ················
08db0 88 00 00 00 00 00 00 00-24 00 00 00 00 00 01 00 ········$·······
08dc0 68 00 52 00 00 00 00 00-23 00 00 00 00 00 01 00 h·R·····#·······
08dd0 1E 7D 41 05 88 E8 CE 01-76 E6 46 FF 87 E8 CE 01 ·}A··èÎ·væFÿ·èÎ·
08de0 1E 7D 41 05 88 E8 CE 01-1E 7D 41 05 88 E8 CE 01 ·}A··èÎ··}A··èÎ·
08df0 08 00 00 00 00 00 00 00-05 00 00 00 00 00 02 00 ················
08e00 20 00 00 00 00 00 00 00-08 03 74 00 65 00 73 00 ··········t·e·s·
08e10 74 00 2E 00 74 00 78 00-74 00 00 00 00 00 00 00 t·.·t·x·t·······
08e20 00 00 00 00 00 00 00 00-10 00 00 00 02 00 00 00 ················
08e30 FF FF FF FF 82 79 47 11-00 00 00 00 00 00 00 00 ÿÿÿÿ·yG·········
```

The 16 bytes before the end-of-record marker are the last node entry, and is an empty record. The flag at offset 180 is 0x02, indicating this is the last record.

```
08d70 31 00 00 00 00 00 00 00-90 00 00 00 B8 00 00 00 1···········¸···
08d80 00 04 18 00 00 00 01 00-98 00 00 00 20 00 00 00 ················
08d90 24 00 49 00 33 00 30 00-30 00 00 00 01 00 00 00 $·I·3·0·0·······
08da0 00 10 00 00 01 00 00 00-10 00 00 00 88 00 00 00 ················
08db0 88 00 00 00 00 00 00 00-24 00 00 00 00 00 01 00 ········$·······
08dc0 68 00 52 00 00 00 00 00-23 00 00 00 00 00 01 00 h·R·····#·······
08dd0 1E 7D 41 05 88 E8 CE 01-76 E6 46 FF 87 E8 CE 01 ·}A··èÎ·væFÿ·èÎ·
08de0 1E 7D 41 05 88 E8 CE 01-1E 7D 41 05 88 E8 CE 01 ·}A··èÎ··}A··èÎ·
08df0 08 00 00 00 00 00 00 00-05 00 00 00 00 00 02 00 ················
08e00 20 00 00 00 00 00 00 00-08 03 74 00 65 00 73 00 ··········t·e·s·
08e10 74 00 2E 00 74 00 78 00-74 00 00 00 00 00 00 00 t·.·t·x·t·······
08e20 00 00 00 00 00 00 00 00-10 00 00 00 02 00 00 00 ················
08e30 FF FF FF FF 82 79 47 11-00 00 00 00 00 00 00 00 ÿÿÿÿ·yG·········
```

PRACTICAL EXERCISE 1

Examine file 12_Pract.E01 with FTK Imager and complete the table below.

INDEX Root Attribute (0x90 00 00 00)	Record 40	Record 42	Record 42	Record 42	Record 43
Folder Name is:					
Length of the Attribute is:					
Resident or Non-Resident:					
Stream Name:					
Type of Attribute Stored in the Index:					
Size of each INDX record in bytes:					
Number of Clusters per INDEX record:					
$MFT record number of file:					
$MFT record number of the parent:					
Created Date/Time (UTC):					
Last Modified Date/Time (UTC):					
Record Modified Date/Time (UTC):					
Last Accessed Date/Time (UTC):					
Allocated Size of the file:					
Actual Size of the file:					
File Attributes (see Chapter 11 FNA):					
Length of the filename:					
Filename type:					
Filename:					

Next we will examine what occurs when there are too many entries in the Index Root and how that data is stored.

Taking the folder used above and adding three additional files to it will make it so the contents will no longer fit inside the $MFT record. In the case of folders, it is not quite as simple as making the attribute Non-Resident and storing the contents in an available cluster. It is similar, but two additional attributes are needed to complete this.

First, let's look at the attributes.

```
08c00 46 49 4C 45 30 00 03 00-5C 4A 10 00 00 00 00 00 FILE0···\J······
08c10 01 00 02 00 38 00 03 00-50 02 00 00 00 04 00 00 ····8···P·······
08c20 00 00 00 00 00 00 00 00-07 00 00 00 23 00 00 00 ············#···
08c30 03 00 00 00 00 00 00 00-10 00 00 00 60 00 00 00 ············`···
08c40 00 00 00 00 00 00 00 00-48 00 00 00 18 00 00 00 ········H·······
08c50 1E 7D 41 05 88 E8 CE 01-AA 1E 53 1F A3 E8 CE 01 ·}A··èÎ·ª·S·£èÎ·
08c60 AA 1E 53 1F A3 E8 CE 01-AA 1E 53 1F A3 E8 CE 01 ª·S·£èÎ·ª·S·£èÎ·
08c70 00 00 00 00 00 00 00 00-00 00 00 00 00 00 00 00 ················
08c80 00 00 00 00 05 01 00 00-00 00 00 00 00 00 00 00 ················
08c90 00 00 00 00 00 00 00 00-30 00 00 00 70 00 00 00 ········0···p···
08ca0 00 00 00 00 00 00 02 00-52 00 00 00 18 00 01 00 ········R·······
08cb0 05 00 00 00 00 00 05 00-1E 7D 41 05 88 E8 CE 01 ·········}A··èÎ·
08cc0 1E 7D 41 05 88 E8 CE 01-1E 7D 41 05 88 E8 CE 01 ·}A··èÎ··}A··èÎ·
08cd0 1E 7D 41 05 88 E8 CE 01-00 00 00 00 00 00 00 00 ·}A··èÎ·········
08ce0 00 00 00 00 00 00 00 00-00 00 00 10 00 00 00 00 ················
08cf0 08 01 4D 00 79 00 20 00-46 00 69 00 6C 00 65 00 ··M·y· ·F·i·l·e·
08d00 73 00 00 00 00 00 00 00-30 00 00 00 70 00 00 00 s·······0···p···
08d10 00 00 00 00 00 00 03 00-52 00 00 00 18 00 01 00 ········R·······
08d20 05 00 00 00 00 00 05 00-1E 7D 41 05 88 E8 CE 01 ·········}A··èÎ·
08d30 1E 7D 41 05 88 E8 CE 01-1E 7D 41 05 88 E8 CE 01 ·}A··èÎ··}A··èÎ·
08d40 1E 7D 41 05 88 E8 CE 01-00 00 00 00 00 00 00 00 ·}A··èÎ·········
08d50 00 00 00 00 00 00 00 00-00 00 00 10 00 00 00 00 ················
08d60 08 02 4D 00 59 00 46 00-49 00 4C 00 45 00 7E 00 ··M·Y·F·I·L·E·~·
08d70 31 00 00 00 00 00 00 00-90 00 00 00 58 00 00 00 1···········X···
08d80 00 04 18 00 00 00 06 00-38 00 00 00 20 00 00 00 ········8··· ···
08d90 24 00 49 00 33 00 30 00-30 00 00 00 01 00 00 00 $·I·3·0·0·······
08da0 00 10 00 00 01 00 00 00-10 00 00 00 28 00 00 00 ············(···
08db0 28 00 00 00 01 00 00 00-00 00 00 00 00 00 00 00 (···············
08dc0 18 00 00 00 03 00 00 00-00 00 00 00 00 00 00 00 ················
08dd0 A0 00 00 00 50 00 00 00-01 04 40 00 00 00 04 00 ····P·····@·····
08de0 00 00 00 00 00 00 00 00-00 00 00 00 00 00 00 00 ················
08df0 48 00 00 00 00 00 00 00-00 10 00 00 00 00 03 00 H···············
08e00 00 10 00 00 00 00 00 00-00 10 00 00 00 00 00 00 ················
08e10 24 00 49 00 33 00 30 00-11 01 25 00 01 00 00 00 $·I·3·0···%·····
08e20 B0 00 00 00 28 00 00 00-00 04 18 00 00 00 05 00 °···(···········
08e30 08 00 00 00 20 00 00 00-24 00 49 00 33 00 30 00 ···· ···$·I·3·0·
08e40 01 00 00 00 00 00 00 00-FF FF FF FF 82 79 47 11 ········ÿÿÿÿ·yG·
```

Note that there is a Standard Information Attribute, two Filename Attributes, an Index Root Attribute, and two new attributes – Index_Allocation and Bitmap Attributes[4]. These two additional attributes handle the storage of the Non-Resident data.

The Index Root layout is the same as what we looked at above with the exception that it stops at the beginning of the entry content because there is no entry content. The references to the $MFT record number and the parent's $MFT record number are 0 because there are no filenames listed in the attribute. This attribute is typically 88 bytes in length (0x58) when the filenames are Non-Resident.

The breakdown of the Index_Allocation Attribute is below[5].

Index_Allocation Attribute (A0 00 00 00)			
DEC OFFSET	**HEX OFFSET**	**SIZE (BYTES)**	**DESCRIPTION**
0	0	4	Attribute Type Identifier
4	4	4	Length of the Attribute
8	8	1	Resident (0x00) or Non-Resident Flag (0x01)
9	9	1	Length of Stream Name in Unicode characters
10	0A	2	Offset to the Stream Name
12	0C	2	Flags (Compressed, Sparse, Encrypted)
14	0E	2	Attribute Identifier
16	10	8	Starting VCN of runlist
24	18	8	Ending VCN of runlist
32	20	2	Offset to runlist in bytes
34	22	2	Used for compression
36	24	4	Unused
40	28	8	Allocated size for content in bytes (physical size)
48	30	8	Actual size of content in bytes (logical size)
56	38	8	Initialized size of content in bytes
64	40	8	Stream Name $I30
72	48	varies	Runlist

We will now parse through the Index_Allocation Attribute, which is almost identical to the Non-Resident Data Attribute we examined in Chapter 11. The only difference is the stream name of $I30 just before the runlist.

We will start with Offsets 0-3 for the attribute type identifier of 0xA0 00 00 00.

```
08dd0 A0 00 00 00 50 00 00 00-01 04 40 00 00 00 04 00  ···P·····@·····
08de0 00 00 00 00 00 00 00 00-00 00 00 00 00 00 00 00  ················
08df0 48 00 00 00 00 00 00 00-00 10 00 00 00 00 03 00  H···············
08e00 00 10 00 00 00 00 00 00-00 10 00 00 00 00 00 00  ················
08e10 24 00 49 00 33 00 30 00-11 01 25 00 01 00 00 00  $·I·3·0···%·····
```

Offsets 4-7 are for the size of the attribute, 0x50 00 00 00 or 80 bytes.

```
08dd0 A0 00 00 00 50 00 00 00-01 04 40 00 00 00 04 00  ···P·····@·····
08de0 00 00 00 00 00 00 00 00-00 00 00 00 00 00 00 00  ················
08df0 48 00 00 00 00 00 00 00-00 10 00 00 00 00 03 00  H···············
08e00 00 10 00 00 00 00 00 00-00 10 00 00 00 00 00 00  ················
08e10 24 00 49 00 33 00 30 00-11 01 25 00 01 00 00 00  $·I·3·0···%·····
```

Offset 8 is for Resident or Non-Resident. This attribute is always Non-Resident.

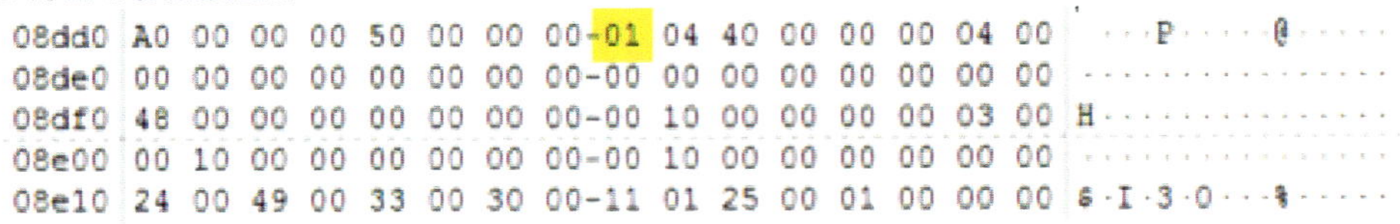

```
08dd0 A0 00 00 00 50 00 00 00-01 04 40 00 00 00 04 00  ···P·····@·····
08de0 00 00 00 00 00 00 00 00-00 00 00 00 00 00 00 00  ················
08df0 48 00 00 00 00 00 00 00-00 10 00 00 00 00 03 00  H···············
08e00 00 10 00 00 00 00 00 00-00 10 00 00 00 00 00 00  ················
08e10 24 00 49 00 33 00 30 00-11 01 25 00 01 00 00 00  $·I·3·0···%·····
```

Offset 9 is the length of the stream name, which in this case is 4 bytes ($I30). Offsets 10-11 have the offset to the name (0x40 00), meaning it is 64 bytes from the beginning of the attribute to the name.

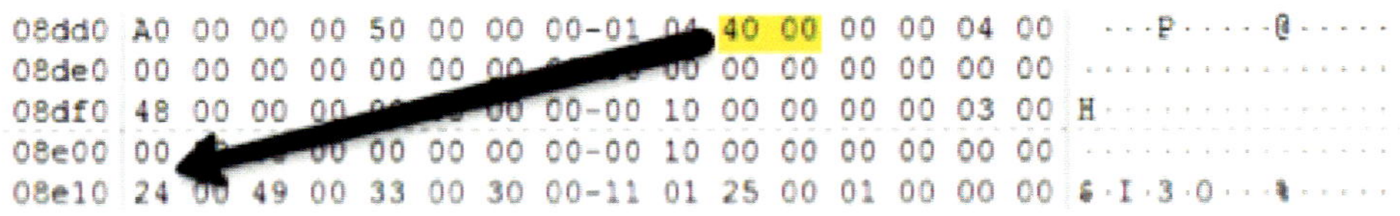

```
08dd0 A0 00 00 00 50 00 00 00-01 04 40 00 00 00 04 00  ···P·····@·····
08de0 00 00 00 00 00 00 00 00-00 00 00 00 00 00 00 00  ················
08df0 48 00 00 00 00 00 00 00-00 10 00 00 00 00 03 00  H···············
08e00 00 10 00 00 00 00 00 00-00 10 00 00 00 00 00 00  ················
08e10 24 00 49 00 33 00 30 00-11 01 25 00 01 00 00 00  $·I·3·0···%·····
```

Offsets 12-13 are for the flags, which there are none for this attribute (0x00 00)
Offsets 14-15 are for the attribute identifier. Since this is the fifth attribute added and counting starts with 0, this attribute's identity is 4 (0x04 00).

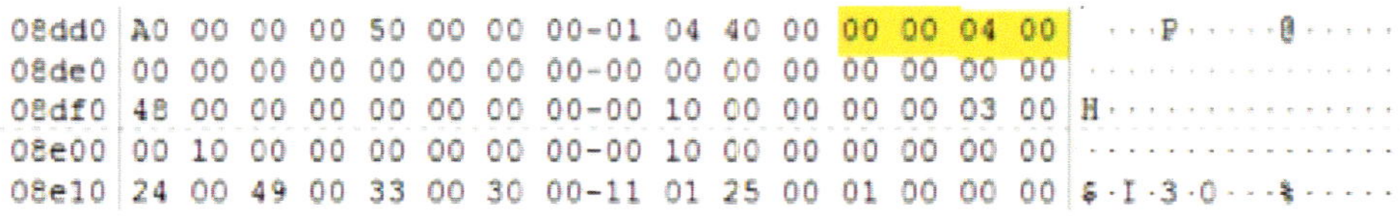

```
08dd0 A0 00 00 00 50 00 00 00-01 04 40 00 00 00 04 00  ···P·····@·····
08de0 00 00 00 00 00 00 00 00-00 00 00 00 00 00 00 00  ················
08df0 48 00 00 00 00 00 00 00-00 10 00 00 00 00 03 00  H···············
08e00 00 10 00 00 00 00 00 00-00 10 00 00 00 00 00 00  ················
08e10 24 00 49 00 33 00 30 00-11 01 25 00 01 00 00 00  $·I·3·0···%·····
```

Offsets 16-31 are for the starting and ending Virtual Cluster Numbers, which are not used in the Index_Allocation Attribute.

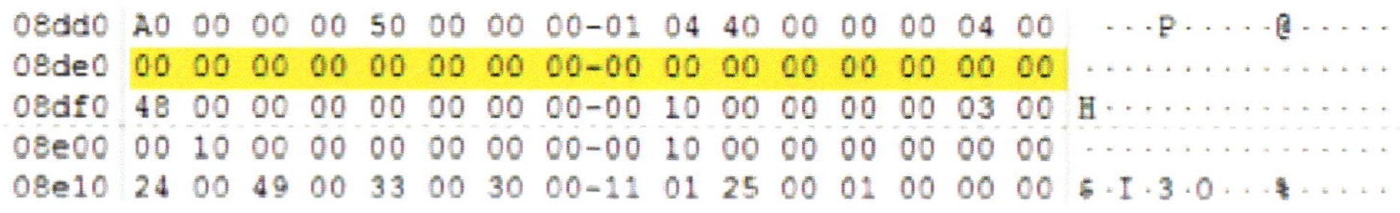

```
08dd0 A0 00 00 00 50 00 00 00-01 04 40 00 00 00 04 00  ···P·····@·····
08de0 00 00 00 00 00 00 00 00-00 00 00 00 00 00 00 00  ················
08df0 48 00 00 00 00 00 00 00-00 10 00 00 00 00 03 00  H···············
08e00 00 10 00 00 00 00 00 00-00 10 00 00 00 00 00 00  ················
08e10 24 00 49 00 33 00 30 00-11 01 25 00 01 00 00 00  $·I·3·0···%·····
```

Offsets 32-33 are the offset to the runlist. In this case it is 72 bytes (0x48 00).

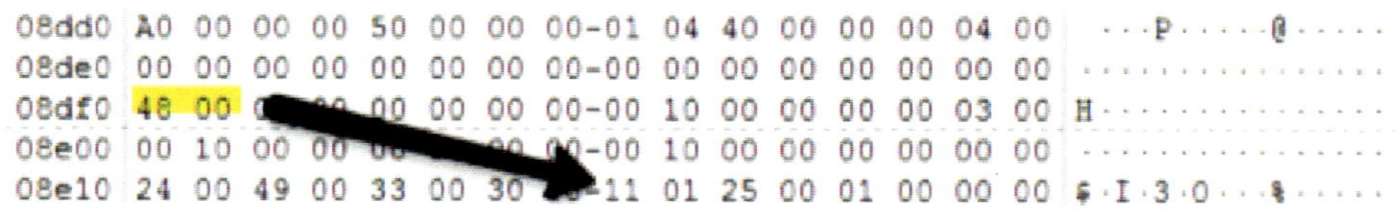

```
08dd0 A0 00 00 00 50 00 00 00-01 04 40 00 00 00 04 00  ···P·····@·····
08de0 00 00 00 00 00 00 00 00-00 00 00 00 00 00 00 00  ················
08df0 48 00 00 00 00 00 00 00-00 10 00 00 00 00 03 00  H···············
08e00 00 10 00 00 00 00 00 00-00 10 00 00 00 00 00 00  ················
08e10 24 00 49 00 33 00 30 00-11 01 25 00 01 00 00 00  $·I·3·0···%·····
```

Offsets 34-39 are for compression and padding, which are not used.

```
08dd0 A0 00 00 00 50 00 00 00-01 04 40 00 00 00 04 00   ···P·····@·····
08de0 00 00 00 00 00 00 00 00-00 00 00 00 00 00 00 00   ················
08df0 48 00 00 00 00 00 00 00-00 10 00 00 00 00 03 00  H···············
08e00 00 10 00 00 00 00 00 00-00 10 00 00 00 00 00 00  ················
08e10 24 00 49 00 33 00 30 00-11 01 25 00 01 00 00 00  $·I·3·0···%·····
```

Offsets 40-47 are for the Allocated Size. Offsets 48-55 are for the Actual Size and offsets 56-63 are for the Initialized Size, which are all the same size of 4096 bytes (0x00 10 00 00). Index Records are always 4096 bytes. Note that in offsets 46-47 there are fixup codes (0x03 00) that must be replaced.

```
08dd0 A0 00 00 00 50 00 00 00-01 04 40 00 00 00 04 00   ···P·····@·····
08de0 00 00 00 00 00 00 00 00-00 00 00 00 00 00 00 00   ················
08df0 48 00 00 00 00 00 00 00-00 10 00 00 00 00 03 00  H···············
08e00 00 10 00 00 00 00 00 00-00 10 00 00 00 00 00 00  ················
08e10 24 00 49 00 33 00 30 00-11 01 25 00 01 00 00 00  $·I·3·0···%·····
```

Offsets 64-71 are for the stream name of $I30 in Unicode.

```
08dd0 A0 00 00 00 50 00 00 00-01 04 40 00 00 00 04 00   ···P·····@·····
08de0 00 00 00 00 00 00 00 00-00 00 00 00 00 00 00 00   ················
08df0 48 00 00 00 00 00 00 00-00 10 00 00 00 00 03 00  H···············
08e00 00 10 00 00 00 00 00 00-00 10 00 00 00 00 00 00  ················
08e10 24 00 49 00 33 00 30 00-11 01 25 00 01 00 00 00  $·I·3·0···%·····
```

Offset 72 is the beginning of the runlist. In this case there is a single run of 11 01 25.
There is 1 byte for the length (0x01) and 1 byte for the location (0x25 or cluster 37).

The remainder of the attribute is padding.

```
08dd0 A0 00 00 00 50 00 00 00-01 04 40 00 00 00 04 00   ···P·····@·····
08de0 00 00 00 00 00 00 00 00-00 00 00 00 00 00 00 00   ················
08df0 48 00 00 00 00 00 00 00-00 10 00 00 00 00 03 00  H···············
08e00 00 10 00 00 00 00 00 00-00 10 00 00 00 00 00 00  ················
08e10 24 00 49 00 33 00 30 00-11 01 25 00 01 00 00 00  $·I·3·0···%·····
```

The next attribute is the Bitmap Attribute. This attribute is for allocated indices[6]. The attribute is fairly simple; this is the 24-byte attribute header, 8-byte stream name ($I30), and the 8-byte bitmap. The breakdown is below[7].

Bitmap Attribute (B0 00 00 00)			
DEC OFFSET	**HEX OFFSET**	**SIZE (BYTES)**	**DESCRIPTION**
0	0	4	Attribute Type Identifier
4	4	4	Length of the Attribute
8	8	1	Resident (0x00) or Non-Resident Flag (0x01)
9	9	1	Length of Stream Name in Unicode characters
10	0A	2	Offset to the Stream Name
12	0C	2	Flags (Compressed, Sparse, Encrypted)
14	0E	2	Attribute Identifier
16	10	4	Size of Resident data
20	14	2	Offset to Resident data
22	16	2	Padding
24	18	8	Stream Name in Unicode
32	20	8	Bitmap

Offsets 0-23 are the standard Resident Attribute Header with an attribute type identifier of 0xB0 00 00 00.

```
08e20 B0 00 00 00 28 00 00 00-00 04 18 00 00 00 05 00  °···(···········
08e30 08 00 00 00 20 00 00 00-24 00 49 00 33 00 30 00  ········$·I·3·0·
08e40 01 00 00 00 00 00 00 00-FF FF FF FF 82 79 47 11  ········ÿÿÿÿ·yG·
```

Offsets 24-31 have the stream name in Unicode ($I30).

```
08e20 B0 00 00 00 28 00 00 00-00 04 18 00 00 00 05 00  °···(···········
08e30 08 00 00 00 20 00 00 00-24 00 49 00 33 00 30 00  ········$·I·3·0·
08e40 01 00 00 00 00 00 00 00-FF FF FF FF 82 79 47 11  ········ÿÿÿÿ·yG·
```

Offsets 32-39 have the Bitmap bytes (0x01 or 00000000 00000001 for a single allocated index). We saw above in the Index_Allocation Attribute that Index records are 4096 bytes. This followed by the end of record marker.

```
08e20 B0 00 00 00 28 00 00 00-00 04 18 00 00 00 05 00  °···(···········
08e30 08 00 00 00 20 00 00 00-24 00 49 00 33 00 30 00  ········$·I·3·0·
08e40 01 00 00 00 00 00 00 00-FF FF FF FF 82 79 47 11  ········ÿÿÿÿ·yG·
```

Finally, we will look at the actual Non-Resident Index record. The record begins with a 60-byte header, similar to the $MFT record header. These records always begin with INDX. Following the header will be the index entries like those we examined in the Index Root Attribute. The screen capture below has the header information, followed by entries in various colors.

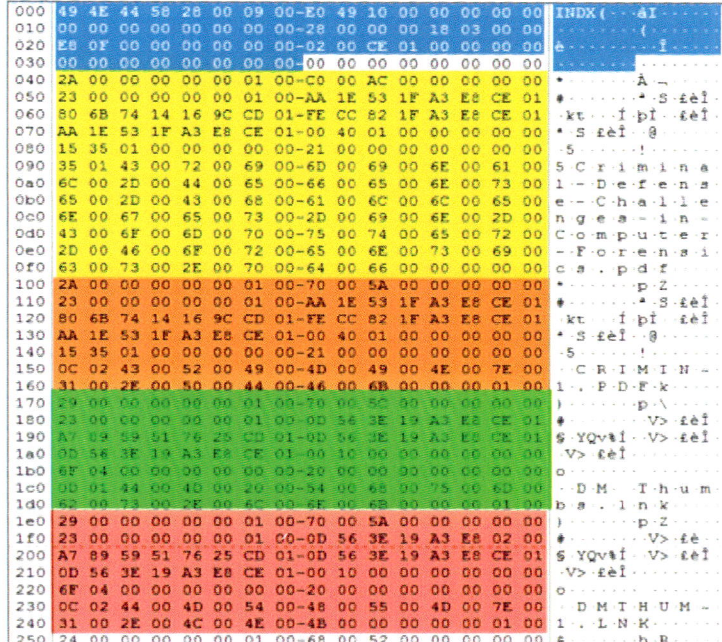
```
000 49 4E 44 58 28 00 09 00-E0 49 10 00 00 00 00 00  INDX(···àI······
010 00 00 00 00 00 00 00 00-28 00 00 00 18 03 00 00  ········(·······
020 E8 0F 00 00 00 00 00 00-02 00 CE 01 00 00 00 00  è·········Î·····
030 00 00 00 00 00 00 00 00-00 00 00 00 00 00 00 00  ················
040 2A 00 00 00 00 00 01 00-C0 00 AC 00 00 00 00 00  *·······À·¬·····
050 23 00 00 00 00 00 01 00-AA 1E 53 1F A3 E8 CE 01  #·······ª·S·£èÎ·
060 80 6B 74 14 16 9C CD 01-FE CC 82 1F A3 E8 CE 01  ·kt···Í·þÌ··£èÎ·
070 AA 1E 53 1F A3 E8 CE 01-00 40 01 00 00 00 00 00  ª·S·£èÎ··@······
080 15 35 01 00 00 00 00 00-21 00 00 00 00 00 00 00  ·5······!·······
090 35 01 43 00 72 00 69 00-6D 00 69 00 6E 00 61 00  5·C·r·i·m·i·n·a·
0a0 6C 00 2D 00 44 00 65 00-66 00 65 00 6E 00 73 00  l·-·D·e·f·e·n·s·
0b0 65 00 2D 00 43 00 68 00-61 00 6C 00 6C 00 65 00  e·-·C·h·a·l·l·e·
0c0 6E 00 67 00 65 00 73 00-2D 00 69 00 6E 00 2D 00  n·g·e·s·-·i·n·-·
0d0 43 00 6F 00 6D 00 70 00-75 00 74 00 65 00 72 00  C·o·m·p·u·t·e·r·
0e0 2D 00 46 00 6F 00 72 00-65 00 6E 00 73 00 69 00  -·F·o·r·e·n·s·i·
0f0 63 00 73 00 2E 00 70 00-64 00 66 00 00 00 00 00  c·s·.·p·d·f·····
100 2A 00 00 00 00 00 01 00-70 00 5A 00 00 00 00 00  *·······p·Z·····
110 23 00 00 00 00 00 01 00-AA 1E 53 1F A3 E8 CE 01  #·······ª·S·£èÎ·
120 80 6B 74 14 16 9C CD 01-FE CC 82 1F A3 E8 CE 01  ·kt···Í·þÌ··£èÎ·
130 AA 1E 53 1F A3 E8 CE 01-00 40 01 00 00 00 00 00  ª·S·£èÎ··@······
140 15 35 01 00 00 00 00 00-21 00 00 00 00 00 00 00  ·5······!·······
150 0C 02 43 00 52 00 49 00-4D 00 49 00 4E 00 7E 00  ··C·R·I·M·I·N·~·
160 31 00 2E 00 50 00 44 00-46 00 6B 00 00 00 01 00  1·.·P·D·F·k·····
170 29 00 00 00 00 00 01 00-70 00 5C 00 00 00 00 00  )·······p·\·····
180 23 00 00 00 00 00 01 00-0D 56 3E 19 A3 E8 CE 01  #········V>·£èÎ·
190 A7 89 59 51 76 25 CD 01-0D 56 3E 19 A3 E8 CE 01  §·YQv%Í··V>·£èÎ·
1a0 0D 56 3E 19 A3 E8 CE 01-00 10 00 00 00 00 00 00  ·V>·£èÎ·········
1b0 6F 04 00 00 00 00 00 00-20 00 00 00 00 00 00 00  o···············
1c0 0D 01 44 00 4D 00 20 00-54 00 68 00 75 00 6D 00  ··D·M· ·T·h·u·m·
1d0 62 00 73 00 2E 00 6C 00-6E 00 6B 00 00 00 01 00  b·s·.·l·n·k·····
1e0 29 00 00 00 00 00 01 00-70 00 5A 00 00 00 00 00  )·······p·Z·····
1f0 23 00 00 00 00 00 01 C0-0D 56 3E 19 A3 E8 02 00  #········V>·£è··
200 A7 89 59 51 76 25 CD 01-0D 56 3E 19 A3 E8 CE 01  §·YQv%Í··V>·£èÎ·
210 0D 56 3E 19 A3 E8 CE 01-00 10 00 00 00 00 00 00  ·V>·£èÎ·········
220 6F 04 00 00 00 00 00 00-20 00 00 00 00 00 00 00  o···············
230 0C 02 44 00 4D 00 54 00-48 00 55 00 4D 00 7E 00  ··D·M·T·H·U·M·~·
240 31 00 2E 00 4C 00 4E 00-4B 00 00 00 00 00 01 00  1·.·L·N·K·······
250 24 00 00 00 00 00 01 00-68 00 52 00 00 00 00 00  $·······h·R·····
```

INDEX RECORD HEADER			
DEC OFFSET	HEX OFFSET	SIZE (BYTES)	DESCRIPTION
0	0	4	"INDX" SIGNATURE
4	4	2	Offset to update sequence (fixup array)
6	6	2	Number of entries in the update sequence (fixup) array
8	8	8	$Log File Sequence Number
16	10	8	Virtual Cluster Number
24	18	4	Offset to Index Entry header
28	1C	4	Offset to End of the Last Entry
32	20	4	Allocated Size of Index Entries
36	24	1	Index Type Flag (small or large)
37	25	3	Padding
40	28	2	Update Sequence Number
42	2A	16	Update Sequence Array
58	3A	6	Padding
Index (Directory) Entry			
64	40	8	MFT Record of Entry (6 bytes)
72	48	2	Length of the Entire Entry
74	4A	2	Length of the Content of the Entry
76	4C	4	Flags - 0x00 Resident Only 0x01 Resident and Non-Resident 0x01 No entries 0x02 Last entry 0x03 All Non-Resident
80	50	8	MFT Record of the Parent (6 bytes)
88	58	8	Creation Date/Time
96	60	8	Last Modified Date/Time
104	68	8	MFT Record Modified Date/Time
112	70	8	Last Accessed Date/Time
120	78	8	Allocated Size of the File
128	80	8	Actual Size of the File
136	88	8	File Attributes (System, Hidden etc)
144	90	1	Length of the Filename
145	91	1	Filename Type
146	92	varies	Filename
Entries will be repeated for each filename, even LFN and SFN			

The runlist in the Index_Allocation Attribute had the Index record located in cluster 37. Breaking down this index, starting at offset 0 is the signature of INDX.

```
000 49 4E 44 58 28 00 09 00-E0 49 10 00 00 00 00 00  INDX(···àI······
010 00 00 00 00 00 00 00 00-28 00 00 00 18 03 00 00  ········(·······
020 E8 0F 00 00 00 00 00 00-02 00 CE 01 00 00 00 00  è·········Î·····
030 00 00 00 00 00 00 00 00-00 00 00 00 00 00 00 00  ················
```

Offsets 4-5 are for the offset to the Update Sequence Array. Again, this is just like in the $MFT Record header. The offset is 56 bytes (0x28 00).

```
000 49 4E 44 58 28 00 09 00-E0 49 10 00 00 00 00 00  INDX(···àI······
010 00 00 00 00 00 00 00 00-28 00 00 00 18 03 00 00  ········(·······
020 E8 0F 00 00 00 00 00 00-02 00 CE 01 00 00 00 00  è·········Î·····
030 00 00 00 00 00 00 00 00-00 00 00 00 00 00 00 00  ················
```

Offsets 6-7 are for the number entries in the Update Sequence Array. In this case, it is 9 (0x09 00). The index is 4096 bytes, so there are 8 sectors. The array will have the fixup codes and the bytes from each of the 8 sectors.

```
000 49 4E 44 58 28 00 09 00-E0 49 10 00 00 00 00 00  INDX(···àI······
010 00 00 00 00 00 00 00 00-28 00 00 00 18 03 00 00  ········(·······
020 E8 0F 00 00 00 00 00 00-02 00 CE 01 00 00 00 00  è·········Î·····
030 00 00 00 00 00 00 00 00-00 00 00 00 00 00 00 00  ················
```

Offsets 8-15 are for the $Logfile Sequence Number value.

```
000 49 4E 44 58 28 00 09 00-E0 49 10 00 00 00 00 00  INDX(···àI······
010 00 00 00 00 00 00 00 00-28 00 00 00 18 03 00 00  ········(·······
020 E8 0F 00 00 00 00 00 00-02 00 CE 01 00 00 00 00  è·········Î·····
030 00 00 00 00 00 00 00 00-00 00 00 00 00 00 00 00  ················
```

Offsets 16-23 are for the Virtual Cluster Number, which is 0 in this case.

```
000 49 4E 44 58 28 00 09 00-E0 49 10 00 00 00 00 00  INDX(···àI······
010 00 00 00 00 00 00 00 00-28 00 00 00 18 03 00 00  ········(·······
020 E8 0F 00 00 00 00 00 00-02 00 CE 01 00 00 00 00  è·········Î·····
030 00 00 00 00 00 00 00 00-00 00 00 00 00 00 00 00  ················
```

Offsets 24-27 are for the offset to the Index Entry Header. This is 40 bytes (0x28 00).

```
000 49 4E 44 58 28 00 09 00-E0 49 10 00 00 00 00 00  INDX(···àI······
010 00 00 00 00 00 00 00 00-28 00 00 00 18 03 00 00  ········(·······
020 E8 0F 00 00 00 00 00 00-02 00 CE 01 00 00 00 00  è·········Î·····
030 00 00 00 00 00 00 00 00-00 00 00 00 00 00 00 00  ················
```

Offsets 28-31 are for the offset to the end of the Last entry.

```
000 49 4E 44 58 28 00 09 00-E0 49 10 00 00 00 00 00 INDX(···àI······
010 00 00 00 00 00 00 00 00-28 00 00 00 18 03 00 00 ········(·······
020 E8 0F 00 00 00 00 00 00-02 00 CE 01 00 00 00 00 è·········Î·····
030 00 00 00 00 00 00 00 00-00 00 00 00 00 00 00 00 ················
```

Offsets 32-35 are for the allocated size of the Index Entries. 0xE8 0F 00 00 = 4072 bytes; 4096 – 24-byte header = 4072.

```
000 49 4E 44 58 28 00 09 00-E0 49 10 00 00 00 00 00 INDX(···àI······
010 00 00 00 00 00 00 00 00-28 00 00 00 18 03 00 00 ········(·······
020 E8 0F 00 00 00 00 00 00-02 00 CE 01 00 00 00 00 è·········Î·····
030 00 00 00 00 00 00 00 00-00 00 00 00 00 00 00 00 ················
```

Offset 36 is for the small or large flag. Small is like Resident and large is Non-Resident. These are small entries. Offsets 37-39 are padding.

```
000 49 4E 44 58 28 00 09 00-E0 49 10 00 00 00 00 00 INDX(···àI······
010 00 00 00 00 00 00 00 00-28 00 00 00 18 03 00 00 ········(·······
020 E8 0F 00 00 00 00 00 00-02 00 CE 01 00 00 00 00 è·········Î·····
030 00 00 00 00 00 00 00 00-00 00 00 00 00 00 00 00 ················
```

Offsets 40-41 are the beginning of the Update Sequence Array and contain the fixup codes (0x02 00).

```
000 49 4E 44 58 28 00 09 00-E0 49 10 00 00 00 00 00 INDX(···àI······
010 00 00 00 00 00 00 00 00-28 00 00 00 18 03 00 00 ········(·······
020 E8 0F 00 00 00 00 00 00-02 00 CE 01 00 00 00 00 è·········Î·····
030 00 00 00 00 00 00 00 00-00 00 00 00 00 00 00 00 ················
```

Offsets 42-57 contain the values from the end of each sector in the index. This followed by 6 bytes of padding.

```
000 49 4E 44 58 28 00 09 00-E0 49 10 00 00 00 00 00 INDX(···àI······
010 00 00 00 00 00 00 00 00-28 00 00 00 18 03 00 00 ········(·······
020 E8 0F 00 00 00 00 00 00-02 00 CE 01 00 00 00 00 è·········Î·····
030 00 00 00 00 00 00 00 00-00 00 00 00 00 00 00 00 ················
```

The first Index Entry begins at offset 64 with the 8-byte $MFT record number and sequence of the first file. The $MFT record number is 42 (0x2A 00 00 00 00 00 00 00). The entries here have the same structure as the entries in the resident Index Root Attribute.

```
040  2A 00 00 00 00 00 01 00-C0 00 AC 00 00 00 00 00  *·······À·¬·····
050  23 00 00 00 00 00 01 00-AA 1E 53 1F A3 E8 CE 01  #·······ª·S·£èÎ·
060  80 6B 74 14 16 9C CD 01-FE CC 82 1F A3 E8 CE 01  ·kt···Í·þÌ··£èÎ·
070  AA 1E 53 1F A3 E8 CE 01-00 40 01 00 00 00 00 00  ª·S·£èÎ··@······
080  15 35 01 00 00 00 00 00-21 00 00 00 00 00 00 00  ·5······!·······
090  35 01 43 00 72 00 69 00-6D 00 69 00 6E 00 61 00  5·C·r·i·m·i·n·a·
0a0  6C 00 2D 00 44 00 65 00-66 00 65 00 6E 00 73 00  l·-·D·e·f·e·n·s·
0b0  65 00 2D 00 43 00 68 00-61 00 6C 00 6C 00 65 00  e·-·C·h·a·l·l·e·
0c0  6E 00 67 00 65 00 73 00-2D 00 69 00 6E 00 2D 00  n·g·e·s·-·i·n·-·
0d0  43 00 6F 00 6D 00 70 00-75 00 74 00 65 00 72 00  C·o·m·p·u·t·e·r·
0e0  2D 00 46 00 6F 00 72 00-65 00 6E 00 73 00 69 00  -·F·o·r·e·n·s·i·
0f0  63 00 73 00 2E 00 70 00-64 00 66 00 00 00 00 00  c·s·.·p·d·f·····
```

Offsets 72-73 have the length of the entry, 192 bytes (0xC0 00). This is the number of bytes in the screen capture.

```
040  2A 00 00 00 00 00 01 00-C0 00 AC 00 00 00 00 00  *·······À·¬·····
050  23 00 00 00 00 00 01 00-AA 1E 53 1F A3 E8 CE 01  #·······ª·S·£èÎ·
060  80 6B 74 14 16 9C CD 01-FE CC 82 1F A3 E8 CE 01  ·kt···Í·þÌ··£èÎ·
070  AA 1E 53 1F A3 E8 CE 01-00 40 01 00 00 00 00 00  ª·S·£èÎ··@······
080  15 35 01 00 00 00 00 00-21 00 00 00 00 00 00 00  ·5······!·······
090  35 01 43 00 72 00 69 00-6D 00 69 00 6E 00 61 00  5·C·r·i·m·i·n·a·
0a0  6C 00 2D 00 44 00 65 00-66 00 65 00 6E 00 73 00  l·-·D·e·f·e·n·s·
0b0  65 00 2D 00 43 00 68 00-61 00 6C 00 6C 00 65 00  e·-·C·h·a·l·l·e·
0c0  6E 00 67 00 65 00 73 00-2D 00 69 00 6E 00 2D 00  n·g·e·s·-·i·n·-·
0d0  43 00 6F 00 6D 00 70 00-75 00 74 00 65 00 72 00  C·o·m·p·u·t·e·r·
0e0  2D 00 46 00 6F 00 72 00-65 00 6E 00 73 00 69 00  -·F·o·r·e·n·s·i·
0f0  63 00 73 00 2E 00 70 00-64 00 66 00 00 00 00 00  c·s·.·p·d·f·····
```

Offsets 74-75 are for the length of the content from the parent $MFT record through the filename, or 172 bytes (0xAC 00).

```
040  2A 00 00 00 00 00 01 00-C0 00 AC 00 00 00 00 00  *·······À·¬·····
050  23 00 00 00 00 00 01 00-AA 1E 53 1F A3 E8 CE 01  #·······ª·S·£èÎ·
060  80 6B 74 14 16 9C CD 01-FE CC 82 1F A3 E8 CE 01  ·kt···Í·þÌ··£èÎ·
070  AA 1E 53 1F A3 E8 CE 01-00 40 01 00 00 00 00 00  ª·S·£èÎ··@······
080  15 35 01 00 00 00 00 00-21 00 00 00 00 00 00 00  ·5······!·······
090  35 01 43 00 72 00 69 00-6D 00 69 00 6E 00 61 00  5·C·r·i·m·i·n·a·
0a0  6C 00 2D 00 44 00 65 00-66 00 65 00 6E 00 73 00  l·-·D·e·f·e·n·s·
0b0  65 00 2D 00 43 00 68 00-61 00 6C 00 6C 00 65 00  e·-·C·h·a·l·l·e·
0c0  6E 00 67 00 65 00 73 00-2D 00 69 00 6E 00 2D 00  n·g·e·s·-·i·n·-·
0d0  43 00 6F 00 6D 00 70 00-75 00 74 00 65 00 72 00  C·o·m·p·u·t·e·r·
0e0  2D 00 46 00 6F 00 72 00-65 00 6E 00 73 00 69 00  -·F·o·r·e·n·s·i·
0f0  63 00 73 00 2E 00 70 00-64 00 66 00 00 00 00 00  c·s·.·p·d·f·····
```

Offsets 76-79 are for the flag and padding. The flag of 0x00 indicates the contents are Resident in this record.

```
040  2A 00 00 00 00 00 01 00-C0 00 AC 00 00 00 00 00  *·······À·¬·····
050  23 00 00 00 00 00 01 00-AA 1E 53 1F A3 E8 CE 01  #·······ª·S·£èÎ·
060  80 6B 74 14 16 9C CD 01-FE CC 82 1F A3 E8 CE 01  ·kt···Í·þÌ··£èÎ·
070  AA 1E 53 1F A3 E8 CE 01-00 40 01 00 00 00 00 00  ª·S·£èÎ··@······
080  15 35 01 00 00 00 00 00-21 00 00 00 00 00 00 00  ·5······!·······
090  35 01 43 00 72 00 69 00-6D 00 69 00 6E 00 61 00  5·C·r·i·m·i·n·a·
0a0  6C 00 2D 00 44 00 65 00-66 00 65 00 6E 00 73 00  l·-·D·e·f·e·n·s·
0b0  65 00 2D 00 43 00 68 00-61 00 6C 00 6C 00 65 00  e·-·C·h·a·l·l·e·
0c0  6E 00 67 00 65 00 73 00-2D 00 69 00 6E 00 2D 00  n·g·e·s·-·i·n·-·
0d0  43 00 6F 00 6D 00 70 00-75 00 74 00 65 00 72 00  C·o·m·p·u·t·e·r·
0e0  2D 00 46 00 6F 00 72 00-65 00 6E 00 73 00 69 00  -·F·o·r·e·n·s·i·
0f0  63 00 73 00 2E 00 70 00-64 00 66 00 00 00 00 00  c·s·.·p·d·f·····
```

Offsets 80-87 are for the $MFT record number of the file's parent and sequence number. In this case it is record number 35 (0x23 00 00 00 00 00 00 00).

```
040  2A 00 00 00 00 00 01 00-C0 00 AC 00 00 00 00 00  *·······À·¬·····
050  23 00 00 00 00 00 01 00-AA 1E 53 1F A3 E8 CE 01  #·······ª·S·£èÎ·
060  80 6B 74 14 16 9C CD 01-FE CC 82 1F A3 E8 CE 01  ·kt···Í·þÌ··£èÎ·
070  AA 1E 53 1F A3 E8 CE 01-00 40 01 00 00 00 00 00  ª·S·£èÎ··@······
080  15 35 01 00 00 00 00 00-21 00 00 00 00 00 00 00  ·5······!·······
090  35 01 43 00 72 00 69 00-6D 00 69 00 6E 00 61 00  5·C·r·i·m·i·n·a·
0a0  6C 00 2D 00 44 00 65 00-66 00 65 00 6E 00 73 00  l·-·D·e·f·e·n·s·
0b0  65 00 2D 00 43 00 68 00-61 00 6C 00 6C 00 65 00  e·-·C·h·a·l·l·e·
0c0  6E 00 67 00 65 00 73 00-2D 00 69 00 6E 00 2D 00  n·g·e·s·-·i·n·-·
0d0  43 00 6F 00 6D 00 70 00-75 00 74 00 65 00 72 00  C·o·m·p·u·t·e·r·
0e0  2D 00 46 00 6F 00 72 00-65 00 6E 00 73 00 69 00  -·F·o·r·e·n·s·i·
0f0  63 00 73 00 2E 00 70 00-64 00 66 00 00 00 00 00  c·s·.·p·d·f·····
```

Offsets 88-119 have the Created, Last Modified, Record Modified, and Last Accessed Dates and Times for the file.

Created:	11/23/13 11:24:14 PM (UTC)
Last Modificed:	09/26/12 06:38:11 PM (UTC)
Record Modified:	11/23/13 11:24:14 PM (UTC)
Last Accessed:	11/23/13 11:24:14 PM (UTC)

```
040  2A 00 00 00 00 00 01 00-C0 00 AC 00 00 00 00 00  *·······À·¬·····
050  23 00 00 00 00 00 01 00-AA 1E 53 1F A3 E8 CE 01  #·······ª·S·£èÎ·
060  80 6B 74 14 16 9C CD 01-FE CC 82 1F A3 E8 CE 01  ·kt···Í·þÌ··£èÎ·
070  AA 1E 53 1F A3 E8 CE 01-00 40 01 00 00 00 00 00  ª·S·£èÎ··@······
080  15 35 01 00 00 00 00 00-21 00 00 00 00 00 00 00  ·5······!·······
090  35 01 43 00 72 00 69 00-6D 00 69 00 6E 00 61 00  5·C·r·i·m·i·n·a·
0a0  6C 00 2D 00 44 00 65 00-66 00 65 00 6E 00 73 00  l·-·D·e·f·e·n·s·
0b0  65 00 2D 00 43 00 68 00-61 00 6C 00 6C 00 65 00  e·-·C·h·a·l·l·e·
0c0  6E 00 67 00 65 00 73 00-2D 00 69 00 6E 00 2D 00  n·g·e·s·-·i·n·-·
0d0  43 00 6F 00 6D 00 70 00-75 00 74 00 65 00 72 00  C·o·m·p·u·t·e·r·
0e0  2D 00 46 00 6F 00 72 00-65 00 6E 00 73 00 69 00  -·F·o·r·e·n·s·i·
0f0  63 00 73 00 2E 00 70 00-64 00 66 00 00 00 00 00  c·s·.·p·d·f·····
```

Offsets 120-127 are for the allocated size of the file. 0x00 40 01 00 00 00 00 00 = 81920 bytes.

```
040  2A 00 00 00 00 00 01 00-C0 00 AC 00 00 00 00 00  *·······À·¬·····
050  23 00 00 00 00 00 01 00-AA 1E 53 1F A3 E8 CE 01  #·······ª·S·£èÎ·
060  80 6B 74 14 16 9C CD 01-FE CC 82 1F A3 E8 CE 01  ·kt···Í·þÌ··£èÎ·
070  AA 1E 53 1F A3 E8 CE 01-00 40 01 00 00 00 00 00  ª·S·£èÎ··@······
080  15 35 01 00 00 00 00 00-21 00 00 00 00 00 00 00  ·5······!·······
090  35 01 43 00 72 00 69 00-6D 00 69 00 6E 00 61 00  5·C·r·i·m·i·n·a·
0a0  6C 00 2D 00 44 00 65 00-66 00 65 00 6E 00 73 00  l·-·D·e·f·e·n·s·
0b0  65 00 2D 00 43 00 68 00-61 00 6C 00 6C 00 65 00  e·-·C·h·a·l·l·e·
0c0  6E 00 67 00 65 00 73 00-2D 00 69 00 6E 00 2D 00  n·g·e·s·-·i·n·-·
0d0  43 00 6F 00 6D 00 70 00-75 00 74 00 65 00 72 00  C·o·m·p·u·t·e·r·
0e0  2D 00 46 00 6F 00 72 00-65 00 6E 00 73 00 69 00  -·F·o·r·e·n·s·i·
0f0  63 00 73 00 2E 00 70 00-64 00 66 00 00 00 00 00  c·s·.·p·d·f·····
```

Offsets 128-135 are for the actual size of the files. 0x15 35 01 00 00 00 00 00 = 79125 bytes.

```
040  2A 00 00 00 00 00 01 00-C0 00 AC 00 00 00 00 00  *·······À·¬·····
050  23 00 00 00 00 00 01 00-AA 1E 53 1F A3 E8 CE 01  #·······ª·S·£èÎ·
060  80 6B 74 14 16 9C CD 01-FE CC 82 1F A3 E8 CE 01  ·kt···Í·þÌ··£èÎ·
070  AA 1E 53 1F A3 E8 CE 01-00 40 01 00 00 00 00 00  ª·S·£èÎ··@······
080  15 35 01 00 00 00 00 00-21 00 00 00 00 00 00 00  ·5······!·······
090  35 01 43 00 72 00 69 00-6D 00 69 00 6E 00 61 00  5·C·r·i·m·i·n·a·
0a0  6C 00 2D 00 44 00 65 00-66 00 65 00 6E 00 73 00  l·-·D·e·f·e·n·s·
0b0  65 00 2D 00 43 00 68 00-61 00 6C 00 6C 00 65 00  e·-·C·h·a·l·l·e·
0c0  6E 00 67 00 65 00 73 00-2D 00 69 00 6E 00 2D 00  n·g·e·s·-·i·n·-·
0d0  43 00 6F 00 6D 00 70 00-75 00 74 00 65 00 72 00  C·o·m·p·u·t·e·r·
0e0  2D 00 46 00 6F 00 72 00-65 00 6E 00 73 00 69 00  -·F·o·r·e·n·s·i·
0f0  63 00 73 00 2E 00 70 00-64 00 66 00 00 00 00 00  c·s·.·p·d·f·····
```

Offsets 136-143 are for the file attributes. In this case, the attributes are Archive and Read-Only (0x21) with padding.

```
040  2A 00 00 00 00 00 01 00-C0 00 AC 00 00 00 00 00  *·······À·¬·····
050  23 00 00 00 00 00 01 00-AA 1E 53 1F A3 E8 CE 01  #·······ª·S·£èÎ·
060  80 6B 74 14 16 9C CD 01-FE CC 82 1F A3 E8 CE 01  ·kt···Í·þÌ··£èÎ·
070  AA 1E 53 1F A3 E8 CE 01-00 40 01 00 00 00 00 00  ª·S·£èÎ··@······
080  15 35 01 00 00 00 00 00-21 00 00 00 00 00 00 00  ·5······!·······
090  35 01 43 00 72 00 69 00-6D 00 69 00 6E 00 61 00  5·C·r·i·m·i·n·a·
0a0  6C 00 2D 00 44 00 65 00-66 00 65 00 6E 00 73 00  l·-·D·e·f·e·n·s·
0b0  65 00 2D 00 43 00 68 00-61 00 6C 00 6C 00 65 00  e·-·C·h·a·l·l·e·
0c0  6E 00 67 00 65 00 73 00-2D 00 69 00 6E 00 2D 00  n·g·e·s·-·i·n·-·
0d0  43 00 6F 00 6D 00 70 00-75 00 74 00 65 00 72 00  C·o·m·p·u·t·e·r·
0e0  2D 00 46 00 6F 00 72 00-65 00 6E 00 73 00 69 00  -·F·o·r·e·n·s·i·
0f0  63 00 73 00 2E 00 70 00-64 00 66 00 00 00 00 00  c·s·.·p·d·f·····
```

Offset 144 is the length of the filename, which is 53 bytes (0x35).

```
040  2A 00 00 00 00 00 01 00-C0 00 AC 00 00 00 00 00  *·······À·¬·····
050  23 00 00 00 00 00 01 00-AA 1E 53 1F A3 E8 CE 01  #·······ª·S·£èÎ·
060  80 6B 74 14 16 9C CD 01-FE CC 82 1F A3 E8 CE 01  ·kt···Í·þÌ··£èÎ·
070  AA 1E 53 1F A3 E8 CE 01-00 40 01 00 00 00 00 00  ª·S·£èÎ··@······
080  15 35 01 00 00 00 00 00-21 00 00 00 00 00 00 00  ·5······!·······
090  35 01 43 00 72 00 69 00-6D 00 69 00 6E 00 61 00  5·C·r·i·m·i·n·a·
0a0  6C 00 2D 00 44 00 65 00-66 00 65 00 6E 00 73 00  l·-·D·e·f·e·n·s·
0b0  65 00 2D 00 43 00 68 00-61 00 6C 00 6C 00 65 00  e·-·C·h·a·l·l·e·
0c0  6E 00 67 00 65 00 73 00-2D 00 69 00 6E 00 2D 00  n·g·e·s·-·i·n·-·
0d0  43 00 6F 00 6D 00 70 00-75 00 74 00 65 00 72 00  C·o·m·p·u·t·e·r·
0e0  2D 00 46 00 6F 00 72 00-65 00 6E 00 73 00 69 00  -·F·o·r·e·n·s·i·
0f0  63 00 73 00 2E 00 70 00-64 00 66 00 00 00 00 00  c·s·.·p·d·f·····
```

Offset 145 is the filename type. In this case, the filename is a Win32 name (0x01).

```
040  2A 00 00 00 00 00 01 00-C0 00 AC 00 00 00 00 00  *·······À·¬·····
050  23 00 00 00 00 00 01 00-AA 1E 53 1F A3 E8 CE 01  #·······ª·S·£èÎ·
060  80 6B 74 14 16 9C CD 01-FE CC 82 1F A3 E8 CE 01  ·kt···Í·þÌ··£èÎ·
070  AA 1E 53 1F A3 E8 CE 01-00 40 01 00 00 00 00 00  ª·S·£èÎ··@······
080  15 35 01 00 00 00 00 00-21 00 00 00 00 00 00 00  ·5······!·······
090  35 01 43 00 72 00 69 00-6D 00 69 00 6E 00 61 00  5·C·r·i·m·i·n·a·
0a0  6C 00 2D 00 44 00 65 00-66 00 65 00 6E 00 73 00  l·-·D·e·f·e·n·s·
0b0  65 00 2D 00 43 00 68 00-61 00 6C 00 6C 00 65 00  e·-·C·h·a·l·l·e·
0c0  6E 00 67 00 65 00 73 00-2D 00 69 00 6E 00 2D 00  n·g·e·s·-·i·n·-·
0d0  43 00 6F 00 6D 00 70 00-75 00 74 00 65 00 72 00  C·o·m·p·u·t·e·r·
0e0  2D 00 46 00 6F 00 72 00-65 00 6E 00 73 00 69 00  -·F·o·r·e·n·s·i·
0f0  63 00 73 00 2E 00 70 00-64 00 66 00 00 00 00 00  c·s·.·p·d·f·····
```

Finally, at offset 146 is the filename: Criminal–Defense–Challeng-es-Computer-Forensics.pdf.

```
040 2A 00 00 00 00 00 01 00-C0 00 AC 00 00 00 00 00 *·······À·—·····
050 23 00 00 00 00 00 01 00-AA 1E 53 1F A3 E8 CE 01 #·······ª·S·£èÎ·
060 80 6B 74 14 16 9C CD 01-FE CC 82 1F A3 E8 CE 01 ·kt···Í·þÌ··£èÎ·
070 AA 1E 53 1F A3 E8 CE 01-00 40 01 00 00 00 00 00 ª·S·£èÎ··@······
080 15 35 01 00 00 00 00 00-21 00 00 00 00 00 00 00 ·5······!·······
090 35 01 43 00 72 00 69 00-6D 00 69 00 6E 00 61 00 5·C·r·i·m·i·n·a·
0a0 6C 00 2D 00 44 00 65 00-66 00 65 00 6E 00 73 00 l·-·D·e·f·e·n·s·
0b0 65 00 2D 00 43 00 68 00-61 00 6C 00 6C 00 65 00 e·-·C·h·a·l·l·e·
0c0 6E 00 67 00 65 00 73 00-2D 00 69 00 6E 00 2D 00 n·g·e·s·-·i·n·-·
0d0 43 00 6F 00 6D 00 70 00-75 00 74 00 65 00 72 00 C·o·m·p·u·t·e·r·
0e0 2D 00 46 00 6F 00 72 00-65 00 6E 00 73 00 69 00 -·F·o·r·e·n·s·i·
0f0 63 00 73 00 2E 00 70 00-64 00 66 00 00 00 00 00 c·s·.·p·d·f·····
```

This structure is repeated for each of the entries in the index.

This is just scratching the surface of the NTFS folder structure. There is much more that could be examined.

PRACTICAL EXERCISE 2

Examine file 12_Pract.E01 with FTK Imager and complete the table below.

INDEX Root Attribute (0x90 00 00 00)	Record 38	Record 44
Folder Name is:		
Length of the Attribute is:		
Resident or Non-Resident:		
Stream Name		
Type of Attribute Stored in the Index:		
Size of each INDX record in bytes:		
Number of Clusters per INDEX record:		

Index_Allocation Attribute (0xA0 00 00 00)	Record 38	Record 44
Allocated size of content:		
Actual size of content:		
Initialized size of content:		
Stream Name:		
Interpret Runlist:		
Bitmap Attribute (0xB0 00 00 00)	Record 38	Record 44
Stream Name:		
Number of indices used:		
INDX Record	Record 38	Record 44
Cluster Number:		
Number of entries in Index:		
$MFT Record # File 1:		
$MFT Record # of Parent File 1:		
Created Date/Time (UTC) File 1:		
Last Modified Date/Time (UTC) File 1:		
Record Modified Date/Time (UTC) File 1:		
Last Accessed Date/Time (UTC) File 1:		
Allocated Size of File 1:		
Actual Size of File 1:		
Length of filename 1:		
Filename 1:		
$MFT Record # File 2:		
$MFT Record # of Parent File 2:		
Created Date/Time (UTC) File 2:		
Last Modified Date/Time (UTC) File 2:		
Record Modified Date/Time (UTC) File 2:		
Last Accessed Date/Time (UTC) File 2:		
Allocated Size of File 2:		
Actual Size of File 2:		
Length of filename 2:		
Filename 2:		
$MFT Record # File 3:		
$MFT Record # of Parent File 3:		
Created Date/Time (UTC) File 3:		
Last Modified Date/Time (UTC) File 3:		
Record Modified Date/Time (UTC) File 3:		
Last Accessed Date/Time (UTC) File 3:		
Allocated Size of File 3:		
Actual Size of File 3:		
Length of filename 3:		
Filename 3:		

Data Attributes associated with Folders

As mentioned in Chapter 10, folders typically do not have Data Attributes; however, they can have an Alternate Data Stream like files. In this case there will be 0x80 00 00 00 attribute header. Professor Rune Nordvik of the Norwegian Police University College brought this information to my attention (R. Nordvik, email, May 2015). I was not aware that this was possible.

Orphan Files

The last NTFS artifact that will be discussed in this text is the concept of Orphan Files. These are files that, as would be guessed, do not have a parent[8]. This occurs when a folder is deleted and subsequently all the files contained witin it and then the $MFT record for the folder is reused by a new file or folder. The deleted files in the original folder are without their parents, so they are orphans.

Start with the folder containing three files. Note the sequence number of the record in the Record Header, which is the number of times the $MFT record has been used.

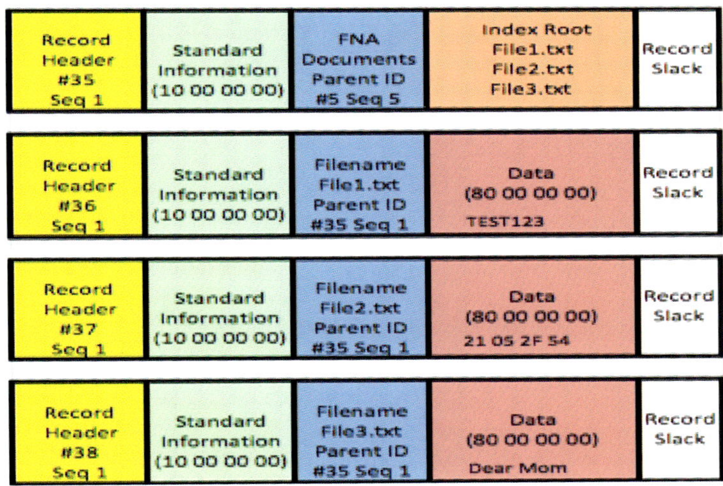

The folder and the contained files are then deleted. The Record Header sequence numbers are incremented upon deletion[9]. The sequence numbers are now 2; however, the parent sequence in the Filename Attribute is not incremented.

The deleted Documents folder sequence is now 2, but in the individual files show that their sequence is just 1.

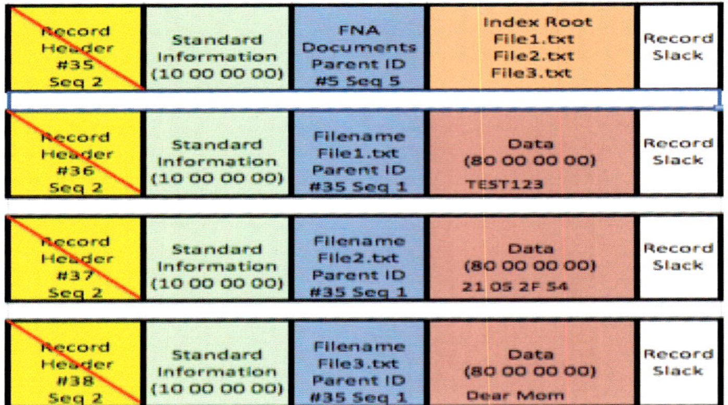

The Documents folder $MFT record is then overwritten by a new folder.

File1.txt, File2.txt, and File3.txt now point to a folder that no longer exists and there is no method to determine what the original folder was. These files are now orphans.

When forensic tools examine the $MFT records, the determination of the status is based upon three criteria[10].

If the sequence number of an active folder and the sequence number of the parent in the Filename Attribute of the file is equal, then the file is a child of the folder.

If the folder is deleted and its sequence is equl to or one more than the sequence number in the Filename Attribute of the file, then it is a deleted child.

If the folder is active and its sequence is at least one more than the sequence number in the Filename Attribute of the file, then it is an orphan.

The forensic utilities such as FTK, FTK Imager, and EnCase interpret orphan files. EnCase refers to them as Lost Files[11].

PRACTICAL EXERCISE 3

Make a determination of the status of the files below based upon the criteria above.

Folder Name	Active or Deleted	Sequence #	Deleted File-name	FNA Sequence #	Child or Orphan or Unknown
My Files	Deleted	3	Test1.doc	2	
Pictures	Active	4	Pic.jpg	2	
Documents	Deleted	2	Letters.doc	2	
Expenses	Deleted	5	Receipts.xls	3	
Temp	Active	3	~1234.TMP	2	
Cache	Deleted	6	CA0346.HTM	6	
Movies	Active	1	ET.MP4	1	
Recent	Deleted	2	Letter.lnk	2	

CHAPTER SUMMARY

Folder structures are much more complex than FAT directory structures. All top-level folders will have an Index Root Attribute. If there are only a couple of files in the folder, then the entries will be Resident. This will include the file's $MFT record number, its parent's $MFT record number, the four dates and times, sizes, and name.

If there are more than three files in the folder, then the entry information is stored in an Index Record in an available cluster. Index records are 4096 bytes in length. There is still an Index Root Attribute present, but has little content. There is an addition of an Index_Allocation Attribute and a Bitmap Attribute.

The Index_Allocation Attribute is a Non-Resident attribute that has a runlist to the Index Record(s). This is similar to the Non-Resident Data attribute.

The Bitmap Attribute is a Resident attribute that simply has a bitmap tracking the allocation of Indices.
The Index Record will have the file-related information mentioned above in the Index Root.

Orphan Files are files where the parent folder has been overwritten.

The status of a file can be determined by examining the sequence numbers of the folder and the value stored in the Filename Attribute of the file.

AT HOME EXERCISE

1. Examine file 12_HW1.E01 with FTK Imager and complete the table below.

INDEX Root Attribute (0x90 00 00 00)	Record 47	Record 35	Record 35	Record 35	Record 35
Folder Name is:					
Length of the Attribute is:					
Resident or Non-Resident:					
Stream Name:					
Type of Attribute Stored in the Index:					
Size of each INDX record in bytes:					
Number of Clusters per INDEX record:					
$MFT record number of file:					
$MFT record number of the parent:					
Created Date/Time (UTC):					
Last Modified Date/Time (UTC):					
Record Modified Date/Time (UTC):					
Last Accessed Date/Time (UTC):					
Allocated Size of the file:					
Actual Size of the file:					
File Attributes (see Chapter 11 FNA):					
Length of the filename:					
Filename type:					
Filename:					

2. Examine file 12_HW1.E01 with FTK Imager and complete the table below.

INDEX Root Attribute (0x90 00 00 00)	Record 39	Record 49
Folder Name is:		
Length of the Attribute is:		
Resident or Non-Resident:		
Stream Name:		
Type of Attribute Stored in the Index:		
Size of each INDX record in bytes:		
Number of Clusters per INDEX record:		
Index_Allocation Attribute (0xA0 00 00 00)	**Record 39**	**Record 49**
Allocated size of content:		
Actual size of content:		
Initialized size of content:		
Stream Name:		
Interpret Runlist:		
Bitmap Attribute (0xB0 00 00 00)	**Record 39**	**Record 49**
Stream Name:		
Number of indices used:		
INDX Record	**Record 39**	**Record 49**
Cluster Number:		
Number of entries in Index:		
$MFT Record # File 1:		
$MFT Record # of Parent File 1:		
Created Date/Time (UTC) File 1:		
Last Modified Date/Time (UTC) File 1:		
Record Modified Date/Time (UTC) File 1:		
Last Accessed Date/Time (UTC) File 1:		
Allocated Size of File 1:		
Actual Size of File 1:		
Length of filename 1:		
Filename 1:		
$MFT Record # File 2:		
$MFT Record # of Parent File 2:		
Created Date/Time (UTC) File 2:		
Last Modified Date/Time (UTC) File 2:		
Record Modified Date/Time (UTC) File 2:		
Last Accessed Date/Time (UTC) File 2:		
Allocated Size of File 2:		
Actual Size of File 2:		
Length of filename 2:		

Filename 2:		
$MFT Record # File 3:		
$MFT Record # of Parent File 3:		
Created Date/Time (UTC) File 3:		
Last Modified Date/Time (UTC) File 3:		
Record Modified Date/Time (UTC) File 3:		
Last Accessed Date/Time (UTC) File 3:		
Allocated Size of File 3:		
Actual Size of File 3:		
Length of filename 3:		
Filename 3:		

ADVANCED HOMEWORK

1. Examine 12_HW1.E01 image and the folder \Users\Kramer\New_Files and note any issues with this folder.

2. Format a flash drive with NTFS. Create a folder named Test1.

Copy File1.txt through File9.txt into Test1 folder.
Provide the $MFT Record numbers for each of the files:

What is the cluster number for the INDX Record used for Test1?

Examine Cluster # ________ with a hex editor.

Delete File3.txt.

Re-examine Cluster # _______ and describe the differences that occurred.

Examine the $MFT # for File3.txt – what changes occurred to this record?

REFERENCES

1. Carrier, B. (2005). File system forensic analysis. (pp. 376-377). Upper Saddle River: Addison-Wesley.

2. Sammes, T., & Jenkinson, B. (2007). Forensic computing, a practitioner's guide. (2nd ed., pp. 404-407). London: Springer Publishing.

3. Carrier, B. (2005). File system forensic analysis. (pp. 290). Upper Saddle River: Addison-Wesley.

4. (n.d.). Retrieved from http://www.c-jump.com/bcc/t256t/Week04NtfsReview/Week04NtfsReview.html.

5. Sammes, T., & Jenkinson, B. (2007). Forensic computing, a practitioner's guide. (2nd ed., pp. 407). London: Springer Publishing.

6. Carrier, B. (2005). File system forensic analysis. (pp. 372-373). Upper Saddle River: Addison-Wesley.

7. Sammes, T., & Jenkinson, B. (2007). Forensic computing, a practitioner's guide. (2nd ed., pp. 408). London: Springer Publishing.

8. Newton, D (2010). Orphaned Files in an NTFS File System. Retrieved from http://dereknewton.com/2010/06/orphaned-files-in-an-ntfs-file-system/.

9. Concept - file record. (n.d.). Retrieved from http://inform.pucp.edu.pe/~inf232/Ntfs/ntfs_doc_v0.5/concepts/file_record.html.

10. Hurlbut, D. (2005). Orphans in the ntfs world. Retrieved from http://ad-pdf.s3.amazonaws.com/papers/wp.NT_Orphan_Files.en_us.pdf.

11.Misner, J. (2007, August 09). What is the lost files folder? Retrieved from https://support.guidancesoftware.com/node/223.

13 FILE SYSTEMS: exFAT

The final file system to be reviewed in this text is the Extended FAT file system or exFAT. This file system is specifically designed to work with the ever-growing flash media market[1]. As flash drives continue to evolve and grow, the limitations of FAT needed to be overcome and this prompted the development of exFAT. NTFS is not well suited for removable media because of the connecting and re-connecting[2]. The exFAT file system was first utilized with Windows CE and then supported by Windows Vista SP1[3]. Jeff Hamm conducted the first publicly documented forensic analysis of exFAT while he was with Paradigm Solutions[4].

The exFAT file system is somewhat of a hybrid between FAT and NTFS. There is still a file allocation table like in FAT, but it is only utilized when the file is fragmented. It uses a bitmap allocation table similar to NTFS for cluster allocation. Times are stored in UTC as opposed to local time in FAT. The directory structure is 32-byte records, but each file has at least three of these records and the names are stored in Unicode.

The number of clusters supported by exFAT is 2^{32} and calling this FAT64 is incorrect[5]. Cluster sizes in exFAT can be as large as 32MB as a limitation set by Microsoft[6]. Theoretically, the volume size supported by exFAT could be 64 ZiB (Zettabytes), but with the limitation set by the Microsoft the volume size can be up to 128 PiB (Petabytes)[7]. To give a drive size reference[8]:

Size	Bytes
Kilobytes	1,024
Megabytes	1,048,576
Gigabytes	1,073,741,824
Terabytes	1,099,511,627,776
Petabytes	1,125,899,906,842,624
Exabytes	1,152,921,504,606,847,000
Zettabytes	1,180,591,620,717,411,303,424

The layout of the file system is similar to that of FAT32 with the exception that there is currently only a single copy of the FAT and no backup copy. There are still two copies of the volume boot record; however, the length is 12 sectors for each copy.

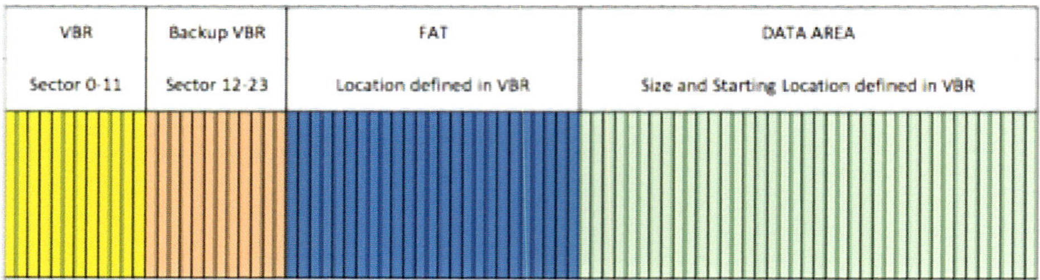

As with the previous file systems, we will start with the examination of the Volume Boot Record. The VBR, as always, begins at physical sector 0. It is 12 sectors in length; however, only the first sector is utilized. The breakdown is below[9].

exFAT Volume Boot Record			
DEC OFFSET	Hex OFFSET	SIZE (BYTES)	DESCRIPTION
0	0x00	3	Jump Instruction
3	0x03	8	OEM ID "EXFAT"
11	0x0B	53	Reserved
64	0x40	8	Partition Sector Offset – 0 for removable drive
72	0x48	8	Size of total volume in Sectors
80	0x50	4	Sector Address of 1st FAT
84	0x54	4	Size of FAT in Sectors
88	0x58	4	Sector address of Data Region
92	0x5C	4	Number of Clusters in Data Region
96	0x60	4	Cluster Address of Root Directory
100	0x64	4	Volume Serial Number
104	0x68	2	File System Revision
106	0x6A	2	Volume Flags: Bit 0 - Active FAT (0=1 1=2) Bit 1 - Dirty Flag (0=Clean 1=Dirty) Bit 2 - Media Failure (0=None 1=Failures)Bit 3 -15 - Reserved
108	0x6C	1	Bytes per Sector
109	0x6D	1	Sectors per Cluster
110	0x6E	1	Number of FATS
111	0x6F	1	Used by INT13
112	0x70	1	Percentage of Data Region In Use
113	0x71	7	Reserved
120	0x72	390	Bootstrap Code
510	0x01FE	42	End of Sector marker (0x55 AA)

A screen capture of the entire first sector is provided below. We will follow this with a look at the individual components of information.

```
000 EB 76 90 45 58 46 41 54-20 20 20 00 00 00 00 00 ëv·EXFAT   ·····
010 00 00 00 00 00 00 00 00-00 00 00 00 00 00 00 00 ················
020 00 00 00 00 00 00 00 00-00 00 00 00 00 00 00 00 ················
030 00 00 00 00 00 00 00 00-00 00 00 00 00 00 00 00 ················
040 00 00 00 00 00 00 00 00-00 70 78 00 00 00 00 00 ·········px·····
050 80 00 00 00 00 04 00 00-80 04 00 00 AE E1 01 00 ············®á··
060 04 00 00 00 C8 CE A1 26-00 01 00 00 09 06 01 80 ····ÈÎ¡&········
070 00 00 00 00 00 00 00 00-33 C9 8E D1 BC F0 7B 8E ········3É·Ñ¼ð{·
080 D9 A0 FB 7D B4 7D 8B F0-AC 98 40 74 0C 48 74 0E Ù û}´}·ð¬·@t·Ht·
090 B4 0E BB 07 00 CD 10 EB-EF A0 FD 7D EB E6 CD 16 ´·»··Í·ëï ý}ëæÍ·
0a0 CD 19 00 00 00 00 00 00-00 00 00 00 00 00 00 00 Í···············
0b0 00 00 00 00 00 00 00 00-00 00 00 00 00 00 00 00 ················
0c0 00 00 00 00 00 00 00 00-00 00 00 00 00 00 00 00 ················
0d0 00 00 00 00 00 00 00 00-00 00 00 00 00 00 00 00 ················
0e0 00 00 00 00 00 00 00 00-00 00 00 00 00 00 00 00 ················
0f0 00 00 00 00 00 00 00 00-00 00 00 00 00 00 00 00 ················
100 0D 0A 52 65 6D 6F 76 65-20 64 69 73 6B 73 20 6F ··Remove disks o
110 72 20 6F 74 68 65 72 20-6D 65 64 69 61 2E FF 0D r other media.ÿ·
120 0A 44 69 73 6B 20 65 72-72 6F 72 FF 0D 0A 50 72 ·Disk errorÿ··Pr
130 65 73 73 20 61 6E 79 20-6B 65 79 20 74 6F 20 72 ess any key to r
140 65 73 74 61 72 74 0D 0A-00 00 00 00 00 00 00 00 estart··········
150 00 00 00 00 00 00 00 00-00 00 00 00 00 00 00 00 ················
160 00 00 00 00 00 00 00 00-00 00 00 00 00 00 00 00 ················
170 00 00 00 00 00 00 00 00-00 00 00 00 00 00 00 00 ················
180 00 00 00 00 00 00 00 00-00 00 00 00 00 00 00 00 ················
190 00 00 00 00 00 00 00 00-00 00 00 00 00 00 00 00 ················
1a0 00 00 00 00 00 00 00 00-00 00 00 00 00 00 00 00 ················
1b0 00 00 00 00 00 00 00 00-00 00 00 00 00 00 FF FF ··············ÿÿ
1c0 FF FF FF FF FF FF FF FF-FF FF FF FF FF FF FF FF ÿÿÿÿÿÿÿÿÿÿÿÿÿÿÿÿ
1d0 FF FF FF FF FF FF FF FF-FF FF FF FF FF FF FF FF ÿÿÿÿÿÿÿÿÿÿÿÿÿÿÿÿ
1e0 FF FF FF FF FF FF FF FF-FF FF FF FF FF FF FF FF ÿÿÿÿÿÿÿÿÿÿÿÿÿÿÿÿ
1f0 FF FF FF FF FF FF FF FF-FF FF FF 00 1F 2C 55 AA ÿÿÿÿÿÿÿÿÿÿÿ··,Uª
```

The VBR starts with the 3-byte jump code and is followed by the 8-byte OEM ID; this is the same as we saw in FAT and NTFS.
The OEM ID, as you can see below, is EXFAT.

```
00000000 EB 76 90 45 58 46 41 54-20 20 20 00 00 00 00 00 ëv·EXFAT   ·····
00000010 00 00 00 00 00 00 00 00-00 00 00 00 00 00 00 00 ················
00000020 00 00 00 00 00 00 00 00-00 00 00 00 00 00 00 00 ················
00000030 00 00 00 00 00 00 00 00-00 00 00 00 00 00 00 00 ················
00000040 00 00 00 00 00 00 00 00-00 70 78 00 00 00 00 00 ·········px·····
00000050 80 00 00 00 00 04 00 00-80 04 00 00 AE E1 01 00 ············®á··
00000060 04 00 00 00 C8 CE A1 26-00 01 00 00 09 06 01 80 ····ÈÎ¡&········
00000070 00 00 00 00 00 00 00 00-33 C9 8E D1 BC F0 7B 8E ········3É·Ñ¼ð{·
```

The next 53 bytes (offsets 12-63) will always be 0 for this version of exFAT. The next 8 bytes are for a partition offset sector, but this is not used for removable media.

```
00000000 EB 76 90 45 58 46 41 54-20 20 20 00 00 00 00 00 ëv·EXFAT   ·····
00000010 00 00 00 00 00 00 00 00-00 00 00 00 00 00 00 00 ················
00000020 00 00 00 00 00 00 00 00-00 00 00 00 00 00 00 00 ················
00000030 00 00 00 00 00 00 00 00-00 00 00 00 00 00 00 00 ················
00000040 00 00 00 00 00 00 00 00-00 70 78 00 00 00 00 00 ·········px·····
00000050 80 00 00 00 00 04 00 00-80 04 00 00 AE E1 01 00 ············®á··
00000060 04 00 00 00 C8 CE A1 26-00 01 00 00 09 06 01 80 ····ÈÎ¡&········
00000070 00 00 00 00 00 00 00 00-33 C9 8E D1 BC F0 7B 8E ········3É·Ñ¼ð{·
```

Offsets 72-79 have the total number of sectors in the volume. In this example, we have 0x00 00 00 00 00 78 70 00 = 7,892,992 sectors or 4041211904 bytes (4 GB).

```
00000000 EB 76 90 45 58 46 41 54-20 20 20 00 00 00 00 00 ëv·EXFAT   ·····
00000010 00 00 00 00 00 00 00 00-00 00 00 00 00 00 00 00 ················
00000020 00 00 00 00 00 00 00 00-00 00 00 00 00 00 00 00 ················
00000030 00 00 00 00 00 00 00 00-00 00 00 00 00 00 00 00 ················
00000040 00 00 00 00 00 00 00 00-00 70 78 00 00 00 00 00 ·········px·····
00000050 80 00 00 00 00 04 00 00-80 04 00 00 AE E1 01 00 ············®á··
00000060 04 00 00 00 C8 CE A1 26-00 01 00 00 09 06 01 80 ····ÈÎ¡&········
00000070 00 00 00 00 00 00 00 00-33 C9 8E D1 BC F0 7B 8E ········3É·Ñ¼ð{·
```

Offsets 80-83 have the starting location of the first FAT. In this case it is 0x00 00 00 80 = Sector 128.

```
00000000 EB 76 90 45 58 46 41 54-20 20 20 00 00 00 00 00 ëv·EXFAT   ·····
00000010 00 00 00 00 00 00 00 00-00 00 00 00 00 00 00 00 ················
00000020 00 00 00 00 00 00 00 00-00 00 00 00 00 00 00 00 ················
00000030 00 00 00 00 00 00 00 00-00 00 00 00 00 00 00 00 ················
00000040 00 00 00 00 00 00 00 00-00 70 78 00 00 00 00 00 ·········px·····
00000050 80 00 00 00 00 04 00 00-80 04 00 00 AE E1 01 00 ············®á··
00000060 04 00 00 00 C8 CE A1 26-00 01 00 00 09 06 01 80 ····ÈÎ¡&········
00000070 00 00 00 00 00 00 00 00-33 C9 8E D1 BC F0 7B 8E ········3É·Ñ¼ð{·
```

Offsets 84-87 have the number of sectors in the FAT. (0x00 00 04 00 = 1024 sectors)

```
00000000 EB 76 90 45 58 46 41 54-20 20 20 00 00 00 00 00 ëv·EXFAT   ·····
00000010 00 00 00 00 00 00 00 00-00 00 00 00 00 00 00 00 ················
00000020 00 00 00 00 00 00 00 00-00 00 00 00 00 00 00 00 ················
00000030 00 00 00 00 00 00 00 00-00 00 00 00 00 00 00 00 ················
00000040 00 00 00 00 00 00 00 00-00 70 78 00 00 00 00 00 ·········px·····
00000050 80 00 00 00 00 04 00 00-80 04 00 00 AE E1 01 00 ············®á··
00000060 04 00 00 00 C8 CE A1 26-00 01 00 00 09 06 01 80 ····ÈÎ¡&········
00000070 00 00 00 00 00 00 00 00-33 C9 8E D1 BC F0 7B 8E ········3É·Ñ¼ð{·
```

Offsets 88-91 have the sector address of the beginning of the data area. This will be assigned to Cluster 2. (0x00 00 04 80 = Sector 1152)

```
00000000 EB 76 90 45 58 46 41 54-20 20 20 00 00 00 00 00 ëv·EXFAT     ·····
00000010 00 00 00 00 00 00 00 00-00 00 00 00 00 00 00 00 ················
00000020 00 00 00 00 00 00 00 00-00 00 00 00 00 00 00 00 ················
00000030 00 00 00 00 00 00 00 00-00 00 00 00 00 00 00 00 ················
00000040 00 00 00 00 00 00 00 00-00 70 78 00 00 00 00 00 ·········px·····
00000050 80 00 00 00 00 04 00 00-80 04 00 00 AE E1 01 00 ············®á··
00000060 04 00 00 00 C8 CE A1 26-00 01 00 00 09 06 01 80 ····ÈÎ¡&········
00000070 00 00 00 00 00 00 00 00-33 C9 8E D1 BC F0 7B 8E ········3É·Ñ¼ð{·
```

Offsets 92-95 have the number of clusters in the volume. (0x 00 01 E1 AE = 123310)

```
00000000 EB 76 90 45 58 46 41 54-20 20 20 00 00 00 00 00 ëv·EXFAT     ·····
00000010 00 00 00 00 00 00 00 00-00 00 00 00 00 00 00 00 ················
00000020 00 00 00 00 00 00 00 00-00 00 00 00 00 00 00 00 ················
00000030 00 00 00 00 00 00 00 00-00 00 00 00 00 00 00 00 ················
00000040 00 00 00 00 00 00 00 00-00 70 78 00 00 00 00 00 ·········px·····
00000050 80 00 00 00 00 04 00 00-80 04 00 00 AE E1 01 00 ············®á··
00000060 04 00 00 00 C8 CE A1 26-00 01 00 00 09 06 01 80 ····ÈÎ¡&········
00000070 00 00 00 00 00 00 00 00-33 C9 8E D1 BC F0 7B 8E ········3É·Ñ¼ð{·
```

Offsets 96-99 have the Cluster number of the Root Directory. In FAT32 this was always 2, but note here it is 0x00 00 00 04 (4).

```
00000000 EB 76 90 45 58 46 41 54-20 20 20 00 00 00 00 00 ëv·EXFAT     ·····
00000010 00 00 00 00 00 00 00 00-00 00 00 00 00 00 00 00 ················
00000020 00 00 00 00 00 00 00 00-00 00 00 00 00 00 00 00 ················
00000030 00 00 00 00 00 00 00 00-00 00 00 00 00 00 00 00 ················
00000040 00 00 00 00 00 00 00 00-00 70 78 00 00 00 00 00 ·········px·····
00000050 80 00 00 00 00 04 00 00-80 04 00 00 AE E1 01 00 ············®á··
00000060 04 00 00 00 C8 CE A1 26-00 01 00 00 09 06 01 80 ····ÈÎ¡&········
00000070 00 00 00 00 00 00 00 00-33 C9 8E D1 BC F0 7B 8E ········3É·Ñ¼ð{·
```

Offsets 100-103 have the Volume Serial Number = 26A1CEC8.

```
00000000 EB 76 90 45 58 46 41 54-20 20 20 00 00 00 00 00 ëv·EXFAT     ·····
00000010 00 00 00 00 00 00 00 00-00 00 00 00 00 00 00 00 ················
00000020 00 00 00 00 00 00 00 00-00 00 00 00 00 00 00 00 ················
00000030 00 00 00 00 00 00 00 00-00 00 00 00 00 00 00 00 ················
00000040 00 00 00 00 00 00 00 00-00 70 78 00 00 00 00 00 ·········px·····
00000050 80 00 00 00 00 04 00 00-80 04 00 00 AE E1 01 00 ············®á··
00000060 04 00 00 00 C8 CE A1 26-00 01 00 00 09 06 01 80 ····ÈÎ¡&········
00000070 00 00 00 00 00 00 00 00-33 C9 8E D1 BC F0 7B 8E ········3É·Ñ¼ð{·
```

Offsets 104-105 have the version of the exFAT file system. This is version 1.0 and not all features, such as transactional logging, have been instituted.

```
00000000 EB 76 90 45 58 46 41 54-20 20 20 00 00 00 00 00 ëv·EXFAT   ·····
00000010 00 00 00 00 00 00 00 00-00 00 00 00 00 00 00 00 ················
00000020 00 00 00 00 00 00 00 00-00 00 00 00 00 00 00 00 ················
00000030 00 00 00 00 00 00 00 00-00 00 00 00 00 00 00 00 ················
00000040 00 00 00 00 00 00 00 00-00 70 78 00 00 00 00 00 ·········px·····
00000050 80 00 00 00 00 04 00 00-80 04 00 00 AE E1 01 00 ············®á··
00000060 04 00 00 00 C8 CE A1 26-00 01 00 00 09 06 01 80 ····ÈÎ¡&········
00000070 00 00 00 00 00 00 00 00-33 C9 8E D1 BC F0 7B 8E ········3É·Ñ¼ð{·
```

Offsets 106-107 have the flags for the volume. Only the lower byte is used, as the high byte is reserved. There are 16 bits in the 2 bytes.
15 14 13 12 11 10 9 8 7 6 5 4 3 2 1 0.

Bit 0: 0 FAT1 is active, FAT2 in inactive
Bit 1: 0 Volume is clean, 1 Volume is dirty
Bit 2: 0 No failures, 1 is for media failures
Bits 3-15: Unused

```
00000000 EB 76 90 45 58 46 41 54-20 20 20 00 00 00 00 00 ëv·EXFAT   ·····
00000010 00 00 00 00 00 00 00 00-00 00 00 00 00 00 00 00 ················
00000020 00 00 00 00 00 00 00 00-00 00 00 00 00 00 00 00 ················
00000030 00 00 00 00 00 00 00 00-00 00 00 00 00 00 00 00 ················
00000040 00 00 00 00 00 00 00 00-00 70 78 00 00 00 00 00 ·········px·····
00000050 80 00 00 00 00 04 00 00-80 04 00 00 AE E1 01 00 ············®á··
00000060 04 00 00 00 C8 CE A1 26-00 01 00 00 09 06 01 80 ····ÈÎ¡&········
00000070 00 00 00 00 00 00 00 00-33 C9 8E D1 BC F0 7B 8E ········3É·Ñ¼ð{·
```

Offset 108 has the size of the sectors. The value is the power that 2 is raised to. In this case it is 2^9 or 512 bytes. The sectors can be as large as 4096 bytes.

```
00000000 EB 76 90 45 58 46 41 54-20 20 20 00 00 00 00 00 ëv·EXFAT   ·····
00000010 00 00 00 00 00 00 00 00-00 00 00 00 00 00 00 00 ················
00000020 00 00 00 00 00 00 00 00-00 00 00 00 00 00 00 00 ················
00000030 00 00 00 00 00 00 00 00-00 00 00 00 00 00 00 00 ················
00000040 00 00 00 00 00 00 00 00-00 70 78 00 00 00 00 00 ·········px·····
00000050 80 00 00 00 00 04 00 00-80 04 00 00 AE E1 01 00 ············®á··
00000060 04 00 00 00 C8 CE A1 26-00 01 00 00 09 06 01 80 ····ÈÎ¡&········
00000070 00 00 00 00 00 00 00 00-33 C9 8E D1 BC F0 7B 8E ········3É·Ñ¼ð{·
```

Offset 109 has the number of sectors per cluster. Again this is the value that 2 is raised to. In this case 2^6 or 64 sectors per cluster, equaling 32768 bytes.

```
00000000 EB 76 90 45 58 46 41 54-20 20 20 00 00 00 00 00 ëv·EXFAT   ·····
00000010 00 00 00 00 00 00 00 00-00 00 00 00 00 00 00 00 ················
00000020 00 00 00 00 00 00 00 00-00 00 00 00 00 00 00 00 ················
00000030 00 00 00 00 00 00 00 00-00 00 00 00 00 00 00 00 ················
00000040 00 00 00 00 00 00 00 00-00 70 78 00 00 00 00 00 ·········px·····
00000050 80 00 00 00 00 04 00 00-80 04 00 00 AE E1 01 00 ············®á··
00000060 04 00 00 00 C8 CE A1 26-00 01 00 00 09 06 01 80 ····ÈÎ¡&········
00000070 00 00 00 00 00 00 00 00-33 C9 8E D1 BC F0 7B 8E ········3É·Ñ¼ð{·
```

Offset 110 has the number of FATs utilized. Version 1.0 of exFAT only uses one copy.

```
00000000 EB 76 90 45 58 46 41 54-20 20 20 00 00 00 00 00 ëv·EXFAT   ·····
00000010 00 00 00 00 00 00 00 00-00 00 00 00 00 00 00 00 ················
00000020 00 00 00 00 00 00 00 00-00 00 00 00 00 00 00 00 ················
00000030 00 00 00 00 00 00 00 00-00 00 00 00 00 00 00 00 ················
00000040 00 00 00 00 00 00 00 00-00 70 78 00 00 00 00 00 ·········px·····
00000050 80 00 00 00 00 04 00 00-80 04 00 00 AE E1 01 00 ············®á··
00000060 04 00 00 00 C8 CE A1 26-00 01 00 00 09 06 01 80 ····ÈÎ¡&········
00000070 42 00 00 00 00 00 00 00-33 C9 8E D1 BC F0 7B 8E B·······3É·Ñ¼ð{·
```

Offset 111 is reportedly utilized by Interrupt 13; however, I am not aware of the purpose.

Offset 112 has the percentage for the volume used. The volume after being formatted is shown below – 0 percent is used.

```
00000000 EB 76 90 45 58 46 41 54-20 20 20 00 00 00 00 00 ëv·EXFAT   ·····
00000010 00 00 00 00 00 00 00 00-00 00 00 00 00 00 00 00 ················
00000020 00 00 00 00 00 00 00 00-00 00 00 00 00 00 00 00 ················
00000030 00 00 00 00 00 00 00 00-00 00 00 00 00 00 00 00 ················
00000040 00 00 00 00 00 00 00 00-00 70 78 00 00 00 00 00 ·········px·····
00000050 80 00 00 00 00 04 00 00-80 04 00 00 AE E1 01 00 ············®á··
00000060 04 00 00 00 C8 CE A1 26-00 01 00 00 09 06 01 80 ····ÈÎ¡&········
00000070 00 00 00 00 00 00 00 00-33 C9 8E D1 BC F0 7B 8E ········3É·Ñ¼ð{·
```

Shown below is the same offset after adding files – 0x42 or 66 percent is used.

```
00000000 EB 76 90 45 58 46 41 54-20 20 20 00 00 00 00 00 ëv·EXFAT   ·····
00000010 00 00 00 00 00 00 00 00-00 00 00 00 00 00 00 00 ················
00000020 00 00 00 00 00 00 00 00-00 00 00 00 00 00 00 00 ················
00000030 00 00 00 00 00 00 00 00-00 00 00 00 00 00 00 00 ················
00000040 00 00 00 00 00 00 00 00-00 70 78 00 00 00 00 00 ·········px·····
00000050 80 00 00 00 00 04 00 00-80 04 00 00 AE E1 01 00 ············®á··
00000060 04 00 00 00 C8 CE A1 26-00 01 00 00 09 06 01 80 ····ÈÎ¡&········
00000070 42 00 00 00 00 00 00 00-33 C9 8E D1 BC F0 7B 8E B·······3É·Ñ¼ð{·
```

The remainder of the sector is boot code until the last two bytes, which have the standard VBR signature of 0x55AA.

```
000001d0 FF FF FF FF FF FF FF FF-FF FF FF FF FF FF FF FF ÿÿÿÿÿÿÿÿÿÿÿÿÿÿÿÿ
000001e0 FF FF FF FF FF FF FF FF-FF FF FF FF FF FF FF FF ÿÿÿÿÿÿÿÿÿÿÿÿÿÿÿÿ
000001f0 FF FF FF FF FF FF FF FF-FF FF FF 00 1F 2C 55 AA ÿÿÿÿÿÿÿÿÿÿÿ··,Uª
```

The next eight sectors (1-8) are all 0 with the exception of the last two bytes of each. They all end in 0x55 AA. Sectors 9 and 10 are all 0 and sector 11 has a repeating checksum value calculated form the VBR. This is for verification of changes to the VBR.

```
00001600  62 F2 F2 D8 62 F2 F2 D8-62 F2 F2 D8 62 F2 F2 D8  bòòØbòòØbòòØbòòØ
00001610  62 F2 F2 D8 62 F2 F2 D8-62 F2 F2 D8 62 F2 F2 D8  bòòØbòòØbòòØbòòØ
00001620  62 F2 F2 D8 62 F2 F2 D8-62 F2 F2 D8 62 F2 F2 D8  bòòØbòòØbòòØbòòØ
00001630  62 F2 F2 D8 62 F2 F2 D8-62 F2 F2 D8 62 F2 F2 D8  bòòØbòòØbòòØbòòØ
00001640  62 F2 F2 D8 62 F2 F2 D8-62 F2 F2 D8 62 F2 F2 D8  bòòØbòòØbòòØbòòØ
00001650  62 F2 F2 D8 62 F2 F2 D8-62 F2 F2 D8 62 F2 F2 D8  bòòØbòòØbòòØbòòØ
00001660  62 F2 F2 D8 62 F2 F2 D8-62 F2 F2 D8 62 F2 F2 D8  bòòØbòòØbòòØbòòØ
00001670  62 F2 F2 D8 62 F2 F2 D8-62 F2 F2 D8 62 F2 F2 D8  bòòØbòòØbòòØbòòØ
00001680  62 F2 F2 D8 62 F2 F2 D8-62 F2 F2 D8 62 F2 F2 D8  bòòØbòòØbòòØbòòØ
00001690  62 F2 F2 D8 62 F2 F2 D8-62 F2 F2 D8 62 F2 F2 D8  bòòØbòòØbòòØbòòØ
000016a0  62 F2 F2 D8 62 F2 F2 D8-62 F2 F2 D8 62 F2 F2 D8  bòòØbòòØbòòØbòòØ
000016b0  62 F2 F2 D8 62 F2 F2 D8-62 F2 F2 D8 62 F2 F2 D8  bòòØbòòØbòòØbòòØ
000016c0  62 F2 F2 D8 62 F2 F2 D8-62 F2 F2 D8 62 F2 F2 D8  bòòØbòòØbòòØbòòØ
000016d0  62 F2 F2 D8 62 F2 F2 D8-62 F2 F2 D8 62 F2 F2 D8  bòòØbòòØbòòØbòòØ
000016e0  62 F2 F2 D8 62 F2 F2 D8-62 F2 F2 D8 62 F2 F2 D8  bòòØbòòØbòòØbòòØ
000016f0  62 F2 F2 D8 62 F2 F2 D8-62 F2 F2 D8 62 F2 F2 D8  bòòØbòòØbòòØbòòØ
00001700  62 F2 F2 D8 62 F2 F2 D8-62 F2 F2 D8 62 F2 F2 D8  bòòØbòòØbòòØbòòØ
00001710  62 F2 F2 D8 62 F2 F2 D8-62 F2 F2 D8 62 F2 F2 D8  bòòØbòòØbòòØbòòØ
00001720  62 F2 F2 D8 62 F2 F2 D8-62 F2 F2 D8 62 F2 F2 D8  bòòØbòòØbòòØbòòØ
00001730  62 F2 F2 D8 62 F2 F2 D8-62 F2 F2 D8 62 F2 F2 D8  bòòØbòòØbòòØbòòØ
00001740  62 F2 F2 D8 62 F2 F2 D8-62 F2 F2 D8 62 F2 F2 D8  bòòØbòòØbòòØbòòØ
00001750  62 F2 F2 D8 62 F2 F2 D8-62 F2 F2 D8 62 F2 F2 D8  bòòØbòòØbòòØbòòØ
00001760  62 F2 F2 D8 62 F2 F2 D8-62 F2 F2 D8 62 F2 F2 D8  bòòØbòòØbòòØbòòØ
00001770  62 F2 F2 D8 62 F2 F2 D8-62 F2 F2 D8 62 F2 F2 D8  bòòØbòòØbòòØbòòØ
00001780  62 F2 F2 D8 62 F2 F2 D8-62 F2 F2 D8 62 F2 F2 D8  bòòØbòòØbòòØbòòØ
00001790  62 F2 F2 D8 62 F2 F2 D8-62 F2 F2 D8 62 F2 F2 D8  bòòØbòòØbòòØbòòØ
000017a0  62 F2 F2 D8 62 F2 F2 D8-62 F2 F2 D8 62 F2 F2 D8  bòòØbòòØbòòØbòòØ
000017b0  62 F2 F2 D8 62 F2 F2 D8-62 F2 F2 D8 62 F2 F2 D8  bòòØbòòØbòòØbòòØ
000017c0  62 F2 F2 D8 62 F2 F2 D8-62 F2 F2 D8 62 F2 F2 D8  bòòØbòòØbòòØbòòØ
000017d0  62 F2 F2 D8 62 F2 F2 D8-62 F2 F2 D8 62 F2 F2 D8  bòòØbòòØbòòØbòòØ
000017e0  62 F2 F2 D8 62 F2 F2 D8-62 F2 F2 D8 62 F2 F2 D8  bòòØbòòØbòòØbòòØ
000017f0  62 F2 F2 D8 62 F2 F2 D8-62 F2 F2 D8 62 F2 F2 D8  bòòØbòòØbòòØbòòØ
```

PRACTICAL EXERCISE 1

Open 13_Pract1.E01 with FTK Imager and complete the table below.

OEM ID	
Total Sectors in the Volume	
Starting Sector of the FAT	
Number of Sectors in the FAT	
First Sector of the Data Area	
Number of Clusters in the Data Area	
Cluster Address of the Root Directory	
Serial Number	
File System Version Number	
Sector Size	
Sectors per Cluster	
Number of FATs	
Percentage of Drive Used	
VBR Checksum	

File Allocation Table

As mentioned above, there is still a File Allocation Table; however, it is only utilized when the file is fragmented. Like with FAT32, there are 4 bytes used to reference each cluster and cluster counting begins with 2[10]. The first 8 bytes of the FAT were reserved for the Media Descriptor (0xF8 FF FF FF) and a reserved byte (0xFF FF FF FF). The Cluster 2 reference below is for the Allocation Bitmap, which we will examine shortly. Cluster 3 is for the UpCase Table file, also to be examined later, and finally Cluster 4 is for the Root Directory. These three items will always be present in this order and the Allocation Bitmap will typically start in Cluster 2, but based upon size, the UpCase Table and the Root Directory may be in different locations.

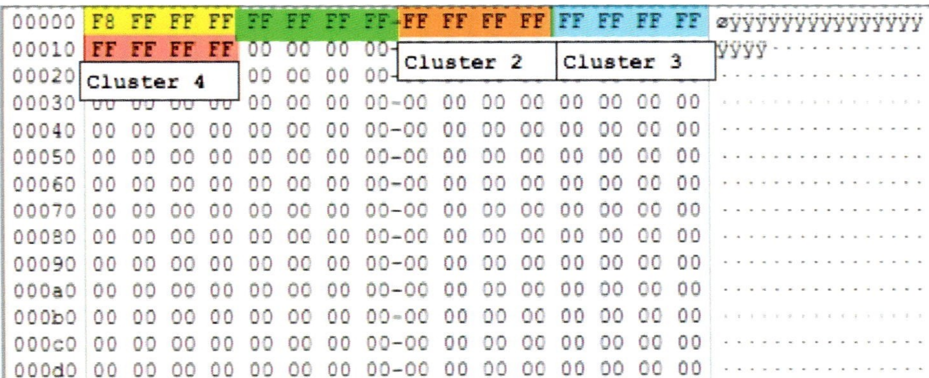

In this example, the drive is 66% filled but you see few cluster references filled. The available entries in the FAT are:

0x00000000 Unused or Unfragmented
0x00000001 Invalid
0x00000002 Valid
.
.
.

.
0xFFFFFFF6 Valid
0xFFFFFFF7 Bad Block
0xFFFFFFF8 Media Descriptor
0xFFFFFFF9 Not Defined
.
.
.
.
0xFFFFFFFE Not Defined
0xFFFFFFFF End of File Marker

Fragmented entries are below and are identical to how FAT32 works. Since the FAT does not track the allocation status of all the clusters, it only provides a link list of clusters.

```
04260 | 99 10 → 9A 10 → 9B 10 → 9C 10 00 00 | ................
04270 | 9D 10 00 00 9E 10 00 00-9F 10 00 00 A0 10 00 00 | ................
04280 | A1 10 00 00 A2 10 00 00-A3 10 00 00 A4 10 00 00 | ¡...¢...£...¤...
04290 | A5 10 00 00 A6 10 00 00-A7 10 00 00 A8 10 00 00 | ¥...¦...§...¨...
042a0 | A9 10 00 00 AA 10 00 00-AB 10 00 00 AC 10 00 00 | ©...ª...«...¬...
042b0 | AD 10 00 00 AE 10 00 00-AF 10 00 00 B0 10 00 00 | -...®...¯...°...
042c0 | B1 10 00 00 B2 10 00 00-B3 10 00 00 FF FF FF FF | ±...²...³...ÿÿÿÿ
```

The non-fragmented files are handled in the directory structure, which will be discussed shortly.

As mentioned above, the Allocation Bitmap is located in Cluster 2. This works in the same manner as the $Bitmap metadata file in NTFS.

```
00000000 | 07 FF FF FF FF FF FF FF-FF FF FF FF FF FF FF FF | ·ÿÿÿÿÿÿÿÿÿÿÿÿÿÿÿ
00000010 | FF FF FF FF FF FF FF FF-FF FF FF FF FF FF FF FF | ÿÿÿÿÿÿÿÿÿÿÿÿÿÿÿÿ
00000020 | FF FF FF FF FF FF FF FF-FF FF FF FF FF FF FF FF | ÿÿÿÿÿÿÿÿÿÿÿÿÿÿÿÿ
00000030 | FF FF FF FF FF FF FF FF-FF FF FF FF FF FF FF FF | ÿÿÿÿÿÿÿÿÿÿÿÿÿÿÿÿ

Cursor pos = 64; clus = 2; phy sec = 1152
```

Note that in the first byte of the Allocation Bitmap, clusters 2, 3, and 4 are allocated and clusters 5, 6, 7, 8, and 9 are unallocated. 0x07 = 00000111

```
9 8 7 6 5 4 3 2  17 16 15 14 13 12 11 10
0 0 0 0 0 1 1 1   1  1  1  1  1  1  1  1
    07                  FF
```

Also mentioned previously was the fact that Cluster 3 contains the UpCase Table file.

```
0000 00 00 01 00 02 00 03 00-04 00 05 00 06 00 07 00 ................
0010 08 00 09 00 0A 00 0B 00-0C 00 0D 00 0E 00 0F 00 ................
0020 10 00 11 00 12 00 13 00-14 00 15 00 16 00 17 00 ................
0030 18 00 19 00 1A 00 1B 00-1C 00 1D 00 1E 00 1F 00 ................
0040 20 00 21 00 22 00 23 00-24 00 25 00 26 00 27 00  .!.".#.$.%.&.'.
0050 28 00 29 00 2A 00 2B 00-2C 00 2D 00 2E 00 2F 00 (.).*.+.,.-.../.
0060 30 00 31 00 32 00 33 00-34 00 35 00 36 00 37 00 0.1.2.3.4.5.6.7.
0070 38 00 39 00 3A 00 3B 00-3C 00 3D 00 3E 00 3F 00 8.9.:.;.<.=.>.?.
0080 40 00 41 00 42 00 43 00-44 00 45 00 46 00 47 00 @.A.B.C.D.E.F.G.
0090 48 00 49 00 4A 00 4B 00-4C 00 4D 00 4E 00 4F 00 H.I.J.K.L.M.N.O.
00a0 50 00 51 00 52 00 53 00-54 00 55 00 56 00 57 00 P.Q.R.S.T.U.V.W.
00b0 58 00 59 00 5A 00 5B 00-5C 00 5D 00 5E 00 5F 00 X.Y.Z.[.\.].^._.
00c0 60 00 41 00 42 00 43 00-44 00 45 00 46 00 47 00 `.A.B.C.D.E.F.G.
00d0 48 00 49 00 4A 00 4B 00-4C 00 4D 00 4E 00 4F 00 H.I.J.K.L.M.N.O.
00e0 50 00 51 00 52 00 53 00-54 00 55 00 56 00 57 00 P.Q.R.S.T.U.V.W.
00f0 58 00 59 00 5A 00 7B 00-7C 00 7D 00 7E 00 7F 00 X.Y.Z.{.|.}.~...
Cursor pos = 191; clus = 3; phy sec = 1216
```

The UpCase Table is like the $Upcase metadata file in NTFS and is used to associate upper- and lower-case values for searching and sorting.

PRACTICAL EXERCISE 2

Open 13_Pract2.E01 with FTK and answer the following.

From the VBR, what percentage of the volume is used?

How many files are in the Root Directory?

Examine the FAT

What cluster(s) are used for the Allocation Bitmap?

What cluster(s) are used for the UpCase Table?

What cluster(s) are used for the Root Directory?

There is one very large 2 GB file, what is its name?

What is the starting cluster? (Either examine the FAT or obtain from FTK Imager Properties)

What is the ending cluster (search the FAT for End of File Markers)?

Examine the Allocation Bitmap. Out of the first 200 clusters, which are unallocated?

Root Directory

The directory structure in exFAT expands upon what we saw in FAT. For all files and folders, with the exception of the Allocation Bitmap, UpCase Table, the Volume Label, and a few other system-related entries not implemented yet, there will be at least three 32-byte entries[11]. We will start our examination with the exceptions and move forward.

Each directory entry begins with a 1-byte Entry Type. This byte must be broken down into its bits[12]:

Bit Offset	**Description**
0-4	Code – Defines the type (there are 10 types)
5	Importance – 0=Critical, 1=Benign
6	*Category – 0=Primary Entry, 1=Secondary Entry
7	In Use – 0=Deleted or unused, 1=Active

There can be only one Primary Entry, but there can be up to 17 secondary entries per file[13]. The Primary and Secondary entries for a file together are referred to as the Directory Entry Set.

Below is the breakdown of the Volume Label entry, which is the first entry in the Root Directory[14].

Volume Label Directory Entry			
DEC OFFSET	HEX OFFSET	SIZE (BYTES)	DESCRIPTION
0	0x00	1	Entry Type (83) Bits 0-4 Code 00011 Bit 5 Importance 0 Bit 6 Category 0 Bit 7 In Use 1 Total 10000011 = 0x83
1	0x01	1	Character Count
2	0x02	22	Volume Label in Unicode
24	0x18	8	Reserved

As discussed earlier, the Root Directory begins in Cluster 4 and the Volume Label is the first 32-byte entry.

Name	Size	Type	Date Modified
[root]	0	Regular File	N/A

```
0000  83 05 65 00 78 00 46 00-41 00 54 00 00 00 00 00  ··e·x·F·A·T·····
0010  00 00 00 00 00 00 00 00-00 00 00 00 00 00 00 00  ················
0020  81 00 00 00 00 00 00 00-00 00 00 00 00 00 00 00  ················
0030  00 00 00 00 02 00 00 00-36 3C 00 00 00 00 00 00  ········6<······
0040  82 00 00 00 0D D3 19 E6-00 00 00 00 00 00 00 00  ·····Ó·æ········
0050  00 00 00 00 03 00 00 00-CC 16 00 00 00 00 00 00  ········Ì·······
0060  85 06 AC 32 20 00 00 00-88 49 89 43 84 49 89 43  ··¬2 ····I·C·I·C
0070  88 49 89 43 23 00 E8 E8-E8 00 00 00 00 00 00 00  ·I·C#·èèè·······
0080  C0 03 00 3D 76 81 00 00-17 00 00 00 00 00 00 00  À··=v···········
0090  00 00 00 00 05 00 00 00-17 00 00 00 00 00 00 00  ················
00a0  C1 00 52 00 65 00 61 00-6C 00 6C 00 79 00 20 00  Á·R·e·a·l·l·y· ·
00b0  52 00 65 00 61 00 6C 00-6C 00 79 00 20 00 52 00  R·e·a·l·l·y· ·R·
00c0  C1 00 65 00 61 00 6C 00-6C 00 79 00 20 00 4C 00  Á·e·a·l·l·y· ·L·
00d0  6F 00 6E 00 67 00 20 00-46 00 69 00 6C 00 65 00  o·n·g· ·F·i·l·e·
00e0  C1 00 6E 00 61 00 6D 00-65 00 20 00 61 00 73 00  Á·n·a·m·e· ·a·s·
00f0  20 00 61 00 6E 00 20 00-45 00 78 00 61 00 6D 00   ·a·n· ·E·x·a·m·
0100  C1 00 70 00 6C 00 65 00-20 00 69 00 6E 00 20 00  Á·p·l·e· ·i·n· ·
0110  65 00 78 00 46 00 41 00-54 00 2E 00 74 00 78 00  e·x·F·A·T·.·t·x·
0120  C1 00 74 00 00 00 00 00-00 00 00 00 00 00 00 00  Á·t·············
```

Parsing the individual entry begins with offset 0 of the entry, which is the Entry Type (0x83) as seen in the table above has the In Use bit (bit 7) as Active and a Code (bits 0-4) of 00011 giving a binary value 10000011 = 83.

```
0000  83 05 65 00 78 00 46 00-41 00 54 00 00 00 00 00  ··e·x·F·A·T·····
0010  00 00 00 00 00 00 00 00-00 00 00 00 00 00 00 00  ················
```

Offset 1 is the number of Unicode characters used in the name. (0x05 or 5 characters)

```
0000  83 05 65 00 78 00 46 00-41 00 54 00 00 00 00 00  ··e·x·F·A·T·····
0010  00 00 00 00 00 00 00 00-00 00 00 00 00 00 00 00  ················
```

Offsets 2-23 are for the volume name, exFAT that is user created, and can be up to 11 Unicode characters.

```
0000  83 05 65 00 78 00 46 00-41 00 54 00 00 00 00 00  ··e·x·F·A·T·····
0010  00 00 00 00 00 00 00 00-00 00 00 00 00 00 00 00  ················
```

Offsets 24-31 are reserved and are all 0.

The next entry is for the Allocation Bitmap and below is the breakdown[15].

Allocation Bitmap Directory Entry			
DEC OFFSET	**HEX OFFSET**	**SIZE (BYTES)**	**DESCRIPTION**
0	0x00	1	Entry Type (81) Bits 0-4 Code: 00001 Bit 5 Importance: 0 Bit 6 Category: 0 Bit 7 In Use: 1 Total 10000001 = 0x81
1	0x01	1	Bitmap Flag (0x00 – 1st Bitmap or 0x01 for 2nd Bitmap
2	0x02	18	Reserved
20	0x14	4	Starting Cluster of the Bitmap
24	0x18	8	Length of the Data

```
[root]                                    0   Regular File       N/A
0000 83 05 65 00 78 00 46 00-41 00 54 00 00 00 00 00  ··e·x·F·A·T·····
0010 00 00 00 00 00 00 00 00-00 00 00 00 00 00 00 00  ················
0020 81 00 00 00 00 00 00 00-00 00 00 00 00 00 00 00  ················
0030 00 00 00 00 02 00 00 00-36 3C 00 00 00 00 00 00  ········6<······
0040 82 00 00 00 0D D3 19 E6-00 00 00 00 00 00 00 00  ····Ó·æ·········
0050 00 00 00 00 03 00 00 00-CC 16 00 00 00 00 00 00  ········Ì·······
0060 85 06 AC 32 20 00 00 00-88 49 89 43 84 49 89 43  ··¬2 ···ˆI‰C„I‰C
0070 88 49 89 43 23 00 E8 E8-E8 00 00 00 00 00 00 00  ˆI‰C#·èèè·······
0080 C0 03 00 3D 76 81 00 00-17 00 00 00 00 00 00 00  À··=v···········
0090 00 00 00 00 05 00 00 00-17 00 00 00 00 00 00 00  ················
00a0 C1 00 52 00 65 00 61 00-6C 00 6C 00 79 00 20 00  Á·R·e·a·l·l·y· ·
00b0 52 00 65 00 61 00 6C 00-6C 00 79 00 20 00 52 00  R·e·a·l·l·y· ·R·
00c0 C1 00 65 00 61 00 6C 00-6C 00 79 00 20 00 4C 00  Á·e·a·l·l·y· ·L·
00d0 6F 00 6E 00 67 00 20 00-46 00 69 00 6C 00 65 00  o·n·g· ·F·i·l·e·
00e0 C1 00 6E 00 61 00 6D 00-65 00 20 00 61 00 73 00  Á·n·a·m·e· ·a·s·
00f0 20 00 61 00 6E 00 20 00-45 00 78 00 61 00 6D 00   ·a·n· ·E·x·a·m·
0100 C1 00 70 00 6C 00 65 00-20 00 69 00 6E 00 20 00  Á·p·l·e· ·i·n· ·
0110 65 00 78 00 46 00 41 00-54 00 2E 00 74 00 78 00  e·x·F·A·T·.·t·x·
0120 C1 00 74 00 00 00 00 00-00 00 00 00 00 00 00 00  Á·t·············
```

The Entry type at offset 0 of the entry is 0x81 or 10000001 binary.

```
0020 81 00 00 00 00 00 00 00-00 00 00 00 00 00 00 00  ················
0030 00 00 00 00 02 00 00 00-36 3C 00 00 00 00 00 00  ········6<······
```

Offset 1 has the flag for the Bitmap being used; there is a bitmap for each copy of the FAT. Since exFAT v 1.0 only uses one FAT, there is only one bitmap (0x00).

```
0020 81 00 00 00 00 00 00 00-00 00 00 00 00 00 00 00  ················
0030 00 00 00 00 02 00 00 00-36 3C 00 00 00 00 00 00  ········6<······
```

The next 18 bytes are reserved so they will be 0. Offsets 20-23 have the starting cluster of the Allocation Bitmap, which is 0x00 00 00 02 or 2. This is consistent with what we saw earlier in examining the Allocation Bitmap.

```
0020  81 00 00 00 00 00 00 00-00 00 00 00 00 00 00 00  ················
0030  00 00 00 00 02 00 00 00-36 3C 00 00 00 00 00 00  ········6<······
```

Offsets 24-31 have the size of the bitmap in bytes (0x00 00 00 00 00 00 3C 36 = 15414).

```
0020  81 00 00 00 00 00 00 00-00 00 00 00 00 00 00 00  ················
0030  00 00 00 00 02 00 00 00-36 3C 00 00 00 00 00 00  ········6<······
```

The next entry is for the UpCase Table and the breakdown is below[16].

UpCase Table Directory Entry			
DEC OFFSET	HEX OFFSET	SIZE (BYTES)	DESCRIPTION
0	0x00	1	Entry Type (82) Bits 0-4 Code: 00010 Bit 5 Importance: 0 Bit 6 Category: 0 Bit 7 In Use: 1 Total 10000010 = 0x82
1	0x01	3	Reserved
4	0x04	4	Table Checksum
8	0x08	12	Reserved
20	0x14	4	Starting Cluster of the Table
24	0x18	8	Length of the Data

```
0000  83 05 65 00 78 00 46 00-41 00 54 00 00 00 00 00  ··e·x·F·A·T·····
0010  00 00 00 00 00 00 00 00-00 00 00 00 00 00 00 00  ················
0020  81 00 00 00 00 00 00 00-00 00 00 00 00 00 00 00  ················
0030  00 00 00 00 02 00 00 00-36 3C 00 00 00 00 00 00  ········6<······
0040  82 00 00 00 0D D3 19 E6-00 00 00 00 00 00 00 00  ·····Ó·æ········
0050  00 00 00 00 03 00 00 00-CC 16 00 00 00 00 00 00  ········Ì·······
0060  85 06 AC 32 20 00 00 00-88 49 89 43 84 49 89 43  ··¬2 ····I·C·I·C
0070  88 49 89 43 23 00 E8 E8-E8 00 00 00 00 00 00 00  ·I·C#·èèè·······
0080  C0 03 00 3D 76 81 00 00-17 00 00 00 00 00 00 00  À··=v···········
0090  00 00 00 00 05 00 00 00-17 00 00 00 00 00 00 00  ················
00a0  C1 00 52 00 65 00 61 00-6C 00 6C 00 79 00 20 00  Á·R·e·a·l·l·y· ·
00b0  52 00 65 00 61 00 6C 00-6C 00 79 00 20 00 52 00  R·e·a·l·l·y· ·R·
00c0  C1 00 65 00 61 00 6C 00-6C 00 79 00 20 00 4C 00  Á·e·a·l·l·y· ·L·
00d0  6F 00 6E 00 67 00 20 00-46 00 69 00 6C 00 65 00  o·n·g· ·F·i·l·e·
00e0  C1 00 6E 00 61 00 6D 00-65 00 20 00 61 00 73 00  Á·n·a·m·e· ·a·s·
00f0  20 00 61 00 6E 00 20 00-45 00 78 00 61 00 6D 00   ·a·n· ·E·x·a·m·
0100  C1 00 70 00 6C 00 65 00-20 00 69 00 6E 00 20 00  Á·p·l·e· ·i·n· ·
0110  65 00 78 00 46 00 41 00-54 00 2E 00 74 00 78 00  e·x·F·A·T·.·t·x·
0120  C1 00 74 00 00 00 00 00-00 00 00 00 00 00 00 00  Á·t·············
```

Parsing this directory entry will give 0x82 as the entry type (10000010).

```
0040 82 00 00 00 0D D3 19 E6-00 00 00 00 00 00 00 00  .....Ó.æ........
0050 00 00 00 00 03 00 00 00-CC 16 00 00 00 00 00 00  ........Ì.......
```

Offsets 1-3 are reserved and offsets 4-7 are a calculated checksum value on the contents (0xE6 19 D3 0D). Offsets 8-19 are also reserved.

```
0040 82 00 00 00 0D D3 19 E6-00 00 00 00 00 00 00 00  .....Ó.æ........
0050 00 00 00 00 03 00 00 00-CC 16 00 00 00 00 00 00  ........Ì.......
```

Offsets 20-23 are for the starting cluster of the file. As we saw during the analysis of this file, it starts on cluster 3.

```
0040 82 00 00 00 0D D3 19 E6-00 00 00 00 00 00 00 00  .....Ó.æ........
0050 00 00 00 00 03 00 00 00-CC 16 00 00 00 00 00 00  ........Ì.......
```

Offsets 24-31 are for the size of the file in bytes. 0x00 00 00 00 00 00 16 CC = 5836.

```
0040 82 00 00 00 0D D3 19 E6-00 00 00 00 00 00 00 00  .....Ó.æ........
0050 00 00 00 00 03 00 00 00-CC 16 00 00 00 00 00 00  ........Ì.......
```

The entries we just parsed are ones that only have a single entry in the set. There are a few other entries that are part of the specification for exFAT, but have not yet been implemented in version 1.0.

Next is the examination of file and folder entries that utilize multiple entries. The primary entry for a file is a type 0x85 and will contain the dates and times. Below are the components[17].

exFAT File Directory Entry			
DEC OFFSET	HEX OFFSET	SIZE (BYTES)	DESCRIPTION
0	0x00	1	Entry Type (85) | Bits 0-4 Code 00101 Bit 5 Importance 0 | Bit 6 - Category 0 Bit 7 In Use 1 | Total 10000101 = 0x85
1	0x01	1	Secondary Entry Count
2	0x02	2	Set Checksum
4	0x04	2	File Attributes Read-Only Bit 0 Hidden Bit 1 System Bit 2 Reserved Bit 3 Directory Bit 4 Archive Bit 5 Reserved Bits 6-16
6	0x06	2	Reserved
8	0x08	4	Creation timestamp

12	0x0C	4	Last modified timestamp
16	0x10	4	Last accessed timestamp
20	0x14	1	Create 10ms increment 0-199
21	0x15	1	Last modified 10ms increment from GMT
22	0x16	1	Create time zone offset from GMT
23	0x17	1	Last modified time zone offset from GMT
24	0x18	1	Last accessed time zone offset from GMT
25	0x19	7	Reserved

```
0000 83 05 65 00 78 00 46 00-41 00 54 00 00 00 00 00  ··e·x·F·A·T·····
0010 00 00 00 00 00 00 00 00-00 00 00 00 00 00 00 00  ················
0020 81 00 00 00 00 00 00 00-00 00 00 00 00 00 00 00  ················
0030 00 00 00 00 02 00 00 00-36 3C 00 00 00 00 00 00  ········6<······
0040 82 00 00 00 0D D3 19 E6-00 00 00 00 00 00 00 00  ·····Ó·æ········
0050 00 00 00 00 03 00 00 00-CC 16 00 00 00 00 00 00  ········Ì·······
0060 85 06 AC 32 20 00 00 00-88 49 89 43 84 49 89 43  ··¬2 ····I·C·I·C
0070 88 49 89 43 23 00 E8 E8-E8 00 00 00 00 00 00 00  ·I·C#·èèè·······
0080 C0 03 00 3D 76 81 00 00-17 00 00 00 00 00 00 00  À··=v···········
0090 00 00 00 00 05 00 00 00-17 00 00 00 00 00 00 00  ················
00a0 C1 00 52 00 65 00 61 00-6C 00 6C 00 79 00 20 00  Á·R·e·a·l·l·y· ·
00b0 52 00 65 00 61 00 6C 00-6C 00 79 00 20 00 52 00  R·e·a·l·l·y· ·R·
00c0 C1 00 65 00 61 00 6C 00-6C 00 79 00 20 00 4C 00  Á·e·a·l·l·y· ·L·
00d0 6F 00 6E 00 67 00 20 00-46 00 69 00 6C 00 65 00  o·n·g· ·F·i·l·e·
00e0 C1 00 6E 00 61 00 6D 00-65 00 20 00 61 00 73 00  Á·n·a·m·e· ·a·s·
00f0 20 00 61 00 6E 00 20 00-45 00 78 00 61 00 6D 00   ·a·n· ·E·x·a·m·
0100 C1 00 70 00 6C 00 65 00-20 00 69 00 6E 00 20 00  Á·p·l·e· ·i·n· ·
0110 65 00 78 00 46 00 41 00-54 00 2E 00 74 00 78 00  e·x·F·A·T·.·t·x·
0120 C1 00 74 00 00 00 00 00-00 00 00 00 00 00 00 00  Á·t·············
```

Offset 0 is the entry type of 0x85 (10000101).

```
0060 85 06 AC 32 20 00 00 00-88 49 89 43 84 49 89 43  ··¬2 ····I·C·I·C
0070 88 49 89 43 23 00 E8 E8-E8 00 00 00 00 00 00 00  ·I·C#·èèè·······
```

Offset 1 has the number of secondary entries that are associated with this primary entry. In this case, there are 0x06 or 6 secondary entries, meaning there are 7 entries in the Entry Set.

```
0060 85 06 AC 32 20 00 00 00-88 49 89 43 84 49 89 43  ··¬2 ····I·C·I·C
0070 88 49 89 43 23 00 E8 E8-E8 00 00 00 00 00 00 00  ·I·C#·èèè·······
```

Offsets 2-3 contain a checksum calculated from the entire Entry Set. (0x32 AC)

```
0060 85 06 AC 32 20 00 00 00-88 49 89 43 84 49 89 43  ··¬2 ····I·C·I·C
0070 88 49 89 43 23 00 E8 E8-E8 00 00 00 00 00 00 00  ·I·C#·èèè·······
```

Offsets 4-5 are for the DOS attributes (0x00 20 = 00000000 00100000). Bit 5 is for the Archive as seen in the table above. The next two bytes are reserved or used as padding.

```
0060 85 06 AC 32 20 00 00 00-88 49 89 43 84 49 89 43  ··¬2 ····I·C·I·C
0070 88 49 89 43 23 00 E8 E8-E8 00 00 00 00 00 00 00  ·I·C#·èèè·······
```

Offsets 8-11 are for the Creation timestamp. This is calculated just like we saw in FAT[18]. The first 2 bytes are for the time (0x49 88) and the next 2 bytes are for the date (0x43 89).

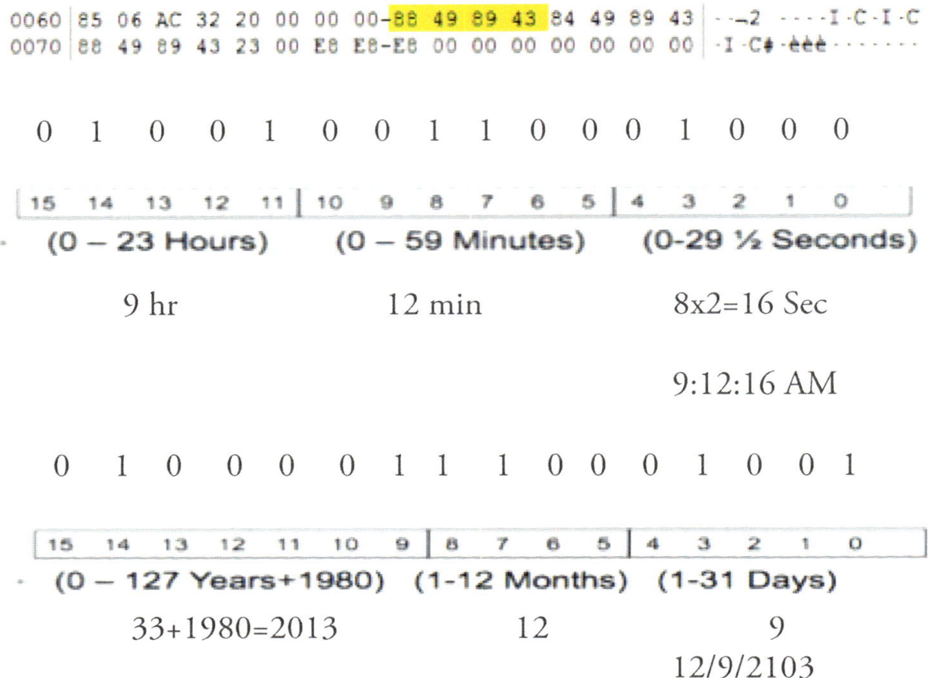

Offsets 12-15 are for the Last Modified timestamp and offsets 16-19 are for the Last Accessed timestamp. In this case, they are the same as the Created timestamp.

```
0060 85 06 AC 32 20 00 00 00-88 49 89 43 84 49 89 43  ··¬2 ····I·C·I·C
0070 88 49 89 43 23 00 E8 E8-E8 00 00 00 00 00 00 00  ·I·C#·èèè·······
```

Offset 20 is for the number of 10 milliseconds for the Created timestamp. Offset 21 is the number of 10 milliseconds for the Last Modified timestamp. In this case, there are 350 milliseconds to add to the Created Time (0x23=35*10). The Last Modified milliseconds are 0. There is no byte for the milliseconds to add to the Last Accessed time.

```
0060 85 06 AC 32 20 00 00 00-88 49 89 43 84 49 89 43  ··¬2 ····I·C·I·C
0070 88 49 89 43 23 00 E8 E8-E8 00 00 00 00 00 00 00  ·I·C#·èèè·······
```

The next three bytes, offsets 22-24, are each the time zone offsets for the Created, Last Modified, and Last Accessed timestamps. Each value is a Signed Integer (positive or negative). The values equate to 15-minute offsets from UTC time[19]. In this case the value is 0xE8 = -24. From the table below, -24 is -6 hours from UTC or Central Standard Time. Note that the time offset is ¼ of the stored value (-6, -24). It is possible for the time zone values to be different for each of the three times, such as when a flash drive was plugged into multiple computers set to different time zones when the file was created, modified, and accessed. The last 7 bytes in the entry are reserved.

```
0060  85 06 AC 32 20 00 00 00-88 49 89 43 84 49 89 43   ··¬2 ····I·C·I·C
0070  88 49 89 43 23 00 E8 E8-E8 00 00 00 00 00 00 00   ·I·C#·èèè·······
```

exFAT Timezone Offset from UTC						
HEX	**BINARY**	**1ST BIT=1**	**2ND BIT =1**	**TWO'S COMPLIMENT**	**7-BIT**	**TIME OFFSET (1/4 OF VALUE)**
		OFFSET USED	**NEGATIVE VALUE**		**VALUE**	**(15 MIN. INTERVAL)**
D0	11010000	Yes	Yes	0110000	-48	-12
D4	11010100	Yes	Yes	0101100	-44	-11
D8	11011000	Yes	Yes	0101000	-40	-10
DA	11011010	Yes	Yes	0100100	-38	-9.5
DC	11011100	Yes	Yes	0100100	-36	-9
E0	11100000	Yes	Yes	0100000	-32	-8
E4	11100100	Yes	Yes	0011100	-28	-7
E8	11101000	Yes	Yes	0011000	-24	-6
EC	11101100	Yes	Yes	0010100	-20	-5
EA	11101110	Yes	Yes	0010010	-18	-4.5
F0	11110000	Yes	Yes	0010000	-16	-4
F2	11110010	Yes	Yes	0001110	-14	-3.5
F4	11110100	Yes	Yes	0001100	-12	-3
F8	11111000	Yes	Yes	0001000	-8	-2
FC	11111100	Yes	Yes	0000100	-4	-1
80	10000000	Yes	No		0	0
84	10000100	Yes	No		4	+1
88	10001000	Yes	No		8	+2
8C	10001100	Yes	No		12	+3
8E	10001110	Yes	No		14	+3.5
90	10010000	Yes	No		16	+4
92	10010010	Yes	No		18	+4.5
94	10010100	Yes	No		20	+5
96	10010110	Yes	No		22	+5.5
97	10010111	Yes	No		23	+5.75

98	10011000	Yes	No		24	+6
9A	10011010	Yes	No		26	+6.5
9C	10011100	Yes	No		28	+7
A0	10100000	Yes	No		32	+8
A2	10100010	Yes	No		34	+8.5
A3	10100011	Yes	No		35	+8.75
A4	10100100	Yes	No		36	+9
A6	101001010	Yes	No		38	+9.5
A8	10101000	Yes	No		40	+10
AA	10101010	Yes	No		42	+10.5
AC	10101100	Yes	No		44	+11
B0	10110000	Yes	No		48	+12
B4	10110100	Yes	No		52	+13
B7	10110111	Yes	No		55	+13.75
B8	10110100	Yes	No		56	+14

The second entry in the file Entry Set is type 0xC0 and is referred to as the Stream Extension Directory Entry[20].

exFAT Stream Extension Directory Entry			
Dec Offset	**Hex Offset**	**Size (Bytes)**	**Description**
0	0x00	1	Entry Type (C0) Bits 0-4 Code 00000 Bit 5 Importance 0 Bit 6 Category 1 Bit 7 In Use 1 Total 11000000 = 0xC0
1	0x01	1	Secondary Flags Allocation Possible Bit 0 (0-No, 1-Yes) No FAT Chain Bit 1 (0-valid, 1-invalid) Reserved Bits 2-7
2	0x02	1	Reserved
3	0x03	1	Name Length
4	0x04	2	Name Hash
6	0x06	2	Reserved
8	0x08	8	Valid Data Length
16	0x10	4	Reserved
20	0x14	4	Cluster Address of 1st Block
24	0x18	8	Length of data

```
0000 83 05 65 00 78 00 46 00-41 00 54 00 00 00 00 00  ··e·x·F·A·T·····
0010 00 00 00 00 00 00 00 00-00 00 00 00 00 00 00 00  ················
0020 81 00 00 00 00 00 00 00-00 00 00 00 00 00 00 00  ················
0030 00 00 00 00 02 00 00 00-36 3C 00 00 00 00 00 00  ········6<······
0040 82 00 00 00 0D D3 19 E6-00 00 00 00 00 00 00 00  ·····Ó·æ········
0050 00 00 00 00 03 00 00 00-CC 16 00 00 00 00 00 00  ········Ì·······
0060 85 06 AC 32 20 00 00 00-88 49 89 43 84 49 89 43  ··¬2 ····I·C·I·C
0070 88 49 89 43 23 00 E8 E8-E8 00 00 00 00 00 00 00  ·I·C#·èèè·······
0080 C0 03 00 3D 76 81 00 00-17 00 00 00 00 00 00 00  À··=v···········
0090 00 00 00 00 05 00 00 00-17 00 00 00 00 00 00 00  ················
00a0 C1 00 52 00 65 00 61 00-6C 00 6C 00 79 00 20 00  Á·R·e·a·l·l·y· ·
00b0 52 00 65 00 61 00 6C 00-6C 00 79 00 20 00 52 00  R·e·a·l·l·y· ·R·
00c0 C1 00 65 00 61 00 6C 00-6C 00 79 00 20 00 4C 00  Á·e·a·l·l·y· ·L·
00d0 6F 00 6E 00 67 00 20 00-46 00 69 00 6C 00 65 00  o·n·g· ·F·i·l·e·
00e0 C1 00 6E 00 61 00 6D 00-65 00 20 00 61 00 73 00  Á·n·a·m·e· ·a·s·
00f0 20 00 61 00 6E 00 20 00-45 00 78 00 61 00 6D 00   ·a·n· ·E·x·a·m·
0100 C1 00 70 00 6C 00 65 00-20 00 69 00 6E 00 20 00  Á·p·l·e· ·i·n· ·
0110 65 00 78 00 46 00 41 00-54 00 2E 00 74 00 78 00  e·x·F·A·T·.·t·x·
0120 C1 00 74 00 00 00 00 00-00 00 00 00 00 00 00 00  Á·t·············
0130 00 00 00 00 00 00 00 00-00 00 00 00 00 00 00 00  ················
```

As stated above, the Entry Type is 0xC0 (11000000), which means it is active and it is a secondary entry.

```
0080 C0 03 00 3D 76 81 00 00-17 00 00 00 00 00 00 00  À··=v···········
0090 00 00 00 00 05 00 00 00-17 00 00 00 00 00 00 00  ················
```

Offset 1 is for a flag for the cluster usage. Two of the bits are used. The first bit is for whether it is possible to use a cluster. The second bit determines whether the file is fragmented and the FAT is needed, or the clusters are contiguous and the FAT is not needed[21]. In this example, 0x03 means both bits are 1, and the clusters are possible and the FAT is not needed.

```
0080 C0 03 00 3D 76 81 00 00-17 00 00 00 00 00 00 00  À··=v···········
0090 00 00 00 00 05 00 00 00-17 00 00 00 00 00 00 00  ················
```

Offset 2 is reserved and offset 3 is the length of the filename. 0x3D equals 61 characters.

```
0080 C0 03 00 3D 76 81 00 00-17 00 00 00 00 00 00 00  À··=v···········
0090 00 00 00 00 05 00 00 00-17 00 00 00 00 00 00 00  ················
```

Offsets 4-5 contain a checksum for the name. If the name changes, the checksum changes. (0x81 76)

```
0080 C0 03 00 3D 76 81 00 00-17 00 00 00 00 00 00 00  À··=v···········
0090 00 00 00 00 05 00 00 00-17 00 00 00 00 00 00 00  ················
```

Offsets 6-7 are reserved and offsets 8-15 are for the file size. 0x00 00 00 00 00 00 00 17 or 23 bytes.

```
0080  C0 03 00 3D 76 81 00 00-17 00 00 00 00 00 00 00  À··=v···········
0090  00 00 00 00 05 00 00 00-17 00 00 00 00 00 00 00  ················
```

Offsets 16-19 are reserved and offsets 20-23 are for the starting cluster of the file. 0x05 is for cluster 5.

```
0080  C0 03 00 3D 76 81 00 00-17 00 00 00 00 00 00 00  À··=v···········
0090  00 00 00 00 05 00 00 00-17 00 00 00 00 00 00 00  ················
```

Offsets 24-31 also contain the size of the file like offsets 8-15. It is unclear why this value is repeated. 0x00 00 00 00 00 00 00 17

```
0080  C0 03 00 3D 76 81 00 00-17 00 00 00 00 00 00 00  À··=v···········
0090  00 00 00 00 05 00 00 00-17 00 00 00 00 00 00 00  ················
```

The next part of the Entry Set is the Name Extension. There will be enough name Extension entries for the filename to fit. Each entry can hold 15 Unicode characters. Since each Unicode character is 2 bytes, this equals 30 bytes for the entry. The Name Extension has an Entry Type of 0xC1[22].

exFAT File Name Extension Directory Entry			
Dec Offset	Hex Offset	Size (Bytes)	Description
0	0x00	1	Entry Type (C1) Bits 0-4 Code: 00001 Bit 5 Importance: 0 Bit 6 Category: 1 Bit 7 In Use: 1 Total 11000001 = 0xC1
1	0x01	1	Secondary Flag Allocation Possible Bit 0 (0-No, 1-Yes) No FAT Chain Bit 1 (0-valid, 1-invalid) Bits 2-7 are reserved
2	0x02	30	15 Unicode characters of File name

We saw earlier in the primary entry that there were 6 secondary entries, 0xC0 was 1, which means there are five 0xC1 entries.

```
0000 83 05 65 00 78 00 46 00-41 00 54 00 00 00 00 00  ··e·x·F·A·T·····
0010 00 00 00 00 00 00 00 00-00 00 00 00 00 00 00 00  ················
0020 81 00 00 00 00 00 00 00-00 00 00 00 00 00 00 00  ················
0030 00 00 00 00 02 00 00 00-36 3C 00 00 00 00 00 00  ········6<······
0040 82 00 00 00 0D D3 19 E6-00 00 00 00 00 00 00 00  ·····Ó·æ········
0050 00 00 00 00 03 00 00 00-CC 16 00 00 00 00 00 00  ········Ì·······
0060 85 06 AC 32 20 00 00 00-88 49 89 43 84 49 89 43  ··¬2 ····I·C·I·C
0070 88 49 89 43 23 00 E8 E8-E8 00 00 00 00 00 00 00  ·I·C#·èèè·······
0080 C0 03 00 3D 76 81 00 00-17 00 00 00 00 00 00 00  À··=v···········
0090 00 00 00 00 05 00 00 00-17 00 00 00 00 00 00 00  ················
00a0 C1 00 52 00 65 00 61 00-6C 00 6C 00 79 00 20 00  Á·R·e·a·l·l·y· ·
00b0 52 00 65 00 61 00 6C 00-6C 00 79 00 20 00 52 00  R·e·a·l·l·y· ·R·
00c0 C1 00 65 00 61 00 6C 00-6C 00 79 00 20 00 4C 00  Á·e·a·l·l·y· ·L·
00d0 6F 00 6E 00 67 00 20 00-46 00 69 00 6C 00 65 00  o·n·g· ·F·i·l·e·
00e0 C1 00 6E 00 61 00 6D 00-65 00 20 00 61 00 73 00  Á·n·a·m·e· ·a·s·
00f0 20 00 61 00 6E 00 20 00-45 00 78 00 61 00 6D 00   ·a·n· ·E·x·a·m·
0100 C1 00 70 00 6C 00 65 00-20 00 69 00 6E 00 20 00  Á·p·l·e· ·i·n· ·
0110 65 00 78 00 46 00 41 00-54 00 2E 00 74 00 78 00  e·x·F·A·T·.·t·x·
0120 C1 00 74 00 00 00 00 00-00 00 00 00 00 00 00 00  Á·t·············
0130 00 00 00 00 00 00 00 00-00 00 00 00 00 00 00 00  ················
```

Each entry begins with the Entry Type of 0xC1 and has a secondary flag of 0x00, just like the Stream Extension Entry. This means there are available clusters and the FAT is not needed. The remainder of the entries is for the filename characters. The file system supports up to 255-character filenames, which means there would be 17 name Extension entries. The filename is Really Really Really Long Filename as an Example in exFAT.txt. This is 61 characters as seen in the Stream Extension entry.

Deleted Files

When files are deleted, the bits in the Allocation Bitmap are flipped from 1 to 0. If the FAT is used, then the references are changed to 0x00 00 00 00. In the directory, the In Use bit is changed from a 1 to a 0. This changes the Entry Type values.

Primary Entry		
Active File	10000101	0x85
Deleted File	00000101	0x05
Stream Extension		
Active File	11000000	0xC0
Deleted File	01000000	0x40
Name Extension		
Active File	11000001	0xC1
Deleted File	01000001	0x41

```
0000 83 05 65 00 78 00 46 00-41 00 54 00 00 00 00 00  ··e·x·F·A·T·····
0010 00 00 00 00 00 00 00 00-00 00 00 00 00 00 00 00  ················
0020 81 00 00 00 00 00 00 00-00 00 00 00 00 00 00 00  ················
0030 00 00 00 00 02 00 00 00-36 3C 00 00 00 00 00 00  ········6<······
0040 82 00 00 00 0D D3 19 E6-00 00 00 00 00 00 00 00  ·····Ó·æ········
0050 00 00 00 00 03 00 00 00-CC 16 00 00 00 00 00 00  ········Ì·······
0060 05 06 AC 32 20 00 00 00-88 49 89 43 84 49 89 43  ··¬2 ····I·C·I·C
0070 88 49 89 43 23 00 E8 E8-E8 00 00 00 00 00 00 00  ·I·C#·èèè·······
0080 40 03 00 3D 76 81 00 00-17 00 00 00 00 00 00 00  @··=v···········
0090 00 00 00 00 05 00 00 00-17 00 00 00 00 00 00 00  ················
00a0 41 00 52 00 65 00 61 00-6C 00 6C 00 79 00 20 00  A·R·e·a·l·l·y· ·
00b0 52 00 65 00 61 00 6C 00-6C 00 79 00 20 00 52 00  R·e·a·l·l·y· ·R·
00c0 41 00 65 00 61 00 6C 00-6C 00 79 00 20 00 4C 00  A·e·a·l·l·y· ·L·
00d0 6F 00 6E 00 67 00 20 00-46 00 69 00 6C 00 65 00  o·n·g· ·F·i·l·e·
00e0 41 00 6E 00 61 00 6D 00-65 00 20 00 61 00 73 00  A·n·a·m·e· ·a·s·
00f0 20 00 61 00 6E 00 20 00-45 00 78 00 61 00 6D 00   ·a·n· ·E·x·a·m·
0100 41 00 70 00 6C 00 65 00-20 00 69 00 6E 00 20 00  A·p·l·e· ·i·n· ·
0110 65 00 78 00 46 00 41 00-54 00 2E 00 74 00 78 00  e·x·F·A·T·.·t·x·
0120 41 00 74 00 00 00 00 00-00 00 00 00 00 00 00 00  A·t·············
0130 00 00 00 00 00 00 00 00-00 00 00 00 00 00 00 00  ················
```

Recovery of Deleted Files

To recover a file, start by updating the Allocation Bitmap. Flip each bit relating to the needed cluster. In this example only cluster 5 is needed.

Below is the Allocation Bitmap after deletion.

F7 01 00 00 00 00 00 00 00 00 00 00 00 00 00 00
00 00 00 00 00 00 00 00 00 00 00 00 00 00 00 00

0xF7 is 11110111 in binary and is related to clusters 2-9. The bit for cluster 5 is the only one that is 0. This needs to be changed to 11111111 or 0xFF.

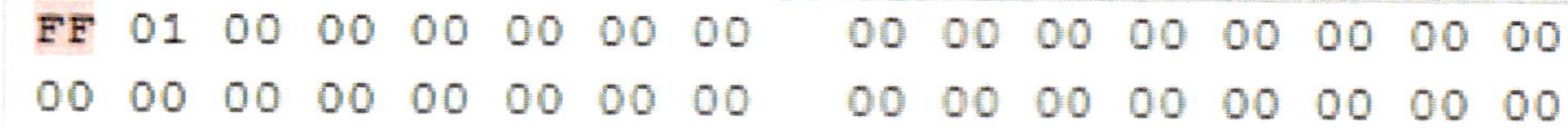
FF 01 00 00 00 00 00 00 00 00 00 00 00 00 00 00
00 00 00 00 00 00 00 00 00 00 00 00 00 00 00 00

The Root Directory Entry Set must be changed as well. The Primary entry is changed from 0x05 to 0x85, the Stream Extension is changed from 0x40 to 0xC0, and the Name Extensions are changed from 0x41 to 0xC1. The changes are conducted with a hex editor like Active@ Disk Editor.

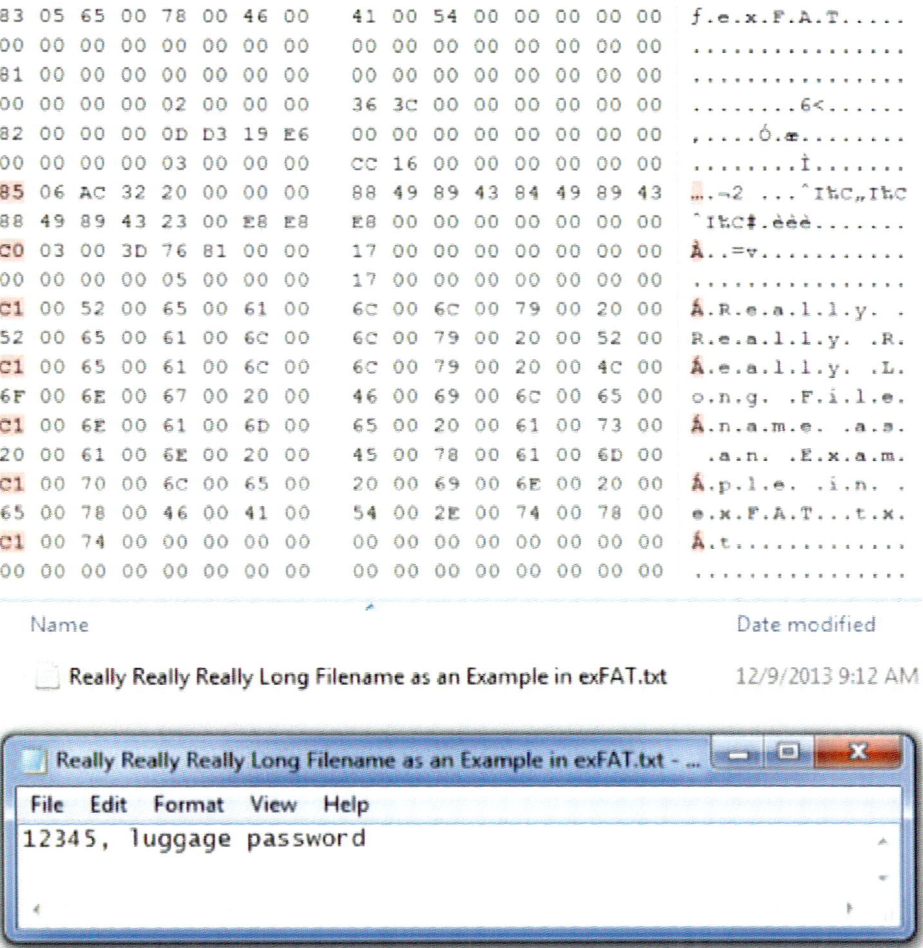

If the file is fragmented and the FAT is needed, then chaining must be done in the same manner as was done with FAT32.

PRACTICAL EXERCISE 3

Open 13_Pract2.E01 in FTK Imager and answer the following questions.

How many Primary Directory Entries are there?

Do any of the files require the use of the FAT? Explain how you know from examining the directory entry.

Which file(s) require more than one Name Extension Entry?

What are the offsets from UTC for the Created, Last Modified, and Last Accessed times?

What file is deleted and how can you tell from the directory entry?

What would be involved in recovering this file? Explain the process.

What is the name hash for battle1.jpg?

For file5.txt, what are the three timestamps, the two 10ms values, and the time zone offsets (number of hours from UTC)? Show your work for the timestamps.

Folder Structure

Finally, we will examine the folder structure within exFAT. It is very similar to FAT and not complicated as with NTFS. Folders are treated like files and will have a Primary Entry, a Stream Extension entry, and one or more Name Extension entries, depending upon the folder name.

Below is a folder in the Root Directory.

Name	Size	Type	Date Modified
Really Really Really Long Folder Name	32	Directory	12/10/2013 2:48:10 PM

We will parse through the directory entries.

```
0000 83 05 65 00 78 00 46 00-41 00 54 00 00 00 00 00  ··e·x·F·A·T·····
0010 00 00 00 00 00 00 00 00-00 00 00 00 00 00 00 00  ················
0020 81 00 00 00 00 00 00 00-00 00 00 00 00 00 00 00  ················
0030 00 00 00 00 02 00 00 00-36 3C 00 00 00 00 00 00  ········6<······
0040 82 00 00 00 0D D3 19 E6-00 00 00 00 00 00 00 00  ·····Ó·æ········
0050 00 00 00 00 03 00 00 00-CC 16 00 00 00 00 00 00  ········Ì·······
0060 85 04 38 15 10 00 00 00-0C 76 8A 43 05 76 8A 43  ··8·······v·C·v·C
0070 0C 76 8A 43 13 00 E8 E8-E8 00 00 00 00 00 00 00  ·v·C··èèè·······
0080 C0 03 00 25 8C F1 00 00-00 80 00 00 00 00 00 00  À··%·ñ··········
0090 00 00 00 00 05 00 00 00-00 80 00 00 00 00 00 00  ················
00a0 C1 00 52 00 65 00 61 00-6C 00 6C 00 79 00 20 00  Á·R·e·a·l·l·y· ·
00b0 52 00 65 00 61 00 6C 00-6C 00 79 00 20 00 52 00  R·e·a·l·l·y· ·R·
00c0 C1 00 65 00 61 00 6C 00-6C 00 79 00 20 00 4C 00  Á·e·a·l·l·y· ·L·
00d0 6F 00 6E 00 67 00 20 00-46 00 6F 00 6C 00 64 00  o·n·g· ·F·o·l·d·
00e0 C1 00 65 00 72 00 20 00-4E 00 61 00 6D 00 65 00  Á·e·r· ·N·a·m·e·
00f0 00 00 00 00 00 00 00 00-00 00 00 00 00 00 00 00  ················
```

The difference between a file and folder can be determined by examining the DOS attributes at offset 4 of the Primary Entry. A directory attribute is the fifth bit – 00010000 or 0x10.

```
0060 85 04 38 15 10 00 00 00-0C 76 8A 43 05 76 8A 43 ··8······v·C·v·C
0070 0C 76 8A 43 13 00 E8 E8-E8 00 00 00 00 00 00 00 ·v·C··èèè·······
0080 C0 03 00 25 8C F1 00 00-00 80 00 00 00 00 00 00 À··%·ñ··········
0090 00 00 00 00 05 00 00 00-00 80 00 00 00 00 00 00 ················
00a0 C1 00 52 00 65 00 61 00-6C 00 6C 00 79 00 20 00 Á·R·e·a·l·l·y· ·
00b0 52 00 65 00 61 00 6C 00-6C 00 79 00 20 00 52 00 R·e·a·l·l·y· ·R·
00c0 C1 00 65 00 61 00 6C 00-6C 00 79 00 20 00 4C 00 Á·e·a·l·l·y· ·L·
00d0 6F 00 6E 00 67 00 20 00-46 00 6F 00 6C 00 64 00 o·n·g· ·F·o·l·d·
00e0 C1 00 65 00 72 00 20 00-4E 00 61 00 6D 00 65 00 Á·e·r· ·N·a·m·e·
00f0 00 00 00 00 00 00 00 00-00 00 00 00 00 00 00 00 ················
```

The starting cluster location of the folder can be found in the Stream Extension entry at offset 20. In this case it is cluster 5, 0x00 00 00 05.

```
0060 85 04 38 15 10 00 00 00-0C 76 8A 43 05 76 8A 43 ··8······v·C·v·C
0070 0C 76 8A 43 13 00 E8 E8-E8 00 00 00 00 00 00 00 ·v·C··èèè·······
0080 C0 03 00 25 8C F1 00 00-00 80 00 00 00 00 00 00 À··%·ñ··········
0090 00 00 00 00 05 00 00 00-00 80 00 00 00 00 00 00 ················
00a0 C1 00 52 00 65 00 61 00-6C 00 6C 00 79 00 20 00 Á·R·e·a·l·l·y· ·
00b0 52 00 65 00 61 00 6C 00-6C 00 79 00 20 00 52 00 R·e·a·l·l·y· ·R·
00c0 C1 00 65 00 61 00 6C 00-6C 00 79 00 20 00 4C 00 Á·e·a·l·l·y· ·L·
00d0 6F 00 6E 00 67 00 20 00-46 00 6F 00 6C 00 64 00 o·n·g· ·F·o·l·d·
00e0 C1 00 65 00 72 00 20 00-4E 00 61 00 6D 00 65 00 Á·e·r· ·N·a·m·e·
00f0 00 00 00 00 00 00 00 00-00 00 00 00 00 00 00 00 ················
```

In FAT the folder size is 0, but in exFAT it is set at full cluster sizes. In this case, only one cluster is needed, so the size is 32768. This can be found in the Stream Extension entry.

```
0060 85 04 38 15 10 00 00 00-0C 76 8A 43 05 76 8A 43 ··8······v·C·v·C
0070 0C 76 8A 43 13 00 E8 E8-E8 00 00 00 00 00 00 00 ·v·C··èèè·······
0080 C0 03 00 25 8C F1 00 00-00 80 00 00 00 00 00 00 À··%·ñ··········
0090 00 00 00 00 05 00 00 00-00 80 00 00 00 00 00 00 ················
00a0 C1 00 52 00 65 00 61 00-6C 00 6C 00 79 00 20 00 Á·R·e·a·l·l·y· ·
00b0 52 00 65 00 61 00 6C 00-6C 00 79 00 20 00 52 00 R·e·a·l·l·y· ·R·
00c0 C1 00 65 00 61 00 6C 00-6C 00 79 00 20 00 4C 00 Á·e·a·l·l·y· ·L·
00d0 6F 00 6E 00 67 00 20 00-46 00 6F 00 6C 00 64 00 o·n·g· ·F·o·l·d·
00e0 C1 00 65 00 72 00 20 00-4E 00 61 00 6D 00 65 00 Á·e·r· ·N·a·m·e·
00f0 00 00 00 00 00 00 00 00-00 00 00 00 00 00 00 00 ················
```

The contents of a folder are just like the contents in the Root Directory. The difference between the contents of a FAT folder and an exFAT folder is there are no "." and ".." entries. Apparently, there are instances where these entries are virtually displayed for consistency, but I have not seen this occur.

Really Really Really Long Folder Name 32 Directory 12/10/201

```
0000 85 03 A0 FD 20 00 00 00-0C 76 8A 43 6B 8E 55 43  ··ý····v·Ck·UC
0010 0C 76 8A 43 19 00 E8 E8-E8 00 00 00 00 00 00 00  ·v·C··èèè·······
0020 C0 03 00 13 5A 97 00 00-D1 51 00 00 00 00 00 00  À··Z···ÑQ······
0030 00 00 00 00 06 00 00 00-D1 51 00 00 00 00 00 00  ········ÑQ······
0040 C1 00 41 00 69 00 72 00-63 00 72 00 61 00 66 00  Á·A·i·r·c·r·a·f·
0050 74 00 43 00 61 00 72 00-72 00 69 00 65 00 72 00  t·C·a·r·r·i·e·r·
0060 C1 00 2E 00 6A 00 70 00-67 00 00 00 00 00 00 00  Á·.·j·p·g·······
0070 00 00 00 00 00 00 00 00-00 00 00 00 00 00 00 00  ················
```

CHAPTER SUMMARY

exFAT was design specifically for flash media and has many advantages over traditional FAT volumes. Most notably, the maximum volume size of 128PB is significantly larger than the 2TB limit of FAT.

exFAT has some of the features of NTFS, such as an Allocation Bitmap and an UpCase Table. The file system also supports Unicode filenames and UTC times.

The Volume Boot Record is very similar to FAT and NTFS. There are 12 sectors assigned, but currently only the first contains data. There is a backup copy immediately following the first copy.

There is still a file allocation table, but it is only utilized when the file is fragmented. Since there is an allocation bitmap, the file allocation table is used only to link the clusters together, not to show whether a cluster is allocated or not. Each cluster reference in the FAT is 4 bytes. This is more efficient for writing as most files are not fragmented.

The directory structure is slightly more complex than FAT, but not nearly as complicated as with NTFS. The Volume Label, the Allocation Bitmap, and the UpCase Table each have a single 32-byte directory entry.

All other files and folders have at least three 32-byte entries. The 3+ entries are referred to as an Entry Set. The first entry is the Primary and contains the file timestamps and a time zone code. The second entry is known as the Stream Extension and contains the size and starting cluster. The next entry or entries contain the filename up to 255 Unicode characters. These are Name Extension entries and each can hold up to 15 Unicode characters.

HOMEWORK EXERCISE 1

Format a USB Flash drive with exFAT, provide a volume label of Homework_1.
Examine the volume with FTK Imager.

View the Volume Boot Record (sector 0).

How many sectors on the volume?

What sector does the FAT start in?

How many clusters are in the data area?

How many sectors per cluster?

What is the volume serial number?

What sector does the backup copy of the VBR start in?

View the FAT

What is the media descriptor?

What cluster does the Allocation Bitmap start in?

How many clusters does the Allocation Bitmap use?

What cluster does the UpCase Table start in?

How many clusters does the UpCase Table use?

What cluster does the Root Directory start in?

Examine the Allocation Bitmap

Which clusters are allocated?

Using Windows Explorer, created a folder named HW_Folder1.

Open that folder and create a text file named exFAT Homework Text File.txt.

Add the text: Homework

Save the file.

Re-add the volume to FTK Imager.

Examine the Root Directory (in the hex/ASCII).

How many entries are there?

What cluster does the HW_Folder1 start in?

Where in the directory entry do you find this information?

Examine the cluster for HW_Folder1.

How many directory entries are there?

How many entries are associated with exFAT Homework Text File.txt?

What are the timestamps for the exFAT Homework Text File.txt file? (show your work)

What are the time zone offset values?

What time zone is this?

What cluster is the file saved in?

Is the FAT used?

What are the first 3 bytes in the Allocation Bitmap?

Go back to Windows Explorer and delete the exFAT Homework Text File.txt file.
Re-Add the volume to FTK Imager.

Examine the HW_Folder1.

What changes occur to the directory entries?
What changes occur in the Allocation Bitmap?

Restore the deleted file and explain your process.

HOMEWORK EXERCISE 2

Open HW_Pract2.001 in FTK Imager.

How many sectors in the volume?

What percentage of the volume is being used?

Is the FAT used for any files?
If yes, how many files?

How many clusters are allocated?

How many deleted directory entries are there (not just Root Directory)?

Describe why there are multiple folders and files pointing to the same starting clusters?

Use Active@ Disk Editor, load HW_Pract2.001, and recover the deleted files and folders.

Open the file again in FTK Imager and describe the content of each of the deleted files.

Which file had its created, last modified, and last accessed timestamps in different time zones?

What are the time zone offsets from UTC?

REFERENCES

1. exfat: a file system for flash memory. (2011). Retrieved from http://www.flashmemorysummit.com/English/Collaterals/Proceedings/2011/20110811_T3A_Prewitt.pdf.
2. Problem ejecting usb mass storage device. (2012, February 15). Retrieved from http://social.technet.microsoft.com/Forums/windows/en-US/74736f2a-1590-4a31-a145-c048a6b01014/problem-ejecting-usb-mass-storage-device.
3. Extended fat file system (windows embedded ce 6.0). (2010, January 6). Retrieved from http://msdn.microsoft.com/en-us/library/ee489968(v=WinEmbedded.60).aspx.
4. Hamm, J. (2009). extended fat file system. Retrieved from http://paradigmsolutions.files.wordpress.com/2009/12/ex-fat-excerpt-1-4.pdf.
5. Ntfs.com/ntfs_vs_fat. (n.d.). Retrieved from http://www.ntfs.com/ntfs_vs_fat.htm.
6. Shullich, R. (2009). Reverse engineering the Microsoft extended fat file system (exfat). (pp 7). SANS Institute InfoSec Reading Room.
7. exfat vs. fat32 comparison. (n.d.). Retrieved from http://www.ntfs.com/exfat-comparison.htm.
8. What's a byte. (n.d.). Retrieved from http://www.whatsabyte.com/.
9. Shullich, R. (2009). Reverse engineering the Microsoft extended fat file system (exfat). (pp 25). SANS Institute InfoSec Reading Room.
10. Shullich, R. (2010, April). Demystifying the Microsoft extended file system (exfat). The computer forensics show, New York, NY.
11. Shullich, R. (2009). Reverse engineering the Microsoft extended fat file system (exfat). (pp 50). SANS Institute InfoSec Reading Room.
12. Shullich, R. (2009). Reverse engineering the Microsoft extended fat file system (exfat). (pp 45). SANS Institute InfoSec Reading Room.
13. Shullich, R. (2009). Reverse engineering the Microsoft extended fat file system (exfat). (pp 46). SANS Institute InfoSec Reading Room.
14. Munegowda, K., Venkatraman, S., & Raju, G. (2011, October). The extended fat file system: Differentiating with fat32 file system. Linux conference, Prague, CZ. (pp 12).
15. Shullich, R. (2009). Reverse engineering the Microsoft extended fat file system (exfat). (pp 47).SANS Institute InfoSec Reading Room.
16. Shullich, R. (2009). Reverse engineering the Microsoft extended fat file system (exfat). (pp 48). SANS Institute InfoSec Reading Room.
17. Hamm, J. (2009). Extended fat file system. (pp 51) Retrieved from http://paradigmsolutions.files.wordpress.com/2009/12/exfat-excerpt-1-4.pdf.
18. unix timestamp to fat timestamp. (n.d.). Retrieved from http://stackoverflow.com/questions/15763259/unix-timestamp-to-fat-timestamp.
19. Shullich, R. (2009). Reverse engineering the Microsoft extended fat file system (exfat). (pp 56). SANS Institute InfoSec Reading Room.

APPENDIX

A - ASCII CHART

B- PARTITION TYPE CODES

C - PARTITION TABLES

D - FAT TABLES

E - NTFS TABLES

F - EXFAT TABLES

INDEX

INDEX

A

B

C

D

E

F

G

L

M

N

O

P

Q

R

S

T

Z

Appendix A - ASCII Chart

Dec	Hex	Oct	Bin	Char
0	0x0	00	00000000	NUL
1	0x1	01	00000001	SOH
2	0x2	02	00000010	STX
3	0x3	03	00000011	ETX
4	0x4	04	00000100	EOT
5	0x5	05	00000101	ENQ
6	0x6	06	00000110	ACK
7	0x7	07	00000111	BEL
8	0x8	010	00001000	BS
9	0x9	011	00001001	HT
10	0xA	012	00001010	LF
11	0xB	013	00001011	VT
12	0xC	014	00001100	FF
13	0xD	015	00001101	CR
14	0xE	016	00001110	SO
15	0xF	017	00001111	SI
16	0x10	020	00010000	DLE
17	0x11	021	00010001	DC1
18	0x12	022	00010010	DC2
19	0x13	023	00010011	DC3
20	0x14	024	00010100	DC4
21	0x15	025	00010101	NAK
22	0x16	026	00010110	SYN
23	0x17	027	00010111	ETB
24	0x18	030	00011000	CAN
25	0x19	031	00011001	EM
26	0x1A	032	00011010	SUB
27	0x1B	033	00011011	ESC
28	0x1C	034	00011100	FS
29	0x1D	035	00011101	GS
30	0x1E	036	00011110	RS
31	0x1F	037	00011111	US
32	0x20	040	00100000	SPC
33	0x21	041	00100001	!

Dec	Hex	Oct	Bin	Char
34	0x22	042	00100010	"
35	0x23	043	00100011	#
36	0x24	044	00100100	$
37	0x25	045	00100101	%
38	0x26	046	00100110	&
39	0x27	047	00100111	'
40	0x28	050	00101000	(
41	0x29	051	00101001	)
42	0x2A	052	00101010	*
43	0x2B	053	00101011	+
44	0x2C	054	00101100	,
45	0x2D	055	00101101	-
46	0x2E	056	00101110	.
47	0x2F	057	00101111	/
48	0x30	060	00110000	0
49	0x31	061	00110001	1
50	0x32	062	00110010	2
51	0x33	063	00110011	3
52	0x34	064	00110100	4
53	0x35	065	00110101	5
54	0x36	066	00110110	6
55	0x37	067	00110111	7
56	0x38	070	00111000	8
57	0x39	071	00111001	9
58	0x3A	072	00111010	:
59	0x3B	073	00111011	;
60	0x3C	074	00111100	<
61	0x3D	075	00111101	=
62	0x3E	076	00111110	>
63	0x3F	077	00111111	?
64	0x40	0100	01000000	@
65	0x41	0101	01000001	A
66	0x42	0102	01000010	B
67	0x43	0103	01000011	C

Dec	Hex	Oct	Bin	Char
68	0x44	0104	01000100	D
69	0x45	0105	01000101	E
70	0x46	0106	01000110	F
71	0x47	0107	01000111	G
72	0x48	0110	01001000	H
73	0x49	0111	01001001	I
74	0x4A	0112	01001010	J
75	0x4B	0113	01001011	K
76	0x4C	0114	01001100	L
77	0x4D	0115	01001101	M
78	0x4E	0116	01001110	N
79	0x4F	0117	01001111	O
80	0x50	0120	01010000	P
81	0x51	0121	01010001	Q
82	0x52	0122	01010010	R
83	0x53	0123	01010011	S
84	0x54	0124	01010100	T
85	0x55	0125	01010101	U
86	0x56	0126	01010110	V
87	0x57	0127	01010111	W
88	0x58	0130	01011000	X
89	0x59	0131	01011001	Y
90	0x5A	0132	01011010	Z
91	0x5B	0133	01011011	[
92	0x5C	0134	01011100	\
93	0x5D	0135	01011101	]
94	0x5E	0136	01011110	^
95	0x5F	0137	01011111	_
96	0x60	0140	01100000	`
97	0x61	0141	01100001	a
98	0x62	0142	01100010	b
99	0x63	0143	01100011	c
100	0x64	0144	01100100	d
101	0x65	0145	01100101	e
102	0x66	0146	01100110	f
103	0x67	0147	01100111	g

Dec	Hex	Oct	Bin	Char
104	0x68	0150	01101000	h
105	0x69	0151	01101001	i
106	0x6A	0152	01101010	j
107	0x6B	0153	01101011	k
108	0x6C	0154	01101100	l
109	0x6D	0155	01101101	m
110	0x6E	0156	01101110	n
111	0x6F	0157	01101111	o
112	0x70	0160	01110000	p
113	0x71	0161	01110001	q
114	0x72	0162	01110010	r
115	0x73	0163	01110011	s
116	0x74	0164	01110100	t
117	0x75	0165	01110101	u
118	0x76	0166	01110110	v
119	0x77	0167	01110111	w
120	0x78	0170	01111000	x
121	0x79	0171	01111001	y
122	0x7A	0172	01111010	z
123	0x7B	0173	01111011	{
124	0x7C	0174	01111100		
125	0x7D	0175	01111101	}
126	0x7E	0176	01111110	~
127	0x7F	0177	01111111	Del
128	0x80	0200	10000000	Ç
129	0x81	0201	10000001	ü
130	0x82	0202	10000010	é
131	0x83	0203	10000011	â
132	0x84	0204	10000100	ä
133	0x85	0205	10000101	à
134	0x86	0206	10000110	Å
135	0x87	0207	10000111	ç
136	0x88	0210	10001000	ê
137	0x89	0211	10001001	ë
138	0x8A	0212	10001010	è
139	0x8B	0213	10001011	ï

Dec	Hex	Oct	Bin	Char
140	0x8C	0214	10001100	î
141	0x8D	0215	10001101	ì
142	0x8E	0216	10001110	Ä
143	0x8F	0217	10001111	Å
144	0x90	0220	10010000	É
145	0x91	0221	10010001	æ
146	0x92	0222	10010010	Æ
147	0x93	0223	10010011	ô
148	0x94	0224	10010100	ö
149	0x95	0225	10010101	ò
150	0x96	0226	10010110	û
151	0x97	0227	10010111	ù
152	0x98	0230	10011000	ÿ
153	0x99	0231	10011001	Ö
154	0x9A	0232	10011010	Ü
155	0x9B	0233	10011011	¢
156	0x9C	0234	10011100	£
157	0x9D	0235	10011101	¥
158	0x9E	0236	10011110	₧
159	0x9F	0237	10011111	ƒ
160	0xA0	0240	10100000	á
161	0xA1	0241	10100001	í
162	0xA2	0242	10100010	ó
163	0xA3	0243	10100011	ú
164	0xA4	0244	10100100	ñ
165	0xA5	0245	10100101	Ñ
166	0xA6	0246	10100110	ª
167	0xA7	0247	10100111	º
168	0xA8	0250	10101000	¿
169	0xA9	0251	10101001	⌐
170	0xAA	0252	10101010	¬
171	0xAB	0253	10101011	½
172	0xAC	0254	10101100	¼
173	0xAD	0255	10101101	¡
174	0xAE	0256	10101110	«
175	0xAF	0257	10101111	»

Dec	Hex	Oct	Bin	Char
176	0xB0	0260	10110000	░
177	0xB1	0261	10110001	▒
178	0xB2	0262	10110010	▓
179	0xB3	0263	10110011	│
180	0xB4	0264	10110100	┤
181	0xB5	0265	10110101	╡
182	0xB6	0266	10110110	╢
183	0xB7	0267	10110111	╖
184	0xB8	0270	10111000	╕
185	0xB9	0271	10111001	╣
186	0xBA	0272	10111010	║
187	0xBB	0273	10111011	╗
188	0xBC	0274	10111100	╝
189	0xBD	0275	10111101	╜
190	0xBE	0276	10111110	╛
191	0xBF	0277	10111111	┐
192	0xC0	0300	11000000	└
193	0xC1	0301	11000001	┴
194	0xC2	0302	11000010	┬
195	0xC3	0303	11000011	├
196	0xC4	0304	11000100	─
197	0xC5	0305	11000101	┼
198	0xC6	0306	11000110	╞
199	0xC7	0307	11000111	╟
200	0xC8	0310	11001000	╚
201	0xC9	0311	11001001	╔
202	0xCA	0312	11001010	╩
203	0xCB	0313	11001011	╦
204	0xCC	0314	11001100	╠
205	0xCD	0315	11001101	═
206	0xCE	0316	11001110	╬
207	0xCF	0317	11001111	╧
208	0xD0	0320	11010000	╨
209	0xD1	0321	11010001	╤
210	0xD2	0322	11010010	╥
211	0xD3	0323	11010011	╙

Dec	Hex	Oct	Bin	Char
212	0xD4	0324	11010100	╘
213	0xD5	0325	11010101	╒
214	0xD6	0326	11010110	╓
215	0xD7	0327	11010111	╫
216	0xD8	0330	11011000	╪
217	0xD9	0331	11011001	┘
218	0xDA	0332	11011010	┌
219	0xDB	0333	11011011	█
220	0xDC	0334	11011100	▄
221	0xDD	0335	11011101	▌
222	0xDE	0336	11011110	▐
223	0xDF	0337	11011111	▀
224	0xE0	0340	11100000	α
225	0xE1	0341	11100001	ß
226	0xE2	0342	11100010	Γ
227	0xE3	0343	11100011	π
228	0xE4	0344	11100100	Σ
229	0xE5	0345	11100101	σ
230	0xE6	0346	11100110	µ
231	0xE7	0347	11100111	τ
232	0xE8	0350	11101000	Φ
233	0xE9	0351	11101001	Θ
234	0xEA	0352	11101010	Ω
Dec	**Hex**	**Oct**	**Bin**	**Char**
235	0xEB	0353	11101011	δ
236	0xEC	0354	11101100	∞
237	0xED	0355	11101101	φ
238	0xEE	0356	11101110	ε
239	0xEF	0357	11101111	∩
240	0xF0	0360	11110000	≡
241	0xF1	0361	11110001	±
242	0xF2	0362	11110010	≥
243	0xF3	0363	11110011	≤
244	0xF4	0364	11110100	⌠
245	0xF5	0365	11110101	⌡
246	0xF6	0366	11110110	÷
247	0xF7	0367	11110111	≈
248	0xF8	0370	11111000	°
249	0xF9	0371	11111001	∙
250	0xFA	0372	11111010	·
251	0xFB	0373	11111011	√
252	0xFC	0374	11111100	^{n}
253	0xFD	0375	11111101	^{2}
254	0xFE	0376	11111110	■
255	0xFF	0377	11111111	

APPENDIX B Partition Type Codes

http://www.win.tue.nl/~aeb/partitions/partition_types-1.html

Type Code	Description
00	Empty
01	DOS 12-bit FAT (up to 15 M)
02	XENIX root
03	XENIX /usr
04	DOS 3.0+ 16-bit FAT (up to 32M)
05	DOS 3.3+ Extended Partition
06	DOS 3.31+ 16-bit FAT (over 32M)
07	OS/2 IFS (e.g., HPFS)
07	Windows NT NTFS
07	Advanced Unix
07	QNX2.x pre-1988
08	OS/2 (v1.0-1.3 only)
08	AIX boot partition
08	SplitDrive
08	Commodore DOS
08	DELL partition spanning multiple drives
08	QNX 1.x and 2.x ("qny")
09	AIX data partition
09	Coherent filesystem
09	QNX 1.x and 2.x ("qnz")
0a	OS/2 Boot Manager
0a	Coherent swap partition
0a	OPUS
0b	WIN95 OSR2 32-bit FAT
0c	WIN95 OSR2 32-bit FAT, LBA-mapped
0e	WIN95: DOS 16-bit FAT, LBA-mapped
0f	WIN95: Extended partition, LBA-mapped
10	OPUS (?)
11	Hidden DOS 12-bit FAT
12	Configuration/diagnostics partition
14	Hidden DOS 16-bit FAT <32M
16	Hidden DOS 16-bit FAT >=32M
17	Hidden IFS (e.g., HPFS)

APPENDIX B Partition Type Codes

http://www.win.tue.nl/~aeb/partitions/partition_types-1.html

18	AST SmartSleep Partition
19	Unused
1b	Hidden WIN95 OSR2 32-bit FAT
1c	Hidden WIN95 OSR2 32-bit FAT, LBA-mapped
1e	Hidden WIN95 16-bit FAT, LBA-mapped
20	Unused
21	Reserved
21	Unused
22	Unused
23	Reserved
24	NEC DOS 3.x
26	Reserved
31	Reserved
32	NOS
33	Reserved
34	Reserved
35	JFS on OS/2 or eCS
36	Reserved
38	THEOS ver 3.2 2gb partition
39	Plan 9 partition
39	THEOS ver 4 spanned partition
3a	THEOS ver 4 4gb partition
3b	THEOS ver 4 extended partition
3c	PartitionMagic recovery partition
3d	Hidden NetWare (According to Powerquest)
40	Venix 80286
41	Linux/MINIX (sharing disk with DRDOS)
41	Personal RISC Boot
41	PPC PReP (Power PC Reference Platform) Boot
42	Linux swap (sharing disk with DRDOS)
42	SFS (Secure Filesystem)
42	Windows 2000 dynamic extended partition marker
43	Linux native (sharing disk with DRDOS)
44	GoBack partition

APPENDIX B Partition Type Codes

http://www.win.tue.nl/~aeb/partitions/partition_types-1.html

45	Boot-US boot manager
45	Priam
45	EUMEL/Elan
46	EUMEL/Elan
47	EUMEL/Elan
48	EUMEL/Elan
4a	Mark Aitchison's ALFS/THIN lightweight filesystem
4a	AdaOS Aquila (Withdrawn)
4c	Oberon partition
4e	QNX4.x 2nd part
4f	QNX4.x 3rd part
4f	Oberon partition
50	OnTrack Disk Manager (older versions) RO
50	Lynx RTOS
50	Native Oberon (alt)
51	OnTrack Disk Manager RW
51	Novell
52	CP/M
52	Microport SysV/A
53	Disk Manager 6.0 Aux3
54	Disk Manager 6.0 Dynamic Drive Overlay
55	EZ-Drive
56	Golden Bow VFeature Partitioned Volume.
56	DM converted to EZ-BIOS
57	DrivePro
57	VNDI Partition
5c	Priam EDisk
61	SpeedStor
63	Unix System V (SCO, ISC Unix, UnixWare,
64	PC-ARMOUR protected partition
64	Novell Netware 286, 2.xx
65	Novell Netware 386, 3.xx or 4.xx
66	Novell Netware SMS Partition
67	Novell

APPENDIX B Partition Type Codes

http://www.win.tue.nl/~aeb/partitions/partition_types-1.html

68	Novell
69	Novell Netware 5+, Novell Netware NSS Partition
70	DiskSecure Multi-Boot
71	Reserved
73	Reserved
74	Reserved
74	Scramdisk partition
75	IBM PC/IX
76	Reserved
77	M2FS/M2CS partition
77	VNDI Partition
78	XOSL FS
7e	Unused
7f	Unused
80	MINIX until 1.4a
81	MINIX since 1.4b, early Linux
81	Mitac disk manager
82	Prime
82	Solaris x86
82	Linux swap
83	Linux native partition
84	OS/2 hidden C: drive
84	Hibernation partition
85	Linux extended partition
86	Old Linux RAID partition superblock
86	NTFS volume set
87	NTFS volume set
8a	Linux Kernel Partition (used by AiR-BOOT)
8b	Legacy Fault Tolerant FAT32 volume
8c	Legacy Fault Tolerant FAT32
8d	Free FDISK hidden Primary DOS FAT12 partitition
8e	Linux Logical Volume Manager partition
90	Free FDISK hidden Primary DOS FAT16 partitition
91	Free FDISK hidden DOS extended partitition

APPENDIX B Partition Type Codes

http://www.win.tue.nl/~aeb/partitions/partition_types-1.html

92	Free FDISK hidden Primary DOS large FAT16 partitition
93	Hidden Linux native partition
93	Amoeba
94	Amoeba bad block table
95	MIT EXOPC native partitions
97	Free FDISK hidden Primary DOS FAT32 partitition
98	Free FDISK hidden Primary DOS FAT32 partitition
98	Datalight ROM-DOS Super-Boot Partition
99	DCE376 logical drive
9a	Free FDISK hidden Primary DOS FAT16 partitition (LBA)
9b	Free FDISK hidden DOS extended partitition (LBA)
9f	BSD/OS
a0	Laptop hibernation partition
a1	Laptop hibernation partition
a1	HP Volume Expansion (SpeedStor variant)
a3	Reserved
a4	Reserved
a5	BSD/386, 386BSD, NetBSD, FreeBSD
a6	OpenBSD
a7	NEXTSTEP
a8	Mac OS-X
a9	NetBSD
aa	Olivetti Fat 12 1.44MB Service Partition
ab	Mac OS-X Boot partition
ab	GO! partition
ae	ShagOS filesystem
af	ShagOS swap partition
b0	BootStar Dummy
b1	Reserved
b3	Reserved
b4	Reserved
b6	Reserved
b6	Windows NT mirror set (master), FAT16 file system
b7	Windows NT mirror set (master), NTFS file system

APPENDIX B Partition Type Codes

http://www.win.tue.nl/~aeb/partitions/partition_types-1.html

b7	BSDI BSD/386 filesystem
b8	BSDI BSD/386 swap partition
bb	Boot Wizard hidden
be	Solaris 8 boot partition
c0	CTOS
c0	REAL/32 secure small partition
c0	NTFT Partition
c0	DR-DOS/Novell DOS secured partition
c1	DRDOS/secured (FAT-12)
c2	Reserved for DR-DOS 7+
c2	Hidden Linux
c3	Hidden Linux swap
c4	DRDOS/secured (FAT-16, < 32M)
c5	DRDOS/secured (extended)
c6	DRDOS/secured (FAT-16, >= 32M)
c6	Windows NT corrupted FAT16 volume/stripe set
c7	Windows NT corrupted NTFS volume/stripe set
c7	Syrinx boot
c8	Reserved
c9	Reserved ca Reserved
cb	reserved for DRDOS/secured (FAT32)
cc	reserved for DRDOS/secured (FAT32, LBA)
cd	CTOS Memdump?
ce	reserved for DRDOS/secured (FAT16, LBA)
d0	REAL/32 secure big partition
d1	Old Multiuser DOS secured FAT12
d4	Old Multiuser DOS secured FAT16 <32M
d5	Old Multiuser DOS secured extended partition
d6	Old Multiuser DOS secured FAT16 >=32M
d8	CP/M-86
da	Non-FS Data
db	Digital Research CP/M
db	CTOS (Convergent Technologies OS -Unisys)
db	KDG Telemetry SCPU boot

APPENDIX B Partition Type Codes

http://www.win.tue.nl/~aeb/partitions/partition_types-1.html

dd	Hidden CTOS Memdump?
de	Dell PowerEdge Server utilities (FAT fs)
df	DG/UX virtual disk manager partition df BootIt EMBRM
e0	Reserved by STMicroelectronics for ST AVFS.
e1	DOS access or SpeedStor 12-bit FAT extended partition
e3	DOS R/O or SpeedStor
e4	SpeedStor 16-bit FAT extended partition < 1024 cyl.
e5	Tandy DOS with logical sectored FAT
e5	Reserved
e6	Reserved
eb	BeOS
ed	Reserved for Matthias Paul's Spryt
ee	Indication that this legacy MBR is followed by an EFI header
ef	Partition that contains an EFI file system
f0	Linux/PA-RISC boot loader
f1	SpeedStor
f2	DOS 3.3+ secondary partition
f3	Reserved
f4	SpeedStor large partition
f4	Prologue single-volume partition
f5	Prologue multi-volume partition f6 Reserved
fa	Bochs
fb	VMware File System partition
fc	VMware Swap partition fd Linux raid partition
fe	SpeedStor > 1024 cyl. fe LANstep
fe	IBM PS/2 IML (Initial Microcode Load) partition
fe	Windows NT Disk Administrator hidden partition
fe	Linux Logical Volume Manager partition (old)
ff	Xenix Bad Block Table

Appendix C Partition Tables

Master Boot Record Partitioning (MBR)

MBR - Physical Sector 0			
DEC OFFSET	HEX OFFSET	Size (BYTES)	DESCRIPTION
0	00	446	Boot code
446	1BE	64	Four - 16 byte entries used.
510	1FE	2	0x55 AA Signature

16 Byte Partition Table Entry			
0	00	1	Boot Indication (0x00-not bootable 0x80-bootable)
1	01	3	Starting Head-8 bits, Sector-6 bits, Cylinder-10 bits (Data not used for drive over 8.4 gig)
4	04	1	File system type ex. (0B-Fat32, 07-NTFS) See Partition Type listing
5	05	3	Ending Head-8 bits, Sector-6 bits, Cylinder-10 bits (Data not used for drive over 8.4 gig)
9	09	4	Relative Sectors (Starting physical sector of the partition)
12	0C	4	Number of Sectors in the Partition
Reserved Sectors:			1-62 if partitioned with Windows XP 1-2047 if partitioned with Windows Vista/7

Appendix C Partition Tables

GUID Partitioning Table (GPT)

Protective MBR - Physical Sector 0			
DEC OFFSET	HEX OFFSET	Size (BYTES)	DESCRIPTION
0	00	446	Boot code
446	1BE	64	Only 1 - 16 byte entry used.
510	1FE	2	0x55 AA Signature

16 Byte Partition Table Record			
0	00	1	Boot Indication (0x00-not bootable)
1	01	3	Starting Head-8 bits, Sector-6 bits, Cylinder-10 bits - 00 02 00 - CHS 0,0,2
4	04	1	File system type - Type EE
5	05	3	Ending Head-8 bits, Sector-6 bits, Cylinder-10 bits - FF FF FF - CHS 1023, 63, 255
9	09	4	Relative Sectors (Starting physical sector of the partition) 01 00 00 00 - Sector 1
12	0C	4	Number of Sectors in the Partition (FF FF FF FF - 4,294,967,295 (x512 = 2.2 TB)

GPT Header - Physical Sector 1			
DEC OFFSET	**HEX OFFSET**	**SIZE (BYTES)**	**DESCRIPTION**
0	00	8	Signature "EFI PART"
8	08	4	Revision (1)
12	0C	4	Header Size- typically 92 bytes
16	10	4	Header CRC32
20	14	4	Reserved- 00
24	18	8	Current LBA sector
32	20	8	Sector Location of Backup
40	28	8	1st sector for partition (34)
48	30	8	Last sector for partitions
56	38	16	Physical Disk GUID
72	48	8	1st Partition Table sector (2)
80	50	4	# of Partition Table Entries (128)
84	54	4	Size of Partition Table Entries (128 bytes)
88	58	4	Partition Table CRC32

16 Byte GUID Notation:

00 11 22 33	44 55	66 77	88 99	AA BB CC DD EE FF
4 bytes	2	2	2	6
LE	LE	LE	BE	BE

33221100 - 5544 - 7766 - 8899 - AABBCCDDEEFF

GPT Partition Table Entry- Physical Sector 2-33

GPT Partition Table Entry – Physical Sector 2-33			
DEC OFFSET	HEX OFFSET	SIZE (BYTES)	DESCRIPTION
0	00	16	Partition Type GUID
16	10	16	Unique Partition GUID
32	20	8	1st LBA Sector of Partition
40	28	8	Last LBA Sector of Partition
48	30	8	Attributes (typically 00)
56	38	72	Partition Name in Unicode

Partition Type GUIDs	
Unused Entry	{00000000-0000-0000-0000-000000000000}
EFI System	{C12A7328-F81F-11D2-BA4B-00A0C93EC93B}
Microsoft Reserved	{E3C9E316-0B5C-4DB8-817D-F92DF00215AE}
Primary	{EBD0A0A2-B9E5-4433-87C0-68B6B72699C7}
LDM Metadata	{5808C8AA-B9E5-42E0-85D2-E1E90434CFB3}
LDM Data	{AF9B60A0-1431-4F62-BC68-3311714A69AD}

FAT 12/16 VBR			
DEC OFFSET	HEX OFFSET	SIZE (BYTES)	DESCRIPTION
0	00	3	Jump to bootstrap (The position of the bootstrap varies.)
3	03	8	OEM name/version (E.g. "IBM 3.3", "IBM 20.0", "MSDOS5.0", "MSWIN4.0".
11	0B	2	Number of bytes per sector (512) Must be one of 512, 1024, 2048, 4096.
13	0D	1	Number of sectors per cluster (1) Must be one of 1, 2, 4, 8, 16, 32, 64, 128. A cluster should have at most 32768 bytes.
14	0E	2	14-15 Number of reserved sectors (1)
16	10	1	Number of FAT copies (2)
17	11	2	Number of root directory entries (224) 0 for FAT32. 512 is recommended for FAT16.
19	13	2	Total number of sectors in the file system for smaller sector numbers
21	15	1	Media descriptor type (f0: 1.4 MB floppy, f8: hard disk)
22	16	2	Number of sectors per FAT (9)
24	18	2	Number of sectors per track (12)
26	1A	2	Number of heads (2, for diskette)
28	1C	4	Number of hidden sectors (0) Hidden sectors are sectors preceding the partition
32	20	4	Total number of sectors in the file system for larger sector numbers
36	24	1	Logical drive number (00 for floppy and 80 for hard drive)
37	25	1	Reserved
38	26	1	Extended Signature (29)
39	27	4	Volume Serial Number
43	2B	11	Volume Label – “NO NAME”
54	36	8	File system type
62	3E	441	Bootstrap code
510	1FE	2	Signature 55 AA

FAT 32 B R			
DEC OFFSET	HEX OFFSET	SIZE (BYTES)	DESCRIPTION
0	00	31	Identical to FAT12/16
36	24	4	Sectors per FAT
40	28	2	Mirror Flags
42	2A	2	Filesystem Version
44	2C	4	1st Cluster of Root Directory (2)
48	30	2	FS Information sector (usually 1)
50	32	2	Backup Boot Sector
52	34	12	Reserved
64	40	1	Logical Drive Number (0x00 or 0x80)
65	41	1	Reserved
66	42	1	Extended signature (0x29)
67	43	4	Serial number of partition
71	47	11	Volume Label
82	52	8	Filesystem type
90	5A	421	Bootstrap
510	3E	2	Signature 0x55 AA

FAT 32	FS INFO		
DEC OFFSET	HEX OFFSET	SIZE (BYTES)	DESCRIPTION
0	00	4	Signature of 0x52526141
4	04	480	Blank
484	1E4	4	Secondary Signature of 0x71716141
488	1E8	4	Free cluster count
492	1EC	4	Next free count
496	1F0	14	Reserved bytes
510	1FE	2	Signature 0x55 AA

FAT DIRECTORY STRUCTURE			
DEC OFFSET	HEX OFFSET	SIZE (BYTES)	DESCRIPTION
0	00	8	File name (1-8 bytes)
8	08	3	Extension (0-3 bytes)
11	0B	1	Attribute - a bitvector. Bit 0: read only. Bit 1: hidden. Bit 2: system file. Bit 3: volume label. Bit 4: subdirectory. Bit 5: archive. Bits 6-7: unused.
12	0C	1	Case – >0 if needs to be converted to upper case
13	0D	1	Created Time 1/10 of a Second - FAT32 Reserved - FAT12/16
14	0E	2	Created Time - FAT32 Reserved - FAT12/16
16	10	2	Created Date - FAT32 Reserved - FAT12/16
18	12	2	Last Accessed Date - FAT32 Reserved - FAT12/16
20	14	2	High Bytes for Cluster location - FAT32 Reserved - FAT12/16
22	16	2	Modified Time (5/6/5 bits, for hour/minutes/halfseconds)
24	18	2	Modified Date (7/4/5 bits, for year-since-1980/month/day)
26	1A	2	Starting cluster (0 for an empty file) Low Bytes for Cluster location - FAT32
28	1C	4	Filesize in bytes

Long File Nan s			
0	00	1	Sequence Number
1	01	10	Unicode characters 1-5
11	0B	1	Attribute: 0x0F
12	0C	1	Type: 0
13	0D	1	Checksum of short name
14	0E	12	Unicode characters 6-11
26	1A	2	Starting cluster: 0
28	1C	4	Unicode characters 12-13

Appendix E – NTFS Tables

NTFS Volume Boot Record -$Boot			
DEC OFFSET	HEX OFFSET	SIZE (BYTES)	DESCRIPTION
0	0x00	3	Jump Instruction
3	0x03	8	OEM ID
11	0x0B	2	Bytes Per Sector – normally 512 bytes (0x00 02)
13	0x0D	1	Sectors Per Cluster
14	0x0E	2	Reserved sectors – always zero in NTFS
16	0x10	5	Values must be 0x00
21	0x15	1	Media Descriptor
22	0x16	2	Values must be 0x00
24	0x18	8	Not used and not checked by NTFS
32	0x20	4	Values must be 0x00
36	0x24	4	Not used by NTFS
40	0x28	8	Total Sectors in the partition
48	0x30	8	Logical Starting Cluster # for the $MFT
56	0x38	8	Logical Starting Cluster #for the $MFTMirr
64	0x40	1	Clusters Per $MFT Record
65	0x41	3	Not used by NTFS
68	0x44	1	Clusters Per Index Buffer
69	0x45	3	Not used by NTFS
72	0x48	8	Volume Serial Number
80	0x50	4	Not used by NTFS
84	0x54	426	Bootstrap Code
510	0x01FE	42	End of Sector marker (0x55 AA)

Appendix E – NTFS Tables

MFT RECORD HEADER			
DEC OFFSET	HEX OFFSET	SIZE (BYTES)	DESCRIPTION
0	0	4	"FILE" SIGNATURE
4	4	2	Offset to update sequence (fixup array)
6	6	2	Number of entries in the update sequence (fixup) array
8	8	8	$Log File Sequence Number
16	10	2	Sequence Count (number times the record has been used)
18	12	2	Hard Link Count (File names)
20	14	2	Offset to Start of Attributes
22	16	2	Flags (Deleted Files-00 00, Allocated Files-01 00, Deleted Directory-02 00, Allocated Directory-03 00
24	18	4	Amount of space used by $MFT records (bytes)
28	1C	4	Amount of space allocated for $MFT records
32	20	8	Base File Reference
40	28	2	Next Attribute ID
42	2A	2	Reserved
44	2C	4	$MFT Record Number
48	30	>0	Update Sequence Number (WinXP/Vista/Win7)

Appendix E – NTFS Tables

Standard Information Attribute (10 00 00 00)			
DEC OFFSET	**HEX OFFSET**	**SIZE (BYTES)**	**DESCRIPTION**
0	0	4	Attribute Type Identifier
4	4	4	Length of the Attribute
8	8	1	Resident (0x00) or Non-Resident Flag (0x01)
9	9	1	Length of Stream Name in Unicode characters
10	0A	2	Offset to the stream name
12	0C	2	Flags
14	0E	2	Attribute Identifier
16	10	4	Size of Resident Data
20	14	2	Offset to Resident Data
22	16	1	Indexing (00=no, 01=yes)
23	17	1	Padding
24	18	8	Creation Time
32	20	8	Modified Time
40	28	8	$MFT Modified Time
48	30	8	Last Access Time
56	38	4	DOS Flags (See table below)
60	3C	4	Maximum number of versions
64	40	4	Version number
68	44	4	Class ID
72	48	4	Owner ID
76	4C	4	Security ID
80	50	8	Quota Charged
88	58	8	Update Sequence Number

Appendix E – NTFS Tables

DOS ATTRIBUTES		
Hex	**Bina y**	**Description**
0x0001	0000 0000 0000 0001	Read Only
0x0002	0000 0000 0000 0010	Hidden
0x0004	0000 0000 0000 0100	System
0x0010	0000 0000 0000 1010	Directory
0x0020	0000 0000 0010 0000	Archive
0x0040	0000 0000 0100 0000	Device
0x0080	0000 0000 1000 0000	Normal
0x0100	0000 0001 0000 0000	Temporary
0x0200	0000 0010 0000 0000	Sparse File
0x0400	0000 0100 0000 0000	Reparse Point
0x0800	0000 1000 0000 0000	Compressed
0x1000	0001 0000 0000 0000	Offline
0x2000	0010 0000 0000 0000	Not Content Indexed
0x4000	0100 0000 0000 0000	Encrypted

Appendix E – NTFS Tables

File Name Attribute (30 00 00 00)			
DEC OFFSET	**HEX OFFSET**	**SIZE (BYTES)**	**DESCRIPTION**
0	0	4	Attribute Type Identifier
4	4	4	Length of the Attribute
8	8	1	Resident (0x00) or Non-Resident Flag (0x01)
9	9	1	Length of Stream Name in Unicode characters
10	0A	2	Offset to the stream name
12	0C	2	Flags
14	0E	2	Attribute Identifier
16	10	4	Size of Resident Data
20	14	2	Offset to Resident Data-
22	16	1	Indexing (00=no, 01=yes)
23	17	1	Padding of 00
24	18	6	$MFT Record Number of the Parent Directory
30	1E	2	Sequence number of the Parent Directory
32	20	8	Creation Time
40	28	8	Modification Time
48	30	8	$MFT Modification Time
56	38	8	Last Access Time
64	40	8	Allocated size of index (if record is an index)
72	48	8	Actual size of index (if record is an index)
80	50	4	File Type Flags
84	54	4	Reparse Value
88	58	1	File name length in Unicode
89	59	1	File name type: 00-Posix 01- Win32 02-DOS Short Name 03-Win32/DOS
90	5A	varies	File name

Appendix E – NTFS Tables

Data Attribute-Resident (0x80 00 00 00)			
DEC OFFSET	HEX OFFSET	SIZE (BYTES)	DESCRIPTION
0	0	4	Attribute Type Identifier
4	4	4	Length of the Attribute
8	8	1	Resident (0x00) or Non-Resident Flag (0x01)
9	9	1	Length of Stream Name in Unicode characters
10	0A	2	Offset to the stream name
12	0C	2	Flags
14	0E	2	Attribute Identifier
16	10	4	Size of Resident Data
20	14	2	Offset to Resident Data
22	16	1	Indexing (00=no, 01=yes)
23	17	1	Padding
24	18	varies	Data

Appendix E – NTFS Tables

Data Attribute-Non Resident (0 00 00 00)			
DEC OFFSET	HEX OFFSET	SIZE (BYTES)	DESCRIPTION
0	0	4	Attribute Type Identifier
4	4	4	Length of the Attribute
8	8	1	Resident (0x00) or Non-Resident Flag (0x01)
9	9	1	Length of Stream Name in Unicode characters
10	0A	2	Offset to the stream name
12	0C	2	Flags
14	0E	2	Attribute Identifier
16	10	8	Starting VCN of runlist
24	18	8	Ending VCN of runlist
32	20	2	Offset to runlist in bytes
34	22	2	Used for compression
36	24	4	Unused
40	28	8	Allocated size for content in bytes (physical size)
48	30	8	Actual size of content in bytes (logical size)
56	38	8	Initialized size of content in bytes
64	40	varies	Data runs

Object ID Attribute (40 00 00 00)			
DEC OFFSET	**HEX OFFSET**	**SIZE (BYTES)**	**DESCRIPTION**
0	0	4	Attribute Type Identifier
4	4	4	Length of the Attribute
8	8	1	Resident-00 or Non-Resident-01)
9	9	1	Length of Stream Name
10	0A	2	Offset to the stream name
12	0C	2	Flags
14	0E	2	Attribute Identifier
16	10	4	Size of Resident Data
20	14	4	Offset to Resident Data
24	18	16	GUID Object ID
40	28	16	GUID Birth Volume ID
56	38	16	GUID Birth Object ID
72	48	16	GUID Domain ID

Reparse Point Attribute (C0 00 00 00)			
DEC OFFSET	HEX OFFSET	SIZE (BYTES)	DESCRIPTION
0	0	4	Attribute Type Identifier
4	4	4	Length of the Attribute
8	8	1	Resident-00 or Non-Resident-01)
9	9	1	Length of Stream Name
10	0A	2	Offset to the stream name
12	0C	2	Flags
14	0E	2	Attribute Identifier
16	10	4	Size of Resident Data
20	14	4	Offset to Resident Data
24	18	4	Reparse Point Type 0x68000008 DFS 0x88000003 Mount point 0xA0000003 Junction 0xA8000004 HSM 0xE8000000 Symbolic link
28	1C	2	Data Length
30	1E	2	Unused
32	20	2	Offset to target's name starting 16 bytes into the content
34	22	2	Length of target's name
36	24	2	Offset to target's print name starting 16 bytes into the content
38	26	2	Length of target's print name
40	22	varied	Folder Path

Appendix E – NTFS Tables

Index Root Attribute (0x90 00 00 00)			
DEC OFFSET	**HEX OFFSET**	**SIZE (BYTES)**	**DESCRIPTION**
0	0	4	Attribute Type Identifier
4	4	4	Length of the Attribute
8	8	1	Resident (0x00) or Non-Resident Flag (0x01)
9	9	1	Length of Stream Name in Unicode characters
10	0A	2	Offset to the stream name
12	0C	2	Flags (Compressed, Sparse, Encrypted)
14	0E	2	Attribute Identifier
16	10	4	Size of Resident data
20	14	2	Offset to Resident data
22	16	2	Padding
24	18	8	Stream Name in Unicode
Index Header			
32	20	4	Type of attribute stored in index
36	24	4	Collation sorting rule
40	28	4	Size of each index record in bytes
44	2C	1	Size of each index record in clusters
45	2D	3	Padding
Node Header			
48	30	4	Offset to the index node

52	34	4	Node length
56	38	4	Node allocated length
60	3C	4	Flags - Small 0x00 or Large 0x01 Plus padding
Index (Directory) Entry			
64	40	8	MFT Record of Entry (6 bytes)
72	48	2	Length of the Entire Entry
74	4A	2	Length of the Content of the Entry
76	4C	4	Flags - 0x00 Resident Only 0x01 Resident and Non-Resident 0x01 No entries 0x02 Last entry 0x03 All Non-Resident
80	50	8	MFT Record of the Parent (6 bytes)
88	58	8	Creation Date/Time
96	60	8	Last Modified Date/Time
104	68	8	MFT Record Modified Date/Time
112	70	8	Last Accessed Date/Time
120	78	8	Allocated Size of the File
128	80	8	Actual Size of the File
136	88	8	File Attributes (System, Hidden etc)
144	90	1	Length of the Filename
145	91	1	Filename Type
146	92	varies	Filename
Entries will be repeated for each filename, even LFN and SFN			

Index Allocation Attribute (A0 00 00 00)			
DEC OFFSET	HEX OFFSET	SIZE (BYTES)	DESCRIPTION
0	0	4	Attribute Type Identifier
4	4	4	Length of the Attribute
8	8	1	Resident (0x00) or Non-Resident Flag (0x01)
9	9	1	Length of Stream Name in Unicode characters
10	0A	2	Offset to the stream name
12	0C	2	Flags (Compressed, Sparse, Encrypted)
14	0E	2	Attribute Identifier
16	10	8	Starting VCN of runlist
24	18	8	Ending VCN of runlist
32	20	2	Offset to runlist in bytes
34	22	2	Used for compression
36	24	4	Unused
40	28	8	Allocated size for content in bytes (physical size)
48	30	8	Actual size of content in bytes (logical size)
56	38	8	Initialized size of content in bytes
64	40	8	Stream Name $I30
72	48	varies	Runlist

Appendix E – NTFS Tables

Bitmap Attribute (B0 00 00 00)			
DEC OFFSET	HEX OFFSET	SIZE (BYTES)	DESCRIPTION
0	0	4	Attribute Type Identifier
4	4	4	Length of the Attribute
8	8	1	Resident (0x00) or Non-Resident Flag (0x01)
9	9	1	Length of Stream Name in Unicode characters
10	0A	2	Offset to the stream name
12	0C	2	Flags (Compressed, Sparse, Encrypted)
14	0E	2	Attribute Identifier
16	10	4	Size of Resident data
20	14	2	Offset to Resident data
22	16	2	Padding
24	18	8	Stream Name in Unicode
32	20	8	Bitmap

INDEX RECORD HEADER			
DEC OFFSET	HEX OFFSET	SIZE BYTES	DESCRIPTION
0	0	4	"INDX" SIGNATURE
4	4	2	Offset to update sequence (fixup array)
6	6	2	Number of entries in the update sequence (fixup) array
8	8	8	$Log File Sequence Number
16	10	8	Virtual Cluster Number
24	18	4	Offset to Index Entry header
28	1C	4	Offset to End of the Last Entry
32	20	4	Allocated Size of Index Entries
36	24	1	Index Type Flag (small or large)
37	25	3	Padding
40	28	2	Update Sequence Number
42	2A	16	Update Sequence Array
58	3A	6	Padding
Index (Directory) Entry			
64	40	8	MFT Record of Entry (6 bytes)
72	48	2	Length of the Entire Entry
74	4A	2	Length of the Content of the Entry
76	4C	4	Flags - 0x00 Resident Only 0x01 Resident and Non-Resident 0x01 No entries 0x02 Last entry 0x03 All Non-Resident
80	50	8	MFT Record of the Parent (6 bytes)
88	58	8	Creation Date/Time

96	60	8	Last Modified Date/Time
104	68	8	MFT Record Modified Date/Time
112	70	8	Last Accessed Date/Time
120	78	8	Allocated Size of the File
128	80	8	Actual Size of the File
136	88	8	File Attributes (System, Hidden etc)
144	90	1	Length of the Filename
145	91	1	Filename Type
146	92	varies	Filename
Entries will be repeated for each filename, even LFN and SFN			

Appendix F - exFAT Tables

exFAT Volume Boot Record			
DEC OFFSET	**Hex OFFSET**	**SIZE (BYTES)**	**DESCRIPTION**
0	0x00	3	Jump Instruction
3	0x03	8	OEM ID "EXFAT"
11	0x0B	53	Reserved
64	0x40	8	Partition Sector Offset –0 for removable drive
72	0x48	8	Size of total volume in Sectors
80	0x50	4	Sector Address of 1st FAT
84	0x54	4	Size of FAT in Sectors
88	0x58	4	Sector address of Data Region
92	0x5C	4	Number of Clusters in Data Region
96	0x60	4	Cluster Address of Root Directory
100	0x64	4	Volume Serial Number
104	0x68	2	File System Revision
106	0x6A	2	Volume Flags Bit 0 - Active FAT (0=1 1=2) Bit 1 - Dirty Flag (0=Clean 1=Dirty) Bit 2 - Media Failure (0=None 1=Failures) Bit 3 -15 - Reserved
108	0x6C	1	Bytes per Sector
109	0x6D	1	Sectors per Cluster
110	0x6E	1	Number of FATS
111	0x6F	1	Used by INT13
112	0x70	1	Percentage of Data Region In Use
113	0x71	7	Reserved
120	0x72	390	Bootstrap Code
510	0x01FE	42	End of Sector marker (0x55 AA)

Appendix F – exFAT Tables

Volume Label Directory Entry			
DEC OFFSET	**HEX OFFSET**	**SIZE (BYTES)**	**DESCRIPTION**
0	0x00	1	Entry Type (83) Bits 0-4 Code 00011 Bit 5 Importance 0 Bit 6 Category 0 Bit 7 In Use 1 Total 10000011 = 0x83
1	0x01	1	Character Count
2	0x02	22	Volume Label in Unicode
24	0x18	8	Reserved

Allocation Bitmap Directory Entry			
DEC OFFSET	**HEX OFFSET**	**SIZE (BYTES)**	**DESCRIPTION**
0	0x00	1	Entry Type (81) Bits 0-4 Code 00001 Bit 5 Importance 0 Bit 6 Category 0 Bit 7 In Use 1 Total 10000001 = 0x81
1	0x01	1	Bitmap Flag (0x00 – 1 for 2
2	0x02	18	Reserved
20	0x14	4	Starting Cluster of the Bitmap
24	0x18	8	Length of the Data

Appendix F – exFAT Tables

UpCase Table Directory Entry			
DEC OFFSET	**HEX OFFSET**	**SIZE (BYTES)**	**DESCRIPTION**
0	0x00	1	Entry Type (82) Bits 0-4 Code 00010 Bit 5 Importance 0 Bit 6 Category 0 Bit 7 In Use 1 Total 10000010 = 0x82
1	0x01	3	Reserved
4	0x04	4	Table Checksum
8	0x08	12	Reserved
20	0x14	4	Starting Cluster of the Table
24	0x18	8	Length of the Data

Appendix F – exFAT Tables

exFAT File Directory Entry			
DEC OFFSET	**HEX OFFSET**	**SIZE (BYTES)**	**DESCRIPTION**
0	0x00	1	Entry Type (85) Bits 0-4 Code 00101 Bit 5 Importance 0 Bit 6 Category 0 Bit 7 In Use 1 Total 10000101 = 0x85
1	0x01	1	Secondary Entry Count
2	0x02	2	Set Checksum
4	0x04	2	File Attributes Read-Only Bit 0 Hidden Bit 1 System Bit 2 Reserved Bit 3 Directory Bit 4 Archive Bit 5 Reserved Bits 6-16
6	0x06	2	Reserved
8	0x08	4	Creation Timestamp
12	0x0C	4	Last Modified Timestamp
16	0x10	4	Last Accessed Timestamp
20	0x14	1	Create 10ms increment 0-199
21	0x15	1	Last Modified 10ms increment 0-199
22	0x16	1	Create Time zone offset from GMT
23	0x17	1	Last Modified Time zone offset from GMT
24	0x18	1	Last Accessed Time zone offset from GMT
25	0x19	7	Reserved

Appendix F – exFAT Tables

exFAT Stream Extension Directory Entry			
Dec Offset	**Hex Offset**	**Size (Bytes)**	**Description**
0	0x00	1	Entry Type (C0) Bits 0-4 Code 00000 Bit 5 Importance 0 Bit 6 Category 1 Bit 7 In Use 1 Total 11000000 = 0xC0
1	0x01	1	Secondary Flags Allocation Possible Bit 0 (0-No, 1-Yes) No FAT Chain Bit 1 (0-valid, 1-invalid) Reserved Bits 2-7
2	0x02	1	Reserved
3	0x03	1	Name Length
4	0x04	2	Name hash
6	0x06	2	Reserved
8	0x08	8	Valid Data Length
16	0x10	4	Reserved
20	0x14	4	Cluster Address of 1st Block
24	0x18	8	Length of data

Appendix F – exFAT Tables

exFAT File Name Extension Directory Entry			
Dec Offset	**Hex Offset**	**Size (Bytes)**	**Description**
0	0x00	1	Entry Type (C1) Bits 0-4 Code 00001 Bit 5 Importance 0 Bit 6 Category 1 Bit 7 In Use 1 Total 11000001 = 0xC1
1	0x01	1	Secondary Flag Allocation Possible Bit 0 (0-No, 1-Yes) No FAT Chain Bit 1 (0-valid, 1-invalid) Bits 2-7 are reserved
2	0x02	30	15 Unicode characters of File name